Death sentences passed by military courts of the British Army 1914–1924

Gerard Oram has been researching capital sentences passed by courts martial of the First World War for a number of years, firstly as part of an MPhil degree, and more recently as part of a PhD with the assistance of a research grant from the Open University.

Julian Putkowski is a freelance military historian. He is co-author of *Shot at Dawn*, the standard reference work about soldiers executed under the British Army Act during the First World War.

Andrew Mackinlay is the Labour MP for Thurrock. He has campaigned in Parliament for posthumous pardons to be granted to men executed for a range of military offences during the First World War.

Gerard Oram

Death sentences passed by military courts of the British Army 1914–1924

Edited by Julian Putkowski
With a foreword by Andrew Mackinlay MP

Francis
Boutle
Publishers

First published 1998 by
Francis Boutle Publishers
23 Arlington Way
London EC1R 1UY

ISBN 0 9532388 0 6

Printed in Great Britain by Redwood Books

Acknowledgements

Any extended research project such as this relies not solely on one person but also many others without whom it could not have been completed. I owe thanks to many people, but I would like to single out two in particular: my wife Anna, who supported me and assisted both with the research and the computing of the data, and Julian Putkowski who painstakingly corrected my errors and provided much additional material.

Contents

List of tables and graphs

Foreword

by Andrew Mackinlay MP

There has always been public disquiet about the fate of the men who were sentenced to death during the First World War.

As early as March, 1919, Brigadier General Sir Wyndham Childs, Director of Personal Services in the Department of the Adjutant General, was saying: 'Even during the continuance of hostilities, there was very strong feeling both in the country and in the House of Commons against the infliction of the death penalty for military offences.

'Now that hostilities have ceased it can confidently be stated that the effect on this country of a death penalty might lead to an agitation which might be difficult to control and in all probability would jeopardise the prospects of maintaining the death penalty for military offences in time of peace when the Annual Army (Act) comes before the Houses of Parliament.'

Since then, anxiety about the sentences has continued to be expressed. Indeed, in the past ten years, as more has become known about the capital courts martial, moves have been initiated for posthumous pardons to be granted to men executed for military crimes during the war.

However, opposition to the measure has been expressed by the closed ranks of the Establishment, including some peers and a handful of retired senior military officers. Amongst other arguments, these influential figures have affirmed that during the war the military authorities exercised economy, if not mercy, in confirming capital sentences.

Such a claim ignores the facts that military courts convicted virtually ninety per cent of soldiers charged with capital offences and that draconian punishments were inflicted on those who were not executed.

Until now, though, no definitive list has been published to substantiate the latter point. Gerard Oram is to be congratulated on his diligence and scholarship in providing the necessary data and more. As well as tabulating the death sentences passed on civilians in addition to servicemen, his findings also confirm the disproportionate extent to which death sentences were used to punish soldiers, rather than commissioned officers.

Bias aside, as an examination of the thousands of names shows, the process of confirming individual death sentences appears to have been arbitrary – a pitiless devil's lottery. Unpalatable facts such as these have to be addressed in order that history may be written with clarity and precision. Gerard Oram's work is a valuable contribution to the process.

It would also be to the credit of those given to sustaining the officers' version of military justice if, as a consequence of studying this book, they were to advance a more generous measure of compassion to the condemned, and to acknowledge the misery and grief simultaneously inflicted on the innocent families and dependents of the men whose names are recorded herein.

Introduction

The British Army sentenced to death more than 3,000 of its soldiers, plus members of Dominion, Colonial and foreign forces, as well as several British and foreign civilians, at courts martial during, and in the aftermath of, the First World War.

This book makes available, in one convenient volume, the fullest possible facts about those men. It provides an easily accessible source of information about all the death sentences passed by British courts martial between 1914 and 1924, the date of the last one, thereby relieving future researchers of many hours of work.

The issue of capital punishment in the British Army during the First World War was controversial at the time, and has remained so ever since. Its use by the army was never more widespread than between 1914 and 1918. In the forty-four years up to 1914, the army executed just four of its men. All this changed during the First World War. By the end of 1914, just a few months into the war, that figure had already been equalled, and the use of the death penalty continued unabated in each subsequent year of the war. In *Shot at Dawn*[1] Julian Putkowski and Julian Sykes have traced 361 executions carried out by the British Army between 1914 and 1920. Their book remains the most comprehensive source of information about those executions.

The executions, however, were merely the tip of the iceberg. According to official statistics, 3,080 men serving with the army had been sentenced to death by courts martial between 1914 and 1920.[2] Approximately ninety per cent of these sentences had been commuted to other punishments, such as penal servitude or hard labour. Thus, at one time or another, more than 2,500 soldiers in the British Army were under the very real threat of execution. These men, by and large, have remained anonymous; and, although the army recorded their names in registers of courts martial, their identities, their units and the locations where the sentences were imposed have never been published before. By revealing these details, we are able to show with more clarity just how widespread the threat of execution was in the British Army, and how it related to events on the battlefield.

The power to impose a sentence of death was derived from the annually renewable British Army Act. Two types of court martial had jurisdiction to try capital offences. The General Court Martial (GCM), the highest form of military court, could be convened only by the Crown or the Commander-in-Chief. Consequently its use was somewhat limited during wartime. In practice only cases involving officers were normally heard by this court. A judge advocate presided over it, and thirteen officers assisted him, although this number could be reduced to five overseas.

Most cases were heard by the Field General Court Martial (FGCM), which was, as its name implies, normally convened close to the front line. Several features distinguished it from the GCM. Firstly, it was far easier to convene, and, secondly, it did not need the authority of the Crown, or Commander-in-Chief. Again the panel was reduced to three officers, the most senior of whom had to hold the substantive rank of Captain or above. Finally, any death sentence required a unanimous verdict.

Until the introduction of the Court Martial Officer (CMO) in 1916, there was no requirement that any member on the panel be legally trained. Even then, since there was only one CMO per corps, most cases were tried without the presence of a legally trained officer.

A death sentence could not be carried out until it was confirmed by the Commander-in-Chief. This usually took about two weeks, and the unfortunate individual often continued to serve in the trenches, uncertain of his ultimate fate. In the meantime, the file ascended the chain of command, and at each stage the condemned man's commander would add his comments and recommendations. The Commander-in-Chief acted as the final arbiter, so he held the ultimate power of life or death. As most cases arose on the Western Front, this would normally be either Sir John French or Sir Douglas Haig. However, the Commanders-in-Chief in other theatres of the war also had to consider death sentences. Most commanders believed in the deterrent effect of capital punishment. In view of this, it is surprising that so many of the sentences were commuted.

The jurisdiction of courts martial extended beyond the British Army. Death sentences were passed on soldiers from the Dominions and the Colonies, although the Australian Government did not permit any of its soldiers to be executed. In many parts of the world, civilians also came under the jurisdiction of British military courts. The Defence of the Realm Act (DORA) allowed for the prosecution of spies, and several foreign nationals were executed in the Tower of London for espionage. British martial law was applied in Ireland, where fifteen of those involved in the 1916 Easter Rising were executed, and also in Egypt. Surprisingly, enemy prisoners were occasionally sentenced to death, usually for killing British soldiers. Although none of the three Germans sentenced to death was in the event executed, six Turkish prisoners were.

The death sentence was the ultimate disciplinary weapon available to the courts martial. However, only in cases of murder was it mandatory. One would expect, therefore, its use to be restricted to only the most serious cases. But, as Putkowski and Sykes have shown, this was not the case. The first sentence of death was passed just

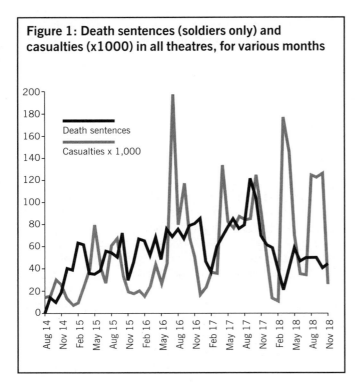

Figure 1: Death sentences (soldiers only) and casualties (x1000) in all theatres, for various months

Death sentences
Casualties x 1,000

(x-axis: Aug 14, Nov 14, Feb 15, May 15, Aug 15, Nov 15, Feb 16, May 16, Aug 16, Nov 16, Feb 17, May 17, Aug 17, Nov 17, Feb 18, May 18, Aug 18, Nov 18)

(y-axis: 0, 20, 40, 60, 80, 100, 120, 140, 160, 180, 200)

one day after the first British action of the war at Mons. The ignominy of being the first British soldier sentenced to death in the First World War fell on a Dragoon, Private Whittle, who had fallen asleep at his post. His sentence was commuted to two years hard labour. The first execution followed little more than two weeks later.

Courts martial continued to pass death sentences with greater frequency until 1918, when the number declined dramatically. This might have been due to the impact of the introduction of the CMO, or to a greater understanding of the medical condition known as shell-shock. It might also have been a consequence of the introduction of conscription, which brought many civilians into the army and resulted in lower standards of discipline being tolerated.

Court martial sentences were influenced in varying degrees by the nature of the war itself. It is beyond the scope of this publication to analyse the course of the war (an extensive debate in itself), but it is essential to place the death sentences within the wider context of the experiences of the British Army. A useful way of doing so is to compare death sentences with casualty returns for the same period. Casualty figures are readily available from official sources.[3] Obviously, their number rose during the more important battles. Figure 1, above, shows the number of all casualties (killed, missing, wounded and taken prisoner) for various months of the war, and directly compares them with the number of death sentences.

The peaks in casualty numbers can be summarised as follows:
- October 1914: First Battle of Ypres. Advancing British troops met by advancing German units.
- April 1915: Second Battle of Ypres. German offensive, and first use of gas on the Western Front (April 23). Also the first troop landings at Gallipoli (April 25).
- August/September 1915: Battle of Loos. Disastrous British offensive.
- April 1916: British garrison surrendered to Turkish Army at Kut in Mesopotamia.
- July 1916: Beginning of the Battle of the Somme. British

offensive with enormous casualties especially on first day (July 1).
- September 1916: Second phase of the Battle of the Somme. British offensive with some (limited) successes.
- April 1917: Battle of Arras, and capture of Vimy Ridge: British contribution to the Nivelle plan.
- October 1917: Third Battle of Ypres: Passchendaele. Another huge British offensive, really a series of battles. Enormous numbers of casualties on both sides.
- March/April 1918: German spring offensive.
- August/September/October 1918: Battle of Amiens and general Allied offensive.

The relationship between these battles, with their large numbers of casualties, and death sentences is clear. Generally, the sentences began to increase in frequency immediately before the big British offensives, and were maintained at a high rate until the battle ended, when they began to tail off. The winter months, when few offensives could be launched, are marked by fewer death sentences. The fact that the peak in casualties in the spring of 1918 is not matched by a corresponding rise in death sentences is explained by the fact that this offensive was started by the Germans. Thus it appears that death sentences were more forcefully applied in the weeks leading up to planned British offensives. The reasons are twofold. Firstly, desertion increasingly was more prevalent as zero-hour approached: tensions were no doubt heightened as the usual preliminary artillery bombardment intensified. Secondly, the courts martial may at such times have adopted a harsher line with alleged deserters, using the death sentence as a deterrent to prevent any evasion of front line duties.

A total of 3,342 death sentences has been traced in the courts martial registers. Civilians and prisoners of war account for 224 of these. The remaining 3,118 relate to soldiers serving with the British Army, a figure comparable to official statistics.

Many of these soldiers came from the Empire: 222 Canadians (25 executed), 113 Australians (none executed), twenty-three New Zealanders (five executed),[4] eleven South Africans (one executed), eight West Indians (four executed), two Nigerians (one executed), nine Ghanaians of the Gold Coast Regiment (three executed) and three West Africans (one executed). Twenty-six labourers and auxiliary workers from China, Egypt and Africa were also sentenced to death, and of these nineteen were executed. It appears that the records of the Indian Army were kept separately, and have not survived. However, the courts martial registers include British soldiers serving with the Indian Army, and these have been included. Thirteen men of the Connaught Rangers who were convicted of mutiny in India fall into this category.

According to Putkowski and Sykes, Lance Corporal William Price and Private Richard Morgan, of 2nd Battalion Welsh Regiment, were executed on February 15, 1915 for the murder of their Company Sergeant-Major. As no record exists of their sentences, neither has been included.

Most of the death sentences were passed for desertion (2,004). Cowardice (213) and sleeping on post (449) also feature highly. Figure 2, on page 15, gives a comprehensive breakdown of offences for which death sentences were passed, and the number of executions actually carried out.

Figure 2: Number of death sentences and executions, by offence

Offence	No. of death sentences	No. of executions
Desertion	2,004	272
Sleeping at post	449	2
Cowardice	213	14
Disobedience	120	4
Murder	106	63
Rebellion (Ireland)	93	15
Quitting post	82	6
Striking senior officer	49	4
Mutiny	55	15
Offence against inhabitant	22	3
Espionage	18	10
Treason	13	5 (all civilians)
Hostile Act	13	3 (all civilians)
Violence	12	2
Insubordination	12	
Absence	8	0
Sedition	8	0
Aiding enemy	8	4 (all civilians)
Casting away arms	6	2
Possessing firearms	6	0
Armed robbery	3	3 (all civilians)
Plundering	3	0
Drunk	4	0
Threatening senior officer	2	1
Offence against martial-law	2	2 (both Egyptian nationals)
Conspiracy	2	2 (both civilians)
Robbery	2	1
Theft	2	0
Attempted assassination	1	1 (civilian)
Attempted murder	4	3
Attempted desertion	1	0
Housebreaking	1	0
Losing army property	1	0
Rape	1	0
Pillaging	1	1 (civilian)
Aiding enemy whilst POW	1	0
Unspecified/Other	14	0
Total	3,342	438

Figure 3: Death sentences and executions (British and Empire Armies) by substantive rank[5]

Rank	No. of death sentences	No. of executions
Private soldiers including: Rifleman, Gunner, Trooper, Driver, Drummer, Sapper, Saddler, Able Seaman, Seaman, Sepoy, Bugler, Pioneer	2,938	316
N. C. O. s (L/Corporal, Corporal, Lance Sergeant, Sergeant, Bombardier)	134	24
2nd & Sub Lieutenant	3	3
Lieutenant	2	0
Total	3,077	343

Figure 2 indicates just how wide was the range of offences for which a sentence of death could be passed. It is also a convenient method by which one can compare the relative seriousness (in the eyes of the High Command) of each offence. As the final arbiter in capital cases the Commander-in-Chief confirmed roughly eleven per cent of the sentences and commuted the rest. This, however, was not evenly distributed. A total of 449 soldiers were sentenced to death for sleeping at their posts, but only two had their sentences confirmed (Privates Burton and Downing). This compares favourably with other offences, such as desertion (2,004 death sentences and 272 executions) and cowardice (213 death sentences and 14 executions). Clearly the Commander-in-Chief was relatively more tolerant of some offences than others.

Only five officers were sentenced to death, and none above the rank of lieutenant. This is a low number compared to the numbers of officers actually serving, and contrasts dramatically with the fate of other ranks, and private soldiers in particular.

Figure 3, above, compares how the confirming authority treated officers, non-commissioned officers and private soldiers. Of the five officers sentences to death, three were executed. The proportion of executions of non-commissioned officers, at fifteen per cent was greater than that of privates (eleven per cent), many of whom may also have been acting in the rank of Lance Corporal. It appears, therefore, that the Commander-in-Chief's expectations differed according to the rank of the soldier whose case he was reviewing, with non-commissioned officers and 2nd Lieutenants being singled out for perhaps the harshest treatment.

There was also a variation between arms, and for that matter between units. A complete breakdown of death sentences and executions in the British regiments has been produced in a tabular form, and may be found in the appendix. It can be summarised thus:

- All British cavalry units – twenty-six death sentences; no executions
- All British artillery – 104 death sentences; thirteen executions
- All British infantry – 2,452 death sentences; 271 executions

Other units such as the Medical Corps, the Machine Gun Corps and the Royal Engineers, which do not fit into any of the three categories above, have been omitted from this summary again. Fuller details may be found in the appendix. The figures relating to Dominion and Colonial units have been cited separately (on page 14).

The official statistics of courts martial, death sentences and executions, produced by the War Office and published in 1922,[6] are slightly at variance with the public records, which form the basis of this volume. This does not imply that the official statistics are incorrect: some records may have been lost or destroyed since the 1920s. Therefore, this publication, which represents the most complete information currently available concerning death sentences in the British Army, should be used in conjunction with, and not instead of, the official statistics.

The details have been collated from a variety of sources, including the courts martial registers kept by the army. Consequently, the information given is very much as it appears in the official records, most of which were hand-written. Undoubtedly, some errors crept in, and some are difficult to read. Therefore, every effort has been made to verify and cross-refer each entry. It is apparent that some false names were recorded. It was not uncommon for men to enlist under a pseudonym. Some were under age, others may have been previously rejected on grounds of poor health or physique. In the case of civilians there may have been a reluctance to co-operate with a military court. Where it is known that a false name has been used, the legal one has been added, with the pseudonym preserved.

Some inconsistencies have emerged from the process of cross-referencing. There are occasions when the available data does not correspond with information available elsewhere. The Easter Rising in Dublin in April 1916 is one example. The courts martial registers contain details of eighty-eight death sentences arising from the uprising, with fifteen of those resulting in execution. This appears to be contradicted by the *Catholic Bulletin*, published in August 1917, which cites figures of ninety-seven and sixteen respectively.[7] However, the *Sinn Fein Rebellion Handbook*, published in 1917, records the names of all those convicted by courts martial as a consequence of the revolt.[8] Generally, these names correspond with those in the courts martial register, thereby supporting its accuracy, although, somewhat mysteriously, the registers record one additional name (Slattery) which does not appear in the Sinn Fein list.

It is also possible that some records are simply missing or that details were not recorded. This appears to be so in the case of New Zealand soldiers. Twenty-three death sentences against men serving with the New Zealand Expeditionary Force are recorded, including five executions, in the courts martial registers at the Public Record Office. All are included in this volume. However, Christopher Pugsley, having studied records kept in New Zealand, has identified a further five cases where death sentences were commuted.[9] This volume is restricted to those cases that I have personally been able to verify, and readers are directed to Pugsley's study for information on those further cases in the New Zealand Expeditionary Force.

Additional information, such as the ages of men or the next of kin, not included in the registers but which may assist in the identification of individuals, has been added wherever possible. Another example of this additional information is the location of each court martial, which was often omitted from the registers. It appears to have been normal practice to record the location as 'in the field'. The inclusion of the theatre of war in which each relevant unit was serving at the time of the trial has compensated for this omission.[10] This is shown as Gallipoli, Salonika, Italy, Mesopotamia and so on. In the case of the Western Front, or France and Flanders, the precedent set by the numerous volumes of *Soldiers Died in the Great War*[11] has been followed, and this information is recorded as 'F&F'.

Inevitably, a resource such as this asks many questions and provides few answers. It is outside the scope of this introduction to address these questions in any detail, but some statistical signposts have been provided enabling readers to analyse the material themselves.[12]

Notes

1   J. Putkowski and J. Sykes, *Shot at Dawn* (Barnsley, 1992).
2   War Office, *Statistics of the Military Effort of the British Empire During the Great War 1914–1920* (London, 1922), Part XXIII – Discipline.
3   War Office, *Statistics of the Military Effort of the British Empire During the Great War 1914–1920* (London, 1922)
4   C. Pugsley, *On the Fringe of Hell* (Auckland, 1991) has identified a further five cases of New Zealand soldiers sentenced to death who do not appear in the records at the Public Record Office. See below.
5   There were also a number of labourers, muleteers, camp followers and coolies sentenced to death, including some which resulted in execution, and a small number where the rank was not recorded.
6   War Office, *Statistics of the Military Effort of the British Empire During the Great War 1914–1920* (London, 1922), Part XXIII – Discipline.
7   *Catholic Bulletin* (Dublin, August 1917).
8   *Sinn Fein Rebellion Handbook*. Easter 1916 (Dublin, 1917)
9   C. Pugsley, *On the Fringe of Hell* (Auckland, 1991).
10 The location of each unit is based on E. A. James (Brig.), *British Regiments, 1914–18*, 4th edition (London, 1993).
11 War Office, *Soldiers Died in the Great War* (London, 1920). Names of most British soldiers killed in the war were recorded in one of the eighty volumes. Significantly, almost all of the executed soldiers were omitted from these records.
12 The author's own ideas and analysis are contained in an unpublished MPhil thesis at the University of Hertfordshire.

How to use the material in this book

There are two sections to the main body of the book. The first is arranged in chronological order by date of sentence, the second in alphabetical order by surname.

The data has been presented in a convenient format, and it should be obvious how to use it. However, here are one or two notes to make things even clearer. The following guidelines have been used in completing the column entries.

Name: Surname first, followed by forenames or initials if available.

Unit: Name of unit prefixed by battalion or battery number (if known). Most of the abbreviations used are obvious, but the following should act as a guide:
ASC – Army Service Corps
Bdrs – Borderers
DAC – Divisional Ammunition Column
EF – Expeditionary Force
Fus – Fusiliers
IF – Imperial Force
Hdrs – Highlanders
KO – King's Own
LI – Light Infantry (e.g. KOYLI – King's Own Yorkshire Light Infantry)
MGC – Machine Gun Corps
R – Royal (e.g. KOR Lancaster – King's Own Royal Lancaster Regiment)
RAMC – Royal Army Medical Corps
RE – Royal Engineers
RFA – Royal Field Artillery
RGA – Royal Garrison Artillery
RHA – Royal Horse Artillery
RMLI – Royal Marine Light Infantry
RND – Royal Naval Division
Civilians are also denoted in this column, as are soldiers serving in other armies such as the German, Turkish or Egyptian. Irish insurgents sentenced to death following the Easter Rising in 1916 are included as civilians. This is merely for convenience, and is not intended to imply any status or lack of it.

Rank: The substantive rank of each soldier is shown in this column. Occasionally a temporary rank may also be given in brackets. Irish insurgents were recorded by the British Army, often incorrectly, as being members of Sinn Fein. For consistency, they are denoted as such here. The abbreviations used are:
A/B – Able Seaman
Bmdr – Bombardier
Capt – Captain
Cpl – Corporal
Dmr – Drummer
Dvr – Driver
Gnr – Gunner
Lbr – Labourer
L/Bmdr – Lance Bombardier
L/Cpl – Lance Corporal
L/Sgt – Lance Sergeant
Lt. – Lieutenant (prefixed by 2 if 2nd Lieutenant or Sub if Sub Lieutenant)
Mltr – Muleteer
Pnr – Pioneer
Pte – Private
Rfm – Rifleman
Sepoy – Indian Private
Sgt – Sergeant
S/man – Seaman
Spr – Sapper
Tpr – Trooper

Date: The date given is the date of the death sentence. Occasionally this differs from the date of the trial and/or conviction. It is invariably different to the date of execution (if applicable).

Offence: The offence for which the sentence of death was passed. Sometimes the man had been convicted of a lesser offence as well. Generally, lesser non-capital offences have been omitted. Most offences are self-explanatory; the exception is most likely to be offences 'against inhabitant'. These were usually burglary, robbery or rape. Murder tended to be a substantive offence in its own right. Where there is more than one offence, this has been indicated by a + sign and the further

offence shown in the Notes on page 121. The letters 'esc' indicate that the prisoner was also convicted of escaping, or attempting to escape.

Final sentence: This is the final sentence as confirmed by the Commander-in-Chief. It could include a period of hard labour (HL), penal servitude (PS), or imprisonment (impt). It may also include a period of Field Punishment Number One (FP1), which entailed being tied to a fixed object for many hours each day. Some cases, of course, ended in execution, and this is indicated here by the symbol 'XXX'. The date of execution has also been included if it is known. Other cases were not confirmed by the Commander-in-Chief and occasionally he 'quashed' the conviction. If an offence was not confirmed or quashed, it may be an indication that the conviction and/or sentence was not a sound one. On at least one occasion the Commander-in-Chief quashed a conviction because of a subsequent act of gallantry by the defendant.

Location: The theatre of war is indicated here. Where this was not included in the records it has been possible to obtain an idea from E A James' *British Regiments 1914–18*. Anomalies occur when units were redeployed, and death sentences were passed before the unit arrived at its next destination. In such cases the last identifiable location has been given.

Ref: This is the reference number of the volume at the Public Record Office containing the relevant entry, and should be prefixed by the letters PRO WO.

Notes: Any other information is contained in this section, which starts on page 121. Further offences or references are included. If the

sentence has been commuted, not
confirmed or quashed, an indication
of the reason for this is given if it is
known. The abbreviation 'GOA' means
'guilty of absence', a lesser offence
than desertion. All executed British
soldiers should have a PRO WO71
reference number in addition to the
PRO WO number. The theatre of war
is also shown if this information is
available (F&F refers to the Western
Front). Details of next of kin may also
be included here. These details have
been obtained from the registers of
war graves, and are therefore rather
limited, but may help to identify
individuals. Other offences may also
be included here.

Death sentences in chronological order

Name	Unit	Rank	Date	Offence	Final sentence	Location	Ref	Note
Melin Ernest W	Civilian	Alien	20/08/14	Espionage	XXX 18/9/15	UK	92/3	1
Roggen Augusto Alfredo	Civilian	Alien	20/08/14	Espionage	XXX 17/9/15	UK	92/3	2
Whittle A	2 Dragoon Gds	Pte	23/08/14	Sleeping	2yrs HL	F&F	213/2	
Buschman Fernando	Civilian	Alien	29/08/14	Espionage	XXX 19/10/14	UK	92/3	3
Brown H	ASC	Dvr	04/09/14	Sleeping	2yrs HL		213/2	
O'Gara John	Manchester	Pte	04/09/14	Housebreaking	Quashed		213/2	
Parsons JA	RFA	Dvr	04/09/14	Sleeping	2yrs HL		213/2	
Roach William	RFA	Dvr	04/09/14	Sleeping	2yrs HL		213/2	
Whincup A	4 Dragoon Gds	Pte	04/09/14	Sleeping	2yrs HL	F&F	213/2	4
Highgate Thomas	R W Kent	Pte	06/09/14	Desertion	XXX 08/09/14	F&F	213/2	5
Cooper A	2 Essex	Pte	20/09/14	Cowardice	3yrs PS	F&F	213/2	
Harvey JC	1 KOR Lancaster	Cpl	20/09/14	Cowardice	3yrs PS	F&F	213/2	
Chadwick	1 KO Yorks LI	Pte	22/09/14	Cowardice	Quashed	Singapore	213/2	
Groves Henry	4 Hussars	Pte	24/09/14	Cowardice	2yrs HL	F&F	213/2	
Prior V	1 R Berkshire	Cpl	24/09/14	Cowardice	2yrs HL/Red in rank	F&F	213/2	
Ward G	1 R Berkshire	Pte	24/09/14	Cowardice	XXX 26/09/14	F&F	213/2	6
Baker Benjamin	2 Grenadier Gds	Pte	25/09/14	Sleeping	5yrs PS	F&F	213/2	
Butler	R Scots Fus	Pte	28/09/14	Desertion	Not Conf		213/2	
Mackie Alexander	2 Highland LI	Pte	01/10/14	AWOL	2yrs HL	F&F	213/2	
Williams W	16 Lancers	Pte	01/10/14	Sleeping	2yrs HL	F&F	213/2	
Godfrey Albert	1 R W Surrey	Pte	04/10/14	Sleeping	2yrs HL		213/2	
O'Keefe D	2 Essex	Pte	06/10/14	Sleeping	2yrs HL	F&F	213/2	
Cotterill J	2 Oxon & Bucks LI	Pte	08/10/14	Sleeping	2yrs HL	F&F	213/1	
Holmes Samuel	2 Grenadier Gds	Pte	09/10/14	Sleeping	2yrs HL	F&F	213/2	
Tanner Edward	1 Wiltshire	Pte	13/10/14	Desertion	XXX 27/10/14	F&F	213/2	7
Powell W	Worcestershire	Pte	18/10/14	Sleeping	2yrs HL		213/1	
Neill Gordon	6 Dragoon Gds	Pte	24/10/14	Sleeping	2yrs HL	F&F	213/2	8
Smith H	4 Dragoon Gds	Pte	24/10/14	Sleeping	2yrs HL	F&F	213/2	9
Plant D	1 N Staffordshire	Pte	25/10/14	Cowardice	2yrs HL	F&F	213/2	
Barrett H	2 Leinster	Dmr	02/11/14	Cowardice	2 HL	F&F	213/2	
Lody Carl Hans	Civilian	Alien	02/11/14	Espionage	XXX 06/11/14	UK	92/3	10
Dwyer Percy	6 Dragoon Gds	Pte	04/11/14	Sleeping	2yrs HL	F&F	213/2	
Livingstone John	RFA	Gnr	04/11/14	Sleeping	2yrs HL		213/2	
Turner Percy	6 Dragoon Gds	Pte	04/11/14	Sleeping	2yrs HL	F&F	213/2	11
Holywood T	1 Cheshire	Pte	10/11/14	Quitting	2yrs HL	F&F	213/1	
Page F	2 Worcestershire	Pte	10/11/14	Desertion	Not Conf	F&F	213/1	
Royle J	1 Cheshire	Pte	10/11/14	Quitting	2yrs HL	F&F	213/1	
Bailey Thomas	1 Life Gds	Tpr	11/11/14	Sleeping	2yrs HL	F&F	213/2	
Fagence P	2 Middlesex	Pte	19/11/14	Sleeping	1yr HL	F&F	213/2	
Rowe T	2 Middlesex	Pte	19/11/14	Sleeping	1yr HL	F&F	213/2	
Corbett J	3 Rifle Bde	Rfm	20/11/14	Sleeping	Quashed	F&F	213/2	
Vale Samuel	RFA	Gnr	20/11/14	Sleeping	2yrs HL		213/2	
Anderton	1 Manchester	Pte	21/11/14	Cowardice	2yrs HL	F&F	213/2	
McNella James	RFA	Dvr	21/11/14	Rape	Quashed		213/2	
Davis F	KOR Lancaster	Pte	24/11/14	Cowardice	2yrs HL		213/1	
Kay L	13 Hussars	Tpr	24/11/14	Desertion	5yrs PS	F&F	213/1	
Bradshaw P	6 Dragoons	Tpr	25/11/14	Desertion	5yrs PS	F&F	213/1	12
Gayson WE	6 Dragoons	Pte	25/11/14	Desertion	5yrs PS	F&F	213/1	13
Heron S	3 Dragoons	Pte	25/11/14	Desertion	5yrs PS	F&F	213/1	14
King AE	2 Leicestershire	Pte	02/12/14	Sleeping	2yrs HL	Mesopotamia	213/2	
Shorthus William	2 Leicestershire	Pte	02/12/14	Sleeping	2yrs HL	Mesopotamia	213/2	
Affleck C	1 E Lancs	Pte	05/12/14	Cowardice	2yrs HL	F&F	213/3	
Gregson J	1 E Lancs	Pte	05/12/14	Cowardice	2yrs HL	F&F	213/3	
Abuary Abdulla	Civilian (Enemy officer?)		07/12/14	Espionage	PS Life	Port Sudan	90/6	
Argyle A	2 Leicestershire	Pte	07/12/14	Sleeping	5yrs PS	Mesopotamia	213/1	
Payne T	2 Leicestershire	Pte	07/12/14	Sleeping	5yrs PS	Mesopotamia	213/1	

Name	Unit	Rank	Date	Offence	Final sentence	Location	Ref	Note
Reed F	2 Leicestershire	Pte	07/12/14	Sleeping	5yrs PS	Mesopotamia	213/1	
Freestone B	2 Middlesex	Pte	08/12/14	Sleeping	Quashed		213/1	
Johnson A	1 Liverpool	Pte	08/12/14	Desertion	2yrs HL	F&F	213/1	
Browne Archibald	2 Essex	Pte	09/12/14	Desertion	XXX 19/12/14	F&F	213/1	15
May W	RFA	Gnr	09/12/14	Desertion	2yrs HL		213/1	
Martin S	1 Lincolnshire	Pte	12/12/14	AWOL	Quashed	F&F	213/3	
Wheeldon JF	1 Lincolnshire	Pte	12/12/14	Quitting/Sleeping	5yrs PS	F&F	213/3	
Davis G	2 Leicestershire	Pte	13/12/14	Sleeping	5yrs PS	Mesopotamia	213/1	
Kay W	2 Lancs Fus	Pte	13/12/14	Quitting	2yrs HL	F&F	213/1	
Hargreaves F	2 R Warwickshire	Pte	14/12/14	Desertion	2yrs HL	F&F	213/3	
Jones R	2 R Warwickshire	Pte	14/12/14	Desertion	2yrs HL	F&F	213/3	
Pannell C	2 R Warwickshire	Pte	14/12/14	Desertion	2yrs HL	F&F	213/3	
Carter AE	2 Bedfordshire	Pte	15/12/14	Quitting/Sleeping	2yrs HL	F&F	213/3	
Clark HFG	2 Bedfordshire	Pte	15/12/14	Quitting/Sleeping	2yrs HL	F&F	213/3	
Simpson	R Scots Fus	Pte	18/12/14	Cowardice	2yrs HL		213/3	
Murphy P	1 R Irish Fus	Pte	21/12/14	Disob + Inhab	5yrs PS	F&F	213/3	
Reavy F	1 R Irish Fus	Pte	21/12/14	Against Inhab	5yrs PS	F&F	213/3	
Coles F	1 Grenadier Gds	Cpl	24/12/14	Sleeping/Quitting	2yrs HL	F&F	213/3	
Orme H	1 Leicestershire	Pte	24/12/14	Quitting/Sleeping	3mos FP1	F&F	213/3	
Barlow C	1 Hampshire	Pte	26/12/14	Sleeping	5yrs PS	F&F	213/3	
Nicol J	2 Scottish Rifles	Pte	26/12/14	Sleeping	2yrs HL	F&F	213/3	
Stevenson J	2 Scottish Rifles	Pte	26/12/14	Drunk x2	2yrs HL	F&F	213/3	
Sanford C	2 Lincolnshire	Pte	27/12/14	Sleeping/Quitting	2yrs HL	F&F	213/3	
Longman M	1 Rifle Bde	Rfm	28/12/14	Sleeping	3mos FP1	F&F	213/3	
Matheson J	R Scots Fus	Cpl	28/12/14	Cowardice	2yrs HL		213/3	
Ball Joseph	2 Middlesex	Pte	30/12/14	Desertion	XXX 12/01/15	F&F	213/3	16
Martin CEJ	1 Bedfordshire	Pte	30/12/14	Sleeping	2yrs HL	F&F	213/3	
Sheffield F	2 Middlesex	Pte	30/12/14	Desertion	XXX 12/01/15	F&F	213/3	17
Cunningham F	1 Lincolnshire	Pte	31/12/14	Cowardice	10yrs PS	F&F	213/3	
Radford J	1 Lincolnshire	Pte	31/12/14	Cowardice	10yrs PS	F&F	213/3	
Shaw H	1 Lincolnshire	Pte	31/12/14	Cowardice	10yrs PS	F&F	213/3	
Underwood JT	1 Lincolnshire	Pte	31/12/14	Cowardice	5yrs PS	F&F	213/3	
Wheat H	1 Lincolnshire	Pte	31/12/14	Cowardice	5yrs PS	F&F	213/3	
Wood H	1 Lincolnshire	Pte	31/12/14	Cowardice	10yrs PS	F&F	213/3	
Bramwell PJ	2 Bedfordshire	Pte	05/01/15	Sleeping	2yrs HL	F&F	213/3	
Neal E	Border	Pte	08/01/15	Insubordination	2yrs HL		213/3	18
Hapted E	2 Rifle Bde	Rfm	09/01/15	Sleeping	2yrs HL	F&F	213/3	
Lawler T	1 KRRC	Pte	09/01/15	Sleeping	2yrs HL	F&F	213/3	
Cunningham D	2 Essex	Pte	11/01/15	Quitting x2	10 yrs PS	F&F	213/3	
Greaves S	1 R Warwickshire	Pte	11/01/15	Sleeping	3yrs PS	F&F	213/3	
Latham George	2 Lancs Fus	Cpl	11/01/15	Desertion	XXX 22/01/15	F&F	213/3	19
Lock TW	2 E Surrey	Pte	11/01/15	Desertion +	2yrs HL	F&F	213/3	20
Wright AE	RFA	Gnr	11/01/15	Sleeping	10yrs PS		213/3	
Mitchell W	1 R Scots Fus	Pte	15/01/15	Cowardice	15yrs PS	F&F	213/4	
Russell C	1 Loyal N Lancs	Pte	15/01/15	Sleeping	2yrs HL	F&F	213/3	
Turner G	1 E Yorks	Pte	15/01/15	Against Inhab	3mos FP1		213/3	
Ward L	1 Loyal N Lancs	Pte	15/01/15	Sleeping	2yrs HL	F&F	213/3	
Walker T	1 Loyal N Lancs	Pte	16/01/15	Sleeping	2yrs HL	F&F	213/3	
Collins H	2 R Warwickshire	Pte	18/01/15	Desertion	5yrs PS	F&F	213/3	21
Godwin J	2 KRRC	Rfm	18/01/15	Quitting	2yrs HL	F&F	213/3	
Hooper G	1 R Welsh Fus	Pte	18/01/15	Desertion	2yrs HL	F&F	213/3	
Linnett F	2 R Warwickshire	Pte	18/01/15	Desertion +	5yrs PS	F&F	213/3	22
Cummings Thomas	1 Irish Gds	Pte	19/01/15	Desertion	XXX 28/01/15	F&F	213/3	23
Smythe Alfred (Albert)	1 Irish Gds	Pte	19/01/15	Desertion	XXX 28/01/15	F&F	213/3	24
Chapman W	1 N Staffordshire	Pte	20/01/15	Desertion	10yrs PS	F&F	213/3	
Flannagan R	1 R Welsh Fus	Pte	20/01/15	Desertion	2yrs HL	F&F	213/3	
Hawkins CH	1 N Staffordshire	Pte	20/01/15	Desertion	10yrs PS	F&F	213/3	
Burrell FG	2 R Warwickshire	Pte	23/01/15	Desertion	2yrs HL	F&F	213/3	
Harrison P	2 R Warwickshire	Pte	23/01/15	Desertion	5yrs PS	F&F	213/3	
Moore W	2 R Warwickshire	Pte	23/01/15	Desertion	2yrs HL	F&F	213/3	
Troughton W	2 R Warwickshire	Pte	23/01/15	Desertion	2yrs HL	F&F	213/3	
Elsdon J	2 R Warwickshire	Pte	24/01/15	Desertion	5yrs PS	F&F	213/3	
Gould M	2 R Warwickshire	Pte	24/01/15	Desertion	5yrs PS	F&F	213/3	
Hargraves J	2 D Cornwall LI	Pte	25/01/15	Against inhab	20yrs PS	F&F	213/3	
Morris T	106 Bty RFA	Gnr	25/01/15	Desertion	5yrs PS		213/3	
Thomas C	1 R Welsh Fus	Pte	25/01/15	Desertion	2yrs HL	F&F	213/3	
McLuskie J	1 Cameron Hdrs	Pte	28/01/15	Quitting x2	5yrs PS	F&F	213/3	
Scotton William	4 Middlesex	Pte	28/01/15	Desertion	XXX 09/02/15	F&F	213/3	25

Name	Unit	Rank	Date	Offence	Final sentence	Location	Ref	Note
Senior H	11 Hussars	Pte	28/01/15	Desertion	Quashed	F&F	213/3	
Byers Joseph	1 R Scots Fus	Pte	30/01/15	Desertion	XXX 06/02/15	F&F	213/3	26
Cooper T	3 Rifle Bde	Pte	30/01/15	Striking	5yrs PS	F&F	213/3	
Evans Andrew	1 R Scots Fus	Pte	30/01/15	Desertion	XXX 06/02/15	F&F	213/3	27
Pitts A	2 R Warwickshire	Pte	30/01/15	Desertion	XXX 08/02/15	F&F	213/3	28
Farey H	2 Middlesex	Pte	31/01/15	Sleeping	2yrs HL	F&F	213/3	
Price H	2 R Welsh Fus	Pte	01/02/15	Desertion	10yrs PS	F&F	213/3	
Hudson F	2 Bedfordshire	Pte	02/02/15	Sleeping	3mos FP1	F&F	213/3	
Sutton A	2 Wiltshire	Pte	02/02/15	Sleeping	Not Conf	F&F	213/3	
Caller A	2 RW Surrey	Pte	03/02/15	AWOL+	3mos FP1	F&F	213/3	29
Povey George H	1 Cheshire	Cpl	03/02/15	Quitting	XXX 11/02/15	F&F	213/3	30
Underhill RB	13 London	Pte	03/02/15	Disobedience+	3mos FP1	F&F	213/3	31
Hope Thomas	2 Leinster	Pte	04/02/15	Desertion	XXX 02/03/15	F&F	213/3	32
McKie S	2 R Irish Rifles	Pte	04/02/15	Cowardice	Quashed	F&F	213/3	
Moran J	1 Irish Gds	Pte	04/02/15	Desertion	2yrs HL	F&F	213/3	
Sterling P	2 R Irish Rifles	Pte	04/02/15	Cowardice	Not Conf	F&F	213/3	
Harvey W	1 Sherwood Fstrs	Pte	05/02/15	Desertion	2yrs HL	F&F	213/3	
Seymour H	1 Grenadier Gds	Pte	05/02/15	Disobedience	3mos FP1	F&F	213/3	
Knight M	2 Middlesex	Pte	06/02/15	Sleeping	3mos FP1	F&F	213/3	
Richardson T	1 D Cornwall LI	Pte	06/02/15	Desertion	10yrs PS	F&F	213/3	
Tero Charles	1 Northants	Pte	06/02/15	Sleeping	2yrs HL	F&F	213/3	33
Collins George E	1 Lincolnshire	Pte	07/02/15	Desertion	XXX 15/02/15	F&F	213/3	34
Davies WJ	1 Manchester	Pte	07/02/15	Desertion	5yrs PS	F&F	213/3	
Joyce J	2 R Warwickshire	Pte	07/02/15	Desertion	3mos FP1	F&F	213/3	
Piper W	2 R Warwickshire	Pte	07/02/15	Desertion+	3mos FP1	F&F	213/3	35
Wilks H	2 R Warwickshire	Pte	07/02/15	Desertion+	3mos FP1	F&F	213/3	36
Brand J	1 Northumb Fus	Pte	08/02/15	Disobedience+	10yrs PS	F&F	213/3	37
Dalgetty G	2 Highland LI	Pte	08/02/15	Cowardice +	Not Conf	F&F	213/3	38
Fitzgerald P	2 Highland LI	Pte	08/02/15	Cowardice	Not Conf	F&F	213/3	39
Gadsby A	1 Northants	Pte	08/02/15	Desertion	Not Conf	F&F	213/3	
Dalgetty G	2 Highland LI	Pte	10/02/15	Cowardice +	1yr HL	F&F	213/3	40
Fitzgerald P	2 Highland LI	Pte	10/02/15	Cowardice +	1yr HL	F&F	213/3	41
Freeman H	1 Rifle Bde	Rfm	10/02/15	Sleeping	10yrs PS	F&F	213/3	
Jackson A	2 S Lancs	Pte	10/02/15	Cowardice	3yrs PS	F&F	213/3	
Desborough W	2 E Surrey	Pte	11/02/15	Sleeping	84days FP1	F&F	213/3	
Hastie C	2 Welsh	Pte	12/02/15	Desertion	2yrs HL	F&F	213/3	
Kelly T	3 R Inniskilling Fus	Pte	12/02/15	Desertion x2	2yrs PS	Ireland	213/3	42
Lloyd H	2 KO Scottish Bdrs	Pte	12/02/15	Desertion	5yrs PS	F&F	213/3	
Walls L	2 KO Scottish Bdrs	Pte	12/02/15	Desertion	5yrs PS	F&F	213/3	
Bridle W	2 E Surrey	Pte	14/02/15	Desertion	2yrs HL	F&F	213/3	
Buckley M	2 R Irish Rifles	Rfm	14/02/15	Desertion	Quashed	F&F	213/3	
Hammond W	2 E Surrey	Pte	14/02/15	Desertion	3yrs HL	F&F	213/3	
March J	2 E Surrey	Pte	14/02/15	Sleeping	84days FP1	F&F	213/3	
Williams L	2 E Surrey	Pte	14/02/15	Desertion	1yr HL	F&F	213/3	
Dunford S	RFA	Dvr	15/02/15	Desertion	2yrs HL		213/3	
Lyons P	1 KRRC	Pte	15/02/15	Sleeping	2yrs HL	F&F	213/3	
Selby J	1 KRRC	Pte	15/02/15	Sleeping	2yrs HL	F&F	213/3	
Strachan A	6 Gordon Hdrs	Pte	15/02/15	Sleeping	84days FP1	F&F	213/3	43
Waite J	2 R Warwickshire	Pte	15/02/15	Desertion	2yrs HL	F&F	213/3	
Shaw C	Royal Fus	L/Cpl	16/02/15	Desertion	10yrs PS		213/3	
Duncan John	1 Cameron Hdrs	Pte	18/02/15	Desertion	XXX 07/03/15	F&F	213/3	44
Briggs James	2 Border	Pte	19/02/15	Desertion	XXX 06/03/15	F&F	213/3	45
Gardner J	2 Border	Pte	19/02/15	Desertion	5yrs PS	F&F	213/3	
Atkinson Alfred	1 W Yorks	L/Cpl	20/02/15	Desertion	XXX 02/03/15	F&F	213/3	46
Green A	1 N Staffordshire	Pte	20/02/15	Desertion	5yrs PS	F&F	213/3	
Lock J	2 E Surrey	Pte	20/02/15	Desertion	84days	F&F	213/3	
McConville J	2 R Irish Rifles	Pte	20/02/15	Sleeping	2yrs HL	F&F	213/3	
McNamara J	1 E Lancs	Pte	20/02/15	Desertion	10yrs PS	F&F	213/3	
Richardson A	1 E Lancs	Pte	20/02/15	Desertion	10yrs PS	F&F	213/3	
Maddison T	2 W Yorks	Pte	21/02/15	Sleeping	3mos FP1	F&F	213/3	
Mayo A	2 E Surrey	Pte	21/02/15	Sleeping	84days FP1	F&F	213/3	
Sharp H	2 A&S Hdrs	Pte	24/02/15	Quitting	2yrs HL	F&F	213/3	
Jenkinson C	1 York & Lancaster	Pte	25/02/15	Desertion	10yrs PS	F&F	213/3	
Jones R	2 R Warwickshire	Pte	25/02/15	Desertion	2yrs HL	F&F	213/3	
Gibbin A	1 Loyal N Lancs	Pte	26/02/15	Desertion	2yrs HL	F&F	213/3	
Kirk Ernest	1 W Yorks	Pte	26/02/15	Desertion	XXX 06/03/15	F&F	213/3	47
Sweetapple W	1 Hampshire	Pte	26/02/15	Desertion	10yrs PS	F&F	213/3	
Taggart J	1 N Staffordshire	Pte	26/02/15	Drunk	3yrs PS	F&F	213/3	

Name	Unit	Rank	Date	Offence	Final sentence	Location	Ref	Note
Turner H	1 Worcestershire	Pte	28/02/15	Desertion +	Not Conf	F&F	213/3	48
Hayes T	1 Cheshire	Pte	01/03/15	Sleeping	10yrs PS	F&F	213/3	
Jude A	1 R W Kent	Pte	01/03/15	Desertion	Quashed	F&F	213/3	
Kelly G	2 Scottish Rifles	Pte	05/03/15	Sleeping	3mos FP1	F&F	213/3	
McClarnon H	1 R Irish Rifles	Rfm	05/03/15	Desertion	2yrs HL	F&F	213/3	
Drennan A	2 R Irish Rifles	Rfm	08/03/15	Desertion	10yrs PS	F&F	213/3	
Forrest J	2 A&S Hdrs	Pte	09/03/15	Desertion	10yrs PS	F&F	213/3	
Hughes W	4 Royal Fus	Pte	09/03/15	Sleeping	10yrs PS	F&F	213/3	
Bell P	1 R Scots Fus	Pte	10/03/15	Desertion	10yrs PS	F&F	213/3	
Casey E	1 R Scots Fus	Pte	10/03/15	Desertion	10yrs PS	F&F	213/3	
King W	1 R Scots Fus	Pte	10/03/15	Desertion	10yrs PS	F&F	213/3	
O'Sullivan J	2 R Irish Rifles	Bugler	10/03/15	Desertion	Qyashed	F&F	213/3	
Taylor T	1 Scottish Rifles	Pte	10/03/15	Desertion	10yrs PS	F&F	213/3	
Dunbar R	2 KOR Lancaster	Pte	11/03/15	Desertion	Quashed	F&F	213/3	
Walton William	2 KRRC	L/Sgt	12/03/15	Desertion	XXX 23/03/15	F&F	213/3	49
Brooke R	4 Rifle Bde	Rfm	13/03/15	Sleeping	Not Conf	F&F	213/3	
Shalders H	12 R Lancers	Pte	14/03/15	Desertion	Quashed	F&F	213/3	50
Bradford F	2 Durham LI	Pte	15/03/15	Disobedience	15yrs PS	F&F	213/3	
Patrick W	1 R Berkshire	Pte	16/03/15	Desertion	2yrs HL	F&F	213/3	
Marienfeld	German Infantry	POW	17/03/15	Hostile Act	Not Conf		213/3	51
Jones W	1 N Staffordshire	Pte	18/03/15	Cowardice	10yrs PS	F&F	213/3	
Towey W	1 N Staffordshire	Sgt	18/03/15	Cowardice	10yrs PS	F&F	213/3	
Welsh M	1 N Staffordshire	Pte	18/03/15	Cowardice	10yrs PS	F&F	213/3	
Brown A	2 KOR Lancaster	Pte	19/03/15	Sleeping	2yrs HL	F&F	213/3	
Griffin W	2 KOR Lancaster	Pte	19/03/15	Sleeping	2yrs HL	F&F	213/3	
Harwood R	2 KOR Lancaster	Pte	19/03/15	Sleeping	Quashed	F&F	213/3	
Jarman G	2 KOR Lancaster	L/Cpl	19/03/15	Sleeping	5yrs PS	F&F	213/3	
Smith G	2 E Surrey	Pte	19/03/15	Sleeping	3mos FP1	F&F	213/3	
Turnbull W	2 KOR Lancaster	Pte	19/03/15	Sleeping	2yrs HL	F&F	213/3	
Fuller R	2 E Surrey	Cpl	20/03/15	Desertion	5yrs PS	F&F	213/3	
Hearnden A	2 E Surrey	Pte	20/03/15	Desertion	Quashed	F&F	213/4	
Hood T	2 E Surrey	Pte	20/03/15	Sleeping	5yrs PS	F&F	213/3	
King H	2 E Surrey	L/Cpl	20/03/15	Sleeping	5yrs PS	F&F	213/3	
Skinner P	2 E Surrey	Pte	20/03/15	Sleeping	5yrs PS	F&F	213/3	
Spencer T	2 E Surrey	Pte	20/03/15	Sleeping	5yrs PS	F&F	213/3	
Walker R	2 E Surrey	Pte	20/03/15	Sleeping	5yrs PS	F&F	213/3	
Driver F	2 E Surrey	L/Cpl	23/03/15	Quitting	5yrs PS	F&F	213/3	52
Capel T	2 E Surrey	Pte	24/03/15	Sleeping	3mos FP1	F&F	213/3	
Dunk J	2 E Surrey	Pte	24/03/15	Sleeping	42days FP1	F&F	213/3	
Miles EJ	2 E Surrey	Pte	24/03/15	Sleeping	3mos FP1	F&F	213/3	
Robinson H	2 E Surrey	Pte	24/03/15	Sleeping	3mos FP1	F&F	213/3	
Couzens A	4 Royal Fus	Sgt	25/03/15	Cowardice	3yrs PS	F&F	213/3	
Pullen W	4 Royal Fus	Pte	25/03/15	Desertion	10yrs PS	F&F	213/3	
Reid Isaac	2 Scots Gds	Pte	26/03/15	Desertion	XXX 09/04/15	F&F	213/3	53
Brown A	1 E Yorks	Pte	27/03/15	Sleeping	2yrs HL	F&F	213/3	
Doyle T	2 Manchester	Pte	27/03/15	Desertion	Not Conf	F&F	213/3	
Greenhalgh H	2 Manchester	Pte	27/03/15	Desertion	10yrs PS	F&F	213/3	
Marlow CJ	68 Bty RFA	Gnr	27/03/15	Striking	5yrs PS		213/3	
McGovern T	2 A & S Hdrs	Pte	27/03/15	Desertion	10yrs PS	F&F	213/3	
Miller G	2 A & S Hdrs	Pte	27/03/15	Desertion	10yrs PS	F&F	213/3	
Wilson H	4 A&S Hdrs	Pte	27/03/15	Desertion	15yrs PS	UK	213/3	54
Young G	2 R Irish Rifles	Rfm	27/03/15	Desertion	15yrs PS	F&F	213/3	
Barnes H	2 KO Yorks LI	Pte	28/03/15	Desertion	15yrs PS	F&F	213/3	
Burford GH	2 KO Yorks LI	Pte	28/03/15	Desertion	15yrs PS	F&F	213/3	
Mills F	1 KRRC	Pte	28/03/15	Sleeping	3mos FP1	F&F	213/3	
Begg C	1 Highland L I	Pte	29/03/15	Desertion	5yrs PS	F&F	213/3	
Fone MH	RFA	Gnr	29/03/15	Sleeping	3mos FP		213/4	
Milloy J	4 Liverpool	L/Cpl	29/03/15	Desertion	5yrs PS	F&F	213/3	
Mooney J	2 R Irish Rifles	Pte	29/03/15	Desertion	Quashed	F&F	213/3	
Thompson J	2 R Irish Rifles	Pte	29/03/15	Desertion x2	Quashed	F&F	213/3	
Watson G	1 Highland LI	Pte	29/03/15	Desertion	5yrs PS	F&F	213/3	
Steben G	14 Canadian Bn	Pte	30/03/15	Desertion	Not Conf	F&F	213/3	
Banks G	1 N Staffordshire	Pte	31/03/15	Sleeping	2yrs HL	F&F	213/3	
Gracey A	1 N Staffordshire	Pte	31/03/15	Sleeping	Quashed	F&F	213/3	
Broad T	2 E Surrey	Pte	03/04/15	Desertion	3mos FP1	F&F	213/4	
Stewart Stanley	2 R Scots Fus	Pte	04/04/15	Desertion +	Not Conf	F&F	213/3	55
Irvine William J	KOR Lancaster	L/Cpl	05/04/15	Desertion x2	XXX 20/04/15	F&F	213/3	56
Wright J	York & Lancaster	Pte	05/04/15	Sleeping	5yrs PS	F&F	213/4	

Name	Unit	Rank	Date	Offence	Final sentence	Location	Ref	Note
Fox Joseph Stanley Victor	1 Wiltshire	L/Cpl	06/04/15	Desertion	XXX 20/04/15	F&F	213/3	57
Gordon J	1 Scottish Rifles	Pte	06/04/15	Desertion	10yrs PS	F&F	213/3	
Jones William	43 Bty RFA	Gnr	06/04/15	Desertion +	XXX 20/04/15		213/3	58
Cowell J	1 Devon	Pte	07/04/15	Desertion	10yrs PS	F&F	213/4	
Penn Major	1 R Welsh Fus	Pte	07/04/15	Desertion	XXX 22/04/15	F&F	213/3	59
Troughton Albert	1 R Welsh Fus	Pte	07/04/15	Desertion	XXX 22/04/15	F&F	213/3	60
Walters G	1 Devon	Pte	07/04/15	Desertion	15yrs PS	F&F	213/4	
Wootton G	1 Devon	Pte	07/04/15	Desertion	10yrs PS	F&F	213/4	
Brewster J	2 R Irish Rifles	Rfm	08/04/15	Desertion	Quashed	F&F	213/3	
McDonald J	2 Highland LI	Pte	08/04/15	Desertion x2	10yrs PS	F&F	213/3	
Burton J	1 Northumb Fus	Pte	09/04/15	Desertion	10yrs PS	F&F	213/4	
Burke W	2 R Inniskilling Fus	Pte	10/04/15	Desertion+	15yrs PS	F&F	213/4	61
Dalziel J	1 Highland LI	Pte	10/04/15	Sleeping	2yrs HL	F&F	213/3	
Mohamad Ahmed El Sufi	Civilian		10/04/15	Murder	XXX	Egypt	213/3	
Traynor J	1 Highland LI	Pte	10/04/15	Sleeping	2yrs HL	F&F	213/3	
Draper A	1 R W Kent	Pte	11/04/15	Sleeping	Remitted	F&F	213/4	
Anderson W	1 R Irish Rifles	Rfm	14/04/15	Sleeping	3mos FP1	F&F	213/3	
Kershaw James	KOR Lancaster	Pte	14/04/15	Desertion	XXX 26/04/15	F&F	213/3	62
Sparkes E	13 Hussars	Tpr	15/04/15	Desertion	Not Conf	F&F	213/3	
Bell John	57 Bty RFA	Dvr	16/04/15	Desertion x3	XXX 25/04/15	F&F	213/3	63
Wilkinson W	RFA	Dvr	16/04/15	Desertion	5yrs PS	F&F	213/3	64
McAuley J	2 Highland LI	Pte	18/04/15	Desertion	5yrs PS	F&F	213/4	
Turner SC	1 Gloucestershire	Pte	18/04/15	Cowardice	2yrs HL	F&F	213/3	
Mohammed Khalil	Civilian		19/04/15	Att Murder	XXX	Egypt	213/3	65
Hobbs RF	3 Royal Fus	Pte	20/04/15	Desertion	10yrs PS	F&F	213/4	
Fraser G	2 R Scots	Pte	21/04/15	Desertion	Quashed	F&F	213/4	
Heyes A	5 S Lancs	Rfm	21/04/15	Sleeping	3yrs PS	F&F	213/4	
Sullivan	1 KOR Lancaster	Pte	21/04/15	Desertion	15yrs PS	F&F	213/4	
Lacey F	2 Grenadier Gds	Pte	23/04/15	Sleeping	2yrs HL	F&F	213/3	
Chapman T	2 Lincolnshire	Pte	26/04/15	Desertion	5yrs PS	F&F	213/4	
FitzGerald A	2 R Irish	Pte	27/04/15	Sleeping	5yrs PS	F&F	213/4	
Hinton A	2 Manchester	Pte	27/04/15	Desertion	15yrs PS	F&F	213/4	
Massey T	2 R Irish	Pte	27/04/15	Sleeping	5yrs PS	F&F	213/4	
Burrell William Henry	2 R Sussex	Pte	30/04/15	Desertion	5yrs PS	F&F	213/4	66
Evans DL	1 R Munster Fus	Sgt	03/05/15	Cowardice	10yrs PS	Gallipoli	213/4	
O'Mahoney C	1 R Munster Fus	Cpl	03/05/15	Cowardice	10yrs PS	Mesopotamia	213/4	
Quill	1 R Munster Fus	Pte	04/05/15	Cowardice	10yrs PS	Mesopotamia	213/4	
Battersby WR	1/5 Liverpool	Rfm	05/05/15	Sleeping	2yrs HL	F&F	213/4	
Perry J	4 Worcestershire	Pte	05/05/15	Cowardice	10yrs PS	Mesopotamia	213/4	
Sheppard F	51 Australian IF	Pte	07/05/15	Desertion	10yrs PS		213/15	
Fraser Evan	2 R Scots	Pte	09/05/15	Desertion x3	XXX 02/08/15	F&F	213/4	67
Randall G	1 E Surrey	Pte	09/05/15	Sleeping	5yrs PS	F&F	213/4	
Chisholm Alexander	20 Army Troop Coy RE	Cpl	10/05/15	Murder	XXX 17/05/15	F&F	90/6	68
Brown G	2 KO Yorks LI	Pte	14/05/15	Desertion	15yrs PS	F&F	213/4	
Graham J	2 KO Yorks LI	Pte	14/05/15	Desertion	15yrs PS	F&F	213/4	
Holmes J	2 KO Yorks LI	Pte	14/05/15	Desertion	15yrs PS	F&F	213/4	
Iveson H	2 KO Yorks LI	Pte	14/05/15	Desertion	15yrs PS	F&F	213/4	
Turner G	2 Durham LI	Pte	14/05/15	Sleeping	5yrs PS	F&F	213/4	
Wakefield J	2 KO Yorks LI	Pte	14/05/15	Desertion	15yrs PS	F&F	213/4	
Willoughby HO	5 Lincolnshire	Pte	15/05/15	Sleeping	3yrs PS	F&F	213/4	
Davison F	2 KO Yorks LI	Pte	17/05/15	Desertion	15yrs PS	F&F	213/4	
Skinner	2 Rifle Bde	Rfm	17/05/15	Desertion	2yrs HL	F&F	213/4	
Ward J	2 KO Yorks LI	Pte	17/05/15	Desertion	15yrs PS	F&F	213/4	
Bird William G	1/5 S Staffordshire	Pte	18/05/15	Sleeping	2yrs HL	F&F	213/4	
Day W	1/5 S Lancs	Rfm	20/05/15	Sleeping	5yrs PS	F&F	213/4	
Findley T	1 Loyal N Lancs	Pte	20/05/15	Desertion+	5yrs PS	F&F	213/4	69
Richardson A	1 York & Lancaster	Pte	20/05/15	Desertion	5yrs PS	F&F	213/4	
Bristow W	2 Rifle Bde	Rfm	21/05/15	Striking	3mos FP1	F&F	213/4	
Coghlan T	1 R Irish Rifles	Rfm	21/05/15	Desertion	5yrs PS	F&F	213/4	
Robinson W	1 R Irish Rifles	Rfm	21/05/15	Striking	3mos FP1	F&F	213/4	
Hodgetts Oliver	1 Worcestershire	Pte	22/05/15	Cowardice	XXX 04/06/15	F&F	213/4	70
Debuse G	4 Royal Fus	Pte	25/05/15	Sleeping	3yrs PS	F&F	213/4	
Morgan A	4 Royal Fus	Pte	25/05/15	Sleeping	3yrs PS	F&F	213/4	
Roberts W	4 Royal Fus	Pte	25/05/15	Desertion	5yrs PS	F&F	213/4	
Roe George	2 KO Yorks LI	Pte	26/05/15	Desertion	XXX 10/06/15	F&F	213/4	71
Chase Herbert	2 Lancs Fus	Pte	29/05/15	Cowardice	XXX 12/06/15	F&F	213/4	72
Mills W	1/10 Manchester	Pte	29/05/15	Cowardice	5yrs PS	Mesopotamia	213/4	
Whitehead H	1/10 Manchester	Pte	29/05/15	Cowardice	5yrs PS	Mesopotamia	213/4	

Name	Unit	Rank	Date	Offence	Final sentence	Location	Ref	Note
Townsend T	2 E Surrey	Pte	31/05/15	Desertion	5yrs PS	F&F	213/4	
Bray Walter W	6 Dragoon Gds	Pte	02/06/15	Sleeping	5yrs PS	F&F	213/4	
Paley A	2 Welsh	Pte	03/06/15	Desertion	5yrs PS	F&F	213/4	
Fillingham A	2 Lancs Fus	Sgt	04/06/15	Cowardice	Quashed	F&F	213/4	
Lunny	2 Lancs Fus	Pte	04/06/15	Cowardice	Quashed	F&F	213/4	
Sykes W	2 Essex	Pte	04/06/15	Cowardice	Quashed	F&F	213/4	
Tilbrook W	2 Essex	Pte	04/06/15	Cowardice	Quashed	F&F	213/4	
Wright	KOR Lancaster	Pte	04/06/15	Cowardice	Quashed		213/4	
McCarthy J	1 R Irish Rifles	Rfm	05/06/15	Desertion	2yrs HL	F&F	213/4	
Willoughby JW	2 R Berkshire	Pte	05/06/15	Sleeping	2yrs HL	F&F	213/4	
Molyneaux J	1 Loyal N Lancs	Pte	06/06/15	Desertion	5yrs PS	F&F	213/4	
Taylor ED	Lord Strathcona's Horse	Pte	06/06/15	Desertion	5yrs PS		213/4	
Cox W	2 Gloucestershire	Pte	07/06/15	Sleeping	3yrs PS	F&F	213/4	
Swann F	139 MGC	Pte	09/06/15	Sleeping	5yrs PS		213/15	
Wilson HF	16 Lancers	Pte	10/06/15	Sleeping	2yrs HL	F&F	213/4	73
Beaumont Ernest Alfred	2 Leicestershire	Pte	11/06/15	Desertion	XXX 24/06/15	F&F	213/4	74
Harris Thomas	1 R W Kent	Pte	12/06/15	Desertion	XXX 21/06/15	F&F	213/4	75
Pelly A	3 Royal Fus	Pte	12/06/15	Desertion	5yrs PS	F&F	213/4	
Swann T	3 Royal Fus	Pte	12/06/15	Desertion	10yrs PS	F&F	213/4	
Brennan G	1 Leinster	Pte	14/06/15	Sleeping	3yrs PS	F&F	213/4	
Callow H	1 E Surrey	Pte	14/06/15	Sleeping	2yrs HL	F&F	213/4	
Cozens A	1 E Surrey	Pte	14/06/15	Sleeping	2yrs HL	F&F	213/4	
Fay M	1 Leinster	Pte	14/06/15	Sleeping	3yrs PS	F&F	213/4	
Hookins A	1 E Surrey	Pte	14/06/15	Sleeping	2yrs HL	F&F	213/4	
Mullins M	1 Leinster	Pte	14/06/15	Sleeping+	3yrs PS	F&F	213/4	76
Winter F	1 R Scots Fus	Pte	15/06/15	Desertion	10yrs PS	F&F	213/4	
Chapman V	3 Middlesex	L/Cpl	16/06/15	Desertion	15yrs PS	F&F	213/4	
Gibbs T	3 Essex	Pte	16/06/15	Desertion	15yrs PS	UK	213/4	77
Hodgetts W	3 Worcestershire	Pte	19/06/15	Desertion	10yrs PS	F&F	213/4	
McSally William	3 Worcestershire	Pte	19/06/15	Desertion	10yrs PS	F&F	213/4	
Turpie William	2 E Surrey	Pte	19/06/15	Desertion	XXX 01/07/15	F&F	213/4	78
Appleby A	1 D Cornwall LI	Pte	22/06/15	Striking	3yrs PS	F&F	213/4	
Davis Thomas	1 R Munster Fus	Pte	22/06/15	Quitting	XXX 02/07/15	Gallipoli	213/4	79
Hodgson A	2 KO Yorks LI	Pte	24/06/15	Desertion	5yrs PS	F&F	213/4	
Mulvihill J	4 Liverpool	Pte	24/06/15	Quitting	5yrs PS	F&F	213/4	
Bacon MA	88 Coy RGA	Sgt	25/06/15	Desertion	XXX [?]	Hong Kong	213/4	
White J	1 R Irish Fus	Pte	26/06/15	Desertion	2yrs HL	F&F	213/4	
Quinn F	4 Rifle Bde	Rfm	29/06/15	Desertion	5yrs PS	F&F	213/4	
Brady	2 Lancs Fus	Pte	30/06/15	Desertion	5yrs PS	F&F	213/4	
Henshall	2 Lancs Fus	Pte	30/06/15	Desertion	5yrs PS	F&F	213/4	
Currington C	2 Essex	Pte	01/07/15	Desertion	3yrs PS	F&F	213/4	
Johnson W	1 Welsh	Pte	01/07/15	Sleeping	5yrs PS	F&F	213/4	
Salmon J	2 Essex	Pte	01/07/15	Desertion	Quashed	F&F	213/4	
Wilkinson G	2 Essex	Pte	01/07/15	Desertion	3yrs PS	F&F	213/4	
Beaumont K	1 KO Yorks LI	Pte	02/07/15	Sleeping	5yrs PS	F&F	213/4	
Bellamy W	1 KRRC	Rfm	02/07/15	Cowardice	XXX 16/07/15	F&F	213/4	80
Burden Herbert	1 Northumb Fus	Pte	02/07/15	Desertion	XXX 21/07/15	F&F	213/4	81
Coleman John	2 Sherwood Fstrs	Pte	02/07/15	Desertion	10yrs PS	F&F	213/4	
Middleton J	1 KO Yorks LI	Pte	02/07/15	Sleeping	5yrs PS	F&F	213/4	
Davis P	1 R Munster Fus	Pte	04/07/15	Cowardice	10yrs PS	Mesopotamia	213/4	
Docherty Thomas	2 KO Scottish Bdrs	Pte	04/07/15	Desertion	XXX 16/07/15	F&F	213/4	82
Kerridge J	RAMC	Pte	04/07/15	Desertion	10yrs PS		213/4	
O'Leary	1 R Munster Fus	Pte	04/07/15	Cowardice	10yrs PS	Mesopotamia	213/4	
Evans E	RE	Spr	05/07/15	Desertion	Not Conf		213/4	
Fatoma	W African Regt	Pte	05/07/15	Cowardice	XXX 19/07/15	Cameroon	213/4	83
Sinna	W African	Pte	05/07/15	Cowardice	5yrs PS	Cameroon	213/4	
Rosenthal Robert	Civilian		06/07/15	Espionage	XXX (Hanged)	UK	92/3	84
Ives Frederick	3 Worcestershire	Cpl	07/07/15	Desertion	XXX 26/07/15	F&F	213/4	85
Mitchell David	2 R Scots	Pte	07/07/15	Desertion	5yrs PS	F&F	213/4	
Braithwaite A	7 Liverpool	Pte	08/07/15	Sleeping+	6 Mos HL	F&F	213/4	86
Hayes R	1 Liverpool	Rfm	08/07/15	Striking x2	6mos HL	F&F	213/4	
McDermott J	12 Australian IF	Pte	09/07/15	Sleeping	5yrs PS		213/5	
Stainthorpe H	1 W Yorks	Pte	09/07/15	Desertion	10yrs PS	F&F	213/4	
Baldwin F	3 Middlesex	Pte	10/07/15	Sleeping	3yrs PS	F&F	213/4	
Bearman W	3 Middlesex	Pte	10/07/15	Sleeping	3yrs PS	F&F	213/4	
Bryant C	3 Middlesex	Pte	10/07/15	Sleeping	3yrs PS	F&F	213/4	
Edwards A	3 Middlesex	Pte	10/07/15	Sleeping	6mos HL	F&F	213/4	
Hilton AJ	7 Liverpool	Pte	10/07/15	Sleeping+	1yr HL	F&F	213/4	87

Name	Unit	Rank	Date	Offence	Final sentence	Location	Ref	Note
Mason W	3 Middlesex	Pte	10/07/15	Sleeping	3yrs PS	F&F	213/4	
Wells A	3 Middlesex	Pte	10/07/15	Sleeping	3yrs PS	F&F	213/4	
Rue J	2 Essex	Pte	12/07/15	Quitting	3yrs PS	F&F	213/4	
Bowyer E	1 Welsh	Pte	13/07/15	Sleeping	3yrs PS	F&F	213/4	
Riddle A	1 Welsh	Pte	13/07/15	Sleeping	3yrs PS	F&F	213/4	
Fellows Ernest	3 Worcestershire	Pte	14/07/15	Desertion	XXX 26/07/15	F&F	213/4	88
Hartells Bert	3 Worcestershire	Pte	14/07/15	Desertion	XXX 26/07/15	F&F	213/4	89
Hollingsworth W	2 Essex	Pte	14/07/15	Desertion	Not Conf	F&F	213/4	
Robinson John	3 Worcestershire	Pte	14/07/15	Desertion	XXX 26/07/15	F&F	213/4	90
Thompson Alfred	3 Worcestershire	Pte	14/07/15	Desertion	XXX 26/07/15	F&F	213/4	91
Crowther FE	1 KO Yorks LI	Pte	15/07/15	Sleeping	3yrs PS	F&F	213/4	
Janssen Haicke MP	Civilian	Alien	15/07/15	Espionage	XXX 29/07/15	UK	92/3	92
Roos Willem Johannes	Civilian	Alien	15/07/15	Espionage	XXX 29/07/15	UK	92/3	93
Gilmore Patrick	2 Durham LI	Pte	16/07/15	Desertion	10yrs PS	F&F	213/4	
Dunn J	New Zealand EF	Pte	18/07/15	Sleeping	Commuted		213/5	94
McAteer W	1 A&S Hdrs	Pte	19/07/15	Sleeping	5yrs PS	F&F	213/4	
Standed G	2 E Kent (Buffs)	Pte	19/07/15	Sleeping	3yrs PS	F&F	213/4	
Middleton A	2 R Scots Fus	Pte	20/07/15	Desertion	2yrs HL	F&F	213/4	
Veasey T	2 R Scots Fus	Pte	20/07/15	Desertion	2yrs HL	F&F	213/4	
Hand J	2 Gloucestershire	Pte	21/07/15	Sleeping	5yrs PS	F&F	213/4	
Stevens W	2 Gloucestershire	Pte	21/07/15	Sleeping	5yrs PS	F&F	213/4	
Taylor T	2 Gloucestershire	Pte	21/07/15	Sleeping	5yrs PS	F&F	213/4	
Blackbarrow James	2 E Surrey	Pte	24/07/15	Desertion	10yrs PS	F&F	213/4	
Godfrey R	6 S Lancs	Pte	25/07/15	Sleeping	2yrs HL	Gallipoli	213/5	
McCall F	1 Scottish Rifles	Pte	25/07/15	Desertion	5yrs PS	F&F	213/4	
Aldridge W	7 KRRC	Rfm	26/07/15	Cowardice	10yrs PS	F&F	213/4	
Mulvey M	2 R Irish Rifles	Pte	28/07/15	Desertion	3yrs PS	F&F	213/4	
Redmond D	1 R Irish Rifles	Rfm	28/07/15	Sleeping	56days FP1	F&F	213/4	
Ball G	9 Sherwood Fstrs	Pte	31/07/15	Sleeping	2yrs HL	Egypt	213/5	
Burton R	9 Sherwood Fstrs	Pte	31/07/15	Sleeping	2yrs HL	Egypt	213/5	
Shinton G	7 S Staffordshire	L/Cpl	31/07/15	Sleeping	2yrs HL	Gallipoli	213/5	
Chadwick JW	1/7 W Yorks	Rfm	01/08/15	Quitting	5yrs PS	F&F	213/4	95
Dyson P	2 Manchester	Pte	02/08/15	Cowardice	Quashed	F&F	213/5	
MacKenzie J	7 Seaforth Hdrs	Pte	05/08/15	Desertion	2yrs HL	F&F	213/4	
Phillips Lewis R	6 Somerset LI	Pte	08/08/15	Desertion	XXX 19/08/15	F&F	213/4	96
Shaw C	37 Trench How Bty RFA	Gnr	08/08/15	Desertion	10yrs PS		213/4	
Lockwood A	10 W Yorks	Pte	09/08/15	Striking	5yrs PS	F&F	213/4	
Morris T	1 KOR Lancaster	Sgt	09/08/15	Desertion x2	10yrs PS	F&F	213/5	
Noble W	1 R Dragoons	Pte	09/08/15	Striking+	2yrs HL	F&F	213/4	97
Sparkisman A	7 E Yorks	Pte	09/08/15	Sleeping	5yrs PS		213/4	
Halstead E	1 KO Yorks LI	Pte	10/08/15	Sleeping	5yrs PS	F&F	213/4	
Mobbs R	1 KO Yorks LI	Pte	10/08/15	Sleeping	5yrs PS	F&F	213/4	
Rodgers S	1/8 W Yorks	Rfm	10/08/15	Sleeping	3yrs PS	F&F	213/4	98
Bolton E	1 Cheshire	Pte	11/08/15	Desertion	10yrs PS	F&F	213/5	
Cartwright A	1 Cheshire	Sgt	11/08/15	Desertion	10yrs PS	F&F	213/5	
Joseph J	2 Northumb Fus	Pte	11/08/15	Sleeping	3yrs PS	F&F	213/4	
Miller RL	14 Canadian EF	Pte	11/08/15	Desertion	10yrs PS	F&F	213/4	
Barker F	1 Norfolk	Pte	12/08/15	Sleeping	10yrs PS	F&F	213/4	
Brazier R	1 Norfolk	Pte	12/08/15	Sleeping	15yrs PS	F&F	213/4	
Cameron W	1/8 Lancs Fus	Pte	12/08/15	Cowardice	Commuted	Gallipoli	213/5	
Hudson J	1 Norfolk	Pte	12/08/15	Sleeping	15yrs PS	F&F	213/4	
Jones T	1 Cheshire	Pte	12/08/15	Sleeping	Commuted	F&F	213/5	
Lack JB	1 Norfolk	Pte	12/08/15	Sleeping	10yrs PS	F&F	213/4	
Livesay R	5 R Irish	Pte	12/08/15	AWOL	2yrs HL		213/5	99
Rice A	1 Norfolk	Pte	12/08/15	Sleeping	10yrs PS	F&F	213/4	
Johnston A	1 R Irish Rifles	Rfm	13/08/15	Sleeping	2yrs Imp	F&F	213/4	
Barrett F	4 KRRC	Rfm	14/08/15	Desertion	10yrs PS	F&F	213/5	
Saddington JW	5 Leicestershire	Pte	14/08/15	Sleeping	5yrs PS	F&F	213/4	
Foster J	1/8 Manchester	Pte	15/08/15	Cowardice	Not Conf	Gallipoli	213/5	100
John E	10 Australian IF	Pte	17/08/15	Sleeping	2yrs HL		213/5	
Hamilton L	1/6 A&S Hdrs	Pte	19/08/15	Sleeping	10yrs PS	F&F	213/4	101
Berry	2 Manchester	Pte	20/08/15	Cowardice	10yrs PS	F&F	213/5	
Grady W	2 Manchester	Pte	20/08/15	Cowardice	10yrs PS	F&F	213/5	
Hill G	2 Manchester	Pte	20/08/15	Cowardice	10yrs PS	F&F	213/5	
Horsfall R	2 Manchester	Pte	20/08/15	Cowardice	10yrs PS	F&F	213/5	
Mather A	2 Manchester	Pte	20/08/15	Cowardice	10yrs PS	F&F	213/5	
Chapman JW	1 Devon	Pte	21/08/15	Sleeping	10yrs PS	F&F	213/5	
Haggar CW	1 Devon	Pte	21/08/15	Sleeping	10yrs PS	F&F	213/5	

Name	Unit	Rank	Date	Offence	Final sentence	Location	Ref	Note
Robson D	1 Devon	Pte	21/08/15	Sleeping	10yrs PS	F&F	213/5	
Squires T	6 Leicestershire	Cpl	21/08/15	Sleeping	5yrs PS	F&F	213/4	
Garmory W	12 Manchester	Pte	22/08/15	Desertion	2yrs HL	F&F	213/5	102
Hunt R	3 Worcestershire	Pte	23/08/15	Sleeping	5yrs PS	F&F	213/5	
Maloney J	1 Loyal N Lancs	Pte	24/08/15	Sleeping	1yr HL	F&F	213/4	
Webb J	1 Loyal N Lancs	Pte	24/08/15	Sleeping	1yr HL	F&F	213/4	
Scott D	10 Highland LI	Pte	25/08/15	Cowardice+	5yrs PS	F&F	213/5	103
Dwyer E	1 York & Lancaster	Pte	26/08/15	Sleeping	5yrs PS	F&F	213/5	
Purnell G	3 Middlesex	Pte	26/08/15	Sleeping	10yrs PS	F&F	213/5	
Gilbert W	3 Middlesex	Pte	27/08/15	Sleeping	5yrs PS	F&F	213/5	
Crook R	1/6 W Riding	Pte	28/08/15	Sleeping	5yrs PS	F&F	213/5	
Maude G	1/6 W Riding	Pte	28/08/15	Sleeping	5yrs PS	F&F	213/5	
Friel J	2 Highland LI	Pte	29/08/15	Desertion	5yrs PS	F&F	213/5	
Turner A	1 Bedfordshire	Pte	29/08/15	Sleeping x3	Commuted	F&F	213/5	
Whittaker J	1 Dorset	Pte	29/08/15	Sleeping	10yrs PS	F&F	213/5	
Parker H	1/8 Manchester	Pte	30/08/15	Sleeping	1yr HL	Gallipoli	213/5	104
Peterson VH	10 Australian IF	Pte	30/08/15	Sleeping	2yrs HL		213/5	
Sands Peter	1 R Irish Rifles	Rfm	30/08/15	Desertion	XXX 15/09/15	F&F	213/5	105
Baker W	1/5 E Lancs	Pte	01/09/15	Sleeping	5yrs PS	Gallipoli	213/5	
Ryan P	2 R Dublin Fus	Pte	01/09/15	Desertion	10yrs PS	F&F	213/5	
Steele E	1 Highland LI	Pte	01/09/15	Sleeping	2yrs HL	F&F	213/4	
Stannard O	1 Rifle Bde	Rfm	06/09/15	Desertion	15yrs PS	F&F	213/5	
Brooks C	5 Wiltshire	Pte	07/09/15	Disobedience	7yrs PS	Gallipoli	213/5	
Adshead A	1/9 Manchester	Pte	09/09/15	Sleeping	10yrs PS	Gallipoli	213/5	
Bridges W	1/10 London	Pte	09/09/15	Sleeping	2yrs HL	Gallipoli	213/5	106
Brown F	1/5 Bedfordshire	Pte	09/09/15	Sleeping	2yrs HL	Gallipoli	213/5	
Mayberry C	8 Welsh	Pte	09/09/15	Sleeping	1yr HL		213/5	107
Spencer James	RFA	Dvr	09/09/15	Desertion	XXX 29/09/15		213/5	108
Thomas W	8 Welsh	Pte	09/09/15	Sleeping	1yr HL		213/5	109
Mills George	2 D Cornwall LI	Pte	10/09/15	Desertion+	XXX 29/09/15	F&F	213/5	110
Wolfe J	7 R Munster Fus	Pte	12/09/15	Desertion	Not Conf	Gallipoli	213/5	
Abdul Rahim	Civilian		13/09/15	Martial Law	XXX	Egypt	213/3	111
Bailey J	6 KOR Lancaster	Pte	13/09/15	Mutiny	2yrs HL	Gallipoli	213/5	
Leatherbarrow C	1/7 Lancs Fus	Pte	13/09/15	Sleeping	10yrs PS	Gallipoli	213/5	
Taylor R	24 Bty RGA	Gnr	13/09/15	Desertion	18mos HL	F&F	213/4	
Gatercole W	6 R Dublin Fus	Pte	14/09/15	Sleeping	10yrs PS	Gallipoli	213/5	
Kirk A	6 KO Yorks LI	Pte	14/09/15	Civil	20yrs PS	F&F	213/5	
Turner R	1/8 Lancs Fus	Pte	15/09/15	Sleeping	Not Conf		213/5	
Allen J	2 R Dublin Fus	Pte	16/09/15	Desertion	2yrs HL	F&F	213/5	
Cox W	2 R Sussex	Pte	16/09/15	Sleeping	2yrs HL	F&F	213/5	
McConville N	1 A&S Hdrs	Pte	16/09/15	Sleeping	10yrs PS	F&F	213/5	
Ogden T	1/5 Lancs Fus	Pte	17/09/15	Sleeping	10yrs PS	Gallipoli	213/5	
Halsall W	1 Lancs Fus	Pte	18/09/15	Disobedience	10yrs PS	Gallipoli	213/5	
McGowan James	2 Cameron Hdrs	Pte	18/09/15	Sleeping	15yrs PS	F&F	213/5	
Fouracres S	8 Leicestershire	Pte	19/09/15	Sleeping	Not Conf	F&F	213/5	
Hoey R	2 Yorks	Pte	19/09/15	Sleeping	Quashed	F&F	213/5	112
Kay H	2 Yorks	Pte	19/09/15	Sleeping	Quashed	F&F	213/5	113
Lamb Alexander	RFA	Dvr	19/09/15	Desertion	XXX 02/10/15		213/5	114
Moore A	6 Lincolnshire	Pte	20/09/15	Cowardice	5yrs PS	Gallipoli	213/5	
Turner R	1/8 Lancs Fus	Pte	20/09/15	Sleeping	Quashed	Gallipoli	213/5	
Ashwood W	2 KO Scottish Bdrs	Pte	21/09/15	Sleeping	10yrs PS	F&F	213/5	
Hughes E	1 York & Lancaster	Pte	21/09/15	Sleeping	5yrs PS	F&F	213/5	
Kendall H	1 York & Lancaster	Pte	21/09/15	Sleeping	5yrs PS	F&F	213/5	
Lee (Irish) George	2 Rifle Bde	Rfm	21/09/15	Desertion	XXX 03/10/15	F&F	213/5	115
Poole H	2 R Warwickshire	Pte	21/09/15	Desertion	2yrs HL	F&F	213/5	
Smith W	2 Rifle Bde	Rfm	21/09/15	Desertion	XXX 03/10/15	F&F	213/5	116
Cadby J	8 R Welsh Fus	Pte	24/09/15	Sleeping	6 Mos HL	Gallipoli	213/5	
Locke H	11 Manchester	L/Cpl	24/09/15	Cowardice	Quashed	Gallipoli	213/5	
Blackwell J	3 Middlesex	Pte	25/09/15	Sleeping	3yrs PS	F&F	213/5	
Bostock J	2 Cheshire	Pte	25/09/15	Sleeping	2yrs HL	F&F	213/5	
Brown P	1 R Warwickshire	Pte	25/09/15	Desertion	10yrs PS	F&F	213/5	
Haynes A	1/6 Essex	Pte	25/09/15	Sleeping	2yrs HL	Gallipoli	213/5	
Barker T	1/7 Black Watch	Pte	26/09/15	Sleeping	6mos HL	F&F	213/5	117
Armstrong R	11 Manchester	Pte	27/09/15	Striking+	2yrs HL	Gallipoli	213/5	118
Badawi SAL	Civilian		27/09/15	Martial Law	XXX (Hanged)	Egypt	213/3	119
Gisbourne S	1 D Cornwall LI	Pte	27/09/15	Sleeping	10yrs PS	F&F	213/5	
Hutchins C	1 D Cornwall LI	Pte	27/09/15	Sleeping	10yrs PS	F&F	213/5	
Barr J	2 Seaforth Hdrs	Pte	28/09/15	Sleeping	10yrs PS	F&F	213/5	

Name	Unit	Rank	Date	Offence	Final sentence	Location	Ref	Note
White J	RFA	Dvr	28/09/15	Disobedience	Not Conf		213/5	
Brannigan J	6 DAC	Gnr	29/09/15	Desertion	Quashed		213/5	
Ratcliffe F	4 Leicestershire	Pte	30/09/15	Sleeping	1yr HL	F&F	213/5	
Smith A	4 Leicestershire	Pte	30/09/15	Sleeping	15yrs PS	F&F	213/5	
Bird JE	11 Sherwood Fstrs	Pte	01/10/15	Sleeping	2yrs HL	F&F	213/6	
Briscoe T	1/5 S Lancs	Cpl	01/10/15	Cowardice	Not Conf	F&F	213/6	
Clements W	2 Essex	Pte	01/10/15	Sleeping	Not Conf	F&F	213/6	
Attwell AG	5 Wiltshire	Pte	02/10/15	Sleeping	5yrs PS	Gallipoli	213/6	
Bremmer A	D Cornwall LI	Pte	02/10/15	Desertion	10yrs PS	F&F	213/6	
Henshaw T	1 Northumb Fus	Pte	02/10/15	Sleeping	5yrs PS	F&F	213/6	
Cox A	2 Essex	Pte	04/10/15	Sleeping	2yrs HL	F&F	213/6	
Hanna S	6 R Irish Fus	Pte	04/10/15	Desertion	10yrs PS	India	213/6	
Hanna S	6 R Irish Rifles	Pte	04/10/15	Desertion	10yrs PS	Egypt	213/7	
Hanson	6 R Irish Fus	Pte	04/10/15	Desertion	10 yrs PS	Gallipoli	213/7	
Irving W	2 Scottish Rifles	Pte	04/10/15	Sleeping	1yr HL	F&F	213/6	
Ries Irving Guy	Civilian	Alien	04/10/15	Espionage	XXX 27/10/15		92/3	120
Hammond A	1 E Surrey	Pte	05/10/15	Desertion	Quashed	F&F	213/6	
Harris J	7 Gloucestershire	Pte	05/10/15	Sleeping	5yrs PS	Gallipoli	213/6	
Moorcroft S	1 N Staffordshire	Pte	06/10/15	Sleeping	1yr HL	F&F	213/6	
Durston TW	8 S Wales Bdrs	Pte	07/10/15	Sleeping	2yrs HL	F&F	213/6	
Ferguson	1 R Scots Fus	Pte	07/10/15	Desertion	10yrs PS	F&F	213/6	
Wigley J	2 S Staffordshire	Pte	07/10/15	Desertion	10yrs PS	F&F	213/6	
Davies G	7 Gloucestershire	Pte	08/10/15	Sleeping	5yrs PS	Gallipoli	213/6	
Gault A	1/6 A&S Hdrs	Pte	08/10/15	Sleeping	3yrs PS	F&F	213/6	121
Hickton W	7 N Staffordshire	Pte	08/10/15	Sleeping	5yrs PS	Gallipoli	213/6	
McGarry J	9 Rifle Bde	Cpl	08/10/15	Cowardice	Quashed	F&F	213/6	
Hunter M	1 Cameronians	Pte	09/10/15	Desertion	3yrs PS	F&F	213/6	
Mackness Ernest	1 Scottish Rifles	Pte	09/10/15	Desertion	10yrs PS	F&F	213/6	122
Rogers D	1 Lancs Fus	Pte	09/10/15	Sleeping	10yrs PS	Gallipoli	213/6	
Hatherill J	1 Essex	Pte	10/10/15	Sleeping	5yrs PS	Gallipoli	213/6	
Turner R	6 S Lancs	Pte	10/10/15	Sleeping	5yrs PS	Gallipoli	213/6	
Pain Frederick	1/7 Essex	Pte	11/10/15	Sleeping	5yrs PS	Gallipoli	213/6	
Scott F	2 Lovat Scouts (TF)	Pte	11/10/15	Sleeping	5yrs PS	Gallipoli	213/6	
Stewart J	2 Lovat Scouts (TF)	Pte	11/10/15	Sleeping	5yrs PS	Gallipoli	213/6	
Goodchild FW	1 R Munster Fus	Pte	12/10/15	Sleeping	5yrs Ps	Gallipoli	213/6	
Lynch P	1 R Munster Fus	Pte	12/10/15	Sleeping	5yrs PS	Gallipoli	213/6	
Reeves CE	11 KRRC	Rfm	12/10/15	Sleeping	3yrs PS	F&F	213/6	
Adams N	1/5 KO Yorks LI	Pte	13/10/15	Sleeping	5yrs PS	F&F	213/6	
Turner G	2 Royal Fus	Pte	13/10/15	Sleeping	5yrs PS	Gallipoli	213/6	
Wilkinson E	4 KRRC	Rfm	14/10/15	Sleeping	1yr HL	F&F	213/6	
Rudge J	6 Dragoon Gds	Pte	15/10/15	Desertion	10yrs PS	F&F	213/6	123
Colbeck F	10 W Riding	Pte	16/10/15	Sleeping	2yrs HL	F&F	213/6	
Ellis C	7 N Staffordshire	Pte	16/10/15	Sleeping	5yrs PS	Gallipoli	213/6	
Goodfellow T	7 N Staffordshire	Pte	16/10/15	Sleeping	5ysr PS	Gallipoli	213/6	
Hackney D	7 N Staffordshire	Pte	16/10/15	Sleeping	5yrs PS	Gallipoli	213/6	
Roach T	11 W Yorks	Pte	16/10/15	Sleeping	2yrs HL	F&F	213/6	
Trivett VJ	7 N Staffordshire	Pte	16/10/15	Sleeping	5yrs PS	Gallipoli	213/6	
Field T	1 R W Surrey	Pte	17/10/15	Cowardice	Quashed	F&F	213/6	
Godfrey A	1 E Surrey	Pte	17/10/15	Sleeping	3mos FP1	F&F	213/6	
Hutson H	1/4 Norfolk	Pte	17/10/15	Sleeping	5yrs PS	Gallipoli	213/6	
Walker ABC	1 R W Surrey	Pte	17/10/15	Cowardice	Quashed	F&F	213/6	
Birch E	7 N Staffordshire	Pte	18/10/15	Sleeping	5yrs PS	Gallipoli	213/6	
Cottam A	10 Loyal North Lancs	Sgt	18/10/15	Cowardice	10yrs PS	F&F	213/6	
Crawshaw C	9 Loyal North Lancs	Pte	18/10/15	Sleeping	5yrs PS	F&F	213/6	
Murphy R	1 R Scots	Drummer	18/10/15	Sleeping	3yrs PS	F&F	213/6	
O'Connell C	R Canadian HA (RFA)	Gnr	18/10/15	Against Inhab	5yrs PS	F&F	213/6	
Connell	2 Lancs Fus	Pte	19/10/15	Sleeping	5yrs PS	F&F	213/6	
Latimer G	1 Border	Pte	20/10/15	Cowardice	10yrs PS	Gallipoli	213/6	
Partridge R	6 Loyal North Lancs	Pte	20/10/15	Sleeping	5yrs PS	Gallipoli	213/6	
Prince J	2 Welsh	Pte	21/10/15	Desertion	2yrs HL	F&F	213/6	
Brooks T	1 Essex	Pte	22/10/15	Disobedience	5yrs PS	Gallipoli	213/6	
Payne A	7 N Staffordshire	Pte	22/10/15	Sleeping	10yrs PS	Gallipoli	213/6	
Corcoran JW	2 S Wales Bdrs	Pte	24/10/15	Sleeping	5yrs PS	Gallipoli	213/6	
Hancock H	2 S Wales Bdrs	Pte	24/10/15	Sleeping	5yrs PS	Gallipoli	213/6	
Suddick Joseph	2 S Wales Bdrs	Pte	24/10/15	Sleeping	5yrs PS	Gallipoli	213/6	
Thickett J	7 N Staffordshire	Pte	24/10/15	Sleeping	10yrs PS	Gallipoli	213/6	
Brewin H	6 Leicestershire	Pte	25/10/15	Sleeping	5yrs PS	F&F	213/6	
Dowswell A	6 Leicestershire	Pte	25/10/15	Sleeping	5yrs PS	F&F	213/6	

Name	Unit	Rank	Date	Offence	Final sentence	Location	Ref	Note
Dudley J	7 Rifle Bde	Rfm	25/10/15	Desertion	10yrs PS	F&F	213/6	
Turner G	2 Royal Fus	Pte	25/10/15	Sleeping	10yrs PS	Gallipoli	213/6	
Brown H	8 Rifle Bde	Cpl	26/10/15	Desertion	10yrs PS	F&F	213/6	
Feuillade G	8 Rifle Bde	Rfm	26/10/15	Desertion	10yrs PS	F&F	213/6	
Cogdell E	1 E Surrey	Pte	27/10/15	Sleeping	10yrs PS	F&F	213/6	
Evans G	1 Devon	Pte	27/10/15	Sleeping	5yrs PS	F&F	213/6	
Winter E	1 Essex	Pte	29/10/15	Disobedience	3mos FP1	Gallipoli	213/6	
Foster C	2 R Sussex	Pte	30/10/15	Casting Arms	Quashed	F&F	213/6	
Perry F	2 R Sussex	Pte	30/10/15	Losing Property	Quashed	F&F	213/6	
Ward H	11 Rifle Bde	Rfm	30/10/15	Sleeping	2yrs HL	F&F	213/6	
Barnard A	1/4 Norfolk	Pte	31/10/15	Sleeping	5yrs PS	Gallipoli	213/6	
Finney W	7 N Staffordshire	Pte	31/10/15	Sleeping	5yrs PS	Gallipoli	213/6	
Anderberg Anton	8 Rifle Bde	Pte	01/11/15	Disobedience+	2yrs HL	F&F	213/6	124
Fineboy	W African Regt	Pte	01/11/15	Quitting	3yrs PS		213/4	
Sherriff W	9 Sherwood Fstrs	Sgt	01/11/15	Cowardice	10yrs PS	Gallipoli	213/6	
Dale W	6 Loyal North Lancs	Pte	04/11/15	Sleeping	10yrs Ps	Gallipoli	213/6	
Abdallah Mohamed Bin	Civilian		05/11/15	Espionage	14yrs Imp	East Africa	213/34	125
MacPherson Nicol	1/8 A&S Hdrs	Pte	05/11/15	Sleeping	2yrs HL	F&F	213/6	126
Meyer Albert	Civilian	Alien	05/11/15	Espionage	XXX 2/12/15	UK	92/3	127
Knight Charles W	10 R Welsh Fus	Pte	06/11/15	Murder	XXX 15/11/15	F&F	213/6	128
Clark G	1/7 Black Watch	Pte	07/11/15	Sleeping	2yrs HL	F&F	213/6	129
Musa Abdurehman Bin	Civilian		09/11/15	Aiding enemy	XXX	East Africa	213/34	130
Musa Suliman Bin	Civilian		09/11/15	Aiding enemy	XXX	East Africa	213/34	131
Puttock A	1 Royal Fus	Pte	10/11/15	Disobedience	3yrs PS	F&F	213/6	
Evans W	1 KRRC	Pte	12/11/15	Desertion	3yrs PS	F&F	213/6	
Rose Thomas	2 Wiltshire	Pte	12/11/15	Desertion	3yrs PS	F&F	213/6	
Bird W	1 KOR Lancaster	Pte	13/11/15	Sleeping	1yr HL	F&F	213/6	
Davis John	Follower	Carrier	15/11/15	Murder	10yrs PS		213/4	
Smith A	2 Royal Fus	Pte	15/11/15	Sleeping	5yrs PS	Gallipoli	213/7	
Waterhouse A	2 Royal Fus	Pte	15/11/15	Sleeping	Remitted	Gallipoli	213/7	
Sargeant Harry	9 Worcestershire	Pte	16/11/15	Sleeping	5yrs PS	Gallipoli	213/6	
Rigby Thomas Henry Basil	8 S Wales Bdrs	Pte	19/11/15	Desertion	3yrs PS	F&F	213/6	132
Ward AP	4 Grenadier Gds	Sgt	21/11/15	Desertion	3yrs PS	F&F	213/6	
Anderson A	7 Yorks	Pte	22/11/15	Desertion	Not Conf	F&F	213/7	
Cook T	7 Yorks	Pte	22/11/15	Desertion	Not Conf	F&F	213/7	
Haslam GE	6 East Lancs	Pte	22/11/15	Desertion	5yrs PS	Gallipoli	213/6	
Kennedy P	7 Yorks	Pte	22/11/15	Desertion	Not Conf	F&F	213/7	
Salter Harry	6 East Lancs	Pte	22/11/15	Desertion/Esc	XXX 11/12/15	Gallipoli	213/6	133
Reeves W	6 East Lancs	Pte	24/11/15	Sleeping	5yrs PS	Gallipoli	213/6	
Shanahan A	1 R Munster Fus	Cpl	24/11/15	Sleeping	10yrs PS	Gallipoli	213/9	
Watson T	9 Northumb Fus	Pte	25/11/15	Cowardice	10yrs PS	F&F	213/6	
Garrett D	9 R Warwickshire	Pte	26/11/15	Sleeping	5yrs PS	Gallipoli	213/7	
Black P	1/4 Black Watch	Pte	27/11/15	Desertion	3yrs PS	F&F	213/6	134
Gill W	9 Black Watch	Pte	30/11/15	Desertion	2yrs HL	F&F	213/6	
Prince F	1 S Wales Bdrs	Pte	30/11/15	Desertion	10yrs PS	F&F	213/6	
Downey Patrick Joseph	6 Leinster	Pte	01/12/15	Disobedience	XXX 27/12/15	Salonika	213/7	135
Raynor J	6 E Lancs	Pte	01/12/15	Quitting	5yrs PS	Gallipoli	213/7	
Tagg H	7 N Staffordshire	Sgt	01/12/15	Desertion	10yrs PS	Gallipoli	213/7	
Colaluca A	8 E Kent (Buffs)	Pte	02/12/15	Sleeping	Quashed	Salonika	213/6	
Taylor C	8 E Kent (Buffs)	Pte	02/12/15	Sleeping	Quashed	F&F	213/6	
Dennis John James	1 Northants	Pte	03/12/15	Desertion	XXX 30/01/16	F&F	213/7	136
Brook T	9 W Riding	Pte	04/12/15	Quitting	3 mos FP1	F&F	213/7	
Mason JT	7 Leicestershire	Pte	04/12/15	Sleeping	5yrs PS	F&F	213/7	
Bone JW	7 East Yorks	Pte	06/12/15	Desertion	5yrs PS	F&F	213/6	
Canavan WJ	6 R Irish Rifles	Rfm	06/12/15	Sleeping	3yrs PS	Salonika	213/7	
Clarke JW	6 KO Scottish Bdrs	Pte	06/12/15	Sleeping	6 Mos HL	F&F	213/6	
Groates G	7 East Yorks	Pte	06/12/15	Desertion	5yrs PS		213/6	
Hanifin T	6 Leinster	Pte	06/12/15	Insubordination	2yrs HL	Salonika	213/7	
Hayden G	6 R Irish Rifles	Rfm	06/12/15	Sleeping	3yrs PS	Salonika	213/7	
Hollins W	7 N Staffordshire	Pte	07/12/15	Sleeping	5yrs PS	Gallipoli	213/7	
Fitzgerald F	7 Gloucestershire	Pte	08/12/15	Striking+	3yrs PS	Gallipoli	213/7	137
McConnell W	8 R Irish Rifles	Rfm	08/12/15	Sleeping	1yr HL	F&F	213/6	138
Robins John	5 Wiltshire	Sgt	08/12/15	Disobedience	XXX 02/01/16	Gallipoli	213/7	139
Graham J	2 R Munster Fus	Pte	09/12/15	Desertion	XXX 21/12/15	F&F	213/6	140
Owens J	8 R Welsh Fus	Pte	09/12/15	Sleeping	2yrs HL	Gallipoli	213/7	
Shebbeas W	2 Suffolk	Pte	11/12/15	Sleeping	5yrs PS	F&F	213/6	
Cook A	9 W Yorks	Pte	12/12/15	Sleeping	3mos FP1	Gallipoli	213/7	
Archer J	8 R Berkshire	Pte	13/12/15	Sleeping	6 Mos HL	F&F	213/6	

Name	Unit	Rank	Date	Offence	Final sentence	Location	Ref	Note
Collins C	8 R Berkshire	Pte	13/12/15	Sleeping	1yr HL	F&F	213/6	
Anderson A	7 Yorks	Pte	14/12/15	Desertion	10yrs PS	F&F	213/7	
Cook T	7 Yorks	Pte	14/12/15	Desertion	10yrs PS	F&F	213/7	
Field AB	9 Royal Fus	Pte	14/12/15	Desertion	2yrs HL	F&F	213/6	
Lord H	9 Worcestershire	Pte	14/12/15	Sleeping	2mos FP1	Gallipoli	213/7	
Robinson H	9 W Yorks	Pte	14/12/15	Sleeping	2mos FP1	Gallipoli	213/7	
Stevens JE	7 Gloucestershire	Pte	14/12/15	Quitting	2mos FP1	Gallipoli	213/7	
Harris B	9 W Yorks	Pte	17/12/15	Sleeping	2mos FP1	Gallipoli	213/7	
Beck C	6 R Munster Fus	Pte	18/12/15	Sleeping	Not Conf	Salonika	213/7	
Reeves Harry	1 S Staffordshire	Pte	18/12/15	Desertion	2yrs HL	F&F	213/6	
Scourfield D	6 R Munster Fus	Pte	18/12/15	Sleeping	Not Conf	Salonika	213/7	
Bartle H	1 Coldstream Gds	Pte	20/12/15	Desertion	3yrs PS	F&F	213/6	
Creegan J	6 Leinster	Pte	20/12/15	Insubordination	10yrs PS	Salonika	213/7	
Masterson M	5 Connaught Rangers	Pte	20/12/15	Desertion +	10yrs PS	Salonika	213/7	141
Saville JW	1 Coldstream Gds	Pte	20/12/15	Desertion	3yrs PS	F&F	213/6	
Carrington H	7 R Munster Fus	Pte	23/12/15	Misc	Not Conf	Salonika	213/7	
Russell C	9 Black Watch	Pte	23/12/15	Desertion	5yrs PS	F&F	213/7	
Jones A	2 R Welsh Fus	Pte	24/12/15	Desertion	3 yrs PS	F&F	213/7	
Godfrey E	9 KRRC	Rfm	27/12/15	Desertion	10yrs PS	F&F	213/7	
Dawson J	1 Gordon Hdrs	Pte	28/12/15	Sleeping	3yrs PS	F&F	213/7	
Gunn P	1 Gordon Hdrs	Pte	28/12/15	Sleeping	3yrs PS	F&F	213/7	
Peters RA	RAMC	Pte	29/12/15	Desertion	10yrs PS		213/7	
Daly D	4 R Munster Fus	Pte	30/12/15	Desertion	10yrs PS		213/7	
Docherty John	9 Black Watch	Pte	30/12/15	Desertion +	5yrs PS	F&F	213/7	142
Thomas J	2 Welsh	Pte	30/12/15	Desertion	5yrs PS	F&F	213/7	
Armes WH	9 R Warwickshire	Pte	01/01/16	Sleeping	5yrs PS	Mesopotamia	90/7	143
Gallagher D	1 R Inniskilling Fus	Pte	01/01/16	Sleeping	5yrs PS	Gallipoli	213/7	
McGuill J	1/4 E Lancs	Pte	01/01/16	Cowardice	2yrs HL	Gallipoli	213/8	
Perks S	8 S Staffordshire	Pte	01/01/16	Desertion	10yrs PS	F&F	213/7	
Raynor J	1/4 E Lancs	Pte	01/01/16	Cowardice	2yrs HL	Gallipoli	213/8	
Seed Robert	1/4 E Lancs	Pte	01/01/16	Cowardice	2yrs HL	Gallipoli	213/8	
Smith H	8 S Staffordshire	Pte	01/01/16	Desertion	10yrs PS	F&F	213/7	
Whittaker R	1/4 E Lancs	Pte	03/01/16	Cowardice	2yrs HL	Gallipoli	213/8	
Craven F	2 Grenadier Gds	Pte	04/01/16	Desertion	PS Life	F&F	213/8	
Waterworth D	15 R Irish Rifles	Rfm	04/01/16	Desertion	5yrs PS	F&F	213/7	144
Anderson W	10 KO Yorks LI	Pte	05/01/16	Sleeping	5yrs PS	F&F	213/7	
Brown C	2 Scots Gds	Pte	05/01/16	Sleeping	3yrs PS	F&F	213/7	
Eveleigh Alfred	1 E Kent (Buffs)	Pte	05/01/16	Desertion	10yrs PS	F&F	213/7	145
Hobday A	9 Worcestershire	Pte	06/01/16	Quitting +	2mos FP1	Gallipoli	213/7	146
Pedro Clyde	11 R Welsh Fus	Pte	06/01/16	Disobedience	5yrs PS	Salonika	213/7	
Fitzgerald E	4 (att 21) R Munster Fus	Pte	07/01/16	Desertion	5yrs PS		213/7	
Graner J	9 KRRC	Rfm	07/01/16	Desertion	10yrs PS	F&F	213/7	
Hawker F	ASC	Pte	07/01/16	Desertion	Not Conf		213/7	
Murphy J	4 (att 21) R Munster Fus	Pte	07/01/16	Desertion	5yrs PS		213/7	
Wilson J	5 Cameron Hdrs	Pte	07/01/16	Desertion	10yrs PS	F&F	213/7	
Connell H	12 KRRC	Pte	10/01/16	Sleeping	2yrs HL	F&F	213/7	
Hocking J	RFA	Dvr	10/01/16	Desertion	10yrs PS		213/7	
White W	1 Hampshire	Pte	10/01/16	Desertion	10yrs PS		213/7	
Davidson JC	5 Dragoon Gds	Pte	11/01/16	Sleeping	2yrs HL	F&F	213/7	147
Tibble W	6 Northants	Cpl	11/01/16	Desertion	Quashed	F&F	213/7	
Wigmore A	7 Gloucestershire	Pte	12/01/16	Sleeping	5yrs PS	Gallipoli [?]	213/7	148
Jumbo	Camp Follower	Carrier	13/01/16	Theft	3mos FP1	Cameroon	213/8	
Labor John	Camp Follower	Carrier	13/01/16	Theft	3mos FP1	Cameroon	213/8	
Watson J	1 KRRC	Pte	13/01/16	Sleeping	3yrs PS	F&F	213/7	
Beaudoin C	14 Canadian EF	Pte	14/01/16	Desertion	10yrs PS	F&F	213/7	
Harries WM	R Monmouth	Spr	14/01/16	Desertion	10yrs PS		213/7	
Jackson G	2 E Yorks	Pte	14/01/16	Striking +	5yrs PS		213/7	
Haddon W	1 (Garr) Northants	Cpl	15/01/16	Disobedience	Not Conf	Egypt	213/7	
Connelly P	7 Gloucestershire	Pte	16/01/16	Quitting	Not Conf	Gallipoli [?]	213/8	149
Ford H	7 Gloucestershire	Pte	16/01/16	Quitting	Not Conf	Gallipoli [?]	213/8	150
Gunston CA	7 Gloucestershire	Pte	16/01/16	Quitting	Not Conf	Gallipoli [?]	213/8	151
Hodges AG	7 Gloucestershire	Pte	16/01/16	Quitting	Not Conf	Gallipoli [?]	213/8	152
Iles W	7 Gloucestershire	Pte	16/01/16	Quitting	Not Conf	Gallipoli [?]	213/8	153
Latto M	13 Canadian EF	Pte	16/01/16	Desertion	15yrs PS	F&F	213/7	
Hyde B	9 R Warwickshire	Pte	17/01/16	Desertion	10yrs PS	Gallipoli [?]	213/8	154
Brown A	7 N Staffordshire	Pte	18/01/16	Cowardice	7yrs PS	Gallipoli [?]	213/8	155
Davis R	7 N Staffordshire	Pte	18/01/16	Cowardice	7yrs PS	Gallipoli [?]	213/8	156
Dutton F	7 N Staffordshire	Pte	18/01/16	Cowardice	7yrs PS	Gallipoli [?]	213/8	157

Name	Unit	Rank	Date	Offence	Final sentence	Location	Ref	Note
Whittle T	7 N Staffordshire	Pte	18/01/16	Cowardice	7yrs PS	Gallipoli [?]	213/7	158
Carter GL	14 Welsh	Pte	19/01/16	Sleeping	3mos FP1	Egypt	213/7	
Blackman E	1 E Kent (Buffs)	Pte	20/01/16	Desertion	10yrs PS	F&F	213/7	
Webb A	1 E Kent (Buffs)	Pte	20/01/16	Desertion	10yrs PS	F&F	213/7	
Carson A	9 R Irish Rifles	Rfm	21/01/16	Desertion	2yrs HL	F&F	213/7	159
Neil W	1 Black Watch	Pte	21/01/16	Sleeping	Not Conf	F&F	213/7	
Carr James G	2 Welsh	Pte	22/01/16	Desertion/Esc	XXX 07/02/16	F&F	213/7	160
Horgan Dennis	4 R Munster Fus	Pte	22/01/16	Desertion	2yrs HL	F&F	213/7	
Hughes W	2 Welsh	Pte	22/01/16	Desertion	5yrs PS	F&F	213/7	
Law A	13 Canadian EF	Pte	22/01/16	Desertion+	10yrs PS	F&F	213/7	161
Williams DG	14 Welsh	Pte	22/01/16	Sleeping	Quashed	F&F	213/7	162
Dalton H	2 Yorks	Pte	23/01/16	Desertion	5yrs PS	F&F	213/7	
Prior J	9 R Irish Rifles	Rfm	23/01/16	Desertion	2yrs HL	F&F	213/7	163
Rodwell E	2 Yorks	Pte	23/01/16	Desertion	5yrs PS	F&F	213/7	
Robinson AH	9 Northumb Fus	Pte	24/01/16	Desertion	10yrs PS	F&F	213/7	
Cossman CE	13 Canadian EF	Pte	26/01/16	Desertion	Quashed GOA	F&F	213/7	
Godfree C	2 Middlesex	Pte	26/01/16	Desertion	10yrs PS	F&F	213/7	
Holmes T	2 Durham LI	Pte	26/01/16	Desertion	10yrs PS	F&F	213/7	
Hutchinson FH	13 Canadian EF	Pte	26/01/16	Desertion	Quashed GOA	F&F	213/7	
Scott J	2 Durham LI	Pte	26/01/16	Desertion	10yrs PS	F&F	213/7	
Waters W	2 Durham LI	Pte	26/01/16	Desertion	10yrs PS	F&F	213/7	
Jones J	17 R Welsh Fus	Pte	27/01/16	Sleeping	3yrs PS	F&F	213/7	164
Selig M	13 Canadian EF	Pte	27/01/16	Desertion	Quashed	F&F	213/7	165
Bilton S	1 E Kent (Buffs)	Pte	29/01/16	Desertion	10yrs PS	F&F	213/7	
Coffey Denis	2 R Munster Fus	Pte	30/01/16	Desertion	5yrs PS	F&F	213/7	
Richardson TJ	2 KO Yorks LI	Pte	30/01/16	Sleeping	3yrs PS	F&F	213/7	
Wain W	2 KO Yorks LI	Pte	30/01/16	Sleeping	3yrs PS	F&F	213/7	
Watson TE	2 KO Yorks LI	Pte	30/01/16	Sleeping	3yrs PS	F&F	213/7	
Barker W	7 N Staffordshire	Pte	31/01/16	Sleeping	1yr HL	Egypt	213/7	
Dean A	1 KRRC	Pte	02/02/16	Sleeping	3yrs PS	F&F	213/7	
Elson RE	7 N Staffordshire	Pte	02/02/16	Cowardice	7yrs PS	Egypt	213/7	
Jarry D	14 Canadian EF	Pte	02/02/16	Desertion	10yrs PS	F&F	213/8	
Jones J	7 N Staffordshire	Pte	02/02/16	Cowardice	7yrs PS	Egypt	213/7	
Lefebure J E	14 Canadian EF	Pte	02/02/16	Desertion	5yrs PS	F&F	213/8	
Lisney G	1 KRRC	Pte	02/02/16	Sleeping	3yrs PS	F&F	213/7	
Sillitor LR	7 N Staffordshire	Pte	02/02/16	Cowardice	7yrs PS	Egypt	213/7	
Smith W	7 N Staffordshire	Pte	02/02/16	Cowardice	7yrs PS	Egypt	213/7	
Burke W	6 R Dublin Fus	Pte	03/02/16	Quitting	3yrs PS	Salonika	213/7	
Docherty John	9 Black Watch	Pte	03/02/16	Desertion	XXX 15/02/16	F&F	213/7	166
Brompton J	5 R Irish Rifles	Rfm	04/02/16	Desertion	5yrs PS	Ireland	213/8	167
Hunter William	1 Loyal N Lancs	Pte	05/02/16	Desertion/Esc	XXX 21/02/16	F&F	213/7	168
Poynter EA	1 E Kent (Buffs)	Pte	05/02/16	Desertion	10yrs PS	F&F	213/7	
Anderson R	1 Highland LI	Pte	08/02/16	Sleeping	5yrs PS	Mesopotamia	90/7	169
Davies F	13 Welsh	Pte	09/02/16	Sleeping	3yrs PS	F&F	213/7	170
Johnson A	1 Liverpool	Pte	09/02/16	Desertion	10yrs Ps	F&F	213/7	
Mills WE	2 Durham LI	Pte	09/02/16	Desertion	10yrs PS	F&F	213/8	
Watson A	8 R W Kent	Pte	09/02/16	Desertion	10yrs PS	F&F	213/7	
Bonsey R	1 R Dragoons	Pte	10/02/16	Quitting	1yr HL	F&F	213/8	
Boyle W	8 Bedfordshire	Pte	10/02/16	Desertion	10yrs PS	F&F	213/7	
Collins A	7 Canadian EF	Pte	10/02/16	Desertion	10yrs PS	F&F	213/8	
Gawler Robert	1 E Kent (Buffs)	Pte	10/02/16	Desertion x 2	XXX 24/02/16	F&F	213/7	171
Jones John	1 Northants	Pte	10/02/16	Desertion/Esc	XXX 24/02/16	F&F	213/7	172
Mason WE	10 Hussars	Pte	10/02/16	Sleeping	5yrs PS		213/7	
Ridgewell FH	24 Royal Fus	Pte	10/02/16	Sleeping	5yrs PS	F&F	213/7	173
Bickers F	3 Canadian EF	Pte	11/02/16	Desertion	5yrs PS	F&F	213/8	
Britton D	1 Welsh Gds	Pte	11/02/16	Quitting	3yrs PS	F&F	213/7	
Howell FL	8 Lincolnshire	Pte	12/02/16	Desertion	10yrs PS	F&F	213/7	
Eveleigh Alfred	1 E Kent (Buffs)	Pte	13/02/16	Desertion	XXX 24/02/16	F&F	213/7	174
Crozier James	9 R Irish Rifles	Rfm	14/02/16	Desertion	XXX 27/02/16	F&F	213/7	175
Stevenson A	1 R Scots Fus	Cpl	15/02/16	Desertion	10yrs PS	F&F	213/7	
Currie Adam	9 Seaforth Hdrs	Pte	16/02/16	Desertion	10yrs PS	F&F	213/7	176
Evans EE	9 York & Lancaster	Pte	16/02/16	Sleeping	5yrs PS	F&F	213/7	
Todd T	7 Seaforth Hdrs	Pte	16/02/16	Disobedience	5yrs PS	F&F	213/7	
Elley Patrick	2 R Irish Rifles	Rfm	17/02/16	Desertion+	10yrs PS	F&F	213/7	177
Gallagher J	13 Canadian EF	Pte	17/02/16	Desertion	Quashed GOA	F&F	213/7	
Moore Thomas	ASC	Dvr	18/02/16	Murder	XXX 26/02/16	F&F	213/7	178
Barker J	2 KO Yorks LI	Pte	19/02/16	Desertion	3 Mos FP1	F&F	213/7	
Simmonds W	8 Devon	Pte	19/02/16	Desertion	5yrs PS	F&F	213/7	

Name	Unit	Rank	Date	Offence	Final sentence	Location	Ref	Note
Dale Arthur	13 R Scots	Pte	20/02/16	Murder	XXX 03/02/16	F&F	213/7	179
Woodhead J	18 Manchester	Pte	22/02/16	Sleeping	3yrs PS	F&F	213/8	180
Bowran Joseph	2 Lancs Fus	Pte	24/02/16	Desertion	5yrs PS	F&F	213/7	
Connolly	2 Lancs Fus	Pte	24/02/16	Desertion	5yrs PS	F&F	213/7	
Davenport W	2 Lancs Fus	Pte	24/02/16	Desertion	5yrs PS	F&F	213/7	
Graham W	2 Lancs Fus	Pte	24/02/16	Desertion	5yrs Ps	F&F	213/7	
McMillan A	2 Highland LI	Pte	24/02/16	Desertion	10yrs PS	F&F	213/8	
Lewis C	12 Highland LI	Cpl	25/02/16	Desertion	XXX 11/03/16	F&F	213/7	181
Ramage J	12 Highland LI	Pte	25/02/16	Desertion x3	10yrs PS	F&F	213/8	
Adams J	20 Liverpool	Pte	26/02/16	Sleeping	3yrs PS	F&F	213/8	
Carr T	2 Bedfordshire	Pte	26/02/16	Sleeping	3yrs PS	F&F	213/8	
Pringle J	10 Canadian EF	L/Cpl	26/02/16	Cowardice	5yrs PS	F&F	213/8	
Southern W	20 Liverpool	Pte	26/02/16	Sleeping	3yrs PS	F&F	213/8	
Turner W	8 Seaforth Hdrs	Pte	26/02/16	Desertion	10yrs PS	F&F	213/8	
Beattie A	15 R Irish Rifles	Rfm	27/02/16	Desertion	5yrs PS	F&F	213/7	182
Holdcroft C	10 Sherwood Fstrs	Pte	27/02/16	Desertion	10yrs PS	F&F	213/9	
McCracken JF	15 R Irish Rifles	Rfm	27/02/16	Desertion	XXX 19/03/16	F&F	213/7	183
McFarland W J	9 R Irish Rifles	Rfm	27/02/16	Quitting	2yrs HL	F&F	213/8	184
Shooter S	10 Sherwood Fstrs	Pte	27/02/16	Desertion	10yrs PS	F&F	213/9	
Templeton J	15 R Irish Rifles	Rfm	27/02/16	Desertion	XXX 19/03/16	F&F	213/7	185
Berrington C	7 E Yorks	Pte	28/02/16	Cowardice	5yrs PS	F&F	213/8	
Deacons M	2 Irish Gds	Pte	28/02/16	Striking x2	2yrs HL	F&F	213/8	
Kidman E	4 Canadian EF	Pte	28/02/16	Desertion	2yrs HL	F&F	213/8	
King R	2 Durham LI	Pte	28/02/16	Desertion	15yrs PS	F&F	213/7	
Bryan WH	7 Northants	Pte	29/02/16	Desertion	10yrs PS	F&F	213/8	
Taylor R	1 Liverpool	Pte	01/03/16	Desertion	5yrs PS	F&F	213/8	
Deehy Edward	2 R Irish	Pte	02/03/16	Desertion	5yrs PS	F&F	213/8	
Ryan S	2 R Irish	Pte	02/03/16	Desertion	5yrs PS	F&F	213/8	
Brook C	1/6 W Yorks	Pte	03/03/16	Disobedience	2yrs HL	F&F	213/8	
Harris (Beverstein) Abraham	11 Middlesex	Pte	04/03/16	Desertion	XXX 20/03/16	F&F	213/7	186
Martin Harry	9 Essex	Pte	04/03/16	Desertion	XXX 20/03/16	F&F	213/7	187
Coleman J	1 Scottish Rifles	Pte	06/03/16	Desertion	5yrs PS	F&F	213/8	
Seymour John	2 R Inniskilling Fus	Pte	07/03/16	Desertion	10yrs PS	F&F	213/8	188
Bladen Charles FH	10 York & Lancaster	Pte	08/03/16	Desertion	XXX 23/03/16	F&F	213/8	189
Campbell J	RFA	Dvr	08/03/16	Desertion	10yrs PS		213/8	
Edwards F	53 Bty RFA	Saddler	08/03/16	Desertion	10yrs PS		213/8	
Mathews N	3 S African Infantry	Pte	08/03/16	Murder	XXX 03/04/16	Egypt	90/6	190
Tolley T	112 Bty RFA	Gnr	08/03/16	Desertion	10yrs PS		213/8	
Bennett FW	8 R W Surrey	Pte	13/03/16	Desertion	10yrs PS	F&F	213/8	
Monaghan J	9 Black Watch	Pte	13/03/16	Desertion	5yrs PS	F&F	213/8	
Ryder EE	9 Liverpool	Pte	13/03/16	Desertion	Not Conf		213/8	
Smith HJ	2 R Irish Rifles	Rfm	13/03/16	Desertion	10yrs PS	F&F	213/8	
McIntyre D	9 Black Watch	Pte	14/03/16	Desertion	5yrs PS	F&F	213/8	
Auger Fortunat	14 Canadian EF	Pte	15/03/16	Desertion	XXX 26/03/16	F&F	213/8	191
Lawrence W	10 Highland LI	Pte	15/03/16	Cowardice	10yrs PS	F&F	213/8	
Middleton A	2 R Scots Fus	Pte	15/03/16	Striking+	10yrs PS	F&F	213/8	192
Simpson J	ASC	Dvr	15/03/16	Desertion	10yrs PS		213/8	
Cummings J	1 Liverpool	Pte	16/03/16	Desertion	2yrs HL	F&F	213/8	
Crute C	1 Loyal N Lancs	Pte	18/03/16	Desertion	15yrs PS	F&F	213/8	
Carlton F	6 Cameron Hdrs	Pte	20/03/16	Desertion	5yrs PS	F&F	213/8	
Hurwitz-y-Zender Ludovico	Civilian	Alien	20/03/16	Espionage	XXX 11/4/16	UK	92/3	193
Gray T	14 Canadian EF	Pte	21/03/16	Desertion	5yrs PS	F&F	213/8	
Inglis W	1 Gordon Hdrs	Pte	21/03/16	Desertion	10yrs PS	F&F	213/8	
Seed ER	14 Canadian EF	Pte	21/03/16	Desertion	5yrs PS	F&F	213/8	
Donnelly JG	13 R Scots	Pte	22/03/16	Desertion	10yrs PS	F&F	213/8	
Fleet F	RAMC	Pte	22/03/16	Desertion	15yrs PS		213/9	
McLelland C	7 R Scottish Rifles	Pte	22/03/16	Desertion	10yrs PS		213/8	
Friend FG	2 S Staffordshire	Pte	23/03/16	Desertion	15yrs PS	F&F	213/8	
Hiscoke W	1 Rifle Bde	Cpl	23/03/16	Desertion	10yrs PS	F&F	213/8	
Johnson W	2 S Staffordshire	Pte	23/03/16	Desertion	2yrs HL	F&F	213/8	
Queen James	13 R Scots	Pte	23/03/16	Desertion	15yrs PS	F&F	213/8	
Bartrum G	7 Norfolk	Pte	24/03/16	Disobedience	1yr HL	F&F	213/8	
Bolton J Edward	1 Cheshire	Pte	24/03/16	Desertion	XXX 14/04/16	F&F	213/8	194
Fermoy RH	7 Norfolk	Pte	24/03/16	Disobedience	18mos HL	F&F	213/8	
MacAuley W	17 Manchester	Pte	24/03/16	Sleeping	Not Conf	F&F	213/9	195
O'Brien J	14 Canadian EF	Pte	24/03/16	Desertion	10yrs PS	F&F	213/8	
Southern A	1 Loyal N Lancs	Pte	24/03/16	Desertion	10yrs PS	F&F	213/8	
Ayre JA	1 Middlesex	Pte	25/03/16	Striking	3yrs PS	F&F	213/8	

Name	Unit	Rank	Date	Offence	Final sentence	Location	Ref	Note
Hunter GW	7 E Yorks	Pte	25/03/16	Desertion	10yrs PS		213/8	
Balfour J	4 (att 2) A&S Hdrs	Pte	26/03/16	Desertion	3yrs PS	UK	213/8	196
Brannigan P	4 (att 2) A&S Hdrs	Pte	26/03/16	Desertion	5yrs PS	UK	213/8	197
Burns J	8 KO Scottish Bdrs	Gnr	26/03/16	Desertion	15yrs PS	F&F	213/8	
Wilson H	4 A&S Hdrs	Pte	26/03/16	Desertion	PS Life	UK	213/8	198
Bly GH	9 Liverpool	Pte	27/03/16	Sleeping	10yrs PS		213/9	
Parker SA	6 R W Kent	Cpl	28/03/16	Desertion	5yrs PS	F&F	213/8	
Burch HE	5 MGC	Pte	29/03/16	Sleeping+	3yrs PS	F&F	213/8	199
Taylor B	8 Cheshire	Pte	29/03/16	Disobedience	3yrs PS	Egypt	90/7	
Mitchell W	2 Highland LI	L/Cpl	30/03/16	Desertion	Quashed	F&F	213/8	
Turner W	1 Northants	Pte	30/03/16	Sleeping	2yrs HL	F&F	213/8	
Hogg E	110 MGC	Pte	01/04/16	Desertion	Not Conf		213/9	
Murphy M	2 KRRC	Rfm	01/04/16	Desertion	2yrs HL	F&F	213/8	
Goodall TW	1 R Warwickshire	Cpl	03/04/16	Desertion	10yrs PS	F&F	213/8	
Readhead H	1 Yorks	Pte	03/04/16	Desertion	5yrs PS	India	213/8	
White J	1 R Irish Fus	Pte	03/04/16	Desertion	10yrs PS	F&F	213/8	
Ellis T	9 Rifle Bde	Rfm	04/04/16	Sleeping	7yrs PS	F&F	213/8	
Mahoney T	2 R Munster Fus	Pte	04/04/16	Desertion	5yrs PS	F&F	213/8	
O'Neill A	1 S Wales Bdrs	Pte	04/04/16	Desertion	XXX 30/04/16	F&F	213/8	200
Thompson William Landreth	6 E Kent (Buffs)	Pte	04/04/16	Desertion	XXX 22/04/16	F&F	213/8	201
Williams E	1 S Wales Bdrs	Pte	04/04/16	Desertion	5yrs PS	F&F	213/8	
Woods E	9 Rifle Bde	Rfm	04/04/16	Sleeping	5yrs PS	F&F	213/8	
Davis E	Australian IF	Pte	05/04/16	Violence+	2yrs HL		213/8	202
James M	5 Munster Fus	Pte	05/04/16	Desertion	5yrs PS		213/8	
Dickinson GH	1 Northants	Pte	06/04/16	Sleeping	5yrs PS	F&F	213/8	
Swift JC	2 KO Yorks LI	Pte	06/04/16	Desertion	5yrs PS	F&F	213/9	
Beadle E	8 R W Kent	Pte	07/04/16	Sleeping	5yrs PS	F&F	213/8	
Canning A	8 R W Kent	Pte	07/04/16	Sleeping	5yrs PS	F&F	213/8	
Murray JG	3 Canadian EF	Cpl	07/04/16	Desertion	5yrs PS	F&F	213/8	
Stow E	8 R W Kent	Pte	07/04/16	Sleeping	5yrs PS	F&F	213/8	
Jefferson H	7 Suffolk	Pte	09/04/16	Insubordination+	2yrs HL	F&F	213/9	203
Templeton T	2 R Inniskilling Fus	Pte	10/04/16	Desertion	5yrs PS	F&F	213/9	
Carter Henry	11 Middlesex	Pte	12/04/16	Desertion	XXX 26/04/16	F&F	213/8	204
Gillman A	8 Royal Fus	Pte	12/04/16	Desertion	10yrs PS	F&F	213/8	
Lillystone J	6 Wiltshire	Pte	12/04/16	Sleeping	3yrs PS	F&F	213/8	
Lochrie J	10 A&S Hdrs	Pte	13/04/16	Desertion	5yrs PS	F&F	213/8	
Bush James	1 W Yorks	Pte	14/04/16	Desertion	5yrs PS	F&F	213/8	
Fox J	2 Highland LI	Pte	14/04/16	Striking x2	XXX 12/05/16	F&F	213/8	205
Cottier SJ	ASC	Dvr	15/04/16	Desertion x2	10yrs PS		213/8	
Goodhead A	11 KRRC	Rfm	15/04/16	Desertion	5yrs PS	F&F	213/8	
Roberts LL	8 Yorks	Pte	16/04/16	Cowardice	10yrs PS	F&F	213/8	
Meyrick J	1/6 Welsh	Pte	17/04/16	Desertion	3yrs PS	F&F	213/8	
Midley S	6 E Lancs	Pte	17/04/16	Sleeping	5yrs PS	Mesopotamia	90/7	206
Owen S	2 KRRC	Rfm	18/04/16	Desertion	5yrs PS	F&F	213/9	
Watts William	1 Loyal N Lancs	Pte	18/04/16	Desertion	XXX 05/05/16	F&F	213/8	207
Brown R	9 Worcestershire	Pte	19/04/16	Sleeping	5yrs PS	Mesopotamia	90/7	208
Clarke G	RGA	Gnr	19/04/16	Desertion	10yrs PS		213/9	
Smith C	12 Liverpool	Pte	19/04/16	Desertion	10yrs PS		213/9	
Trainer H	1 R W Kent	Pte	19/04/16	Sleeping	5yrs PS	F&F	213/9	
Gribben J	1 R Irish Rifles	Rfm	20/04/16	Cowardice	15yrs PS	F&F	213/9	
Jones J	6 Kings Shropshire LI	Pte	20/04/16	Desertion	15yrs PS	F&F	213/8	
Kane J	1 R Irish Rifles	Rfm	20/04/16	Cowardice	15yrs PS	F&F	213/9	
Bate W	9 Cheshire	Pte	22/04/16	Disobedience	15yrs PS	F&F	213/8	
Cuthbert J	9 Cheshire	Pte	22/04/16	Disobedience	XXX 06/05/16	F&F	213/8	209
Dineen J	9 Cheshire	Pte	22/04/16	Disobedience	15yrs PS	F&F	213/8	
Wallace T	2 Lancs Fus	Pte	22/04/16	Cowardice	2yrs HL	F&F	213/8	
McLaughlin J	8 KO Scottish Bdrs	Pte	23/04/16	Desertion	5yrs PS	F&F	213/9	
Coyle F	4 (att 2) A&S Hdrs	Pte	24/04/16	Desertion	6 Mos HL	F&F	213/9	
Dawson W	1 Loyal N Lancs	Pte	24/04/16	Desertion	5yrs PS	F&F	213/8	
Parry C	1 Loyal N Lancs	Pte	24/04/16	Desertion	10yrs PS	F&F	213/9	
Ravenscroft A	1 KRRC	Rfm	24/04/16	Desertion	10yrs PS	F&F	213/9	
Singh Mula	Hong Kong TMB RGA	A/Naik	24/04/16	Murder+	10yrs PS	Egypt	90/6	210
FitzGerald P	2 Black Watch	L/Cpl	25/04/16	Disobedience	Not Conf	Mesopotamia	90/7	211
King R	1/7 Black Watch	Pte	25/04/16	Quitting	2yrs HL	F&F	213/8	212
Roberts W	1/6 Welsh	Pte	25/04/16	Disobedience	3yrs PS	F&F	213/8	
Halligan J	14 Canadian EF	Cpl	26/04/16	Desertion	Not Conf	F&F	213/9	
Havelin W	14 Canadian EF	Pte	26/04/16	Desertion	Not Conf	F&F	213/9	
Poirat A	14 Canadian EF	Pte	26/04/16	Desertion	Not Conf	F&F	213/9	

Name	Unit	Rank	Date	Offence	Final sentence	Location	Ref	Note
Snell B	7 Norfolk	Pte	26/04/16	Insubordination+	2yrs HL	F&F	213/9	213
Richardson H	3 Canadian EF	Pte	27/04/16	Desertion	10yrs PS	F&F	213/9	
Turner H	9 Liverpool	Pte	27/04/16	Desertion	10yrs PS		213/8	
Clarke T	1 R Berkshire	Pte	28/04/16	Desertion	10yrs PS	F&F	213/9	
Evans W	13 Essex	Pte	28/04/16	Desertion	5yrs PS	F&F	213/9	214
Robinson Arthur H	9 Northumb Fus	Pte	28/04/16	Desertion	XXX 10/05/16	F&F	213/9	215
Summerfield J	1 Liverpool	Pte	28/04/16	Desertion	3yrs PS	F&F	213/9	
Clark T	1 Royal Fus	Pte	29/04/16	Desertion	5yrs PS	F&F	213/9	
O'Neill P	2 Durham LI	Pte	29/04/16	Desertion	15yrs PS	F&F	213/9	
Smith F	2 Durham LI	Pte	29/04/16	Desertion	15yrs PS	F&F	213/9	
Hasemere John William	RFA	Dvr	30/04/16	Threatening	XXX 12/05/16	F&F	213/8	216
Clarke Thomas J	Civilian	Sinn Fein	01/05/16	Rebellion	XXX 03/05/16	Dublin	213/8	217
Davys Richard	Civilian	Sinn Fein	01/05/16	Rebellion	10yrs PS	Dublin	213/8	218
Irvine G	Civilian	Sinn Fein	01/05/16	Rebellion	10yrs PS	Dublin	213/8	219
Jones DG	1 S Wales Bdrs	Pte	01/05/16	Desertion	5yrs PS	F&F	213/9	
Kent Edmund	Civilian	Sinn Fein	01/05/16	Rebellion	XXX 08/05/16	Dublin	213/8	220
MacDonagh Thomas	Civilian	Sinn Fein	01/05/16	Rebellion	XXX 03/05/16	Dublin	213/8	221
McBride John	Civilian	Sinn Fein	01/05/16	Rebellion	XXX 05/05/16	Dublin	213/8	222
Pearse PH	Civilian	Sinn Fein	02/05/16	Rebellion	XXX 03/05/16	Dublin	213/8	223
Bevan Thomas	Civilian	Sinn Fein	03/05/16	Rebellion	10yrs PS	Dublin	213/8	224
Clancy Peter	Civilian	Sinn Fein	03/05/16	Rebellion	10yrs PS	Dublin	213/8	225
Daley Edward	Civilian	Sinn Fein	03/05/16	Rebellion	XXX 04/05/16	Dublin	213/8	226
Dougherty John	Civilian	Sinn Fein	03/05/16	Rebellion	10yrs PS	Dublin	213/8	227
Lynch Finian	Civilian	Sinn Fein	03/05/16	Rebellion	10yrs PS	Dublin	213/8	228
McGarry John	Civilian	Sinn Fein	03/05/16	Rebellion	8yrs PS	Dublin	213/8	229
McNestry Patrick	Civilian	Sinn Fein	03/05/16	Rebellion	10yrs PS	Dublin	213/8	230
Melinn James	Civilian	Sinn Fein	03/05/16	Rebellion	10yrs PS	Dublin	213/8	231
Mervyn Michael	Civilian	Sinn Fein	03/05/16	Rebellion	10yrs PS	Dublin	213/8	232
O'Callaghan Denis	Civilian	Sinn Fein	03/05/16	Rebellion	10yrs PS	Dublin	213/8	233
O'Hanrahan Michael	Civilian	Sinn Fein	03/05/16	Rebellion	XXX 04/05/16	Dublin	213/8	234
Pearse William	Civilian	Sinn Fein	03/05/16	Rebellion	XXX 04/05/16	Dublin	213/8	235
Plunkett Joseph	Civilian	Sinn Fein	03/05/16	Rebellion	XXX 04/05/16	Dublin	213/8	236
Reid John J	Civilian	Sinn Fein	03/05/16	Rebellion	10yrs PS	Dublin	213/8	237
Sweeney PE	Civilian	Sinn Fein	03/05/16	Rebellion	10yrs PS	Dublin	213/8	238
Tobin William	Civilian	Sinn Fein	03/05/16	Rebellion	10yrs PS	Dublin	213/8	239
Walsh JJ	Civilian	Sinn Fein	03/05/16	Rebellion	10yrs PS	Dublin	213/8	240
Welsh Thomas	Civilian	Sinn Fein	03/05/16	Rebellion	10yrs PS	Dublin	213/8	241
Williams John	Civilian	Sinn Fein	03/05/16	Rebellion	10yrs PS	Dublin	213/8	242
Bevan Charles	Civilian	Sinn Fein	04/05/16	Rebellion	3yrs PS	Dublin	213/8	243
Brennan J	Civilian	Sinn Fein	04/05/16	Rebellion	3yrs PS	Dublin	213/8	244
Brooks F	Civilian	Sinn Fein	04/05/16	Rebellion	3yrs PS	Dublin	213/8	245
Byrne J	Civilian	Sinn Fein	04/05/16	Rebellion	3yrs PS	Dublin	213/8	246
Clarke J	Civilian	Sinn Fein	04/05/16	Rebellion	3yrs PS	Dublin	213/8	247
Coleman R	Civilian	Sinn Fein	04/05/16	Rebellion	3yrs PS	Dublin	213/8	248
Cosgrave Phillip B	Civilian	Sinn Fein	04/05/16	Rebellion	5yrs PS	Dublin	213/8	249
Cosgrave William	Civilian	Sinn Fein	04/05/16	Rebellion	PS Life	Dublin	213/8	250
Cronin J	6 Loyal N Lancs	Pte	04/05/16	Desertion	10yrs PS	Mesopotamia	90/7	251
Cullen John F	Civilian	Sinn Fein	04/05/16	Rebellion	3yrs PS	Dublin	213/8	252
Dorrington J	Civilian	Sinn Fein	04/05/16	Rebellion	3yrs PS	Dublin	213/8	253
Hewston JJ	Civilian	Sinn Fein	04/05/16	Rebellion	XXX 08/05/16	Dublin	213/8	254
Hunter Thomas	Civilian	Sinn Fein	04/05/16	Rebellion	PS Life	Dublin	213/8	255
Kelly P	Civilian	Sinn Fein	04/05/16	Rebellion	3yrs PS	Dublin	213/8	256
Kelly R	Civilian	Sinn Fein	04/05/16	Rebellion	3yrs PS	Dublin	213/8	257
Kent Thomas	Civilian	Sinn Fein	04/05/16	Rebellion	XXX	Dublin	213/8	258
Levins G	Civilian	Sinn Fein	04/05/16	Rebellion	3yrs PS	Dublin	213/8	259
Markievicz Constance G	Civilian	Sinn Fein	04/05/16	Rebellion	PS Life	Dublin	213/8	260
Marks J	Civilian	Sinn Fein	04/05/16	Rebellion	3yrs PS	Dublin	213/8	261
Meehan W	Civilian	Sinn Fein	04/05/16	Rebellion	3yrs PS	Dublin	213/8	262
Norton J	Civilian	Sinn Fein	04/05/16	Rebellion	3yrs PS	Dublin	213/8	263
O'Brien John	Civilian	Sinn Fein	04/05/16	Rebellion	3yrs PS	Dublin	213/8	264
O'Colbaird Concabar	Civilian	Sinn Fein	04/05/16	Rebellion	XXX 08/05/16	Dublin	213/8	265
O'Dea W	Civilian	Sinn Fein	04/05/16	Rebellion	3yrs PS	Dublin	213/8	266
O'Hanrahan H	Civilian	Sinn Fein	04/05/16	Rebellion	PS Life	Dublin	213/8	267
O'Kelly T	Civilian	Sinn Fein	04/05/16	Rebellion	3yrs PS	Dublin	213/8	268
Parker Albert Edward	7 KRRC	Rfm	04/05/16	Desertion	XXX 15/05/16	F&F	213/8	269
Peppard T	Civilian	Sinn Fein	04/05/16	Rebellion	3yrs PS	Dublin	213/8	270
Plunkett G	Civilian	Sinn Fein	04/05/16	Rebellion	10yrs PS	Dublin	213/8	271
Plunkett J	Civilian	Sinn Fein	04/05/16	Rebellion	10yrs PS	Dublin	213/8	272

Name	Unit	Rank	Date	Offence	Final sentence	Location	Ref	Note
Poole Vincent	Civilian	Sinn Fein	04/05/16	Rebellion	5yrs PS	Dublin	213/8	273
Wilson P	Civilian	Sinn Fein	04/05/16	Rebellion	3yrs PS	Dublin	213/8	274
Wilson W	Civilian	Sinn Fein	04/05/16	Rebellion	3yrs PS	Dublin	213/8	275
Brennan M	Civilian	Sinn Fein	05/05/16	Rebellion	3yrs PS	Dublin	213/8	276
Burke James	Civilian	Sinn Fein	05/05/16	Rebellion	3yrs PS	Dublin	213/8	277
Burrell William Henry	2 R Sussex	Pte	05/05/16	Desertion	XXX 22/05/16	F&F	213/9	278
Corrigan William	Civilian	Sinn Fein	05/05/16	Rebellion	5yrs PS	Dublin	213/8	279
Dempsey J	Civilian	Sinn Fein	05/05/16	Rebellion	3yrs PS	Dublin	213/8	280
Downey John	Civilian	Sinn Fein	05/05/16	Rebellion	3yrs PS	Dublin	213/8	281
Doyle Gerald	Civilian	Sinn Fein	05/05/16	Rebellion	3yrs PS	Dublin	213/8	282
Mallin Michael	Civilian	Sinn Fein	05/05/16	Rebellion	XXX 08/05/16	Dublin	213/8	283
McGregor W	1/4 Black Watch	Pte	05/05/16	Desertion	3yrs PS	F&F	213/9	284
Morrissy James	Civilian	Sinn Fein	05/05/16	Rebellion	3yrs PS	Dublin	213/8	285
O'Sullivan James	Civilian	Sinn Fein	05/05/16	Rebellion	8yrs PS	Dublin	213/8	286
Slattery Peter	Civilian	Sinn Fein	05/05/16	Rebellion	8yrs PS	Dublin	213/8	287
Brewster A	2 Essex	Pte	06/05/16	Sleeping	5yrs PS	F&F	213/10	
Faulkner J	Civilian	Sinn Fein	06/05/16	Rebellion	3yrs PS	Dublin	213/8	288
Fogarty P	Civilian	Sinn Fein	06/05/16	Rebellion	3yrs PS	Dublin	213/8	289
Gant J	2 Essex	Pte	06/05/16	Sleeping	5yrs PS	F&F	213/10	
Hickey J	8 R Inniskilling Fus	Pte	06/05/16	Sleeping	2yrs HL	F&F	213/9	
O'Donovan C	Civilian	Sinn Fein	06/05/16	Rebellion	5yrs PS	Dublin	213/8	290
Saunders H	8 R Inniskilling Fus	Pte	06/05/16	Sleeping	2yrs HL	F&F	213/9	
Shouldice John	Civilian	Sinn Fein	06/05/16	Rebellion	5yrs PS	Dublin	213/8	291
Hailwood E	2 Border	Pte	07/05/16	Desertion	5yrs PS	F&F	213/10	
Ashe Thomas	Civilian	Sinn Fein	08/05/16	Rebellion	PS Life	Dublin	213/8	292
Brady Michael	Civilian	Sinn Fein	08/05/16	Rebellion	3yrs PS	Dublin	213/8	293
Burgess William	1 Lincolnshire	Pte	08/05/16	Desertion	10yrs PS	F&F	213/10	
Darby A	1 Border	Pte	08/05/16	Quitting	Not Conf	Gallipoli	213/10	
de Valera Edward	Civilian	Sinn Fein	08/05/16	Rebellion	PS Life	Dublin	213/8	294
Lawless Frank	Civilian	Sinn Fein	08/05/16	Rebellion	10yrs PS	Dublin	213/8	295
Lawless James	Civilian	Sinn Fein	08/05/16	Rebellion	10yrs PS	Dublin	213/8	296
McArdle J	Civilian	Sinn Fein	08/05/16	Rebellion	3yrs PS	Dublin	213/8	297
Thomas J	2 Welsh	Pte	08/05/16	Desertion+	XXX 20/05/16	F&F	213/9	298
Connolly James	Civilian	Sinn Fein	09/05/16	Rebellion	XXX 12/05/16	Dublin	213/8	299
McDermott J	Civilian	Sinn Fein	09/05/16	Rebellion	XXX 12/05/16	Dublin	213/8	300
Quigley EJ	1 E Kent (Buffs)	Pte	09/05/16	Desertion	5yrs PS	F&F	213/9	
Brennan Robert	Civilian	Sinn Fein	10/05/16	Rebellion	5yrs PS	Dublin	213/8	301
Doyle James	Civilian	Sinn Fein	10/05/16	Rebellion	5yrs PS	Dublin	213/8	302
Etchingham John R	Civilian	Sinn Fein	10/05/16	Rebellion	5yrs PS	Dublin	213/8	303
King Richard F	Civilian	Sinn Fein	10/05/16	Rebellion	5yrs PS	Dublin	213/8	304
Lacy Michael	Civilian	Sinn Fein	10/05/16	Rebellion	5yrs PS	Dublin	213/8	305
Rafter James	Civilian	Sinn Fein	10/05/16	Rebellion	5yrs PS	Dublin	213/8	306
Downey J	8 R Inniskilling Fus	Pte	11/05/16	Disobedience	Quashed	F&F	213/9	
Nisbet J	8 Leicestershire	Pte	11/05/16	Disobedience x3	10yrs PS	F&F	213/9	
Donohue M	6 Leinster	Cpl	12/05/16	Violence+	3yrs PS	Salonika	213/9	307
Hawkins CH	1 N Staffordshire	Pte	12/05/16	Desertion/Esc	10yrs PS	F&F	213/9	
Highway E	20 Lancs Fus	Pte	12/05/16	Indiscipline	5yrs PS	F&F	213/9	308
Liston C	9 R Dublin Fus	Pte	12/05/16	Desertion	7yrs PS	F&F	213/9	
Molloy Bryan	Civilian	Sinn Fein	12/05/16	Rebellion	10yrs PS	Dublin	213/8	309
Hewitt GH	2 KO Yorks LI	Pte	15/05/16	Violence/striking	1yr HL	F&F	213/10	
Sneddon J	1 Black Watch	Pte	15/05/16	Desertion	2yrs HL	F&F	213/9	
Barkley P	8 R Irish Fus	Pte	16/05/16	Disobedience	Not Conf	F&F	213/9	
Cole J	1 D Cornwall LI	Pte	16/05/16	Sleeping	2yrs HL	F&F	213/9	
Gallighan Peter	Civilian	Sinn Fein	16/05/16	Rebellion	5yrs PS	Dublin	213/8	310
Stammers J	1 D Cornwall LI	Pte	16/05/16	Sleeping	2yrs HL	F&F	213/9	
Lynch Jeremiah C	Civilian	Sinn Fein	17/05/16	Rebellion	10yrs PS	Dublin	213/8	311
Miller C	1(Pioneer) Australian IF	Sgt	17/05/16	Desertion	5yrs PS/Red in rank	F&F	213/9	
Holland James	10 Cheshire	Pte (L/C)	18/05/16	Cowardice+	XXX 30/05/16	F&F	213/9	312
Simpson J	8 Yorks	Pte	18/05/16	Desertion	2yrs HL	F&F	213/9	
Ward J	2 R Scots Fus	Pte	18/05/16	Desertion	2yrs HL	F&F	213/11	
Bowsher A	8 E Kent (Buffs)	Pte	20/05/16	Desertion	10yrs PS	F&F	213/9	
Gosheff P	Civilian		20/05/16	Treason	XXX	Macedonia	213/12	313
Rawlinson B	2 Worcestershire	Pte	20/05/16	Desertion	3yrs PS	F&F	213/9	
Roberts William W	4 Royal Fus	Pte	20/05/16	Desertion/Esc	XXX 29/05/16	F&F	213/9	314
Birtle A	2 W Riding	Pte	21/05/16	Desertion	2yrs HL	F&F	213/10	
Doran J	19 Liverpool	Pte	22/05/16	Desertion	2yrs HL	F&F	213/10	
Lawler F	2 York & Lancaster	Pte (L/C)	22/05/16	Desertion	10yrs PS	F&F	213/9	
Archibald James	17 R Scots	Pte	23/05/16	Desertion	XXX 04/06/16	F&F	213/9	315

Name	Unit	Rank	Date	Offence	Final sentence	Location	Ref	Note
Doyle P	9 R Dublin Fus	Pte	23/05/16	Desertion	10yrs PS	F&F	213/9	
Harris G	3 Rifle Bde	Rfm	23/05/16	Desertion	3yrs PS	F&F	213/9	
Itko CD	Civilian		23/05/16	Treason	XXX	Macedonia	213/12	316
Mullins J	8 MGC	Pte	23/05/16	Cowardice	5yrs PS		213/9	
Petro C	Civilian		23/05/16	Treason	XXX	Macedonia	213/12	317
Yazagi MH	Civilian		23/05/16	Treason	XXX	Macedonia	213/12	318
Kitchen J	1 Loyal N Lancs	Pte	24/05/16	Sleeping	2yrs HL	F&F	213/9	
Phillips WTH	1 Coldstream Gds	Pte	24/05/16	Desertion	XXX 30/05/16	F&F	213/9	319
Plummer WR	4 Royal Fus	Pte	25/05/16	Desertion	10yrs PS	F&F	213/9	
Walsh M	4 Royal Fus	Pte	25/05/16	Desertion	10yrs Ps	F&F	213/9	
Mumun R	Civilian		26/05/16	Treason	XXX	Macedonia	213/12	320
Simpson R	1 Canadian DAC	Bmdr	27/05/16	Desertion	10yrs PS	F&F	213/9	
Burugi S	Civilian		28/05/16	Treason	10yrs PS	Macedonia	213/12	321
Carey A	MGC	Pte	29/05/16	Cowardice	15yrs PS		213/9	
Keiller P	MGC	Pte	29/05/16	Cowardice	15yrs PS		213/9	
Marshall W	4 Grenadier Gds	L/Cpl	29/05/16	Cowardice x2	10yrs PS	F&F	213/9	
McLeod DF	13 Canadian EF	Pte	29/05/16	Desertion	5yrs PS	F&F	213/9	
Swaine James W	RFA	Dvr	29/05/16	Desertion	XXX 09/06/16	F&F	213/9	322
Burke P	1 Gloucestershire	Pte	30/05/16	Disobedience	1yr HL	F&F	213/9	
Campbell GH	1 Canadian FA	Gnr	31/05/16	Desertion	10yrs PS	F&F	213/9	
Hedges L	1 R Scots Fus	Pte	31/05/16	Desertion	10yrs PS	F&F	213/9	
Wakefield W	8 S Lancs	Pte	31/05/16	Desertion	10yrs PS	F&F	213/9	
Robson JR	16 Cheshire	Cpl	01/06/16	Quitting	5yrs PS	F&F	213/9	323
Foister J	East Non Combat Corps	Pte	02/06/16	Disobedience x2	Not Conf	F&F	213/10	324
Marten H	East Non Combat Corps	Pte	02/06/16	Disobedience x2	Not Conf	F&F	213/10	325
Ring J	East Non Combat Corps	Pte	02/06/16	Disobedience x2	Not Conf	F&F	213/10	326
Scullard H	East Non Combat Corps	Pte	02/06/16	Disobedience x2	Not Conf	F&F	213/10	327
Sharp G	12 R Sussex	Pte	02/06/16	Sleeping	3yrs PS	F&F	213/10	328
Walker CE	19 Manchester	Pte	02/06/16	Sleeping	Not Conf	F&F	213/10	329
Hill W	9 E Surrey	Pte	03/06/16	Threatening+	5yrs PS	F&F	213/9	330
Middleton JE	RE	Cpl	03/06/16	Desertion	10yrs PS		213/9	
Andrews A	11 R W Surrey	Pte	04/06/16	Striking	5yrs PS	F&F	213/9	
Molyneaux James	1 Loyal N Lancs	Pte	05/06/16	Desertion	XXX 15/06/16	F&F	213/9	331
Gormley J	2 Worcestershire	Pte	06/06/16	Desertion	2yrs PS	F&F	213/9	
Foister J	East Non Combat Corps	Pte	07/06/16	Disobedience	10yrs PS	F&F	213/9	332
Marten H	East Non Combat Corps	Pte	07/06/16	Disobedience	10yrs PS	F&F	213/9	333
Ring J	East Non Combat Corps	Pte	07/06/16	Disobedience	10yrs PS	F&F	213/9	334
Scullard H	East Non Combat Corps	Pte	07/06/16	Disobedience	10yrs PS	F&F	213/9	335
Barker R	6 London	Rfm	08/06/16	Desertion	5yrs PS	F&F	213/9	
Bunn L	2/7 Worcestershire	Pte	08/06/16	Sleeping	5yrs PS	F&F	213/9	
Pickering G	9 Rifle Bde	Rfm	08/06/16	Quitting	5yrs PS	F&F	213/9	
Powell O	9 Rifle Bde	Rfm	08/06/16	Quitting	5yrs PS	F&F	213/9	
Prescott T	9 Rifle Bde	Rfm	08/06/16	Quitting	5yrs PS	F&F	213/9	
Wright W	7 Lincolnshire	Pte	08/06/16	Striking	5yrs PS	F&F	213/9	
Carberry J	2 S Lancs	Pte	09/06/16	Cowardice+	10yrs PS	F&F	213/9	336
Clinch EW	2 Wiltshire	Pte	09/06/16	Disobedience	Not Conf	F&F	213/10	
Hamilton D	8 R Irish Fus	Pte	09/06/16	Desertion	5yrs PS	F&F	213/9	
Lally James	Civilian		09/06/16	Poss firearms	10yrs PS	Dublin	92/3	337
Leahy Denis	Civilian		09/06/16	Poss firearms	10yrs PS	Dublin	92/3	338
Martin Frank	Civilian		09/06/16	Poss firearms	10yrs PS	Dublin	92/3	339
McEntee John (Sean)	Civilian		09/06/16	Poss firearms	PS Life	Dublin	92/3	340
Woods WJ	7 R Irish Fus	Pte	09/06/16	AWOL	5yrs PS	F&F	213/9	
Barritt C	East Non Combat Corps	Pte	10/06/16	Disobedience	10yrs PS	F&F	213/9	341
Bonner B	East Non Combat Corps	Pte	10/06/16	Disobedience	10yrs PS	F&F	213/9	342
Brewster HF	East Non Combat Corps	Pte	10/06/16	Disobedience	10yrs PS	F&F	213/9	343
Hicks GE	East Non Combat Corps	Pte	10/06/16	Disobedience	10yrs PS	F&F	213/9	344
King T	1/4 Dragoon Gds	Pte	10/06/16	Disobedience	2yrs HL		213/9	
Priestley A	East Non Combat Corps	Pte	10/06/16	Disobedience	10yrs PS	F&F	213/9	345
Ricketts OG	East Non Combat Corps	Pte	10/06/16	Disobedience	10yrs PS	F&F	213/9	346
Seed TG	1/4 Dragoon Gds	Pte	10/06/16	Disobedience	2yrs HL		213/9	
Stanton HE	East Non Combat Corps	Pte	10/06/16	Disobedience	10yrs PS	F&F	213/9	347
Ward T	1/4 Dragoon Gds	Pte	10/06/16	Disobedience	2yrs HL		213/9	
Giles H	1/5 R Warwickshire	Pte	11/06/16	Quitting	2yrs HL	F&F	213/10	
Hatton A	1/5 R Warwckshire	Pte	11/06/16	Quitting	2yrs HL		213/10	
Rea TG	8 R Irish Rifles	Rfm	11/06/16	Sleeping	2yrs PS	F&F	213/10	348
Scrivener J	1/5 R Warwickshire	Pte	11/06/16	Quitting	2yrs HL	F&F	213/10	
Whitehouse AE	1 Worcestershire	Pte	11/06/16	Desertion	15yrs PS	F&F	213/9	
Anderson J	4 W Riding	Pte	12/06/16	Disobedience	2yrs HL	F&F	213/10	

Name	Unit	Rank	Date	Offence	Final sentence	Location	Ref	Note
Cartwright C	2 North Non Combat Corps	Pte	12/06/16	Disobedience	10yrs PS	F&F	213/9	349
Cryer CE	2 North Non Combat Corps	Pte	12/06/16	Disobedience	10yrs PS	F&F	213/9	350
Hall S	2 North Non Combat Corps	Pte	12/06/16	Disobedience	10yrs PS	F&F	213/9	351
Law HG	2 North Non Combat Corps	Pte	12/06/16	Disobedience	10yrs PS		213/9	352
Law William E	2 North Non Combat Corps	Pte	12/06/16	Disobedience	10yrs PS	F&F	213/9	353
Lown RA	2 North Non Combat Corps	Pte	12/06/16	Disobedience	10yrs PS	F&F	213/9	354
Martlew A	2 North Non Combat Corps	Pte	12/06/16	Disobedience	10yrs PS	F&F	213/9	355
Myers A	2 North Non Combat Corps	Pte	12/06/16	Disobedience	10yrs PS		213/9	356
Renton L	2 North Non Combat Corps	Pte	12/06/16	Disobedience	10yrs PS	F&F	213/9	357
Senior CH	2 North Non Combat Corps	Pte	12/06/16	Disobedience	10yrs PS	F&F	213/9	358
Spencer ES	2 North Non Combat Corps	Pte	12/06/16	Disobedience	10yrs PS		213/9	359
Beavis GHS	3 East Non Combat Corps	Pte	13/06/16	Disobedience	10yrs PS	F&F	213/9	360
Brocklesby JH	2 North Non Combat Corps	Pte	13/06/16	Disobedience	10yrs PS	F&F	213/9	361
Frear WT	3 East Non Combat Corps	Pte	13/06/16	Disobedience	10yrs PS	F&F	213/9	362
Gaudie N	2 North Non Combat Corps	Pte	13/06/16	Disobedience	10yrs PS	F&F	213/9	363
Hall C	2 North Non Combat Corps	Pte	13/06/16	Disobedience	10yrs PS	F&F	213/9	364
Jackson CR	2 North Non Combat Corps	Pte	13/06/16	Disobedience	10yrs PS	F&F	213/9	365
Jordan PB	3 East Non Combat Corps	Pte	13/06/16	Disobedience	10yrs PS	F&F	213/9	366
Murfin FJ	3 East Non Combat Corps	Pte	13/06/16	Disobedience	10yrs PS	F&F	213/9	367
Routledge JW	2 North Non Combat Corps	Pte	13/06/16	Disobedience	10yrs PS	F&F	213/9	368
Taylor AW	3 East Non Combat Corps	Pte	13/06/16	Disobedience	10yrs PS	F&F	213/9	369
Walker EH	3 East Non Combat Corps	Pte	13/06/16	Disobedience	10yrs PS	F&F	213/9	370
Walling AF	3 East Non Combat Corps	Pte	13/06/16	Disobedience	10yrs PS	F&F	213/9	371
Kent W	Civilian		14/06/16	Poss firearms	5yrs PS	Dublin	92/3	372
Coster J	1/5 D Cornwall LI	Pte	15/06/16	Desertion	5yrs PS	F&F	213/9	373
Evans DW	1 Welsh Gds	Pte	15/06/16	Sleeping	Not Conf	F&F	213/9	
Harding Frederick	1 KRRC	Rfm	15/06/16	Desertion	XXX 29/06/16	F&F	213/9	374
McGrory J	4 (att 2) Argyle & Sutherland	Pte	15/06/16	Desertion	2yrs HL	F&F	213/9	
Hamilton A	1 Scottish Rifles	Pte	16/06/16	Desertion	Not Conf	F&F	213/9	
Yarnold Anthony	3 Worcestershire	Pte	16/06/16	Desertion	2yrs HL	F&F	213/10	
Boulton RO	1 Canadian MGC	Cpl	17/06/16	Desertion	5yrs PS	F&F	213/10	
Hampsey J	2 A&S Hdrs	Pte	17/06/16	Striking	10yrs PS	F&F	213/9	
Hubbard W	2 Leicestershire	Pte	17/06/16	Sleeping	2yrs HL	Mesopotamia	90/7	375
Knighton W	1 Northants	Pte	17/06/16	Desertion	5yrs PS	F&F	213/9	
McDermott JF	20 Manchester	Pte	17/06/16	Sleeping	2yrs PS	F&F	213/10	376
Smith John	1 Loyal N Lancs	Pte	17/06/16	Desertion	XXX 02/07/16	F&F	213/9	377
Weightman J	9 Black Watch	Pte	18/06/16	Desertion	5yrs PS	F&F	213/9	
Jennings John	2 S Lancs	Pte	20/06/16	Desertion	XXX 26/06/16	F&F	213/9	378
Lewis Griffith	2 S Lancs	Pte	20/06/16	Desertion	XXX 26/06/16	F&F	213/9	379
Middleton H	5 DAC	Dvr	20/06/16	Desertion	10yrs PS		213/9	
Stone EF	9 KRRC	Rfm	21/06/16	Desertion	10yrs Ps	F&F	213/9	
Wilson James H	4 Canadian EF	Pte	21/06/16	Desertion	XXX 09/07/16	F&F	213/9	380
Craig W	RAMC	Pte	22/06/16	Desertion	10yrs PS		213/9	
Deboi C	RAMC	Pte	22/06/16	Desertion	10yrs PS		213/9	
Hunter George	2 Durham LI	Pte	22/06/16	Desertion	XXX 02/07/16	F&F	213/9	381
Rossiter H	2 Durham LI	Pte	22/06/16	Desertion	10yrs PS	F&F	213/9	
Smith J	10 Lancs Fus	Cpl	22/06/16	Cowardice	5yrs PS	F&F	213/10	
Stewart A	6/7 R Scots Fus	Pte (L/C)	22/06/16	Desertion	15yrs PS	F&F	213/9	
Crump F	2 London	Pte	23/06/16	Desertion	5yrs PS	F&F	213/9	382
Butler Alexander	R Canadian Dragoons	Tpr	24/06/16	Murder	XXX 02/07/16	F&F	90/6	383
Evans AW	2 East Non Combat Corps	Pte	24/06/16	Disobedience	10yrs PS	F&F	213/9	
Brown A	ASC	Dvr	25/06/16	Desertion	5yrs PS		213/10	
Boag E	6 KO Scottish Bdrs	Pte	26/06/16	Desertion	Not Conf	F&F	213/11	
Collins JA	2 S Lancs	Pte	26/06/16	Desertion	5yrs PS	F&F	213/10	
Driver T	RE	Spr	26/06/16	Desertion	5yrs PS		213/9	
Kelly J	2 Manchester	Pte	26/06/16	Disobedience	15yrs PS	F&F	213/11	
Taylor J	19 London	Pte	26/06/16	Desertion	10yrs PS	F&F	213/9	384
Voice William	6 R W Surrey	Pte	26/06/16	Desertion	5yrs PS	F&F	213/10	
Woodhouse J	12 KRRC	Rfm	26/06/16	Desertion	10yrs PS	F&F	213/9	
Donovan HJ	11 E Yorks	Pte	27/06/16	Quitting	5yrs PS		213/10	
Hogan P	49 MGC	Pte	28/06/16	Desertion	5yrs PS		213/9	
Carberry M	6 R Irish Rifles	Rfm	29/06/16	Violence	18mos HL	Salonika	213/10	
Haynes W	6 R Irish Rifles	Rfm	29/06/16	Striking+	5yrs PS	Salonika	213/10	385
Monroe J	1 Canadian EF	Pte	29/06/16	Desertion	5yrs PS	F&F	213/10	
Morris N	12 S Wales Bdrs	Pte	29/06/16	Desertion	10yrs PS	F&F	213/9	386
Roberts J	1/8 Liverpool	Pte	29/06/16	Desertion	10yrs PS	F&F	213/9	387
Russell J	1/8 Liverpool	Pte	29/06/16	Desertion	10yrs PS	F&F	213/10	388
Sloane J	1/4 KOR Lancaster	Pte	29/06/16	Desertion	XXX 16/07/16	F&F	213/9	389

Name	Unit	Rank	Date	Offence	Final sentence	Location	Ref	Note
Beveridge A	24 DAC	Dvr	30/06/16	Striking	2yrs HL		213/9	
Brennan Joseph	1/8 Liverpool	Pte	30/06/16	Desertion	XXX 16/07/16	F&F	213/9	390
Clifton J	2 York & Lancaster	Pte	30/06/16	Desertion	10yrs PS	F&F	213/10	
Wiggham S	2 York & Lancaster	Pte	30/06/16	Desertion	10yrs PS	F&F	213/10	
Bannister H	7 Rifle Bde	Rfm	01/07/16	Sleeping	2yrs HL	F&F	213/9	
Perrin T	1/8 Liverpool	Pte	01/07/16	Desertion	10yrs PS	F&F	213/9	391
Buchanan A	4 Canadian EF	Pte	02/07/16	Desertion +	10yrs PS	F&F	213/10	392
Florence JR	48 Australian IF	Pte	02/07/16	Desertion	10yrs PS	F&F	213/16	
Parker A	13 Rifle Bde	Rfm	02/07/16	Sleeping	2yrs HL	F&F	213/10	
Allison J	4 Canadian EF	Pte	03/07/16	Desertion	5yrs PS	F&F	213/10	
Barry J	4 R Munster Fus	Pte	03/07/16	Desertion	3yrs PS		213/10	
Bulman T	4 (att 2) R Munster Fus	Pte	03/07/16	Desertion	3yrs PS	F&F	213/10	
Drummond A	2 A&S Hdrs	Pte	03/07/16	Desertion	10yrs PS	F&F	213/10	
Kelleher T	4 R Munster Fus	Pte	03/07/16	Desertion	3yrs PS		213/10	
Lane F	4 Canadian EF	Pte	03/07/16	Desertion	10yrs PS	F&F	213/10	
Millard P	4 R Munster Fus	Pte	03/07/16	Desertion	3yrs PS		213/10	
Sparkes JB	4 R Munster Fus	Pte	03/07/16	Desertion	3yrs PS		213/10	
Arnold Frederick S	Canadian FA	Dvr	05/07/16	Desertion	XXX 25/07/16	F&F	213/10	393
Hauptman KG	German Army	POW	05/07/16	Hostile Act	Not Conf		213/9	394
Ward E	2 York & Lancaster	Pte	05/07/16	Desertion	10yrs PS	F&F	213/10	
Legg H	2 DAC	Dvr	06/07/16	Desertion	5yrs PS		213/9	
Nolan J	9 R Dublin Fus	Pte	06/07/16	Desertion	5yrs PS	F&F	213/10	
Earp Arthur Grove	1/5 R Warwickshire	Pte	10/07/16	Desertion	XXX 22/07/16	F&F	213/10	395
Hewitt W	1 DAC	Dvr	10/07/16	Desertion	2yrs HL		213/10	
Chandler SE	42 Canadian EF	Pte	11/07/16	Desertion	10yrs PS	F&F	213/10	
Eaton J	7 N Staffordshire	Pte	11/07/16	Casting Arms	10yrs PS	Mesopotamia	90/7	396
Holloway Albert	2 R W Surrey	Pte	11/07/16	Cowardice	Not Conf	F&F	213/10	
Jeffries William	12 Middlesex	Pte	11/07/16	Desertion	5yrs PS	F&F	213/11	
Weston G	12 Middlesex	Pte	11/07/16	Desertion	5yrs PS	F&F	213/11	
Bacon A	10 Essex	Pte	12/07/16	Desertion	Not Conf	F&F	213/11	
Featherstone C	14 York & Lancaster	Pte	12/07/16	Desertion	15yrs PS	F&F	213/10	397
Hont Frederick	1 Liverpool	Pte	12/07/16	Desertion	3yrs PS	F&F	213/11	
Byrnes AJ	25 Australian IF	Pte	15/07/16	Violence	10yrs PS		213/10	
Cassidy James	1 R Inniskilling Fus	Pte	15/07/16	Desertion	XXX 23/07/16	F&F	213/10	398
Hawkins J	25 Australian IF	Pte	15/07/16	Striking	10yrs PS		213/10	
McMurdie J	1 R Inniskilling Fus	Pte	15/07/16	Desertion	3yrs PS	F&F	213/10	
Roberts John William	1 Canadian Mtd Rifles	Pte	15/07/16	Desertion	XXX 30/07/16	F&F	213/10	399
Young N	2 Canadian EF	Pte	15/07/16	Disobedience	2yrs HL	F&F	213/10	
Dickenson F	18 MGC	Pte	16/07/16	Striking	10yrs PS		213/10	
Griffiths B	18 MGC	Pte	16/07/16	Striking	10yrs PS		213/10	
Newall J	18 MGC	Pte	16/07/16	Striking	10yrs PS		213/10	
Bassett J	12 Royal Fus	Pte	17/07/16	Desertion	10 yrs PS	F&F	213/10	
Dennis T	5 Leicestershire	Pte	17/07/16	Desertion	10yrs PS	F&F	213/10	
Gill William J	8 Sherwood Fstrs	Pte	17/07/16	Desertion	10yrs PS	F&F	213/10	
Halsall J	7 Liverpool	Pte	17/07/16	Sleeping	2yrs HL	Salonika	213/11	400
Smith W	Div Am Sub Park	Pte	18/07/16	Indecency	Quashed		213/10	401
Lowton G	17 Sherwood Fstrs	Pte	19/07/16	Desertion	XXX 30/07/16	F&F	213/10	402
McCubbin Bertie	17 Sherwood Fstrs	Pte	19/07/16	Desertion	XXX 30/07/16	F&F	213/10	403
Potts William	2 Durham LI	Pte	19/07/16	Desertion	2yrs HL	F&F	213/10	
Bell AA	2/20 London	Pte	20/07/16	Sleeping	5yrs PS	F&F	213/10	
Cummings William H	2/20 London	Pte	20/07/16	Sleeping	5yrs PS	F&F	213/10	
Davies J	18 Welsh	Pte	20/07/16	Sleeping	3yrs PS	F&F	213/10	404
Bold R	3 Canadian EF	Pte	21/07/16	Desertion	10yrs PS	F&F	213/10	
Docherty J	1/4 Seaforth Hdrs	Pte	21/07/16	Desertion	5yrs PS	F&F	213/16	405
Scott J	1/5 E Kent (Buffs)	Pte	21/07/16	Sleeping	5yrs PS	Mesopotamia	90/7	406
Tempest J	RFA	Gnr	22/07/16	Desertion	5yrs PS		213/11	
Correy Frederick De B	2 Canadian Tunnelling Coy	Spr	24/07/16	Desertion	10yrs PS	F&F	213/10	
Jacobs J	7 D Cornwall LI	L/Cpl	24/07/16	Desertion	2yrs HL	F&F	213/10	
Mangham M	3 Canadian EF	Pte	24/07/16	Desertion	10yrs PS	F&F	213/10	
Robinson RJ	12 Durham LI	Pte	24/07/16	Desertion	Quashed	F&F	213/11	
Buttle AE	2 KO Yorks LI	Pte	25/07/16	Desertion	10yrs PS	F&F	213/10	
LaLiberte Come	3 Canadian EF	Pte	25/07/16	Desertion	XXX 04/08/16	F&F	213/10	407
Norman F	2 KO Yorks LI	Pte	25/07/16	Desertion	15yrs PS	F&F	213/10	
Godson C	12 E Yorks	Pte	26/07/16	Desertion	10yrs PS		213/10	
Shaw J	54 MGC	Pte	26/07/16	Desertion	Not Conf		213/10	
Costin W	6 Liverpool	Rfm	27/07/16	Sleeping	6mos HL		213/11	
Grimes A	1 R W Surrey	Pte (L/C)	27/07/16	Desertion	5yrs PS	F&F	213/11	
Hartfield HJ	RGA	Gnr	29/07/16	Desertion	10yrs PS		213/10	

Name	Unit	Rank	Date	Offence	Final sentence	Location	Ref	Note
Miller J	2 KO Scottish Bdrs	Pte	29/07/16	Desertion	5yrs PS	F&F	213/11	
Pugh P	7 W Riding	Pte	29/07/16	Cowardice	Not Conf	F&F	213/10	
Leary J	9 Scottish Rifles	Pte	30/07/16	Desertion	10yrs PS	F&F	213/10	408
McKay A	11 R Scots	Pte	30/07/16	Cowardice	Not Conf	F&F	213/10	
Murphy Allan	9 Scottish Rifles	Pte	30/07/16	Desertion	XXX 17/08/16	F&F	213/10	409
Ronan J	9 Sherwood Fstrs	Pte	30/07/16	Against Inhab	3yrs PS	F&F	213/10	
Fairhead S	7 Norfolk	Cpl	31/07/16	Cowardice	5yrs PS	F&F	213/11	
Hawthorne Frederick	1/5 S Staffordshire	Pte (L/C)	31/07/16	Cowardice	XXX 11/08/16	F&F	213/10	410
Randall C	9 Leicestershire	Pte	31/07/16	Desertion	10yrs PS	F&F	213/10	
Nelson William Barry	14 Durham LI	Pte	01/08/16	Desertion	XXX 11/08/16	F&F	213/10	411
Freer J	2 Lancs Fus	Pte	02/08/16	Desertion	10yrs PS	F&F	213/10	
Grainger S	1 Worcestershire	Pte	02/08/16	Desertion	10yrs PS	F&F	213/10	
Knightly R	2 KO Yorks LI	Pte	02/08/16	Desertion	2yrs HL	F&F	213/11	
Moffit J	15 Sherwood Fstrs	Pte	02/08/16	Quitting	5yrs PS	F&F	213/11	412
Wilson H	7 R Irish Fus	Pte	02/08/16	Desertion	5yrs PS	F&F	213/10	
Wilton Jesse	15 Sherwood Fstrs	Cpl	02/08/16	Quitting	XXX 17/08/16	F&F	213/10	413
Carden H	22 Manchester	Pte	03/08/16	Desertion	3yrs PS	F&F	213/11	
Hunter GW	2 Coldstream Gds	Pte	03/08/16	Desertion	2yrs HL	F&F	213/10	
O'Shea J	RGA	Cpl	03/08/16	Murder	10yrs PS		213/10	
Whitfield S	6 R W Kent	Pte	03/08/16	Cowardice+	10yrs PS	F&F	213/11	414
Woods CM	55 Canadian EF	Pte	03/08/16	Insubordination	5yrs PS	F&F	213/10	
Connor J	1 R Irish Fus	Pte	04/08/16	Desertion	10yrs PS	F&F	213/10	
Gregory T	4 Canadian EF	Pte	04/08/16	Desertion	10yrs PS	F&F	213/10	
Marsh EA	2/4 R Berkshire	Pte	04/08/16	Desertion	5yrs PS	F&F	213/10	
Morrison TC	2 New Zealand EF	Pte	04/08/16	Quitting+	5yrs PS		213/10	415
Spencer J	9 Worcestershire	Pte	04/08/16	Sleeping	3yrs PS	Mesopotamia	90/7	416
Sharpe WL	14 York & Lancaster	Pte	05/08/16	Cowardice	10yrs PS		213/10	417
Kane Thomas	2 R Irish Rifles	Rfm	06/08/16	Desertion	1yr HL	F&F	213/10	
Lavender G	4 Australian IF	L/Cpl	06/08/16	Desertion	15yrs PS		213/10	
Allison CF	20 Middlesex	Pte	07/08/16	Desertion	Not Conf	F&F	213/10	418
Collins T	5 Northumb Fus	Pte	08/08/16	Desertion	5yrs PS	F&F	213/11	
Reynolds EJ	3 Canadian EF	Pte	08/08/16	Desertion	XXX 23/08/16	F&F	213/10	419
Smith E	6 Northumb Fus	Pte	08/08/16	Desertion	5yrs PS	F&F	213/11	
Clarke A	2 Worcestershire	Pte	09/08/16	Desertion	5yrs PS	F&F	213/11	
Lindridge R	20 KRRC	Rfm	10/08/16	Desertion	5yrs PS		213/11	420
Simons H	13 Canadian EF	Pte	10/08/16	Desertion	10yrs PS	F&F	213/10	
Tilley S	1 Loyal N Lancs	Pte	10/08/16	Desertion	2yrs HL	F&F	213/11	
Wallace P	2 R Scots	Sgt	11/08/16	Desertion	5yrs PS	F&F	213/11	421
Barnett W	1 New Zealand EF	Pte	12/08/16	Desertion	5yrs PS		213/10	422
Hughes Frank	2 New Zealand EF	Pte	12/08/16	Desertion	XXX 25/08/16		213/10	423
Newton W	9 Lancs Fus	Pte	12/08/16	Sleeping	5yrs PS	F&F	213/11	
Ellison J	18 Canadian EF	Pte	13/08/16	Desertion	5yrs PS	F&F	213/10	
Evans D	2 Welsh	Pte	13/08/16	Desertion	5yrs PS	F&F	213/11	
Calderwood W	5 R Irish	Pte	15/08/16	Striking	3yrs PS	Salonika	213/11	424
Giles Peter	14 Northumb Fus	Pte	15/08/16	Desertion	XXX 24/08/16		213/10	425
Hall E	25 RFA	Dvr	15/08/16	Desertion	10yrs PS		213/11	
Pither A	1 R Berkshire	Pte	15/08/16	Desertion	3yrs PS	F&F	213/10	
Bennett John	1 Hampshire	Pte	16/08/16	Cowardice	XXX 28/08/16	F&F	213/10	426
Cottingham J	6 E Kent (Buffs)	Pte	18/08/16	Sleeping	5yrs PS	F&F	213/10	
Daniels William T	18 MGC	Pte	18/08/16	Sleeping	3yrs PS		213/10	
Capener A	9 Worcestershire	Pte	19/08/16	Sleeping	3yrs PS	Mesopotamia	90/7	427
Hallam T	9 Worcestershire	Pte	19/08/16	Sleeping	3yrs PS	Mesopotamia	90/7	
Higgins J	1/9 A&S Hdrs	Pte	19/08/16	Desertion	XXX 26/08/16	F&F	213/10	428
Holderness William	11 Royal Fus	Pte	19/08/16	Desertion	10yrs PS	F&F	213/10	
Hopkins JT	2 York & Lancaster	Pte	19/08/16	Desertion	2yrs HL	F&F	213/10	
Ashby H	1 Grenadier Gds	Pte	21/08/16	Desertion	5yrs PS	F&F	213/11	
Barton Granville W	1 R Irish Rifles	Rfm	21/08/16	Desertion	3yrs PS	F&F	213/10	
Crimmins Herbert	18 W Yorks	Pte	21/08/16	Desertion	XXX 05/09/16	F&F	213/10	429
Hancock E	12 Suffolk	Pte	21/08/16	Desertion	10yrs PS	F&F	213/10	430
Turnbull G	2 Rifle Bde	Rfm	21/08/16	Desertion	10yrs PS	F&F	213/10	
Welsh C	8 Canadian EF	Pte	21/08/16	Desertion	5yrs PS	F&F	213/11	431
Wild Arthur	18 W Yorks	Pte	21/08/16	Desertion	XXX 05/09/16	F&F	213/10	432
Carey Joseph	7 R Irish Fus	Pte	22/08/16	Desertion x2	XXX 15/09/16	F&F	213/11	433
Creighton H	RFA	Pte	22/08/16	Desertion	5yrs PS		213/11	
de Fehr B	1 Canadian Reserve Park	Dvr	22/08/16	Murder	XXX 25/08/16	F&F	213/10	
Geoghegan T	7 R Irish Fus	Pte	22/08/16	Disobedience+	3yrs PS	F&F	213/11	434
Lewis J	2/20 London	Pte	22/08/16	Sleeping	5yrs PS	F&F	213/11	
Long D	8 R Irish Fus	Pte	22/08/16	Sleeping	3yrs PS	F&F	213/11	

Name	Unit	Rank	Date	Offence	Final sentence	Location	Ref	Note
Cleasby T	9 Lancs Fus	Pte	23/08/16	Sleeping	2yrs HL	F&F	213/10	
Howard J	1/7 W Riding	Pte	23/08/16	Sleeping	2yrs HL	F&F	213/10	
Roberts A	1 R Warwickshire	Sgt	23/08/16	Desertion	10yrs PS	F&F	213/11	
Smoothy F	147 MGC	Pte	23/08/16	Sleeping	2yrs HL		213/10	
Haddock James A	12 York & Lancaster	Pte	24/08/16	Desertion	XXX 16/09/16	F&F	213/11	435
Harley WM	9 Essex	Sgt	24/08/16	Desertion	Not Conf	F&F	213/11	
Scholes R	11 E Lancs	Pte	24/08/16	Desertion	2yrs HL	F&F	213/11	436
Wadsworth A	64 MCG	Pte	24/08/16	Sleeping/Quitting	5yrs PS	F&F	213/11	
Adams T	8 R W Kent	Pte	25/08/16	Sleeping	5yrs PS	F&F	213/11	
Attwell FN	7 Wiltshire	Pte	25/08/16	Sleeping	1yr HL	Salonika	213/11	
Dowling A	2 Yorks	Pte	25/08/16	Sleeping	3yrs PS	F&F	213/10	
Langridge A	2 R Sussex	Pte	25/08/16	Desertion+	Not Conf	F&F	213/11	437
Jackson E	55 DAC RFA	Gnr	26/08/16	Desertion	5yrs PS		213/11	
Letten S	RFA	Gnr	26/08/16	Desertion	10yrs PS		213/11	
Mann RC	1/5 Gloucestershire	Pte	26/08/16	Cowardice	5yrs PS	F&F	213/10	
Saunders W	14 DAC RFA	Gnr	26/08/16	Desertion	5yrs PS	F&F	213/11	
Clee R	9 S Staffordshire	Pte	28/08/16	Desertion	10yrs PS	F&F	213/11	
O'Sullivan J	8/10 Gordon Hdrs (att RE)	Pte	28/08/16	Mutiny	5yrs PS	F&F	213/11	
Watts A	1 R Irish	Pte	28/08/16	Violence	10yrs PS	Salonika	213/11	
Hampden A	1 New Zealand EF	Pte	30/08/16	Desertion	Not Conf		213/11	438
Staunton M	24 Bty RFA	Pte	30/08/16	Sleeping	5yrs PS		213/11	
Donnelly Thomas	1 W Yorks	Pte	31/08/16	Desertion	5yrs PS	F&F	213/11	
O'Hagan JT	1 W Yorks	Pte	31/08/16	Desertion	5yrs PS	F&F	213/11	
Allen TF	2 Leicestershire	Pte	01/09/16	Sleeping	2yrs HL	Mesopotamia 90/7		439
Walls FR	21 Australian IF	Pte	01/09/16	Desertion	Not Conf		213/11	
Cruse HS	ASC	Pte	02/09/16	Desertion	10yrs PS		213/11	
Depper Charles	1/4 R Berkshire	Pte	02/09/16	Desertion	XXX 13/09/16	F&F	213/11	440
Schulman B	1/1 Oxon & Bucks LI	Pte	02/09/16	Cowardice	Not Conf	F&F	213/11	
Anderson James	12 Liverpool	Pte	03/09/16	Cowardice	XXX 12/09/16	F&F	213/10	441
Black Peter	1/4 (att 1/7) Black Watch	Pte	03/09/16	Desertion	XXX 18/09/16	F&F	213/11	442
Hussein MS	Civilian		03/09/16	War treason	Acquitted		213/12	
Pounder J	RE	Spr	03/09/16	Desertion	15yrs PS		213/11	
Cartwright L	9 Worcestershire	Pte	04/09/16	Sleeping	3yrs PS	Mesopotamia 90/7		443
Walsh M	4 Royal Fus	Pte	04/09/16	Desertion	10yrs PS	F&F	213/11	
Morin G	52 Canadian EF	Pte	05/09/16	Desertion	5yrs PS	F&F	213/11	444
Wyman A	60 Canadian EF	L/Cpl	05/09/16	Quitting	5yrs PS	F&F	213/11	
Rickman Albert	1 R Dublin Fus	Pte	07/09/16	Desertion	XXX 15/09/16	F&F	213/10	445
Rielly WG	18 Australian IF	Pte	07/09/16	Desertion	Not Conf	F&F	213/11	
Hall G	2 E Lancs	Pte	08/09/16	Cowardice	15yrs PS	F&F	213/11	
Middleton J	1 Northumb Fus	Pte	08/09/16	Cowardice	10yrs PS		213/11	
Card Edward A	20 KRRC	Rfm	09/09/16	Desertion	XXX 22/09/16	F&F	213/11	446
Fields JT	2 York & Lancaster	Pte	09/09/16	Desertion	Not Conf	F&F	213/11	
Ryecroft W	1 Northumb Fus	Pte	09/09/16	Desertion	5yrs PS	F&F	213/11	
Baxter HJ	9 Suffolk	Pte	10/09/16	Striking	5yrs PS	F&F	213/11	
Williams W	8 Somerset LI	Pte	10/09/16	Desertion	3yrs PS	F&F	213/11	
Berry F	6 E Kent (Buffs)	Pte	11/09/16	Sleeping	5yrs PS	F&F	213/11	
Charnock W	8 KOR Lancaster	Pte	11/09/16	Desertion	5yrs PS	F&F	213/11	
Cunningham T	11 S Lancs	Pte	11/09/16	Desertion x2	Not Conf	F&F	213/11	447
Woodhouse G	7 Border	Pte	11/09/16	Desertion	5yrs PS	F&F	213/11	
Allison A	7 Norfolk	Pte (L/C)	12/09/16	Sleeping	5yrs PS	F&F	213/11	
Phillips T	5 DAC	Dvr	12/09/16	Desertion	5yrs PS		213/11	
Barton GW	13 Middlesex	Sgt	13/09/16	Desertion	Not Conf	F&F	213/11	
O'Brien D	1 Middlesex	Pte	13/09/16	Desertion	10yrs PS	F&F	213/11	
Sweeney John J	1 New Zealand EF	Pte	13/09/16	Desertion	XXX 02/10/16		213/11	448
Hall V	2 West Indies	Pte	14/09/16	Sleeping	10yrs PS		213/11	
O'Neill J	1/4 Black Watch	Pte	15/09/16	Disobedience	5yrs PS	F&F	213/11	449
Galfin E	1 Liverpool	Pte	17/09/16	Desertion	3yrs PS	F&F	213/11	
Wheelton C	1 Middlesex	Pte	17/09/16	Desertion	5yrs PS	F&F	213/11	
Barnes T	6 S Lancs	Pte (L/C)	18/09/16	Desertion	5yrs PS	Mesopotamia 90/7		450
Morris M	2 Leinster	Pte	18/09/16	Desertion	10yrs PS	F&F	213/11	
Smith H	3 (att 11) Suffolk	Pte	18/09/16	Desertion	10yrs PS	UK	213/11	451
Weightman J	9 Black Watch	Pte	18/09/16	Desertion	5yrs PS	F&F	213/11	
Whitehead EG	13 R Welsh Fus	Pte	18/09/16	Quitting	10yrs PS	F&F	213/11	452
Badger W	1/5 S Staffordshire	Pte	19/09/16	Sleeping	2yrs HL	F&F	213/11	
Frafra Aziberi	Gold Coast Regt	Pte	19/09/16	Casting Arms +	XXX 28/09/16	East Africa	213/11	453
Butler J	8 Cheshire	Pte	20/09/16	Quitting	3yrs PS	Mesopotamia 90/7		454
Fox H	2 KOR Lancaster	L/Cpl	20/09/16	Desertion	2yrs HL	Salonika	213/11	
Hamilton Thomas Grant	38 RFA	Dvr	20/09/16	Striking	XXX 03/10/16	F&F	213/11	455

Name	Unit	Rank	Date	Offence	Final sentence	Location	Ref	Note
Mullany James	RFA	Dvr	20/09/16	Striking	XXX 03/10/16		213/11	456
Sloan S	10 A&S Hdrs	Pte	20/09/16	Desertion	5yrs PS	F&F	213/11	
Turley G	94 MGC	Pte	20/09/16	Sleeping	2yrs HL		213/11	
Webster J	2 KOR Lancaster	L/Cpl	20/09/16	Desertion	5yrs PS	Salonika	213/11	
Baker EC	2/20 London	Pte	21/09/16	Sleeping	10yrs PS	F&F	213/11	
Redfern W	16 Northumb Fus	Pte	21/09/16	Desertion	15yrs PS	F&F	213/11	
Rix RH	10 Welsh (att 2 RW Fus)	Pte	21/09/16	Desertion	5yrs PS	F&F	213/11	
Harvey T	19 Manchester	Pte	23/09/16	Sleeping	Not Conf	F&F	213/11	457
Mann TW	ASC	Pte	23/09/16	Striking x2	10yrs PS		213/11	
Murray Francis	9 Gordon Hdrs (att RE)	Pte	24/09/16	Murder x2	XXX 01/10/16		213/11	458
Izatt William	9 Essex	Pte	25/09/16	Sleeping	5yrs PS	F&F	213/11	
Perris J	6 KOR Lancaster	Pte	25/09/16	Desertion	5yrs PS	Mesopotamia	90/7	459
Wardlaw P	13 R Scots	Pte	25/09/16	Desertion	5yrs PS	F&F	213/11	
Sweeney C	17 Highland LI	Pte	26/09/16	Cowardice	2yrs HL	F&F	213/11	460
Maidment J	8 KOR Lancaster	Pte	27/09/16	Desertion	6mos HL	F&F	213/11	
Thomas J	3 Liverpool (att 8 E Lancs)	Pte	27/09/16	Desertion	10yrs PS		213/11	
Walton H	8 S Staffordshire	Pte	27/09/16	Desertion	10yrs PS	F&F	213/11	
Barker Robert Loveless	6 Royal Fus (London)	Rfm	28/09/16	Desertion	XXX 04/11/16	F&F	213/11	461
Lynch H	26 Australian IF	Pte	28/09/16	Desertion/Esc	Not Conf		213/11	
Spowart W	26 Ausralian IF	Pte	28/09/16	Desertion/Esc	Not Conf	F&F	213/11	
Kelly J	2 (Gn) R Irish Fus	Pte	29/09/16	Quitting	2yrs HL	Salonika	213/11	
McLaren J	6 Cameron Hdrs	Pte	29/09/16	Desertion	5yrs PS	F&F	213/11	
Smith T	13 R Scots	Pte	29/09/16	Desertion	5yrs PS	F&F	213/11	
Timmins G	26 Australian IF	Pte	29/09/16	Desertion	Not Conf		213/11	
Dimes Frank	181 Bde RFA	Dvr	30/09/16	Disobedience	10yrs PS		213/11	
Botfield Albert	9 S Staffordshire	Pte	01/10/16	Cowardice+	XXX 18/10/16	F&F	213/12	462
Harris J	10 Lancs Fus	Pte	01/10/16	Desertion	5yrs PS	F&F	213/12	
Hopley JW	11 KRRC	Pte	01/10/16	Desertion	Not Conf	F&F	213/12	
Major JP	1 R Scots Fus	Pte	01/10/16	Desertion	3yrs PS	F&F	213/12	
Morris R	18 Australian IF	Pte	01/10/16	Desertion	2yrs HL		213/13	
Farr Harry	1 W Yorks	Pte	02/10/16	Cowardice	XXX 18/10/16	F&F	213/12	463
Rix JW	7 KOR Lancaster	Pte	04/10/16	Desertion	Not Conf	F&F	213/12	
Bellet J	1 R Berkshire	Pte	05/10/16	Desertion	10yrs PS	F&F	213/12	
Delaney James	2 A&S Hdrs	Pte	05/10/16	Mutiny	2yrs HL	F&F	90/6	464
Garden James	1 Highland LI	Pte	05/10/16	Mutiny	15yrs PS	F&F	90/6	465
Lewis William E	124 RFA	Gnr	05/10/16	Mutiny	XXX 29/10/16	F&F	90/6	466
Little Alexander	10 Australian IF	Pte	05/10/16	Striking	2yrs HL	F&F	90/6	467
McCaffery V	8 R Irish Fus	Pte	05/10/16	Cowardice	Not Conf	F&F	213/12	
McCorkindale Daniel	11 R Scots	Pte	05/10/16	Mutiny	15yrs PS	F&F	90/6	468
Murphy Michael J	6 Connaught Rangers	Pte	05/10/16	Mutiny	10yrs PS	F&F	90/6	469
Peden William	ASC	Dvr	05/10/16	Mutiny	2yrs HL	F&F	90/6	470
Bernard A	11 Essex	Pte	06/10/16	Desertion	5yrs PS	F&F	213/12	
Chapman S	HQ 1 Canadian DT	Pte	06/10/16	Disobedience	3yrs PS	F&F	213/12	
Marples T	2 Coldstream Gds	Pte	06/10/16	Desertion	5yrs PS	F&F	213/12	
Boak G	1 Seaforth Hdrs	Pte	07/10/16	Insubordination	3yrs PS	Mesopotamia	213/12	
Dyckhoff J	2/24 London	Pte	07/10/16	Sleeping	15yrs PS	F&F	213/12	
Green C	Kings Shropshire LI	L/Cpl	07/10/16	Desertion	7yrs PS		213/12	
Warrington E	2 Leicestershire	Pte	07/10/16	Sleeping	3mos FP1	Mesopotamia	90/7	471
Birch F	1 Worcestershire	Pte	08/10/16	Desertion	5yrs PS	F&F	213/12	
Jefferies Alfred Leonard	6 Somerset LI	Pte	09/10/16	Desertion	XXX 01/11/16	F&F	213/12	472
Jung J	66 MGC	Pte	09/10/16	Sleeping	3yrs PS		213/12	
Insley J	7 KRRC	Rfm	10/10/16	Desertion	Not Conf	F&F	213/12	
Knight E	9 KRRC	Rfm	10/10/16	Quitting	5yrs PS	F&F	213/12	
McQuade John	18 Highland LI	Pte	10/10/16	Desertion x2	XXX 06/11/16	F&F	213/12	473
Smith W	7 KRRC	Rfm	10/10/16	Desertion	Not Conf	F&F	213/12	
Sweeney P	2 R Munster Fus	Pte	10/10/16	Disobedience	10yrs PS	F&F	213/12	
Woodfield A	9 Rifle Bde	Rfm	10/10/16	Cowardice	10yrs PS	F&F	213/12	
Braithwaite John	New Zealand Rifle Bde	Pte	11/10/16	Mutiny	XXX 29/10/16	F&F	90/6	474
Le Guier Bertie	14 Australian IF	Pte	11/10/16	Mutiny	2yrs HL	F&F	90/6	475
Lingard J	6 Northumb Fus	Pte	11/10/16	Desertion	5yrs PS	F&F	213/12	
Mitchell Frederick W	57 Australian IF	Pte	11/10/16	Mutiny	2yrs HL	F&F	90/6	476
Palmer Henry	5 Northumb Fus	Pte	11/10/16	Desertion	XXX 27/10/16	F&F	213/12	477
Poole Harry	7 Yorks	Pte	11/10/16	Desertion+	XXX 09/12/16	F&F	213/12	478
Sheffield Sidney A	4 Australian IF	Pte	11/10/16	Mutiny	2yrs HL	F&F	90/6	479
Stevenson Richard	1/4 Loyal N Lancs	Pte	11/10/16	Desertion	XXX 25/10/16	F&F	213/12	480
Atkinson G	2 R Scots	Pte	12/10/16	Desertion	3yrs PS	F&F	213/12	
Girling A	1/4 Suffolk	Pte	12/10/16	Desertion	10yrs PS	F&F	213/12	
Plummer WR	4 Royal Fus	Pte	12/10/16	Desertion	Not Conf	F&F	213/13	

Name	Unit	Rank	Date	Offence	Final sentence	Location	Ref	Note
Wilson T	1/5 W Riding	Pte	12/10/16	Desertion	5yrs PS	F&F	213/12	
Course SG	1/13 London	Pte	14/10/16	Cowardice	Not Conf	F&F	213/12	481
Gardiner William	1/13 London	Pte	14/10/16	Cowardice	5yrs PS	F&F	213/12	482
McGhee H	1/5 Highland LI	Pte	14/10/16	Sleeping	2yrs HL	Egypt	213/13	483
O'Conner F	7 D Cornwall LI	Pte	14/10/16	Cowardice	Not Conf	F&F	213/12	
James W	13 Welsh	Pte	15/10/16	Cowardice	15yrs PS	F&F	213/12	484
French J	8 R Inniskilling Fus	Pte	16/10/16	Desertion	5yrs PS	F&F	213/12	
Murray A	1 R W Surrey	Pte	16/10/16	Striking	5yrs PS	F&F	213/12	
Smith G	7 D Cornwall LI	Pte	16/10/16	Desertion	5yrs PS	F&F	213/12	
Larginson S	1/8 Liverpool	Pte	17/10/16	Desertion	15yrs PS	F&F	213/12	485
Roberts E	20 Liverpool	Pte	17/10/16	Cowardice	5yrs PS	F&F	213/12	
White J	9 Rifle Bde	Rfm	18/10/16	Desertion	10yrs PS	F&F	213/12	
Litters HJ	48 Australian IF	Pte	19/10/16	Disobedience x2	5yrs PS		213/12	
Young Elsworth	25 Canadian EF	Pte	19/10/16	Desertion	XXX 29/10/16	F&F	213/12	486
Hinchem J	2 KO Yorks LI	Pte	20/10/16	Desertion	1yr HL	F&F	213/12	
McGeehan Bernard	1/8 Liverpool	Pte	21/10/16	Desertion	XXX 02/11/16	F&F	213/12	487
Nicholson D	11 RFA	Gnr	21/10/16	Desertion	Not Conf		213/12	
Wardlaw P	13 R Scots	Pte	21/10/16	Desertion	1yr HL	F&F	213/12	
Gordon E	8 R W Surrey	L/Cpl	23/10/16	Striking	2yrs HL	F&F	213/12	
Worgan F	5 Loyal N Lancs	Pte	23/10/16	Desertion	10yrs PS	F&F	213/12	
MacDonald Henry [Harry]	12 W Yorks	Pte	24/10/16	Desertion	XXX 04/11/16	F&F	213/12	488
Bayliss C	42 RFA	Dvr	25/10/16	Desertion	5yrs PS		213/12	
Gates W	1 Leicestershire	Pte	26/10/16	Desertion	5yrs PS	F&F	213/12	
Hiskey E	9 Suffolk	Pte	26/10/16	Desertion	5yrs PS	F&F	213/12	
Lane JH	5 S Lancs	Rfm	26/10/16	Disobedience	10yrs PS	F&F	213/12	
Ollerenshaw N	5 S Lancs	Rfm	26/10/16	Disobedience	2yrs HL	F&F	213/12	
Sawyer C	1 Leicestershire	Pte	26/10/16	Desertion	5yrs PS	F&F	213/12	
Urwin WA	14 Durham LI	Pte	26/10/16	Desertion	5yrs PS	F&F	213/12	
Flynn Hugh	18 Highland LI	Pte	27/10/16	Desertion	XXX 15/11/16	F&F	213/12	489
Keeson WH	1 E Surrey	Pte	28/10/16	Desertion	15yrs PS	F&F	213/13	
Mulgrew Edward	2 RHA	Dvr	28/10/16	Desertion	10yrs PS		213/12	
Reeson WH	1 E Surrey	Pte	28/10/16	Desertion	15yrs PS	F&F	213/12	
Ryan J	11 W Yorks	Cpl	28/10/16	Desertion	10yrs PS	F&F	213/12	
Weatherspoon P	20 Liverpool	Pte	29/10/16	Desertion	10yrs PS	F&F	213/12	490
Bass GA	13 Essex	Pte	30/10/16	Desertion	5yrs PS	F&F	213/12	491
Fraser J	1 Canadian EF	Pte	30/10/16	Desertion	Not Conf	F&F	213/12	
Nolan M	6 R Dublin Fus	Pte	30/10/16	Desertion	15yrs PS	Salonika	213/12	
Bishop TA	7 Canadian EF	Pte	31/10/16	Desertion	5yrs PS	F&F	213/12	
Bodnarchuk B	1 Canadian EF	Pte	31/10/16	Desertion	5yrs PS	F&F	213/12	
Coley J	1 S Staffordshire	Pte	01/11/16	Desertion	Quashed	F&F	213/12	
Lewin F	11 Sherwood Fstrs	Pte	01/11/16	Cowardice	Not Conf	F&F	213/12	
Penman J	6/7 R Scots Fus	Cpl	01/11/16	Desertion	5yrs PS	F&F	213/12	
Rookes TW	2 Yorks	Pte	01/11/16	Desertion	15yrs PS	F&F	213/12	
Thompson G	12 Northumb Fus	Pte	01/11/16	Desertion	5yrs PS	F&F	213/12	
Wales EJ	8 KO Yorks LI	Pte	01/11/16	Cowardice	Not Conf	F&F	213/12	
Archer J	20 Durham LI	Pte	02/11/16	Desertion	Not Conf	F&F	213/12	492
Hopper JR	20 Durham LI	Pte	02/11/16	Desertion	Not Conf	F&F	213/12	493
Hunt William G	18 Manchester	Pte	02/11/16	Desertion	XXX 14/11/16	F&F	213/12	494
Rogers E	26 Ausralian IF	Pte	02/11/16	Desertion x2	10yrs PS	F&F	213/13	
Roundstein R	2 S Wales Bdrs	Pte	02/11/16	Desertion	5yrs PS	F&F	213/12	
Searle F	1 E Surrey	Pte	02/11/16	Desertion	5yrs PS	F&F	213/12	
Tighe JJ	9 R Irish Rifles	Rfm	02/11/16	Sleeping	5yrs PS	F&F	213/12	495
Tite Reginald T	13 R Sussex	Pte	02/11/16	Desertion	XXX 25/11/16	F&F	213/12	496
Willmot B	1 E Surrey	Pte	02/11/16	Desertion	3yrs PS	F&F	213/12	
Maguire J	2 R Dublin Fus	Pte	03/11/16	Disobedience	5yrs PS	F&F	213/12	
Mulvey M	1 Australian IF	Pte	03/11/16	Desertion	Not Conf		213/13	
Thomas H	2 Yorks	Pte	03/11/16	Desertion	Not Conf	F&F	213/12	
Allen B	2/6 Gloucestershire	Pte	04/11/16	Sleeping	10yrs PS	F&F	213/12	
Gilham Harry	1 E Kent (Buffs)	Pte	04/11/16	Desertion	Not Conf	F&F	213/12	
Anstead [?] Alfred Thomas	4 Royal Fus	Pte	05/11/16	Desertion	XXX 15/11/16	F&F	213/12	497
Benians A	14 Highland LI	Pte	05/11/16	Sleeping	2yrs HL	F&F	213/12	498
Footner AE	2 Hampshire	Pte	05/11/16	Desertion	5yrs PS	F&F	213/12	
Kennedy J	104 RFA	Dvr	06/11/16	Desertion	10yrs PS		213/12	
Roberts T	1 R Welsh Fus	Pte	06/11/16	Sleeping	2yrs HL	F&F	213/12	
Kerr Henry H	7 Canadian EF	Pte	07/11/16	Desertion	XXX 21/11/16	F&F	213/12	499
Thorpe W	17 Lancs Fus	Pte	07/11/16	Sleeping	10yrs PS	F&F	213/12	500
Barnaby A	148 RFA	Gnr	08/11/16	Desertion	5yrs PS		213/12	
Blyth F	148 RFA	Gnr	08/11/16	Desertion	5yrs PS		213/12	

Name	Unit	Rank	Date	Offence	Final sentence	Location	Ref	Note
Clarke Wilfred	2 Durham LI	Pte	08/11/16	Desertion	10yrs PS	F&F	213/12	501
Randle William H	10 Sherwood Fstrs	Pte	08/11/16	Desertion	XXX 25/11/16	F&F	213/12	502
Hannon W	7 R Dublin Fus	Pte	09/11/16	Sleeping	5yrs PS	Salonika	213/12	
Hughes George E	7 KOR Lancaster	L/Cpl	09/11/16	Desertion	XXX 23/11/16	F&F	213/12	503
MacMillan J	RAMC	Pte	09/11/16	Desertion	15yrs PS		213/7	
Moorhouse C	2 W Riding	Pte	09/11/16	Desertion	5yrs PS	F&F	213/12	
Kempton H	148 RFA	Gnr	10/11/16	Desertion	5yrs PS		213/13	
Law W	1/19 London	Pte	11/11/16	Desertion	5yrs PS	F&F	213/12	504
Moon William Alfred	11 Cheshire	Pte (L/C)	11/11/16	Desertion	XXX 21/11/16	F&F	213/12	505
Townsend HO	1 Canadian Mtd Rifles	Pte	11/11/16	Desertion	5yrs PS	F&F	213/12	
Wallen G	1 Sherwood Fstrs	Pte	11/11/16	Sleeping	2yrs HL	F&F	213/12	
Davidson H	(Hawke) R Naval Div	S'man	12/11/16	Desertion	3yrs PS		213/12	
Foster CW	19 Manchester	Pte	13/11/16	Cowardice	10yrs PS	F&F	213/12	506
Osborne P	19 Manchester	Pte	13/11/16	Cowardice	10yrs PS	F&F	213/12	507
Scott EH	19 Manchester	Pte	13/11/16	Cowardice	10yrs PS	F&F	213/12	508
Skuse SJ	19 Manchester	Pte	13/11/16	Cowardice	10yrs PS	F&F	213/12	509
Taffs J	ASC	Pte	13/11/16	Desertion	10yrs PS	F&F	213/12	
Viejra (Rikard) Leopold	Civilian	Alien	14/11/16	Espionage	PS Life	UK	92/3	510
Beeby Ernest	212 RE	Pnr	15/11/16	Desertion	XXX 09/12/16		213/12	511
McDougall A	2 A&S Hdrs	Pte	15/11/16	Desertion	5yrs PS	F&F	213/12	
Bishop CB	2 R Sussex	Pte	16/11/16	Desertion	5yrs PS	F&F	213/12	
Edwards M	1/4 York & Lancaster	Pte	17/11/16	Desertion	10yrs PS	F&F	213/12	
Hartley S	1/5 York & Lancaster	Pte	17/11/16	Desertion	10yrs PS	F&F	213/12	
Brooks C	6 Wiltshire	Pte	18/11/16	Desertion	15yrs PS	F&F	213/12	
Mark F	2 W Yorks	Pte	18/11/16	Desertion	5yrs PS	F&F	213/12	
Speers D	9 R Inniskilling Fus	Pte	18/11/16	Sleeping	5yrs PS	F&F	213/12	512
Simmonds William Henry	23 Middlesex	Pte	19/11/16	Desertion	XXX 01/12/16	F&F	213/12	513
Tootle TE	10 R Irish Rifles	Rfm	19/11/16	Sleeping	5yrs PS	F&F	213/12	514
Dunbavin J	4 Liverpool	Sgt	20/11/16	Cowardice	5yrs PS	F&F	213/13	
Field A	20 Royal Fus	Pte	20/11/16	Desertion	5yrs PS	F&F	213/12	515
Ingham Albert	18 Manchester	Pte	20/11/16	Desertion	XXX 01/12/16	F&F	213/12	516
Kennedy J	RFA	Dvr	20/11/16	Desertion	5yrs PS		213/12	
Longshaw Alfred	18 Manchester	Pte	20/11/16	Desertion	XXX 01/12/16	F&F	213/12	517
Murray J	1 Scottish Rifles	Pte	20/11/16	Cowardice	10yrs PS	F&F	213/12	
Semple G	1 Scottish Rifles	Pte	20/11/16	Cowardice	10yrs PS	F&F	213/12	
Stead F	2 W Riding	Pte	21/11/16	Desertion	5yrs PS	F&F	213/13	
Gibbons J	6 R Irish Rifles	Rfn	23/11/16	Desertion	15yrs PS	Salonika	213/13	
Thorne FR	2 Royal Fus	Cpl	23/11/16	Desertion	5yrs PS	F&F	213/13	
Cameron John	1/5 Northumb Fus	Pte	24/11/16	Desertion	XXX 04/12/16	F&F	213/12	518
Cuthbertson J	5 Northumb Fus	Pte	24/11/16	Desertion	15yrs PS	F&F	213/12	
Poole Eric Skeffington	11 W Yorks	2 Lt	24/11/16	Desertion	XXX 10/12/16	F&F	90/6	519
Powell FB	18 Middlesex	Pte	24/11/16	Desertion	Quashed		213/13	520
Stovin E	14 E Yorks	Pte	24/11/16	Desertion	5yrs PS	F&F	213/12	521
Bright B	9 R Irish Rifles	Rfm	25/11/16	Desertion	15yrs PS	F&F	213/12	522
Griffiths S	2 KO Yorks LI	Pte	25/11/16	Desertion	10yrs PS	F&F	213/12	
McBride S	2 R Irish Rifles	Rfm	25/11/16	Desertion	XXX 07/12/16	F&F	213/12	523
Higgins John Morris	1 Canadian EF	Pte	26/11/16	Desertion	XXX 07/12/16	F&F	213/12	524
Crichton J	32 MGC	Pte	27/11/16	Desertion	3yrs PS		213/12	
Baxter W	3 Middlesex	Pte	28/11/16	Sleeping	3yrs PS	Salonika	213/13	
Bedford G	4 Bedfordshire	Pte	28/11/16	Cowardice	Not Conf	F&F	213/12	525
Lingard J	6 Northumb Fus	Pte	28/11/16	Desertion	15yrs PS	F&F	213/13	
Youll G	18 Northumb Fus	Pte	28/11/16	Desertion	10yrs PS	F&F	213/12	
Leader FM	72 Canadian EF	Lt	29/11/16	Disobedience	10yrs PS + Cash'd	F&F	90/6	526
Bailey L	1 Liverpool	Pte	30/11/16	Desertion	5yrs PS	F&F	213/12	
Burke W	1 Liverpool	Pte	30/11/16	Desertion	5yrs PS	F&F	213/12	
Bartholemew H	25 Australian IF	Pte	01/12/16	Desertion	10yrs PS		213/13	
Burt John	2 New Zealand Rifle Bde	Pte	01/12/16	Desertion	10yrs PS		213/12	
Walker HH	1 New Zealand Rifle Bde	Pte	01/12/16	Desertion	10yrs PS		213/12	
White E	25 Australian IF	Pte	01/12/16	Desertion	10yrs PS		213/13	
Dyett Edwin LA	2 Nelson Bn R Naval Div	Sub Lt	02/12/16	Desertion	XXX 05/01/17	F&F	90/6	527
Clarke WP	7/8 KO Scottish Bdrs	Pte	05/12/16	Desertion	2yrs HL	F&F	213/13	
Bowsher A	8 E Kent (Buffs)	Pte	06/12/16	Desertion	10yrs PS	F&F	213/13	
Findler JF	8 N Staffordshire	Pte	07/12/16	Disobedience	15yrs PS	F&F	213/12	
Grundy F	8 N Staffordshire	Pte	07/12/16	Disobedience	15yrs PS	F&F	213/12	
Wilkes H	8 N Staffordshire	Pte	07/12/16	Disobedience	15yrs PS	F&F	213/12	
Packer HA	1/9 London	Rfm	09/12/16	Sleeping	5yrs PS	F&F	213/13	
Putz PG	1/9 London	Rfm	09/12/16	Sleeping	5yrs PS	F&F	213/13	
Skilton Charles WF	22 Royal Fus	Pte	09/12/16	Desertion	XXX 26/12/16	F&F	213/12	528

Name	Unit	Rank	Date	Offence	Final sentence	Location	Ref	Note
Frith H	3 Australian IF	Pte	11/12/16	Desertion	10yrs PS		213/13	
Terrington F	8 R W Surrey	Pte	11/12/16	Desertion	2yrs HL	F&F	213/13	
Walker H	10 W Yorks	Pte	11/12/16	Desertion	2yrs HL	F&F	213/13	
Hallett G	8 S Lancs	Pte	12/12/16	Cowardice	3yrs PS	F&F	213/13	
Pyper D	1 Gordon Hdrs	Pte	12/12/16	Cowardice	10yrs PS	F&F	213/13	
Brennan W	RAMC	Pte	13/12/16	Desertion	5yrs PS		213/13	
Stanton P	RFA	Gnr	13/12/16	Desertion	2yrs HL		213/12	
Ballock J	R Scots Fus	Pte	15/12/16	Desertion x2	5yrs PS		213/12	
Cairnie Peter W	1 R Scots Fus	Pte	15/12/16	Desertion	XXX 28/12/16	F&F	213/12	529
Hanna George	2 R Irish Fus	Pte	15/12/16	Desertion	7yrs PS	F&F	213/13	530
Hurd A	9 Essex	Pte	15/12/16	Sleeping	5yrs PS	F&F	213/13	
Oddy FW	17 Lancs Fus	Pte	15/12/16	Quitting	15yrs PS	F&F	213/13	531
Robinson R	17 Lancs Fus	Pte	15/12/16	Quitting	15yrs PS	F&F	213/13	532
Wain H	10 Sherwood Fstrs	Pte	15/12/16	Desertion	2yrs HL	F&F	213/13	
Worsley J	17 Lancs Fus	Pte	15/12/16	Quitting	15yrs PS	F&F	213/13	533
Farrell J	1 Northumb Fus	Pte	16/12/16	Desertion	10yrs PS	F&F	213/13	
Aldridge H	5 Wiltshire	Pte	19/12/16	Sleeping	5yrs PS	Mesopotamia	90/7	534
Clarke W	8 Devon	Pte	19/12/16	Desertion	15yrs PS	F&F	213/13	
Jarvis WE	1/8 Worcestershire	Pte	19/12/16	Desertion	5yrs PS	F&F	213/13	
Lester R	19 Australian IF	Pte	19/12/16	Desertion	10yrs PS		213/13	
Taylor E	2/5 Lancs Fus	Pte	19/12/16	Sleeping	5yrs PS	F&F	213/13	
Woodhouse G	7 Border	Pte	21/12/16	Desertion	5yrs PS	F&F	213/13	
Hamling J	45 Australian IF	Pte	22/12/16	Desertion	10yrs PS		213/13	
Moran J	45 Australian IF	Pte	22/12/16	Desertion	10yrs PS		213/13	
Webber W	45 Australian IF	Pte	22/12/16	Desertion	10yrs PS		213/13	
Craig T	3 E Lancs	Pte	23/12/16	Desertion	18 Mos HL	UK	213/13	535
Watchorn H	10 R Warwickshire	Pte	23/12/16	Desertion	10yrs PS	F&F	213/13	
Hopkinson E	19 Durham LI	L/Cpl	24/12/16	Quitting	15yrs PS	F&F	213/13	536
Stones Joseph W	19 Durham LI	L/Sgt	24/12/16	Casting Arms	XXX 18/01/17	F&F	213/13	537
Atkinson F	1/7 W Riding	Pte	26/12/16	Sleeping	2yrs HL	F&F	213/13	
Barrett FA	5 Australian IF	Pte	26/12/16	Desertion	2yrs HL		213/13	
Farrell J	2/5 Northumb Fus	Pte	26/12/16	Desertion	Not Conf	UK	213/13	
Lowry T	2 New Zealand EF	Pte	26/12/16	Desertion	15yrs PS		213/13	538
Torevell J	25 Northumb Fus	Pte	26/12/16	Desertion	Not Conf	F&F	213/13	539
Barr CA	59 Australian IF	Pte	27/12/16	Desertion	5yrs PS		213/13	
Brannon JT	11 Sherwood Fstrs	Pte	27/12/16	Sleeping	5yrs PS	F&F	213/13	
Kucer A	4 S African Infantry	Pte	27/12/16	Desertion	15yrs PS		213/13	
McMillan J	58 Australian IF	Pte	27/12/16	Striking	2yrs HL		213/13	
Milbourne W	2 Suffolk	Pte	27/12/16	Desertion	10yrs PS	F&F	213/13	
Presnell TW	11 Essex	Pte	27/12/16	Sleeping	10yrs PS	F&F	213/13	
Richman W	58 Australian IF	Pte	27/12/16	Striking	2yrs HL		213/13	
Davies A	19 Durham LI	Pte	28/12/16	Quitting	15yrs PS	F&F	213/13	540
Dowsey H	19 Durham LI	Pte	28/12/16	Quitting	15yrs PS	F&F	213/13	541
Fenn T	9 Royal Fus	Pte	28/12/16	Sleeping	5yrs PS	F&F	213/13	
Forrest D	19 Durham LI	Pte	28/12/16	Quitting	15yrs PS	F&F	213/13	542
Goggins Peter	19 Durham LI	L/Cpl	28/12/16	Quitting	XXX 18/01/17	F&F	213/13	543
MacDonald John	19 Durham LI	L/Cpl	28/12/16	Quitting	XXX 18/01/17	F&F	213/13	544
Ritchie T	19 Durham LI	Pte	28/12/16	Quitting	15yrs PS	F&F	213/13	545
Shannahan AJ	7 Australian IF	Pte	28/12/16	Desertion	5yrs PS		213/13	
Allen W	1 KO Yorks LI	Pte	29/12/16	Sleeping	2yrs HL	Salonika	213/13	
Hale A	2 R Inniskilling Fus	Pte	29/12/16	Desertion x2	5yrs PS	F&F	213/13	
Herbert J	2 E Kent (Buffs)	Pte	29/12/16	Sleeping	2yrs HL	Salonika	213/13	
Ling Wilson N	2 Canadian EF	Pte	29/12/16	Desertion	2yrs HL	F&F	213/13	546
Stevenson F	15 Lancs Fus	Pte	29/12/16	Desertion	10yrs PS	F&F	213/13	547
Anderson J	19 Durham LI	Pte	30/12/16	Cowardice	10yrs PS	F&F	213/13	548
Bates W	19 Durham LI	Pte	30/12/16	Cowardice	10yrs PS	F&F	213/13	549
Dempsey M	19 Durham LI	L/Cpl	30/12/16	Cowardice	10yrs PS	F&F	213/13	550
Dunn JS	19 Durham LI	Pte	30/12/16	Cowardice	10yrs PS	F&F	213/13	551
Garrity TA	19 Durham LI	Pte	30/12/16	Cowardice	10yrs PS	F&F	213/13	552
Giggins GW	19 Durham LI	Pte	30/12/16	Cowardice	10yrs PS	F&F	213/13	553
Greaves H	19 Durham LI	Pte	30/12/16	Cowardice	10yrs PS	F&F	213/13	554
Hewitt BB	19 Durham LI	Pte	30/12/16	Cowardice	10yrs PS	F&F	213/13	555
Lumley JG	19 Durham LI	Pte	30/12/16	Cowardice	10yrs PS	F&F	213/13	556
Mann JG	19 Durham LI	Pte	30/12/16	Cowardice	10yrs PS	F&F	213/13	557
Oldknow J	19 Durham LI	Pte	30/12/16	Cowardice	10yrs PS	F&F	213/13	558
Pattison J	19 Australian LI	Pte	30/12/16	Cowardice	10yrs PS	F&F	213/13	559
Potts W	19 Durham LI	Pte	30/12/16	Cowardice	10yrs PS	F&F	213/13	560
Proudfoot H	19 Durham LI	Pte	30/12/16	Cowardice	10yrs PS	F&F	213/13	561

Name	Unit	Rank	Date	Offence	Final sentence	Location	Ref	Note
Richardson JW	19 Durham LI	Pte (L/C)	30/12/16	Cowardice	10yrs PS	F&F	213/13	562
Surtees T	19 Durham LI	Pte	30/12/16	Cowardice	10yrs PS	F&F	213/13	563
Taylor John	15 Lancs Fus	Pte	30/12/16	Desertion	XXX 27/01/17	F&F	213/13	564
Wilson PC	19 Durham LI	Pte	30/12/16	Cowardice	10yrs PS	F&F	213/13	565
Cray H	15 Cheshire	Sgt	31/12/16	Desertion	10yrs PS	F&F	213/13	566
Reen W	1 E Surrey	Pte	31/12/16	Cowardice	15yrs PS	F&F	213/13	
Walton W	3 Rifle Bde	Pte	31/12/16	Sleeping	2yrs HL	F&F	213/13	
Rumley R	19 Durham LI	Sgt	01/01/17	Cowardice	10yrs PS	F&F	213/13	567
Hawkins T	7 R W Surrey	Pte	03/01/17	Desertion	10yrs PS	F&F	213/13	568
Knight AF	14 Hampshire	Pte	03/01/17	Desertion	Not Conf	F&F	213/13	
Williams T	13 Welsh	Pte	03/01/17	Desertion	10yrs PS	F&F	213/13	569
Brookes W	8 KRRC	Sgt	04/01/17	Desertion	5yrs PS	F&F	213/13	
Roberts T	96 MGC	Pte	04/01/17	Desertion	10yrs PS		213/13	
Thornton G	1 R W Kent	Pte	04/01/17	Desertion+	15yrs PS	F&F	213/13	570
Hatcher G	2 S Wales Bdrs	Pte	06/01/17	Desertion	2yrs HL	F&F	213/13	
Kendrick EG	6 Lincolnshire	Pte	06/01/17	Desertion	10yrs PS	F&F	213/13	
Phillips E	7 Gloucestershire	Pte	09/01/17	Sleeping	5yrs PS	Mesopotamia	90/7	571
Tompkins CF	1 Canadian EF	Pte	09/01/17	Quitting	15yrs PS	F&F	213/13	
French J	8 R Inniskilling Fus	Pte	10/01/17	Desertion	10yrs PS	F&F	213/13	
Wright Frederick	1 R W Surrey	Pte	10/01/17	Desertion	XXX 28/01/17	F&F	213/13	572
Aitchison B	66 RFA	Gnr	11/01/17	Disobedience	5yrs PS	Mesopotamia	90/7	573
Connor J	1 R Irish Fus	Pte	11/01/17	Desertion	15yrs PS	F&F	213/14	
Stead Frederick	2 W Riding	Pte	11/01/17	Desertion	XXX 12/02/17	F&F	213/13	574
Ames S	4 Liverpool	Pte (L/C)	12/01/17	Desertion	5yrs PS	F&F	213/13	
Budworth JT	2 KRRC	Rfm	13/01/17	Desertion	5yrs PS	F&F	213/13	
Grice S	7 Border	Pte	13/01/17	Desertion	5yrs PS	F&F	213/13	
Arkinson W	11 A&S Hdrs	Pte	14/01/17	Desertion	5yrs PS	F&F	213/13	
Dawes J	1 N Staffordshire	Pte	14/01/17	Quitting	5yrs PS	F&F	213/13	
Evans A	6 Cameron Hdrs	Pte	14/01/17	Desertion	10yrs PS	F&F	213/13	
Francis J	13 R Scots	Pte	14/01/17	Desertion	5yrs PS	F&F	213/13	
Bradford S	2 York & Lancaster	Pte	15/01/17	Sleeping	2yrs HL	F&F	213/13	
Pearson T	15 Highland LI	Pte	15/01/17	Desertion	10yrs PS	F&F	213/14	575
Reid Alexander	16 Highland LI	Pte	18/01/17	Murder	XXX 31/01/17	F&F	213/13	576
Bellamy E	1 KRRC	Rfm	19/01/17	Desertion	10yrs PS	F&F	213/13	
Murray Robert	81 RFA	Gnr	19/01/17	Desertion	XXX 03/02/17	F&F	213/13	577
Rigby H	2 Rifle Bde	Rfm	19/01/17	Desertion	5yrs PS	F&F	213/13	
Shields EF	51 Australian IF	Pte (L/C)	19/01/17	Desertion/Esc	10yrs PS		213/13	
Pritchett WJ	8 E Yorks	Pte	20/01/17	Desertion	10yrs PS		213/14	
Newsome H	6 Durham LI	Pte	21/01/17	Desertion	5yrs PS		213/14	
Tongue James (Joseph)	1 Liverpool	Pte	22/01/17	Desertion	XXX 31/01/17	F&F	213/13	578
Blewitt J	10 D Cornwall LI	Pte	23/01/17	Desertion	10yrs PS	F&F	213/13	579
Foster JA	59 Australian IF	Pte	23/01/17	Cowardice	Not Conf		213/14	
Grampton James	9 York & Lancaster	Pte	23/01/17	Desertion	XXX 04/02/17	F&F	213/13	580
Harris Ernest Walter [Jack]	10 Lancs Fus	Pte	23/01/17	Desertion	XXX 03/02/17	F&F	213/13	581
Sekum H	4 Canadian Mtd Rifles	Pte	23/01/17	Desertion	5yrs PS	F&F	213/13	
McDonald J	8/10 Gordon Hdrs	Pte	24/01/17	Desertion x2	5yrs PS	F&F	213/13	
Lister R	13 R Scots	Pte	25/01/17	Desertion	5yrs PS	F&F	213/13	
Buchanan J	1/6 Black Watch	Pte	26/01/17	Desertion	10yrs PS	F&F	213/13	582
Clark F	1 Northants	Pte	26/01/17	Desertion	5yrs PS	F&F	213/13	
Liversidge PH	2 KRRC	Rfm	26/01/17	Desertion	5yrs PS	F&F	213/13	
Hart Benjamin Albert	1/4 Suffolk	Pte	28/01/17	Desertion	XXX 06/02/17	F&F	213/13	583
Murphy William	5/6 R Scots	Pte	28/01/17	Desertion	XXX 07/02/17	F&F	213/13	584
Locke G	25 Australian IF	Pte	29/01/17	Desertion	5yrs PS		213/13	
Beal EJ	7 E Yorks	Pte	31/01/17	Desertion	5yrs PS	F&F	213/13	
Sullivan RP	10 Royal Fus	Pte	31/01/17	Mutiny+	Not Conf	F&F	213/13	585
Condon S	52 Australian IF	Pte	01/02/17	Desertion	10yrs PS		213/14	
Broadrick F	11 R Warwickshire	Pte	02/02/17	Desertion	10yrs PS	F&F	213/13	
Cunliffe J	8 W Riding	Pte	03/02/17	Desertion	5yrs PS	F&F	213/13	
Ryan J	2 Leinster	Pte	03/02/17	Desertion	2yrs HL	F&F	213/13	
Timson GA	11 Northumb Fus	Pte	03/02/17	Desertion	10yrs PS	F&F	213/13	
Granderson W	79 RFA	Gnr	05/02/17	Desertion	5yrs PS		213/13	
Holt Ellis	19 Manchester	Pte	05/02/17	Desertion x2	XXX 04/03/17	F&F	213/13	586
Orme CE	2 Sherwood Fstrs	Pte	05/02/17	Desertion	15yrs PS	F&F	213/14	
Gooch Robert W	1/4 Suffolk	Pte	06/02/17	Desertion	10yrs PS	F&F	213/13	
Burton Robert	6 S Lancs	Pte	07/02/17	Sleeping	XXX 19/02/17	Mesopotamia	90/7	587
Downing Thomas	6 S Lancs	Pte	07/02/17	Sleeping	XXX 19/02/17	Mesopotamia	90/7	588
Jones Richard M	6 S Lancs	Pte	07/02/17	Desertion	XXX 21/02/17	Mesopotamia	90/7	589
Payne FJ	5 Dorset	Pte (L/C)	08/02/17	Desertion	10yrs PS	F&F	213/13	

Name	Unit	Rank	Date	Offence	Final sentence	Location	Ref	Note
Smith H	2/7 W Yorks	Rfn	09/02/17	Desertion	Not Conf	F&F	213/14	590
Hall H	25 Northumb Fus	Pte	10/02/17	Sleeping	10yrs PS	F&F	213/13	591
Prinn J	12 Gloucestershire	Pte	10/02/17	Quitting	15yrs PS	F&F	213/13	592
Maddison G	9 Durham LI	Pte	11/02/17	Desertion	5yrs PS		213/14	
Fletcher F	88 MGC	Pte	13/02/17	Desertion	5yrs PS		213/13	
Hamilton Arthur	14 Durham LI	Pte	15/02/17	Desertion	XXX 27/03/17	F&F	213/14	593
Rose Frederick	2 Yorks	Dmr	18/02/17	Desertion	XXX 04/03/17	F&F	213/13	594
Pearson JH	9 Yorks	Pte	19/02/17	Desertion	15yrs PS	F&F	213/14	
Blanch AJ	4 Australian IF	Pte	20/02/17	Desertion	10yrs PS		213/14	
Gonsalves SF	30 Australian IF	Pte	21/02/17	Desertion	5yrs PS		213/14	
Harris J	9 Welsh	Pte	21/02/17	Desertion	10yrs PS	F&F	213/15	
McCloy R	7/8 R Irish Fus	Pte	21/02/17	Desertion	10yrs PS	F&F	213/14	
Robinson HJ	30 Australian IF	Pte	21/02/17	Desertion	Quashed		213/14	
Buckley WJ	1 Australian IF	Pte	24/02/17	Desertion	10yrs PS		213/14	
Elliot L	2 KO Scottish Bdrs	Sgt	24/02/17	Desertion	15yrs PS	F&F	213/14	
Johnson H	7 Durham LI	Pte	24/02/17	Desertion	5yrs PS		213/14	
Lemay A	22 Canadian EF	Pte	24/02/17	Desertion	5yrs PS	F&F	213/14	595
Walker J	2 KO Scottish Bdrs	Pte	24/02/17	Desertion x2	15yrs PS	F&F	213/14	
Bacon GV	Civilian	Alien	26/02/17	Espionage	PS Life	UK	92/3	596
Emeny CA	1/3 London	Pte	27/02/17	Desertion	10yrs PS	F&F	213/14	
Holderness W	11 Royal Fus	Pte	27/02/17	Desertion	Not Conf	F&F	213/14	
Ingram AA	7 S Lancs	Pte	27/02/17	Desertion	10yrs PS	F&F	213/14	
Stone C	7 R Sussex	Pte	27/02/17	Desertion	10yrs PS	F&F	213/15	
Prince LE	1 W Yorks	Pte	28/02/17	Desertion	5yrs PS	F&F	213/14	
Gleadow George E	1 W Yorks	Sgt	01/03/17	Desertion	XXX 06/04/17	F&F	213/14	597
Mayers James	1/13 London	Pte	01/03/17	Quitting x2	5yrs PS	F&F	213/14	598
Rogers John	2 S Lancs	Pte	01/03/17	Desertion	XXX 09/03/17	F&F	213/14	599
Yeoman W	1/12 London	Rfm	01/03/17	Desertion	15yrs PS	F&F	213/14	600
Carabine E	8 R Inniskilling Fus	Pte	03/03/17	Desertion	10yrs PS	F&F	213/16	
Maynard EA	8 Bedfordshire	Pte	03/03/17	Sleeping	5yrs PS	F&F	213/14	
Boot E	1 S Staffordshire	Pte	05/03/17	Desertion	5yrs PS	F&F	213/14	
Cliffe J	1 S Staffordshire	Pte	05/03/17	Desertion	5yrs PS	F&F	213/14	
Keeble EG	R Marines LI	Pte	05/03/17	Desertion	10yrs PS		213/14	
O'Leary AJ	52 Australian IF	Pte	05/03/17	Desertion	10yrs PS		213/14	
Frost E	13 Cheshire	Pte	06/03/17	Desertion	10yrs PS	F&F	213/14	
Newell A	57 Australian IF	Pte	06/03/17	Desertion	5yrs PS		213/14	
Morley LH	12 Royal Fus	Pte	07/03/17	Sleeping/Quitting	5yrs PS	F&F	213/14	
Bowerman William	1 E Surrey	Pte	08/03/17	Desertion	XXX 24/03/17	F&F	213/14	601
Doherty J	10/11 Highland LI	Pte	08/03/17	Desertion+	15yrs PS	F&F	213/14	602
Watson W	1 Worcestershire	Pte	08/03/17	Desertion	Remitted	F&F	213/14	
Anderson William E	5 Dorset	Pte	09/03/17	Desertion	XXX 31/03/17	F&F	213/14	603
Gibbons M	8 Yorks	Pte	09/03/17	Desertion	10yrs PS	F&F	213/14	
Lewis John	5 Dorset	Pte	09/03/17	Desertion	Not Conf	F&F	213/14	604
Brookfield N	12 S Staffordshire	Pte	10/03/17	Desertion	2yrs HL	F&F	213/14	605
Barr N	10 R Irish Rifles	Rfm	11/03/17	Desertion	10yrs PS	F&F	213/14	606
Sparkes C	2 R Warwickshire	Pte	11/03/17	Desertion	15yrs PS	F&F	213/14	
Heathcote W	8 S Staffordshire	Pte	12/03/17	Desertion x2	10yrs PS	F&F	213/14	
McGrath JP	1 Australian IF	Pte	12/03/17	Desertion	10yrs PS		213/14	
Turner J	1/8 Worcestershire	Pte	12/03/17	Desertion	5yrs PS	F&F	213/14	
Allsop Arthur E	12 KRRC	Rfm	13/03/17	Desertion	5 yrs PS	F&F	213/14	607
Burt A	4 Royal Fus	Pte	13/03/17	Desertion	10yrs PS	F&F	213/14	
Johnson LE	10 Essex	Pte	14/03/17	Desertion	10yrs PS	F&F	213/14	
Denzell W	3 Australian IF	Pte	15/03/17	Desertion	10yrs PS		213/14	
Locke EJ	57 Australian IF	Pte	15/03/17	Desertion	10yrs PS		213/14	
McGuire JH	4 Australian IF	Pte	15/03/17	Desertion	10yrs PS		213/14	
Paget J	3 Australian IF	Pte	15/03/17	Desertion	10yrs PS		213/14	
Pennell A	3 Australian IF	Pte	15/03/17	Desertion	10yrs PS		213/14	
Butterley B	25 Northumb Fus	Pte	16/03/17	Desertion	5yrs PS	F&F	213/14	608
Cork WJ	1/1 Monmouth	Rfm	16/03/17	Desertion	15yrs PS	F&F	213/14	
Fraser J	2 A&S Hdrs	Pte	17/03/17	Desertion	2yrs HL	F&F	213/14	
Green C	7 Kings Shropshire LI	Pte	18/03/17	Desertion	Quashed	F&F	213/15	
McDonnell H	4 Canadian EF	Pte	19/03/17	Desertion	2yrs HL	F&F	213/14	
Lambert W	22 Manchester	Pte (L/C)	20/03/17	Desertion	Not Conf	F&F	213/15	609
Ramage J	12 Highland LI	Pte	20/03/17	Desertion	15yrs PS	F&F	213/14	
Harrigan LJ	34 Australian IF	Pte	21/03/17	Disobedience x2	Not Conf		213/14	
Malyon Frederick	12 RE (att RFA)	Spr	21/03/17	Desertion	XXX 04/04/17		213/14	610
Kempson HG	10 Rifle Bde	Rfm	23/03/17	Disobedience	5yrs PS	F&F	213/14	
Ferguson Joseph	1 R Scots Fus (att RE)	Pte	24/03/17	Desertion	XXX 20/04/17	F&F	213/14	611

Name	Unit	Rank	Date	Offence	Final sentence	Location	Ref	Note
Robinson William	1 Sherwood Fstrs	Pte	24/03/17	Desertion	XXX 10/04/17	F&F	213/14	612
Thompson G	20 Durham LI	Pte	24/03/17	Desertion	15yrs PS	F&F	213/14	613
Balmbro C	8 KO Yorks LI	Pte	25/03/17	Desertion	10yrs PS	F&F	213/15	
Hodgkiss G	2 Leinster	Pte	25/03/17	Desertion	15yrs PS	F&F	213/14	
Millar WH	13 Welsh	Pte	26/03/17	Desertion+	Not Conf	F&F	213/14	614
Hughes P	10/11 Highland LI	Pte	27/03/17	Desertion	15yrs PS	F&F	213/14	
Lemay A	22 Canadian EF	Pte	27/03/17	Desertion x2	5yrs PS	F&F	213/14	
Benard B	22 Canadian EF	Pte	28/03/17	Desertion x2	15yrs PS	F&F	213/14	
Coleman M	2 Leinster	Pte	28/03/17	Striking	5yrs PS	F&F	213/16	
Fagan G	2 Leicestershire	Pte	28/03/17	Cowardice	3yrs PS	Mesopotamia	213/14	
Peloquin J	22 Canadian EF	Pte	28/03/17	Desertion	15yrs PS	F&F	213/14	
Crane J	10 R W Surrey	Pte	29/03/17	Desertion	10yrs PS	F&F	213/14	
Reilly T	1 Scottish Rifles	Pte	29/03/17	Desertion	1yr HL	F&F	213/15	
Webster JA	32 Royal Fus	Pte	29/03/17	Desertion	10yrs PS	F&F	213/14	615
Wood H	12 KRRC	Rfm	29/03/17	Desertion	5yrs PS	F&F	213/15	
George TE	7 Northumb Fus	Pte	30/03/17	Insubordinaion	Not Conf	F&F	213/15	
Weeks H	15 R Irish Rifles	Rfm	30/03/17	Desertion	15yrs PS	F&F	213/14	616
Hamilton W	93 MGC	Pte	31/03/17	Desertion	5yrs PS		213/14	
Marflitt JB	1/4 KO Yorks LI	Pte	01/04/17	Desertion	5yrs PS	F&F	213/14	
Phipps GE	3 Worcestershire	Pte	01/04/17	Desertion	10yrs PS	F&F	213/14	
Brogan J	2 R Munster Fus	Pte	02/04/17	Desertion	5yrs PS	F&F	213/14	
Jones W	9 R Welsh Fus	Pte	02/04/17	Desertion	10yrs PS	F&F	213/14	617
Shields J	2 R Munster Fus	Pte	02/04/17	Desertion	5yrs PS	F&F	213/14	
Smith H	6 R Dublin Fus	Pte	02/04/17	Desertion	15yrs PS	Salonika	213/14	
Sutton F	1 Liverpool	Pte	02/04/17	Sleeping	2yrs HL	F&F	213/14	
Johnson A	1 Liverpool	Pte	03/04/17	Desertion	2yrs PS	F&F	213/14	
Perry Eugene	22 Canadian EF	Pte	03/04/17	Desertion	XXX 11/04/17	F&F	213/14	618
Ratelle A	22 Canadian EF	Pte	03/04/17	Desertion	15yrs PS	F&F	213/15	
Bond JW	13 York and Lancaster	Pte	04/04/17	Desertion	10yrs PS	F&F	213/14	619
Christie T	6 R Munster Fus	Pte	04/04/17	Cowardice+	10yrs PS	Salonika	213/15	620
Connell P	6 R Munster Fus	Pte	04/04/17	Cowardice+	10yrs PS	Salonika	213/15	621
Connors M	6 R Munster Fus	Pte	04/04/17	Cowardice+	10yrs PS	Salonika	213/15	622
Cross F	13 York and Lancaster	Pte	04/04/17	Desertion	10yrs PS	F&F	213/14	623
Dawson A	6 R Munster Fus	Pte	04/04/17	Cowardice+	10yrs PS	Salonika	213/15	624
Leahy F	6 R Munster Fus	Pte	04/04/17	Cowardice+	10yrs PS	Salonika	213/15	625
Mosey W	7 R Dublin Fus	Pte	04/04/17	Cowardice	10yrs PS	Salonika	213/15	
Robson R	7 Liverpool	Pte	04/04/17	Desertion	10yrs PS	Salonika	213/14	626
Shea C	10 W Yorks	Pte	04/04/17	Desertion	10yrs PS	F&F	213/15	
Carter Harold George	73 Canadian EF	Pte	05/04/17	Desertion	XXX 20/04/17	F&F	213/14	627
Lewis John	5 Dorset	Pte	06/04/17	Desertion	XXX 19/04/17	F&F	213/14	628
Warren H	17 KRRC	Rfm	07/04/17	Sleeping	5yrs PS		213/14	629
Young P J	58 Canadian EF	Pte	07/04/17	Desertion	15yrs PS	F&F	213/14	
Giles G	1/6 S Staffordshire	Pte	08/04/17	Desertion	5yrs PS	F&F	213/14	
Heslop G	4 Northumberalnd Fus	Pte	08/04/17	Desertion	10yrs PS		213/15	
Haggett J	1 Wiltshire	Pte	10/04/17	Desertion	2 yrs HL	F&F	213/14	
Lane J	35 DAC	Gnr	11/04/17	Desertion	2yrs HL		213/14	
Lawrence R	8 E Surrey	Pte	11/04/17	Desertion	Not Conf	F&F	213/15	
Vaughan T	1/7 W Yorks	Rfm	11/04/17	Desertion	5yrs PS	F&F	213/14	630
Black JW	1 New Zealand EF	Pte	12/04/17	Desertion	10yrs PS		213/14	631
Liggett J	1/35 Trench Mtr Bty	Gnr	12/04/17	Desertion	2yrs HL		213/14	
Pareezer S	21 Manchester	Pte	13/04/17	Desertion	15yrs PS	F&F	213/15	632
Rae C	16 Trench Mtr Bty	Gnr	13/04/17	Desertion	10yrs PS		213/14	
Reeves R	ASC	Dvr	13/04/17	Desertion	2yrs HL		213/14	
Dennington AF	12 E Surrey	Pte	16/04/17	Sleeping	10yrs PS	F&F	213/14	633
Gentry WA	12 E Surrey	Pte	16/04/17	Quitting	10yrs PS	F&F	213/14	634
Currie G	2 R Scots Fus	Pte	17/04/17	Desertion	10yrs PS	F&F	213/15	
Brown J	10 W Riding	Pte	18/04/17	Desertion	10yrs PS	F&F	213/15	
Oldfield J	8 KOR Lancaster	Pte	18/04/17	Desertion	10yrs PS	F&F	213/15	
Curtis F	10 Cheshire	Pte	19/04/17	Desertion	10yrs PS	F&F	213/14	
Marriott F	24 Northumb Fus	Pte	19/04/17	Desertion x2	10yrs PS	F&F	213/15	635
McGoldrick GM	10 Scottish Rifles	Pte	19/04/17	Desertion	10yrs PS	F&F	213/15	
Honeysett GR	6 R Irish	Pte	20/04/17	Cowardice	10yrs PS	F&F	213/14	
Newman JD	1 Canadian EF	Pte	22/04/17	Desertion	10yrs PS	F&F	213/15	
Oram TG	46 Australian IF	Pte	23/04/17	Desertion	10yrs PS		213/15	
Price E	2 Rifle Bde	Rfm	23/04/17	Sleeping	5yrs PS	F&F	213/14	
Mamprusi A	Gold Coast Regt	Pte (L/C)	25/04/17	Desertion+	XXX 28/04/17	East Africa	213/16	636
Riley J	1 Devon	Pte	25/04/17	Desertion	2yrs HL	F&F	213/14	
Wilson H	7/8 R Irish Fus	Pte	25/04/17	Desertion	Not Conf	F&F	213/15	

Name	Unit	Rank	Date	Offence	Final sentence	Location	Ref	Note
Brazier W	104 DAC RFA	Cpl	26/04/17	Against Inhab	10yrs PS		213/15	
Edwards HR	50 Australian IF	Pte	26/04/17	Desertion+	5yrs PS		213/15	637
Potts GC	50 Australian IF	Pte	26/04/17	Desertion+	10yrs PS		213/15	638
Robertson H	47 Australian IF	Pte	26/04/17	Desertion	10yrs PS		213/15	
Cook PH	51 Australian IF	Pte	27/04/17	Desertion	2yrs HL		213/15	
Fitzhenry M	7/8 R Irish Fus	Pte	27/04/17	Desertion+	10yrs PS	F&F	213/15	639
Graham J	11 Border	Pte	27/04/17	Desertion	5yrs PS	F&F	213/15	640
Triptree HW	RFA	Dvr	27/04/17	Desertion	15yrs PS	F&F	213/15	
Williams DH	9 R Welsh Fus	Pte	27/04/17	Desertion	10yrs PS	F&F	213/15	
Strathmere LG	1 Welsh Gds	Pte	28/04/17	Desertion	3yrs PS	F&F	213/15	
Brown W	ASC	Pte	29/04/17	Desertion	15yrs PS		213/15	
Cunnington Samuel H	2 R Warwickshire	Pte	29/04/17	Desertion	XXX 19/05/17	F&F	213/15	641
Mills F	1 R Warwickshire	Pte	29/04/17	Desertion	10yrs PS	F&F	213/15	
Rushworth G	1 Sherwood Fstrs	Pte	29/04/17	Desertion	5yrs PS	F&F	213/15	
Watkins George	13 Welsh	Pte	29/04/17	Desertion	XXX 15/05/17	F&F	213/15	642
Black A	49 Australian IF	Pte	30/04/17	Desertion	5yrs PS		213/15	
Bruce AE	9 E Surrey	Pte	30/04/17	Desertion	3yrs PS	F&F	213/15	
Irvine G	49 Australian IF	Pte	30/04/17	Desertion	10yrs PS		213/15	
Murphy Thomas	9 R Inniskilling Fus	Pte	30/04/17	Desertion	XXX 14/05/17	F&F	213/14	643
Andrews C	1 R Irish Rifles	Rfm	01/05/17	Desertion x2	5yrs PS	F&F	213/15	
McCormick J	51 Australian IF	Pte	01/05/17	Desertion	10yrs PS		213/15	
McLennan JT	49 Australian IF	Pte	01/05/17	Desertion	10yrs PS		213/15	
Walker T	1 Border	Pte	01/05/17	Desertion	Not Conf	F&F	213/15	
Hornick E	2/11 London	Rfm	02/05/17	Desertion	5yrs PS	F&F	213/15	644
Wright FE	9 Gloucestershire	Pte	02/05/17	Violence	5 Yrs PS	Salonika	213/16	645
Gould W	2 R Irish Fus	Pte	03/05/17	Plundering	1yr HL	Salonika	213/15	
Walsh J	2 R Irish Fus	Pte	03/05/17	Plundering	1yr HL	Salonika	213/15	
Weatherall W	2 R Irish Fus	Pte	03/05/17	Plundering	1yr HL	Salonika	213/15	
Ramscar W	18 Welsh	Pte	04/05/17	Desertion	5yrs PS	F&F	213/15	646
Brown J	24 Northumb Fus	Dvr	05/05/17	Desertion	5yrs PS	F&F	213/15	647
McAlinder J	8 R Inniskilling Fus	Pte	05/05/17	Desertion	10yrs PS	F&F	213/15	
Milligan Charles M	10 Scottish Rifles	Pte	05/05/17	Desertion	XXX 03/06/17	F&F	213/15	648
Hayward H	1 R Irish Fus	Pte	06/05/17	Desertion	10yrs PS	F&F	213/15	
Foster JA	51 Australian IF	Pte	07/05/17	Desertion x2	10yrs PS		213/15	
Barber G	2 E Surrey	Pte	09/05/17	Sleeping	3yrs PS	Salonika	213/15	
Beere G	2 E Surrey	Pte	09/05/17	Sleeping	3yrs PS	Salonika	213/15	
Irvine F	5 Northumb Fus	Pte	09/05/17	Desertion	10yrs PS	F&F	213/15	
Neave Walter	10 W Yorks	Pte	09/05/17	Desertion	15yrs PS	F&F	213/15	649
Pearce G	RAMC	Pte	09/05/17	Cowardice x2	10yrs PS		213/15	
Carleton J	38 Canadian EF	L/Cpl	10/05/17	Desertion	10yrs PS	F&F	213/15	
Kremers C	78 Canadian EF	Pte	10/05/17	Desertion x2	15yrs PS	F&F	213/15	
Walsh WP	49 Australian IF	Pte	11/05/17	Desertion	10yrs PS		213/15	
Fitchford S	2 S Staffordshire	Pte	12/05/17	Desertion	10yrs PS	F&F	213/15	
Leavey E	6 R Irish Rifles	Rfm	12/05/17	Desertion	7yrs PS	Salonika	213/15	
Dickson W	10 Black Watch	Pte	13/05/17	Sleeping	2yrs HL	Salonika	213/16	
Murphy JC	49 Australian IF	Pte	13/05/17	Desertion	10yrs PS		213/15	
Smith JL	45 Australian IF	Pte	13/05/17	Desertion	10yrs PS		213/15	
Glover TL	1/11 London	Rfm	15/05/17	Sleeping	2yrs HL	Egypt	213/15	650
Tye AE	10 Lincolnshire	Cpl	15/05/17	Desertion	10yrs PS	F&F	213/15	651
Atwell G	12 Northumb Fus	Pte	16/05/17	Desertion	2yrs HL	F&F	213/15	
Marston E	12 Northumb Fus	Pte	16/05/17	Desertion	Not Conf	F&F	213/15	
Metcalfe WE	12 Northumb Fus	Cpl	16/05/17	Desertion	10yrs PS	F&F	213/15	
Pringle JW	12 Northumb Fus	Pte	16/05/17	Desertion	10yrs PS	F&F	213/15	
Watson J	11 Suffolk	Pte	16/05/17	Cowardice	15yrs PS	F&F	213/15	652
Wilson W	9 Liverpool	Pte	16/05/17	Desertion	10yrs PS		213/15	
Boakes A	11 Suffolk	Pte	17/05/17	Cowardice	15yrs PS	F&F	213/15	
Clarke W	84 RFA	Dvr	17/05/17	Desertion	15yrs PS		213/15	
Halliday E	10 Loyal N Lancs	Pte	17/05/17	Desertion	10yrs PS	F&F	213/15	
Reilly WP	Nelson Bn R Naval VR	A/B	17/05/17	Desertion	Not Conf		213/15	
Tye FG	10 Lincolnshire	Cpl (L/S)	18/05/17	Desertion	10yrs PS	F&F	213/15	653
Wilhams R	1 Somerset LI	Pte	18/05/17	Striking	2yrs HL	F&F	213/15	
Kemp T	1 KOR Lancaster	Pte	19/05/17	Desertion	10yrs PS	F&F	213/15	
Kershaw H	10 Lincolnshire	Cpl	19/05/17	Desertion	10yrs PS	F&F	213/15	654
Robson L	148 RFA	Gnr	19/05/17	Cowardice	2yrs HL		213/15	
Smith J	10 Lincolnshire	Pte (L/C)	19/05/17	Desertion	10yrs PS	F&F	213/15	655
Brown Archibald	10 Black Watch	Pte	20/05/17	Desertion	XXX 01/06/17	Salonika	213/15	656
Ashton Harry	11 Scottish Rifles	L/Sgt	21/05/17	Desertion+	Not Conf	Salonika	213/16	657
Bateman F	1/4 York & Lancaster	Pte	21/05/17	Desertion	15yrs PS	F&F	213/15	658

Name	Unit	Rank	Date	Offence	Final sentence	Location	Ref	Note
Mooney JA	1 Manchester	Pte	21/05/17	Sleeping	5yrs PS	Mesopotamia	90/7	659
Nolan T	7 R Dublin Fus	Pte	21/05/17	Desertion	2yrs HL	Salonika	213/15	
Flynn M	1/8 Liverpool	Pte	22/05/17	Desertion	10yrs PS	F&F	213/15	660
Garner WW	1/4 London	Pte	22/05/17	Desertion	10yrs PS	F&F	213/15	661
Jackson EE	1/8 Liverpool	Pte	22/05/17	Desertion	10yrs PS	F&F	213/15	662
Keightley S	7/8 R Irish Fus	Cpl	22/05/17	Desertion	10yrs PS	F&F	213/15	
Kirkpatrick R	5 Durham LI	Pte	22/05/17	Desertion	5yrs PS	F&F	213/15	
Martin C	11 W Yorks	Pte	22/05/17	Desertion	10yrs PS	F&F	213/15	
Mayers James	1/13 Royal Fus	Pte	22/05/17	Desertion+	XXX 16/06/17	F&F	213/15	663
Adams H	1 Newfdland Canadian EF	Pte	23/05/17	Desertion	10yrs PS	F&F	213/15	
Smith J	Army Veterinary Corps	Pte	23/05/17	Desertion	10yrs PS		213/15	
Dickson A	2 R Scots	Pte	24/05/17	Desertion	5yrs PS	F&F	213/16	
Garswood G	2/5 Lancs Fus	Pte	24/05/17	Desertion	10yrs PS	F&F	213/15	
Hancock J	8 E Yorks	Pte	24/05/17	Desertion	10yrs PS	F&F	213/15	
McCulloch J	1 R Scots Fus	Pte	24/05/17	Desertion	10yrs PS	F&F	213/15	
Ward W	13 Canadian EF	Pte	25/05/17	Desertion	5yrs PS		213/15	
Blakemore D	8 N Staffordshire	Pte	26/05/17	Desertion	15yrs PS	F&F	213/15	
Morgan TG	1/8 Middlesex	Pte	26/05/17	Desertion	2yrs HL	F&F	213/15	
McCulloch D	9 Scottish Rifles	Pte	27/05/17	Desertion	5yrs PS	F&F	213/15	
Smith W	8 Devon	Pte	27/05/17	Desertion	10yrs PS	F&F	213/15	
Davidson D	5 Highland LI	Pte	28/05/17	Sleeping	2yrs HL		213/16	
Logan J	7 Highland LI	Pte	28/05/17	Desertion	5yrs PS	F&F	213/16	
Webber W	1 Border	Pte	28/05/17	Desertion	10yrs PS	F&F	213/15	
Wood W	7 Highland LI	Pte	28/05/17	Desertion	5yrs PS	F&F	213/16	
Cassidy F	2 R Inniskilling Fus	Pte	30/05/17	Desertion x2	Not Conf	F&F	213/19	
Walley W	46 Canadian EF	Pte	30/05/17	Desertion	10yrs PS	F&F	213/15	
Allsop Arthur E	12 KRRC	Rfm	31/05/17	Desertion	XXX 15/06/17	F&F	213/15	664
Gamble J	2 R Inniskilling Fus	Pte	31/05/17	Desertion	10yrs PS	F&F	213/15	
Watchorn H	10 R Warwickshire	Pte	31/05/17	Desertion	15yrs PS	F&F	213/15	
Wishart J	7 R Inniskilling Fus	Pte	31/05/17	Desertion x2	XXX 15/06/17	F&F	213/15	665
Burgoyne A	7 E Surrey	Pte	01/06/17	Desertion	10yrs PS	F&F	213/15	
Fullard T	8 R Dublin Fus	Pte	01/06/17	Desertion	10yrs PS	F&F	213/15	
Grant J	1/5 Gordon Hdrs	Pte	01/06/17	Desertion	10yrs PS	F&F	213/15	
Michael James S	10 Scottish Rifles	Pte	01/06/17	Desertion	XXX 24/08/17	F&F	213/16	666
Chant T	7 R Sussex	Pte	03/06/17	Desertion	10yrs PS	F&F	213/15	
Cross C	11 Liverpool	Pte	03/06/17	Desertion	10yrs PS	F&F	213/15	
Graves H	11 Liverpool	Pte	03/06/17	Desertion+	5yrs PS	F&F	213/15	667
Yeoman Walter	1/12 London	Rfm	03/06/17	Desertion x2	XXX 03/07/17	F&F	213/15	668
Baker W	2 Durham LI	Pte	04/06/17	Cowardice	10yrs PS	F&F	213/15	
Locky A	2 Durham LI	Pte (L/C)	04/06/17	Cowardice	15yrs PS	F&F	213/15	
O'Neill CC	2 Australian IF	Pte	04/06/17	Desertion	15yrs PS		213/17	
Ship CH	1/13 London	Pte	04/06/17	Desertion	5yrs PS	F&F	213/16	669
Thompson JH	93 RFA	Dvr	04/06/17	Desertion	10yrs PS		213/15	
Lamb W	6 R Dublin Fus	Pte	05/06/17	Sleeping	5yrs PS	Salonika	213/16	
Lynch FN	9 KRRC	Rfm	05/06/17	Desertion	10yrs PS	F&F	213/15	
Comte Gustave	22 Canadian EF	Pte	06/06/17	Desertion	XXX 03/07/17	F&F	213/15	670
Gaudy A	22 Canadian EF	Pte	06/06/17	Desertion	15yrs PS	F&F	213/16	
Patterson Robert Gillis	7 E Surrey	Pte	06/06/17	Desertion	XXX 04/07/17	F&F	213/15	671
Blanchette G	22 Canadian EF	Pte	07/06/17	Desertion	15yrs PS	F&F	213/16	
Hampshire F	2/5 W Riding	Pte	07/06/17	Desertion	15yrs PS	F&F	213/15	
LaLancette Joseph	22 Canadian EF	Pte	07/06/17	Desertion	XXX 03/07/17	F&F	213/15	672
Frankhan G	76 MGC	Pte	09/06/17	Desertion	10yrs PS		213/15	
Hepple [Hope] Robert	1 R Inniskilling Fus	Pte	09/06/17	Desertion	XXX 05/07/17	F&F	213/16	673
Norris HG	57 Australian IF	Pte	09/06/17	Desertion	2yrs HL		213/16	
Rodgers C	Nelson Bn R Naval VR	A/B	09/06/17	Desertion	10yrs PS		213/15	
Smith GW	139 MGC	Pte	09/06/17	Sleeping	5yrs PS		213/15	
Walton T	1/7 Lancs Fus	Cpl	09/06/17	Quitting	7yrs PS	F&F	213/15	
Barnes John E	7 R Sussex	Pte	10/06/17	Desertion	XXX 04/07/17	F&F	213/15	674
Fryer John	12 E Surrey	Pte	10/06/17	Desertion	XXX 24/06/17	F&F		675
Hatton C	60 Australian IF	Pte	10/06/17	Desertion	5yrs PS		213/16	
Smith J	RE	Dvr	10/06/17	Disobedience+	10yrs PS		213/15	676
Ballinger H	6 R Berkshire	Pte	11/06/17	Desertion	5yrs PS	F&F	213/15	
Massiter J	1/5 York & Lancaster	Pte	11/06/17	Desertion	5yrs PS	F&F	213/15	
Barron H	55 MGC	Pte	12/06/17	Quitting	10yrs PS		213/15	
Hawkins T	7 R W Surrey	Pte	12/06/17	Desertion	10yrs PS	F&F	213/15	
Thaourides Nicolas A	Muleteer	Foreman	12/06/17	Murder	XXX 06/07/17	Salonika	213/16	677
Bozan K	85 Canadian EF	Pte	13/06/17	Desertion	10yrs PS	F&F	213/16	
Fetterley P	38 Canadian EF	Pte	14/06/17	Desertion x2	15yrs PS	F&F	213/16	

Name	Unit	Rank	Date	Offence	Final sentence	Location	Ref	Note
Toomey N	1/4 London	Pte	14/06/17	Desertion	10yrs PS	F&F	213/15	678
Treveleyn V	38 Canadian EF	Pte	14/06/17	Desertion	15yrs PS	F&F	213/16	
Pond A	7 Norfolk	Pte	15/06/17	Desertion	10yrs PS	F&F	213/15	
Smith GW	146 MGC	Pte	15/06/17	Murder	15yrs PS		213/16	
Barrowclough N	4 Bedfordshire	Pte	16/06/17	Desertion	Not Conf	F&F	213/16	
Donaldson H	9 Yorks	Pte	16/06/17	Desertion	10yrs PS	F&F	213/15	
Rummel C	2 New Zealand EF	Pte	16/06/17	Desertion	10yrs PS		213/15	679
Turner G	11 Sherwood Fstrs	Pte	16/06/17	Desertion	10yrs PS	F&F	213/15	
Randall ST	9 Northumb Fus	Pte	18/06/17	Desertion	5yrs PS	F&F	213/15	
Smith HE	20 Australian IF	Pte	18/06/17	Desertion	15yrs PS		213/15	
Byrne H	6 Northumb Fus	Pte	19/06/17	Desertion x2	5yrs PS	F&F	213/15	
Horsley J	22 Northumb Fus	Cpl	19/06/17	Desertion x2	5yrs PS	F&F	213/15	680
King J	5 Northumb Fus	Pte	19/06/17	Desertion	10yrs PS	F&F	213/15	
Hodgson WJ	28 Canadian EF	Pte	20/06/17	Desertion	10yrs PS	F&F	213/16	
Marshall D	32 MGC	Pte	20/06/17	Desertion	10yrs PS		213/15	
Barratt Frederick Martin	7 KRRC	Rfm	21/06/17	Desertion	XXX 10/07/17	F&F	213/16	681
Laurie W	2 Rifle Bde	Rfm	21/06/17	Desertion	5yrs PS	F&F	213/15	
Newey E	7 KRRC	Rfm	21/06/17	Desertion	10yrs PS	F&F	213/15	
Burrows EW	6 Northumb Fus	Pte	22/06/17	Desertion	5yrs PS	F&F	213/16	
Keegan J	2 S Wales Bdrs	Pte	22/06/17	Desertion	5yrs PS	F&F	213/16	
Bowen J	11 Sherwood Fstrs	Pte	23/06/17	Desertion	10yrs PS	F&F	213/15	
Cherry J	59 Australian IF	Pte	23/06/17	Desertion	90 days FP1		213/16	
Foster H	6 Dorset	Pte	23/06/17	Desertion	5yrs PS	F&F	213/15	
Mooney E	11 S Lancs	Pte	23/06/17	Desertion	10yrs PS		213/15	682
Cross F	13 York and Lancaster	Pte	24/06/17	Desertion	Not Conf	F&F	213/16	683
Doolan J	26 Australian IF	Pte	24/06/17	Desertion	5yrs PS		213/15	
Williams WW	10 KO Yorks LI	Pte	24/06/17	Quitting	10yrs PS	F&F	213/15	
Baker T	12 York & Lancaster	Pte	25/06/17	Desertion	5yrs PS	F&F	213/16	684
Smith W	MGC	Pte	25/06/17	Disobedience	5yrs PS		213/16	
Thompson J	8 N Staffordshire	Pte	25/06/17	Desertion	10yrs PS	F&F	213/15	
Brompton J	1 R Irish Fus	Pte	26/06/17	Desertion	15yrs PS	F&F	213/16	
Smith CE	RFA	Dvr	26/06/17	Desertion	PS Life		213/17	
Stainton T	11 W Yorks	Pte	26/06/17	Desertion	10yrs PS	F&F	213/15	
Stokes RM	9 Durham LI	Pte	26/06/17	Desertion	5yrs PS		213/16	
Evans AJ	46 Australian IF	Pte	27/06/17	Desertion	10yrs PS		213/16	
Hawkins G	46 Australian IF	Pte	27/06/17	Desertion	10yrs PS		213/16	
Wessell M	47 Australian IF	Pte	27/06/17	Cowardice	10yrs PS		213/16	
Blakemore Denis	8 N Staffordshire	Pte	28/06/17	Desertion	XXX 09/07/17	F&F	213/16	685
Clarke FH	46 Australian IF	Pte	28/06/17	Desertion	10yrs PS		213/16	
Clarke FH	46 Australian IF	Pte	28/06/17	Desertion	10yrs PS		213/16	
Lepley JE	48 Australian IF	Pte	28/06/17	Desertion	10yrs PS		213/16	
Stower EC	2/5 S Staffordshire	Pte	28/06/17	Desertion	5yrs PS	F&F	213/17	
Benham William	1/3 London	Pte	29/06/17	Desertion	XXX 12/07/17	F&F	213/16	686
Burns E	2/7 Manchester	Pte	29/06/17	Sleeping	2yrs HL	F&F	213/16	
Raine Henry	2 Durham LI	Pte	29/06/17	Desertion	5yrs PS	F&F	213/16	
Scott H	1 Worcestershire	Pte	29/06/17	Desertion	5yrs PS	F&F	213/16	
Ashton Harry	11 Scottish Rifles	L/Sgt	30/06/17	Desertion	XXX 08/07/17	Salonika	213/16	687
Sneddon HJ	20 Middlesex	Pte	30/06/17	Desertion	5yrs PS	F&F	213/16	688
Valler AJ	13 E Surrey	Pte	30/06/17	Desertion	5yrs PS	F&F	213/16	689
Lynch J	2 R Inniskilling Fus	Pte	01/07/17	Drunk/AWOL	2yrs HL	F&F	213/16	
Teague J	10 R Warwickshire	Pte	01/07/17	Desertion	10yrs PS	F&F	213/16	
Cutmore George	2 Black Watch	Pte	02/07/17	Desertion	XXX 25/07/17	Mesopotamia	90/7	690
Elvin JE	23 Northumb Fus	CSM	02/07/17	Desertion	5yrs PS	F&F	213/16	691
Crawford ER	New Zealand Engineers	Spr	03/07/17	Desertion	5yrs PS		213/16	692
Law J	1/19 London	Pte	03/07/17	Desertion	3 Mos FP1	F&F	213/16	693
Loader Frederick	1/22 London	Pte	03/07/17	Desertion	10yrs PS	F&F	213/16	694
Ollerton G	1/5 S Lancs	Rfm	03/07/17	Murder	3yrs PS	F&F	213/16	
Sabongidda Samuel	3 Nigeria	Pte	03/07/17	Violence	XXX 27/07/17	East Africa	213/17	695
Wilson F	2 Bedfordshire	Pte	03/07/17	Desertion	10yrs PS	F&F	213/16	
Baker FJ	1 New Zealand EF	Pte	04/07/17	Desertion	15yrs PS		213/16	696
Broad P	4 Australian Pnr Bn	Pte	05/07/17	Desertion	10yrs PS		213/16	
Hackett J	7 Leicestershire	Pte	05/07/17	Desertion	5yrs PS	F&F	213/16	
Hammond A	4 Australian Pnr Bn	Pte	05/07/17	Desertion	10yrs PS		213/16	
Jenkins M	4 Australian Pnr Bn	Pte	05/07/17	Desertion	10yrs PS		213/16	
Nicol LP	4 Australian Pnr Bn	Pte	05/07/17	Desertion	10yrs PS		213/16	
Swords M	4 Australian Pnr Bn	Pte	05/07/17	Desertion	10yrs PS		213/16	
Looker H	2 Suffolk	Pte	06/07/17	Desertion	5yrs PS	F&F	213/16	
Smith R	2 Canadian EF	Pte	06/07/17	Desertion	5yrs PS	F&F	213/16	

Name	Unit	Rank	Date	Offence	Final sentence	Location	Ref	Note
Castonguay OA	22 Canadian EF	Pte	07/07/17	Desertion	15yrs PS	F&F	213/16	
Robillard A	22 Canadian EF	Pte	07/07/17	Desertion	15yrs PS	F&F	213/16	
Whicker WH	RE	Spr	07/07/17	Desertion	10yrs PS		213/16	
Sheridan E	48 Australian IF	Pte	08/07/17	Desertion	10yrs PS		213/16	
Caulfield J	13 Highland LI	Pte	09/07/17	Desertion	Not Conf	UK	213/16	697
Holien MT	46 Australian IF	Pte	09/07/17	Desertion	10yrs PS		213/16	
Jenkins P	14 R Warwickshire	Cpl	10/07/17	Desertion	5yrs PS	F&F	213/16	
Foster G	2 S Staffordshire	Pte	11/07/17	Desertion x2	2yrs HL	F&F	213/17	
Benn E	41 MGC	Pte	12/07/17	Desertion	10yrs PS		213/17	
Cornell GJ	38 Canadian EF	Pte	12/07/17	Desertion	15yrs PS	F&F	213/16	
Davies Richard M	11 Sherwood Fstrs	Pte	13/07/17	Desertion	3yrs PS	F&F	213/16	698
Keeling E	11 Sherwood Fstrs	Pte	13/07/17	Desertion	3yrs PS	F&F	213/16	
Mailey T	1/4 R Scots Fus	Pte	13/07/17	Disobedience	5yrs PS	Egypt	213/16	
Simpson T	1/4 R Scots Fus	Pte	13/07/17	Disobedience	5yrs PS	Egypt	213/16	
Ward T	10 Loyal N Lancs	Pte	13/07/17	Desertion	10yrs PS	F&F	213/16	
Latour T	22 Canadian EF	Pte	14/07/17	Desertion	15yrs PS	F&F	213/16	
Mathieson J	9 Black Watch	Pte	14/07/17	Desertion	5yrs PS	F&F	213/16	
Millar J	9 Black Watch	Pte	14/07/17	Desertion	5yrs PS	F&F	213/16	
Doyle F	44 Canadian EF	Pte	15/07/17	Desertion	3yrs PS	F&F	213/16	
Cowley R	11 Sherwood Fstrs	Pte	16/07/17	Desertion	Not Conf	F&F	213/16	
Jones JA	7 Rifle Bde	Pte	16/07/17	Desertion	10yrs PS	F&F	213/16	
Miller P	147 MGC	Pte	16/07/17	Desertion	5yrs PS		213/16	
Mitchell L	8 York & Lancaster	Pte	16/07/17	Desertion	10yrs PS	F&F	213/16	699
Wilson W	2 Scottish Rifles	Pte	16/07/17	Desertion	10yrs PS	F&F	213/16	
Widdows R	19 R Welsh Fus	Pte	17/07/17	Desertion	5yrs PS	F&F	213/16	700
Miller R	2 KO Scottish Bdrs	Pte	18/07/17	Desertion	10yrs PS	F&F	213/16	
Allender J	2 York & Lancaster	Pte	19/07/17	Desertion	15yrs PS	F&F	213/16	
Cole AAJ	1/8 Liverpool	Pte	19/07/17	Desertion	15yrs PS	F&F	213/16	701
Riddell G	5 Highland LI	Pte	19/07/17	Sleeping	5yrs PS		213/17	
Broaderick Frederick	11 R Warwickshire	Pte	20/07/17	Desertion	XXX 01/08/17	F&F	213/16	702
Hood A	11 R Warwickshire	Pte	20/07/17	Desertion	15yrs PS	F&F	213/16	
Wearne CA	1/5 E Lancs	Pte	20/07/17	Desertion	5yrs PS	F&F	213/16	
Graham H	7 Essex	Pte	21/07/17	Sleeping	5yrs PS	F&F	213/17	
Inglis R	2 Black Watch	Pte	21/07/17	Sleeping	5yrs PS	Mesopotamia	90/7	703
Scott C	11 R W Kent	Pte	21/07/17	Desertion	10yrs PS	F&F	213/16	704
Lovitt E	2 R Berkshire	Pte	22/07/17	Desertion	5yrs PS	F&F	213/16	
Masters A	2 R Berkshire	Pte	22/07/17	Cowardice	15yrs PS	F&F	213/16	
Hamilton J	15 Highland LI	Pte	23/07/17	Desertion	5yrs PS	F&F	213/16	705
Metcalfe H	22 Northumb Fus	Pte	23/07/17	Desertion	5yrs PS	F&F	213/17	706
Methven J	1/6 Gordon Hdrs	Pte	23/07/17	Desertion	5yrs PS	F&F	213/16	707
Fagan A	10 Cheshire	Pte	25/07/17	Desertion	5yrs PS	F&F	213/16	
Kimber E	24 Royal Fus	Pte	25/07/17	Cowardice	7yrs PS	F&F	213/16	708
McManus H	3 Worcestershire	Pte	25/07/17	Desertion	2yrs HL	F&F	213/16	
Reed WJ	38 Canadian EF	Pte	25/07/17	Desertion	10yrs PS	F&F	213/16	
Rutter N	38 Canadian EF	Pte	25/07/17	Desertion	10yrs PS	F&F	213/16	
Wilson JH	38 Canadian EF	Pte	25/07/17	Desertion	5yrs PS	F&F	213/16	
Bridges F	2 R Sussex	Pte	26/07/17	Sleeping	2yrs HL	F&F	213/16	
Bernier G	14 Canadian EF	Pte	27/07/17	Desertion	2yrs HL	F&F	213/16	
Fewins G	13 Middlesex	Pte	27/07/17	Cowardice+	15 yrs PS	F&F	213/16	709
Hart A	1/22 London	Pte	27/07/17	Desertion	10yrs PS	F&F	213/17	
Lothian D	48 Australian IF	Pte	27/07/17	Cowardice+	10yrs PS		213/16	710
Crawford SH	16 Australian IF	Pte	28/07/17	Desertion	10yrs PS		213/16	
Auckland A	7 KRRC	Rfm	29/07/17	Violence	10yrs PS	F&F	213/16	
Syrett C	2 Manchester	Pte	29/07/17	Desertion	7 yrs PS	F&F	213/16	
Edwards EG	1/8 Manchester	Pte	30/07/17	Desertion	5yrs PS	F&F	213/16	711
Goody WT	1 Rifle Bde	Pte	30/07/17	Desertion	Not Conf	F&F	213/16	
Sautier EG	35 Australian IF	Pte	30/07/17	Desertion	5yrs PS		213/16	
Vetters J	6/7 R Scottish Rifles	Pte	30/07/17	Desertion	2yrs HL	F&F	213/16	
Hayes JH	8 London	Rfm	01/08/17	Desertion	10yrs PS	F&F	213/16	712
Thorne FR	2 Royal Fus	Pte	01/08/17	Desertion	5yrs PS	F&F	213/16	
Wells F	1/21 London	Rfm	01/08/17	Desertion	10yrs PS	F&F	213/16	713
Livingstone C	1/6 Highland LI	Pte	02/08/17	Sleeping	3yrs PS	Egypt	213/17	714
Loader Frederick	1/22 London	Pte	02/08/17	Desertion	XXX 19/08/17	F&F	213/16	715
Mitchell Arthur	1/6 Lancs	Pte	02/08/17	Desertion	XXX 20/08/17	F&F	213/16	716
Phelps E	1/22 London	Pte	02/08/17	Desertion	10yrs PS	F&F	213/16	
King H	Tank Corps	Cpl (Sgt)	03/08/17	Desertion	5yrs PS	F&F	213/17	717
McPherson J	16 R Scots	Pte	03/08/17	Desertion	5yrs PS	F&F	213/16	
Raynor J	2 New Zealand EF	Pte	03/08/17	Desertion	10yrs PS		213/16	718

Name	Unit	Rank	Date	Offence	Final sentence	Location	Ref	Note
Gill E	52 RFA	Gnr	04/08/17	Desertion	5 yrs PS		213/16	
Shallcross G	1 KO Yorks LI	Pte	04/08/17	Sleeping	2yrs HL	Salonika	213/17	
King John	1 New Zealand EF	Pte	05/08/17	Desertion	XXX 19/08/17		213/16	719
Hozier WG	5 R Berkshire	Pte	06/08/17	Desertion	15yrs PS	F&F	213/17	
Ingersoll RA	24 Canadian EF	Pte	06/08/17	Desertion	10yrs PS	F&F	213/16	
Walker W	7 E Yorks	Pte	06/08/17	Desertion	15yrs PS		213/17	
Clarke Hubert A	2 British West Indies	Pte	07/08/17	Striking +	XXX 11/08/17	Egypt	213/17	720
Barfoot F	14 Australian IF	Pte	08/08/17	Desertion	10yrs PS		213/17	
Hennelbury M	14 Australian IF	Pte	08/08/17	Desertion	10yrs PS		213/17	
Meeguane [?] M	14 Australian IF	Pte	08/08/17	Desertion	10yrs PS		213/17	
Waring H	7 Leicestershire	Pte	08/08/17	Cowardice+	5yrs PS	F&F	213/16	721
Darkiya	2/2 King's African Rifles	Pte	09/08/17	Sleeping	2yrs HL	Egypt	213/17	
Green W	1/4 York & Lancaster	Pte	09/08/17	Desertion	5yrs PS	F&F	213/16	722
Harvey W	2 R Berkshire	Pte	09/08/17	Desertion	10yrs PS	F&F	213/16	
Parry Albert	2 W Yorks	Pte	10/08/17	Desertion	XXX 30/08/17	F&F	213/17	723
Watts Thomas W	7 E Yorks	Pte	10/08/17	Desertion	XXX 30/08/17	F&F	213/17	724
Davies A	RAMC	Pte	11/08/17	Desertion	5yrs PS		213/18	
Hodges WJ	English Civilian	N/A	11/08/17	Espionage	5yrs PS		213/20	
Rutland E	RAMC	Pte	11/08/17	Desertion	5yrs PS		213/18	
Cheeney RL	24 Canadian EF	Pte	12/08/17	Desertion	15yrs PS	F&F	213/16	
Graves H	11 Liverpool	Pte	12/08/17	Desertion	10yrs PS	F&F	213/16	
Latto GS	51 Australian IF	Pte	12/08/17	Desertion	15yrs PS		213/17	
Stewart Stanley	2 R Scots Fus	Pte	12/08/17	Desertion	XXX 29/08/17	F&F	213/16	725
Turner HJ	28 Canadian EF	Pte	12/08/17	Desertion	Not Conf	F&F	213/17	
Butcher J	4 Grenadier Gds	Pte	13/08/17	Desertion	5yrs PS	F&F	213/16	
Crowhurst J	8 R W Surrey	Pte	13/08/17	Cowardice x2	15yrs PS	F&F	213/17	
Leslie A	35 Australian IF	Pte	13/08/17	Desertion+	10yrs PS		213/17	726
McGrath J	9 Liverpool	Sgt	13/08/17	Cowardice	2yrs HL		213/16	
Sherry D	36 Australian IF	Pte	13/08/17	Desertion	10yrs PS		213/17	
Swinton GW	35 Australian IF	Pte	13/08/17	Desertion	10yrs PS		213/17	
Wycherley William	2 Manchester	Pte	13/08/17	Desertion x2	XXX 12/09/17	F&F	213/17	727
Brady D	2 R Scots Fus	Pte	14/08/17	Desertion	15yrs PS	F&F	213/16	
Findlay W	2 R Scots Fus	Pte	14/08/17	Desertion	15yrs PS	F&F	213/16	
Irwin S	2 R Scots Fus	Pte	14/08/17	Desertion	15yrs PS	F&F	213/16	
Mason J	2 R Scots Fus	Pte	14/08/17	Desertion	15yrs PS	F&F	213/16	
Parchiskin E	2 Canadian Pioneers	Pnr	14/08/17	Desertion	2yrs HL	F&F	213/17	728
Parkes E	36 Australian IF	Pte	14/08/17	Desertion	10yrs PS		213/17	
Robertson	Anglo-Indian	Pte	14/08/17	Sleeping	5yrs PS	Mesopotamia	90/7	729
Tilbury J	RFA	Gnr	16/08/17	Striking	5yrs PS		213/17	
Wilson H	11 R Warwickshire	Pte	16/08/17	Desertion	10yrs PS	F&F	213/17	
Fisher-Jones D	3 Canadian EF	Pte	17/08/17	Desertion	10yrs PS	F&F	213/17	
Johnson J	8 York & Lancaster	Pte	17/08/17	Desertion	15yrs PS	F&F	213/17	
Orr B	22 Northumb Fus	Pte	17/08/17	Desertion	5yrs PS	F&F	213/16	
Assister WJ	8 E Kent (Buffs)	Pte	18/08/17	Desertion	2yrs HL	F&F	213/16	730
Burns W	1 Gordon Hdrs	Pte	20/08/17	Desertion	5yrs PS	F&F	213/16	
Hughes J	1/5 A&S Hdrs	Pte	20/08/17	Casting Arms	10yrs PS	Egypt	213/17	731
Morris M	2 Leinster	Pte	20/08/17	Desertion x2	10yrs PS	F&F	213/17	
Ryan J	2 Leinster	Pte	20/08/17	Desertion	10yrs PS	F&F	213/16	
Whitworth W	RFA	Pte	21/08/17	Desertion	5yrs PS		213/16	
Bolton J	17 Liverpool	Pte	22/08/17	Desertion	Not Conf	F&F	213/17	
Smith James	17 Liverpool	Pte	22/08/17	Desertion	XXX 05/09/17	F&F	213/17	732
Abigail John Henry	8 Norfolk	Pte	24/08/17	Desertion	XXX 12/09/17	F&F	213/17	733
Beck JE	8 Norfolk	Pte	24/08/17	Desertion	Not Conf	F&F	213/17	
Best T	6 Northants	Pte	24/08/17	Desertion	10yrs PS	F&F	213/17	
Delargey Edward	1/8 R Scots	Pte	24/08/17	Desertion	XXX 06/09/17	F&F	213/17	734
Burgess C	10 KRRC	Rfm	26/08/17	Desertion	5yrs PS	F&F	213/16	
Hyde John J	10 KRRC	Rfm	26/08/17	Desertion	XXX 05/09/17	F&F	213/17	735
Neave Walter	10 W Yorks	Pte	26/08/17	Desertion	XXX 30/08/17	F&F	213/17	736
Stedman [Steadman] Joseph	117 MGC	Pte	26/08/17	Desertion	XXX 05/09/17	F&F	213/17	737
Thompson JH	RFA	Dvr	26/08/17	Desertion	Not Conf		213/17	
Hagn A	Civilian	Alien	27/08/17	Espionage	PS Life	UK	92/4	738
Hart H	2 British West Indies	Pte	27/08/17	Striking	10yrs PS		213/17	
Makin R	8 Border	Pte	27/08/17	Desertion	5yrs PS	F&F	213/17	
Lucas J	1/7 London	Rfm	28/08/17	Desertion	15yrs PS	F&F	213/17	
Brady JE	4 Australian Pnr Bn	Pte	29/08/17	Desertion	PS Life		213/17	
Frederick OR	49 Australian IF	Pte	29/08/17	Desertion	15yrs PS		213/17	
Fredrick OR	49 Australian LI	Pte	29/08/17	Desertion	15yrs PS		213/17	
Keen William	7 R W Surrey	Pte	29/08/17	Desertion	10yrs PS	F&F	213/17	

Name	Unit	Rank	Date	Offence	Final sentence	Location	Ref	Note
Fitzjohn C	11 Lincolnshire	Pte	30/08/17	Desertion	5yrs PS	F&F	213/17	
Hastings G	8 E Kent (Buffs)	Pte	30/08/17	Desertion	10yrs PS	F&F	213/17	
King JH	13 Rifle Bde	Rfm	30/08/17	Desertion	10yrs PS	F&F	213/18	
Kusasi Allasan	Gold Coast Regt	Pte	30/08/17	Sleeping	5yrs PS		213/19	
Wall John Thomas	3 Worcestershire	Sgt	30/08/17	Desertion	XXX 06/09/17	F&F	213/17	739
Warriner W	7 Lincolnshire	Pte	30/08/17	Desertion	5yrs PS	F&F	213/17	
Britton Charles	1/5 R Warwickshire	Pte	31/08/17	Desertion	XXX 12/09/17	F&F	213/17	740
De Fontenay GA	37 Australian IF	Pte	01/09/17	Desertion	10yrs PS		213/18	
Rees DJ	13 Welsh	Pte	01/09/17	Desertion	2yrs HL	F&F	213/17	741
Walshe D	39 Australian IF	Pte	01/09/17	Desertion	10yrs PS		213/18	
Black W	2 New Zealand EF	Pte	02/09/17	Desertion	10yrs PS		213/17	742
Heathcote H	2 E Lancs	Pte	02/09/17	Desertion +	10yrs PS	F&F	213/17	743
Bullas J	1/7 Worcestershire	Pte	03/09/17	Cowardice	Not Conf	F&F	213/17	
Chandler W	11 Essex	Pte	03/09/17	Desertion	5yrs PS	F&F	213/17	
Collins E	1/4 Gloucestershire	Pte	03/09/17	Desertion	10yrs PS	F&F	213/17	744
Everill George	1 N Staffordshire	Pte	03/09/17	Desertion	XXX 14/09/17	F&F	213/17	745
Bogdanov V	2 Canadian Pnr Bn	Pte	04/09/17	Desertion	5yrs PS	F&F	213/17	
Clarke C	1 Border	Pte	04/09/17	Desertion	5yrs PS	F&F	213/17	
Duncombe S	2 Royal Fus	Pte	04/09/17	Desertion	10yrs PS	F&F	213/17	
Dunn J	2/8 Liverpool	Pte	04/09/17	Desertion	10yrs PS	F&F	213/17	746
Ginn AA	45 Australian IF	Pte	04/09/17	Desertion	PS Life		213/17	
Kerr WA	2 New Zealand EF	Pte	04/09/17	Desertion	10yrs PS		213/17	747
Krivetsky A	2 Canadian Pnr Bn	Pte	04/09/17	Desertion	5yrs PS	F&F	213/17	
Kudatski S	2 Canadian Pnr Bn	Pte	04/09/17	Desertion	5yrs PS		213/17	
Reid CF	46 Australian IF	Pte	04/09/17	Desertion	15yrs PS		213/17	
Steadman WH	9 Worcestershire	Pte	04/09/17	Sleeping	3yrs PS	Mesopotamia	90/7	
Wilson EW	RGA	Gnr	04/09/17	Desertion	5yrs PS		213/17	
Allen J	Canadian EF	Pte	05/09/17	Against Inhab	PS Life	F&F	213/17	
Clarke F	46 Australian	Pte	05/09/17	Desertion	PS Life		213/18	
Clarke J	15 R Irish Rifles	Rfm	05/09/17	Quitting	5yrs PS	F&F	213/17	748
Davey W	11 R W Surrey	Pte	05/09/17	Desertion	10yrs PS	F&F	213/17	
Harding E	46 Australian IF	Pte	05/09/17	Desertion	20yrs PS		213/17	
Hodges J	2 S Wales Bdrs	Pte	05/09/17	Desertion	15yrs PS	F&F	213/17	
Jardine C	15 R Irish Rifles	Rfm	05/09/17	Quitting	5yrs PS	F&F	213/17	749
Johnson O	Canadian EF	Pte	05/09/17	Against Inhab	PS Life	F&F	213/17	
Mitchell Leonard	8 York & Lancaster	Pte	05/09/17	Desertion	XXX 19/09/17	F&F	213/17	750
Ogorodnick J	47 Canadian EF	Pte	05/09/17	Cowardice +	10yrs PS	F&F	213/17	751
Saunders GW	15 R Irish Rifles	Rfm	05/09/17	Quitting	5yrs PS	F&F	213/17	752
Thomas FC	15 R Irish Rifles	Rfm	05/09/17	Quitting	5yrs PS	F&F	213/17	753
Marchuk M	47 Canadian EF	Pte	06/09/17	Cowardice	10yrs PS		213/17	
Oleinik N	38 Canadian EF	Pte	06/09/17	Desertion	5yrs PS	F&F	213/17	
Shefford E	5 R Berkshire	Pte	06/09/17	Desertion	5yrs PS	F&F	213/17	
Wallace J	24 Canadian EF	Pte	06/09/17	Desertion	5yrs PS	F&F	213/17	
Zuk G	38 Canadian EF	Pte	06/09/17	Desertion	5yrs PS	F&F	213/17	
Broomfield E	7 Lincolnshire	L/Cpl	07/09/17	Desertion x2	15yrs PS	F&F	213/17	
Hardaker W	2 R Warwickshire	Pte	07/09/17	Desertion	10yrs PS	F&F	213/17	
Kirman Charles Henry	7 Lincolnshire	Pte	07/09/17	Desertion x2	XXX 23/09/17	F&F	213/17	754
Morris Herbert	British West Indies	Pte	07/09/17	Desertion	XXX 20/09/17	F&F	213/17	755
Day W	7 Rifle Bde	Rfm	08/09/17	Desertion	10yrs PS	F&F	213/17	
Gore Frederick C	7 E Kent (Buffs)	Pte	08/09/17	Desertion	XXX 16/10/17	F&F	213/17	756
Leicester JW	1/15 London	Pte	08/09/17	Desertion	10yrs PS	F&F	213/17	757
McDonald J	RFA	Gnr	08/09/17	Desertion	10yrs PS		213/17	
Schofield E	2/8 Lancs Fus	Pte	08/09/17	Sleeping	5yrs PS	F&F	213/17	
Lever S	Scottish Rifles	Pte	09/09/17	Desertion	10yrs PS		213/17	
Chalk C	3 Rifle Bde	Rfm	10/09/17	Desertion	10yrs PS	F&F	213/17	
Lowen Albert	1 Rifle Bde	Rfm	10/09/17	Desertion	10yrs PS	F&F	213/17	
Smith W	3 Rifle Bde	Rfm	10/09/17	Desertion	10yrs PS	F&F	213/17	
Walker E	10 R Welsh Fus	Pte	10/09/17	Desertion	5yrs PS	F&F	213/17	
Wyniger G	3 Rifle Bde	Rfm	10/09/17	Desertion	10yrs PS	F&F	213/17	
Yates F	4 Grenadier Gds	Pte	10/09/17	Desertion	Not Conf	F&F	213/17	
Court RS	48 Australian IF	Pte	11/09/17	Desertion	PS Life		213/17	
Farrow AW	1/2 London	Pte	12/09/17	Desertion	5yrs PS	F&F	213/17	758
Marshall W	17 Australian IF	Pte	12/09/17	Desertion	5yrs PS		213/18	
Ryan EJ	51 Australian IF	Pte	12/09/17	Desertion	5yrs PS		213/17	
Short Jesse R	24 Northumb Fus	Cpl	12/09/17	Mutiny	XXX 04/10/17	F&F	213/17	759
Sinicky Dimitro	52 Canadian EF	Pte	12/09/17	Cowardice	XXX 09/10/17	F&F	213/17	760
Burtch JA	38 Canadian EF	Pte	13/09/17	Desertion	5yrs PS	F&F	213/17	
Grist JP	14 Australian IF	Pte	13/09/17	Desertion	10yrs PS		213/17	

Name	Unit	Rank	Date	Offence	Final sentence	Location	Ref	Note
Marineau G	22 Canadian EF	Pte	13/09/17	Desertion	10yrs PS	F&F	213/17	
Perkins W	78 Canadian EF	Pte	13/09/17	Desertion	10yrs PS	F&F	213/17	
Saxby F	5 Dorset	Pte	13/09/17	Desertion	5yrs PS	F&F	213/17	
Sewell J	87 Canadian EF	Pte	13/09/17	Desertion	5yrs PS	F&F	213/17	
Stepharnoff A	87 Canadian EF	Pte	13/09/17	Desertion	10yrs PS	F&F	213/17	
Ward H	13 KRRC	Rfm	13/09/17	Desertion	15yrs PS	F&F	213/17	
Dawson E	9 KO Yorks LI	Pte	14/09/17	Desertion	10yrs PS	F&F	213/17	
Grozier AE	1 E Yorks	Cpl	14/09/17	Desertion	10yrs PS		213/17	
Mackness Ernest	1 Scottish Rifles	Pte	14/09/17	Desertion	XXX 01/10/17	F&F	213/17	761
Daley A	4 Canadian Mtd Rifles	Pte	15/09/17	Desertion	15yrs PS	F&F	213/17	
Dumesnil A	22 Canadian EF	Pte	15/09/17	Desertion	15yrs PS	F&F	213/17	
Jones A	4 Royal Fus	Pte	15/09/17	Desertion	15yrs PS	F&F	213/21	
Lewis LA	4 Canadian Mtd Rifles	Pte	15/09/17	Desertion	15yrs PS	F&F	213/17	
Moorhouse J	2 R Irish	Pte	15/09/17	Desertion	5yrs PS	F&F	213/18	
Porter WG	4 Canadian Mtd Rifles	Pte	15/09/17	Desertion	15yrs PS	F&F	213/17	
Tunnicliffe A	RAMC	Pte	15/09/17	Desertion	10yrs PS		213/17	
Mulgrew E	2 Highland LI	Pte	16/09/17	Desertion	15yrs PS	F&F	213/17	
Bell W	1/7 Highland LI	Pte	17/09/17	Drunk	5yrs PS	Egypt	213/18	762
Fedrick G	49 Australian IF	Pte	17/09/17	Desertion	PS Life		213/17	
Harris H	Lab Coy	Pte	17/09/17	Desertion	Not Conf		213/17	
Johnson LE	10 Essex	Pte	17/09/17	Desertion	Not Conf	F&F	213/17	
McCrae A	54 Canadian EF	Pte	17/09/17	Desertion	10yrs PS	F&F	213/17	
McLean C	7 Highland LI	Pte	17/09/17	Casting Arms	4yrs PS	F&F	213/18	
Walker W	52 Australian IF	Pte	17/09/17	Desertion	10yrs PS		213/18	
Woodhouse John	12 KRRC	Rfm	17/09/17	Desertion	XXX 04/10/17	F&F	213/17	763
Mosey W	7 R Dublin Fus	Pte	18/09/17	Disobedience	Not Conf	Salonika	213/18	
Best J	1/4 R Scots Fus	Pte	19/09/17	Disobedience x2	10yrs PS	Egypt	213/18	
Frew J	1/4 R Scots Fus	Pte	19/09/17	Disobedience	10yrs PS	Egypt	213/18	
Latta W	1/4 R Scots Fus	Pte	19/09/17	Disobedience	10yrs PS	Egypt	213/18	
LeDoux L	58 Canadian EF	Pte	19/09/17	Desertion	10yrs PS	F&F	213/17	
McLelland S	1/4 Seaforth Hdrs	Pte	19/09/17	Desertion	5yrs PS	F&F	213/17	764
Penrose E	58 Canadian EF	Pte	19/09/17	Desertion	3yrs PS	F&F	213/17	
Pugh C	52 Canadian EF	Pte	19/09/17	Desertion	2yrs HL	F&F	213/17	765
Tobin A	52 Canadian EF	Pte	19/09/17	Desertion	3yrs PS	F&F	213/17	766
Brown R	13 R Scots	Pte	20/09/17	Desertion	5yrs PS	F&F	213/17	
Holmes W	44 Canadian EF	Pte	20/09/17	Desertion	2yrs HL	F&F	213/17	
Silburn GH	36 Australian IF	Pte	20/09/17	Desertion	10yrs PS		213/17	
Ward Thomas	8/10 Gordon Hdrs	Pte	20/09/17	Desertion	XXX 16/10/17	F&F	213/17	767
Hill W	7 D Cornwall LI	Pte	21/09/17	Desertion	10yrs PS	F&F	213/17	
Clarke AG	13 Essex	Sgt	22/09/17	Desertion	5yrs PS	F&F	213/17	768
Ganley M	1 KO Yorks LI	Pte	22/09/17	Sleeping	2yrs HL	Salonika	213/17	
Sharpe GH	2 W Yorks	Pte	22/09/17	Desertion	10yrs PS	F&F	213/17	
Bryant Ernest	10 Cheshire	Pte	23/09/17	Desertion x2	XXX 27/10/17	F&F	213/18	769
Fletcher WJ	29 Canadian EF	Pte	24/09/17	Desertion	5yrs PS	F&F	213/17	
Goten L	Civilian	Alien	24/09/17	Espionage	PS Life	UK	92/4	770
Jones A	7 R Welsh Fus	Pte	24/09/17	Desertion	5yrs PS	Egypt	213/17	
Pearson AV	8 E Surrey	Pte	24/09/17	Desertion	10yrs PS	F&F	213/17	
Stairs E	5 Canadian Mtd Rifles	Pte	24/09/17	Desertion	5yrs PS	F&F	213/17	
Taysum Norman Henry	9 Black Watch	Pte	24/09/17	Desertion	XXX 16/10/17	F&F	213/17	771
Ashworth E	6 KOR Lancaster	Pte	25/09/17	Desertion/Drunk	5yrs PS	Mesopotamia	90/7	
Cook M	3 Bty RFA	Dvr	25/09/17	Desertion +	5yrs PS	Mesopotamia	90/7	772
Jacques J	18 Canadian EF	Sgt	25/09/17	Desertion	10yrs PS	F&F	213/17	
Jenning C	1/8 Worcestershire	Pte	25/09/17	Cowardice	15yrs PS	F&F	213/19	
Kelly J	3 Bty RFA	Dvr	25/09/17	Desertion/Drunk	5yrs PS	Mesopotamia	90/7	
Roberts FJ	1/8 Worcestershire	Pte	25/09/17	Cowardice	15yrs PS	F&F	213/17	
Rock JT	33 Bty RFA	Dvr	25/09/17	Desertion/Drunk	5yrs PS	Mesopotamia	90/7	
Stephenson JH	6 Durham LI	Pte	25/09/17	Desertion	5yrs PS		213/17	
Watnough J	6 KOR Lancaster	Pte	25/09/17	Desertion/Drunk	5yrs PS	Mesopotamia	90/7	
Bakewell A	RFA	Dvr	26/09/17	Desertion	5yrs PS		213/17	
Ball JH	66 Bde RFA	Gnr	26/09/17	Sleeping	3yrs HL	Mesopotamia	90/7	773
Llewellyn TJ	4 S Wales Bdrs (att RFA)	Pte	26/09/17	Sleeping	3yrs HL	Mesopotamia	90/7	774
McNeilly G	85 Canadian EF	Pte	26/09/17	Desertion x2	10yrs PS	F&F	213/17	
McPhee W	85 Canadian EF	Pte	26/09/17	Desertion	5yrs PS	F&F	213/17	
Murphy J	1/5 Seaforth Hdrs	Pte	26/09/17	Desertion	5yrs PS	F&F	213/18	775
Gilmore A	6/7 R Scots Fus	Pte	27/09/17	Desertion	15yrs PS	F&F	213/18	
Gilmour A	6/7 R Scots Fus	Pte	27/09/17	Desertion	15yrs PS	F&F	213/17	
Harris T	1/9 London	Pte	27/09/17	Desertion	15yrs PS	F&F	213/17	
Woodfield F	1/19 London	Pte	27/09/17	Desertion	5yrs PS	F&F	213/17	776

Name	Unit	Rank	Date	Offence	Final sentence	Location	Ref	Note
Ahmed MM	Egyptian Lab Corps	Lbr	28/09/17	Violence	XXX 10/10/17	F&F	213/17	777
Jones William	9 R Welsh Fus	Pte	28/09/17	Desertion	XXX 25/10/17	F&F	213/17	778
Wood FW	1/6 Manchester (att RE)	Pte	28/09/17	Desertion	10yrs PS	Mesopotamia	90/7	779
Alexander William	10 Canadian EF	CQMSgt	29/09/17	Desertion	XXX 18/10/17	F&F	213/17	780
Fathers E	8 Canadian EF	Pte	30/09/17	Desertion	10yrs PS	F&F	213/19	
Rutley L	7 Canadian EF	Pte	30/09/17	Desertion	5yrs PS	F&F	213/17	
Barre N	4 Canadian EF	Pte	01/10/17	Desertion+	5yrs PS	F&F	213/17	781
Hazelden F	4 Canadian EF	Pte	01/10/17	Desertion	10yrs PS	F&F	213/18	
Masterson R	2 Canadian EF	Pte	01/10/17	Desertion	10yrs PS	F&F	213/18	
Orr M	2 Canadian EF	Pte	02/10/17	Desertion	10yrs PS	F&F	213/18	
Cheeseman Frank William	18 KRRC	Rfm	03/10/17	Desertion	XXX 20/10/17	F&F	213/17	782
Coulby F	38 Canadian EF	Pte	03/10/17	Desertion	5yrs PS	F&F	213/17	
Eakimchuk M	85 Canadian EF	Pte	03/10/17	Desertion	10yrs PS	F&F	213/18	
Rogers SD	1 Liverpool	Pte	03/10/17	Desertion	10yrs PS	F&F	213/17	
Chalk T	8 Bedfordshire	Pte	04/10/17	Desertion	10yrs PS	F&F	213/18	
Eckman A	119 DAC	Gnr	04/10/17	Desertion	10yrs PS		213/17	783
Jones L	22 Northumb Fus	Pte	04/10/17	Cowardice	5yrs PS	F&F	213/18	784
Knight WE	9 York & Lancaster	Pte	04/10/17	Desertion	15yrs PS	F&F	213/17	
Moles Thomas	54 Canadian EF	Pte	04/10/17	Desertion	XXX 22/10/17	F&F	213/17	785
Anderson T	22 Northumb Fus	Pte	05/10/17	Desertion	10yrs PS	F&F	213/18	786
Price M	22 Northumb Fus	Pte	05/10/17	Desertion	5yrs PS	F&F	213/18	787
Doe J	2 Middlesex	Pte	06/10/17	Desertion	10yrs PS	F&F	213/19	
Hedger Frederick	18 KRRC	Rfm	06/10/17	Desertion	5yrs PS	F&F	213/17	788
Lynch J	1 R Irish Rifles	Rfm	06/10/17	Cowardice	15yrs PS	F&F	213/17	
Millburn John B	24 Northumb Fus	Pte	06/10/17	Desertion	XXX 08/11/17	F&F	213/18	789
Rollin W	1 R Irish Rifles	Pte	06/10/17	Cowardice	15yrs PS	F&F	213/17	
Campbell S	2 York & Lancaster	Pte	07/10/17	Desertion	5yrs PS	F&F	213/18	
Bushnell V	8 York & Lancaster	Pte	08/10/17	Desertion	10yrs PS	F&F	213/18	
Gardiner C	1/20 London	Pte	08/10/17	Desertion	15yrs PS	F&F	213/19	790
Massey L	8 York & Lancaster	Pte	08/10/17	Desertion	15yrs PS	F&F	213/17	
Nicholson Charles Bain	8 York & Lancaster	Pte	08/10/17	Desertion	XXX 27/10/17	F&F	213/18	791
Oyns Arthur Philip	RE (Field Search Lt Coy)	Spr	08/10/17	Murder	XXX 20/10/17	F&F	213/17	792
Wilson H	1/20 London	Pte	08/10/17	Desertion	15yrs PS	F&F	213/19	793
Worsley Ernest	2 Middlesex	Pte	08/10/17	Desertion	XXX 22/10/17	F&F	213/17	794
Garnhum C	2 Canadian Heavy Bty	Gnr	09/10/17	Desertion	Not Conf	F&F	213/18	
Holden J	12 Manchester	Pte	09/10/17	Desertion	10yrs PS	F&F	213/17	
Stone AV	1/1 Cambridgeshire	Pte	09/10/17	Desertion	10yrs PS	F&F	213/18	
Turner Frederick	6 Northumb Fus	Pte	11/10/17	Desertion x2	XXX 23/10/17	F&F	213/17	795
Beadle F	2 Royal Fus	Pte	12/10/17	Desertion	15yrs PS	F&F	213/17	
Frafra A	Gold Coast Regt	Pte	12/10/17	Cowardice	14yrs PS		213/19	
Long JD	1/17 London	Pte	12/10/17	Desertion	5yrs PS	F&F	213/17	796
Monaghan M [Byrne S]	1 R Dublin Fus	Pte	12/10/17	Desertion	XXX 28/10/17	F&F	213/18	797
Strevens H	4 Bedfordshire	Pte	12/10/17	Desertion	15yrs PS	F&F	213/18	
Birch A	11 Worcestershire	Pte	13/10/17	Sleeping	5yrs PS	Salonika	213/18	
Daganli D	Gold Coast Regt	Cpl	13/10/17	Cowardice	14yrs PS	East Africa	213/22	
Giles H	11 Worcestershire	Pte	13/10/17	Sleeping	5yrs PS	Salonika	213/18	
Moshi M	Gold Coast Regt	Pte	13/10/17	Cowardice	7yrs PS	East Africa	213/22	
Webb Henry J	2 KO Yorks LI	Pte	13/10/17	Desertion x2	XXX 31/10/17	F&F	213/18	798
Turner H	9 Liverpool	Pte	14/10/17	Desertion	5yrs PS		213/17	
Boylan P	2 Leinster	Pte	15/10/17	Desertion	5yrs PS	F&F	213/17	
Mitchell R	10 Loyal N Lancs	Pte	15/10/17	Desertion	10yrs PS	F&F	213/18	
Stokes W	RFA	Pte	15/10/17	Desertion	10yrs PS		213/18	
Vickers G	10 R Warwickshire	Pte	15/10/17	Desertion	10yrs PS	F&F	213/18	
Lindsay G	12 A&S Hdrs	Pte	16/10/17	Desertion	5yrs PS	Salonika	213/18	
Shepherd T	2 S Staffordshire	Pte	16/10/17	Desertion+	5yrs PS	F&F	213/18	799
Squire J	5 KOR Lancaster	Pte	16/10/17	Desertion	15yrs PS	F&F	213/18	
Dale G	10 Lincolnshire	Pte	17/10/17	Desertion x2	15yrs PS	F&F	213/18	800
Dionne C	15 Canadian EF	Pte	17/10/17	Desertion	5yrs PS	F&F	213/17	
Donovan Thomas	16 KRRC	Rfm	17/10/17	Desertion x3	XXX 31/10/17	F&F	213/18	801
Robson H	2 Lincolnshire	Pte	17/10/17	Desertion	10yrs PS	F&F	213/18	
Rossington J	1 E Yorks	Pte	17/10/17	Desertion	10yrs PS		213/18	
Rowe J	22 Durham LI	Pte	17/10/17	Desertion	10yrs PS	F&F	213/18	802
Sweeney P	10 W Riding	Pte	17/10/17	Desertion	15yrs PS	F&F	213/18	
Taylor John	2 S Staffordshire	Pte	17/10/17	Desertion x2	XXX 06/11/17	F&F	213/18	803
Coward J	1/5 S Lancs	Pte	18/10/17	Striking x2	5yrs PS	F&F	213/17	
James A	2 R Warwickshire	Pte	18/10/17	Desertion	10yrs PS	F&F	213/18	
Wooding E	2 R Warwickshire	Pte	18/10/17	Desertion	10yrs PS	F&F	213/18	
Ammon J	1/5 Sherwood Fstrs	Pte	19/10/17	Quitting	5yrs PS	F&F	213/18	

Name	Unit	Rank	Date	Offence	Final sentence	Location	Ref	Note
Brown T	1/5 Sherwood Fstrs	Pte	19/10/17	Quitting	5yrs PS	F&F	213/18	
Carpenter AE	18 Liverpool	Pte	19/10/17	Quitting	10yrs PS	F&F	213/18	
Dring T	1 E Yorks	Pte	19/10/17	Desertion	10yrs PS		213/18	
Gibbon L	1 E Yorks	Pte	19/10/17	Desertion	10yrs PS		213/20	
Hanna George	1 R Irish Fus	Pte	19/10/17	Desertion	XXX 06/11/17	F&F	213/18	804
Isbister G	52 Canadian EF	Pte	19/10/17	Desertion	10yrs PS	F&F	213/18	805
Sizer B	1 E Yorks	Pte	19/10/17	Desertion	10yrs PS		213/18	
Daikee HO	1 New Zealand EF	Pte	20/10/17	Desertion	Not Conf	F&F	213/18	806
Kinsey F	21 Manchester	Pte	20/10/17	Desertion	10yrs PS	F&F	213/18	807
Moore H	1 Middlesex	Pte	22/10/17	Desertion	10yrs PS	F&F	213/18	
Morrison D	Dragoon Gds	Pte	22/10/17	Desertion	5yrs PS		213/18	
Rigby Thomas Henry Basil	10 S Wales Bdrs	Pte	22/10/17	Desertion	XXX 22/11/17	F&F	213/18	808
Schofield S	1/5 E Lancs	Pte	24/10/17	Desertion	5yrs PS	F&F	213/19	
Davis Richard M	11 Sherwood Fstrs	Pte	25/10/17	Desertion	XXX 15/11/17	F&F	213/18	809
Donnelly J	1 Irish Gds	Pte	25/10/17	Desertion	2yrs HL	F&F	213/18	
Gaylard P	1/15 London	Cpl	25/10/17	Desertion	10yrs PS	F&F	213/18	810
Hopkins T	1 Irish Gds	Pte	25/10/17	Desertion	2yrs HL	F&F	213/18	
Jackson J	2 Coldstream Gds	Pte	25/10/17	Desertion	5yrs PS	F&F	213/18	
Light F	8 R W Surrey	Pte	25/10/17	Cowardice	Not Conf	F&F	213/18	
Dagomba A	Gold Coast Regt	Pte	26/10/17	Sleeping	14yrs PS		213/19	
Dorr C	38 Australian IF	Pte	26/10/17	Desertion x2	10yrs PS		213/18	
Gillam A	40 Australian IF	Pte	26/10/17	Desertion	10yrs PS		213/18	
Holderness HA	1/5 Bedfordshire	Pte	26/10/17	Disobedience	5yrs PS	Egypt	213/19	
Morrison J	9 Yorks	Pte	26/10/17	Desertion	10yrs PS	F&F	213/18	
Days J	7 S Lancs	Pte	27/10/17	Desertion	10yrs PS	F&F	213/18	
Westwood Arthur H	8 E Surrey	Pte	27/10/17	Desertion	XXX 23/11/17	F&F	213/18	811
Mills F	RAMC	Pte	28/10/17	Desertion	10yrs PS		213/18	
Montgomery F	1 Canadian R'way Troops	Spr	28/10/17	Insub+	5yrs PS	F&F	213/18	812
Bedford A	1/7 W Yorks	Rfm	29/10/17	Desertion	10yrs PS	F&F	213/18	813
Doeltz W	German Army	POW	29/10/17	Insubordinaion	168 days HL	Egypt	213/18	
Ibadan A	4 Nigerian Regt	Pte (L/C)	29/10/17	Cowardice x2	14yrs PS	East Africa	213/21	
McCarthy S	MGC	Pte	29/10/17	Desertion	XXX [?]	F&F	213/18	814
McGee P	9 Yorks	Pte	29/10/17	Desertion	15yrs PS	F&F	213/18	
Siman N	German Army	POW	29/10/17	Insubordinaion	168 days HL	Egypt	213/18	
Brookes R	3/5 Lancs Fus	Pte	30/10/17	Desertion	15yrs PS	F&F	213/18	
Lee J	1/10 London	Pte	30/10/17	Striking	10yrs PS	Egypt	213/19	815
North H	3/5 Lancs Fus	Pte	30/10/17	Desertion	15yrs PS	F&F	213/18	
Smith William	3/5 Lancs Fus	Pte	30/10/17	Desertion	XXX 14/11/17	F&F	213/18	816
Adamson JS	7 Cameron Hdrs	Pte	31/10/17	Cowardice	XXX 23/11/17	F&F	213/18	817
Best J	2 Lincolnshire	Sgt	31/10/17	Cowardice	10yrs PS	F&F	213/18	
Conroy P	RFA	Dvr	31/10/17	Desertion	10yrs PS		213/18	
Cowls A	36 Australian IF	Pte	31/10/17	Desertion	10yrs PS		213/18	
Picard H	2 Lincolnshire	Pte	31/10/17	Cowardice	10yrs PS	F&F	213/18	
Bagnell J	36 Australian IF	Pte	01/11/17	Desertion	10yrs PS		213/18	
Foulkes Thomas	1/10 Manchester	Pte	01/11/17	Desertion	XXX 21/11/17	F&F	213/18	818
Ratican P	2 R Welsh Fus	Pte	02/11/17	Desertion	10yrs PS	F&F	213/18	
Bateman Joseph	2 S Staffordshire	Pte	04/11/17	Desertion	XXX 03/12/17	F&F	213/18	819
Garfoot G	Sherwood Fstrs	Pte	04/11/17	Desertion	Not Conf		213/18	
Harris E	2 S Staffordshire	Pte	04/11/17	Desertion	15yrs PS	F&F	213/18	
Ruff N	DAC	Dvr	04/11/17	Desertion x2	5yrs PS		213/18	
Connor P	22 Northumb Fus	Pte	05/11/17	Desertion	3yrs PS	F&F	213/18	820
Maw J	2 Durham LI	Pte	05/11/17	Desertion	5yrs PS	F&F	213/18	
Irvine A	11 A&S Hdrs	Pte	06/11/17	Desertion	5yrs PS	F&F	213/18	
Smith F	58 Canadian EF	Cpl	06/11/17	Desertion	5yrs PS	F&F	213/18	
Dean V	7 R W Surrey	Pte	07/11/17	Desertion	5yrs PS	F&F	213/18	
Goff E	9 Devon	Pte	07/11/17	Desertion	5yrs PS	F&F (?)	213/19	821
Hawkins Thomas	2 R W Surrey	Pte	07/11/17	Desertion	XXX 22/11/17	F&F	213/18	822
Lawrence Ernest	2 Devon	Pte	07/11/17	Desertion x3	XXX 22/11/17	F&F	213/20	823
Parker G	7 R W Surrey	Pte	07/11/17	Desertion	10yrs PS	F&F	213/18	
Wright J	2/2 London	Pte	07/11/17	Insub+	10yrs PS	F&F	213/18	824
Baker H	3 Coldstream Gds	Pte	08/11/17	Desertion	5yrs PS	F&F	213/18	
Brigham T	1/10 Manchester	Pte	08/11/17	Desertion	15yrs PS	F&F	213/18	825
Lewis D	6 Cheshire	Pte	08/11/17	Desertion	5yrs PS	F&F	213/18	
Lloyd J	RE	Spr	08/11/17	Desertion	Not Conf		213/18	
Smith L	4 Royal Fus	Pte	08/11/17	Desertion	5yrs PS	F&F	213/8	
Davidson J	Lab Corps	Pte	09/11/17	Desertion	2yrs HL		213/18	
Gibson H	RFA	Gnr	09/11/17	Desertion	5yrs PS		213/18	
Gibson T	7 R Irish Rifles	Rfm	09/11/17	Desertion	5yrs PS		213/18	

Name	Unit	Rank	Date	Offence	Final sentence	Location	Ref	Note
Pritchard J	8 R Welsh Fus	Pte	09/11/17	Quitting	2yrs HL	Mesopotamia	90/7	826
Sheehan M	RFA	Bmdr	09/11/17	Desertion	10yrs PS		213/18	
Griffin A	197 MGC	Pte	11/11/17	Desertion	15yrs PS		213/18	
Krebs A	78 Canadian EF	Pte	11/11/17	Desertion	15yrs PS	F&F	213/18	
Lewis T	44 Canadian EF	Pte	11/11/17	Desertion x2	10yrs PS	F&F	213/18	
Scrogge E	RFA	Dvr	12/11/17	Desertion	5yrs PS		213/18	
Watson R	10 A&S Hdrs	Pte	12/11/17	Desertion	2yrs HL	F&F	213/20	
Parish W	1/10 London	Pte	13/11/17	Disobedience x2	15yrs PS	Egypt	213/19	827
Rayson A	7 S Wales Bdrs	Pte	13/11/17	Striking	10yrs PS	Salonika	213/18	
Scholes William	2 S Wales Bdrs	Pte	14/11/17	Desertion	5yrs PS	F&F	213/18	828
Slade Frederick W	2/6 London	Rfm	14/11/17	Disobedience x2	XXX 24/11/17	F&F	213/18	829
Buckle J	4 Yorks	Pte	15/11/17	Desertion	5yrs PS	F&F	213/18	
Martin R	115 MGC	Pte	15/11/17	Sleeping	Not Conf		213/18	
Meredith J	2 Highland LI	Pte	15/11/17	Desertion	10yrs PS	F&F	213/18	
Ryan J	20 Lancs Fus	Pte	15/11/17	Quitting	2yrs HL	F&F	213/19	830
Swift J	115 MGC	Cpl	15/11/17	Sleeping	Not Conf		213/18	
Barrington A	2 Manchester	Pte	17/11/17	Desertion	5yrs PS	F&F	213/18	
McIntyre J	12 A&S Hdrs	Pte	17/11/17	Sleeping	3yrs PS	Salonika	213/18	
Cameron W	27 Canadian EF	Pte	18/11/17	Desertion	10yrs PS	F&F	213/18	
Coates G	1/4 York & Lancaster	Pte	19/11/17	Desertion	10yrs PS	F&F	213/18	831
Giles G	1/6 S Staffordshire	Pte	19/11/17	Desertion	10yrs PS	F&F	213/18	
Chemmings J	1 R Marine LI	Pte	20/11/17	Desertion	5yrs PS		213/18	
Turnbull W	85 Canadian EF	Pte	22/11/17	Desertion	10yrs PS	F&F	213/18	
Wilson H	100 MGC	Pte	22/11/17	Desertion x2	5yrs PS		213/19	
Hackett J	7 Leicestershire	Pte	23/11/17	Disobedience	Not Conf	F&F	213/19	
Leins J	Employment Coy	Pte	24/11/17	Desertion	5yrs PS		213/19	
Milligan M	9 Durham LI	Pte	24/11/17	Desertion	5yrs PS		213/19	
Siddall Clyde	2 S Lancs	Pte	24/11/17	Desertion	5yrs PS	F&F	213/18	
Kirk E	10 W Yorks	Pte	26/11/17	Desertion	5yrs PS	F&F	213/19	
Orr B	22 Northumb Fus	Pte	26/11/17	Desertion	5yrs PS	F&F	213/19	832
Stephens A	8/10 Gordon Hdrs	Pte	26/11/17	Desertion x2	5yrs PS	F&F	213/18	
Taylor E	1/6 Welsh	Pte	26/11/17	Desertion	5yrs PS	F&F	213/18	833
Taylor R	2 Canadian EF	Pte	26/11/17	Desertion	5yrs PS	F&F	213/18	
Derritt G	42 Canadian EF	Pte	27/11/17	Desertion	5yrs PS	F&F	213/18	
Lyons W	4 E Yorks	Pte	27/11/17	Desertion	5yrs PS		213/19	
McColl Charles F	4 E Yorks	Pte	27/11/17	Desertion	XXX 28/12/17	F&F	213/19	834
Banks L	7 KOR Lancaster	Pte	28/11/17	Desertion	5yrs PS	F&F	213/18	
Gibbons J	1 R Irish Rifles	Rfm	28/11/17	Desertion	15yrs PS	F&F	213/19	
Greig J	58 Canadian EF	Pte	28/11/17	Desertion	5yrs PS	F&F	213/19	
Hudson W	42 Canadian EF	Pte	28/11/17	Desertion	5yrs PS	F&F	213/19	
Smith B	42 Canadian EF	Pte	28/11/17	Desertion	15yrs PS	F&F	213/19	
Dubue E	52 Canadian EF	Pte	29/11/17	Desertion	10yrs PS	F&F	213/19	835
Gallagher A	4 Liverpool	Pte	29/11/17	Desertion	2yrs HL	F&F	213/19	
Sokol A	44 Canadian EF	Pte	29/11/17	Desertion	10yrs PS	F&F	213/19	
Duce J	9 KO Yorks LI	Pte	30/11/17	Desertion	5yrs PS	F&F	213/18	
Dukes S	16 R Welsh Fus	Pte	30/11/17	Desertion x2	5yrs PS	F&F	213/19	
Hardie JN	52 Canadian EF	Pte	30/11/17	Desertion	5yrs PS	F&F	213/18	836
Bradley J	7 Kings Shropshire LI	Pte	01/12/17	Desertion	5yrs PS	F&F	213/18	
Brooks A	9 Durham LI	Pte	01/12/17	Desertion	5yrs PS		213/19	
Davies W	7 Kings Shropshire LI	Pte	01/12/17	Desertion	5yrs PS	F&F	213/18	
Payne S	87 Canadian EF	Pte	01/12/17	Desertion x2	3yrs PS	F&F	213/19	
Savage EW	52 Canadian EF	Pte	03/12/17	Desertion	5yrs PS	F&F	213/19	837
Edmondstone R	17 R Scots	Pte	05/12/17	Desertion	5yrs PS	F&F	213/19	838
Hopkins Thomas	1/8 Lancs Fus	Pte	05/12/17	Quitting+Esc	XXX 13/02/18	F&F	213/20	839
Jordon TH	7 R W Kent	Pte	05/12/17	Desertion	5yrs PS	F&F	213/19	
Roe W	1/11 London	Rfm	06/12/17	Desertion	5yrs PS	Egypt	213/20	840
Murray E	1/5 Lincolnshire	Pte	07/12/17	Desertion	5yrs PS	F&F	213/19	
Johnston J	1/6 Gordon Hdrs	Pte	08/12/17	Desertion	5yrs PS	F&F	213/18	841
Simpson W	9 Yorks	Pte	08/12/17	Desertion	10yrs PS	Italy	213/19	
Wilkes A	Kings Shropshire LI	Pte	09/12/17	Desertion	5yrs PS		213/19	
Bleasedale W	116 Canadian EF	Pte	10/12/17	Desertion	Not Conf	F&F	213/20	
Grannon J	7 E Yorks	Pte	10/12/17	Desertion	5yrs PS		213/18	
Hughes J	1/5 York & Lancaster	Pte	10/12/17	Desertion	10yrs PS	F&F	213/19	
Fowles SM	44 Canadian EF	Pte	12/12/17	Desertion	15yrs PS	F&F	213/19	842
Mayes J	1/4 E Lancs	Pte	12/12/17	Desertion	5yrs PS	F&F	213/19	
Montgomery P	10 W Riding	Pte	12/12/17	Desertion	15yrs PS	Italy	213/19	
Sharpe HL	50 Canadian EF	Pte	12/12/17	Desertion	7yrs PS	F&F	213/19	
Fuller J	2 R Sussex	Pte	13/12/17	Absence	5yrs PS	F&F	213/19	

Name	Unit	Rank	Date	Offence	Final sentence	Location	Ref	Note
Holmes W	44 Canadian EF	Pte	13/12/17	Desertion	15yrs PS (n/s)	F&F	213/19	
Williams Harry	1/9 London	Rfm	13/12/17	Desertion	XXX 28/12/17	F&F	213/19	843
Ellwood J	2 Leinster	Pte	14/12/17	Desertion	Not Conf	F&F	213/20	
Fewins G	13 Middlesex	Pte	14/12/17	Desertion	10yrs PS	F&F	213/19	
Raine H	2 Durham LI	Pte	14/12/17	Desertion	5yrs PS	F&F	213/19	
Smith S	2 Rifle Bde	Rfm	14/12/17	Desertion	2yrs HL	F&F	213/19	
Thompson A	2 Rifle Bde	Rfm	14/12/17	Desertion	5yrs PS	F&F	213/19	
Agon DW	42 Canadian EF	Pte	15/12/17	Desertion	15yrs PS	F&F	213/19	
Bennett G	2 KO Yorks LI	Pte	15/12/17	Desertion	5yrs PS	F&F	213/19	
Bryant WJ	42 Canadian EF	Pte	15/12/17	Desertion	15yrs PS	F&F	213/19	
Henderson N	78 Canadian EF	Pte	15/12/17	Desertion	10yrs PS	F&F	213/19	
Mathieson A	1/8 A&S Hdrs	Pte	15/12/17	Desertion	5yrs PS	F&F	213/18	844
Mitchell James A	1 British West Indies	Pte	15/12/17	Murder	XXX 22/12/17	Palestine	213/20	845
Birch P	10 Essex	Pte	16/12/17	Desertion	5yrs PS	F&F	213/19	
Darlington J	2/8 Liverpool	Pte	16/12/17	Desertion	5yrs PS	F&F	213/18	846
Clarke F	225 MGC	Pte	17/12/17	Not recorded	5yrs PS		213/21	
Bryan H	13 York and Lancaster	Pte	18/12/17	Desertion x2	10yrs PS	F&F	213/20	847
Corbett SE	14 Welsh	Pte	18/12/17	Cowardice	5yrs PS	F&F	213/19	848
Cross F	13 York and Lancaster	Pte	18/12/17	Desertion	10yrs Ps	F&F	213/20	849
Allsopp G	705 Lab Coy	Pnr	19/12/17	Desertion	5yrs PS		213/19	
Old G	58 DAC	Dvr	19/12/17	Desertion	10yrs PS		213/19	
Stevens A	DAC	Dvr	19/12/17	Desertion x2	5yrs PS		213/19	
Rickett E	10 W Riding	Pte	20/12/17	Desertion	10yrs PS	Italy	213/19	
Callaghan J	8 Seaforth Hdrs	Pte	21/12/17	Desertion	5yrs PS	F&F	213/19	
Stewart F	58 Lab Coy	Pte	21/12/17	Desertion	10yrs PS		213/19	
Stepharnoff A	87 Canadian EF	Pte	22/12/17	Desertion	15yrs PS	F&F	213/19	
Parker J	1 R Scots Fus	Pte	23/12/17	Att Desertion	15yrs PS	F&F	213/19	
Carolan G	2/5 Lancs Fus	Pte	24/12/17	Desertion x2	10yrs PS	F&F	213/19	
Fitzpatrick J	2 R Inniskilling Fus	Pte	24/12/17	Desertion	5yrs PS	F&F	213/19	
Holliday G	RFA	Dvr	24/12/17	Desertion	5yrs PS		213/19	
Lipowich J	8 Canadian EF	Pte	24/12/17	Desertion	5yrs PS	F&F	213/19	
McGrath M	12 Manchester	Pte	24/12/17	Desertion	5yrs PS	F&F	213/19	
Morgan A	D1 Tank Corps	Pte	24/12/17	Desertion	15yrs PS	F&F	213/20	
Smith E	6 Northumb Fus	Pte	24/12/17	Desertion	5yrs PS	F&F	213/19	
Mawdsley JH	20 Lancs Fus	Pte	26/12/17	Desertion	5yrs PS	F&F	213/19	850
Gerrard WJ	1/4 Norfolk	Pte	27/12/17	Cowardice	10yrs PS	Egypt	213/20	851
Hanson E	4 E Yorks	Pte	27/12/17	Desertion	5yrs PS	F&F	213/19	
Anderson A	5 Yorks	Pte	28/12/17	Desertion	5yrs PS	F&F	213/19	
Burton G	2 E Kent (Buffs)	Pte	29/12/17	Sleeping	2yrs HL	Salonika	213/13	
Fox H	9 Sherwood Fstrs	Pte	29/12/17	Desertion	10yrs PS	F&F	213/19	
Poulter F	58 Canadian EF	Pte	30/12/17	Desertion	10yrs PS	F&F	213/19	
Magill J	R Irish Rifles	L/Cpl	31/12/17	Desertion	3yrs PS		213/19	
Buntin J	1/7 Highland LI	Pte	02/01/18	Desertion	Not Conf	Egypt	213/20	
Donnelly M	1/7 Highland LI	Pte	02/01/18	Desertion	Not Conf	Egypt	213/20	
Logan J	7 Highland LI	Pte	02/01/18	Cowardice	10yrs PS	Egypt	213/21	
Muir C	27 Canadian EF	Pte	02/01/18	Desertion	7yrs PS	F&F	213/19	
O'Connor C	2 Leinster	Pte	02/01/18	Desertion	5yrs PS	F&F	213/19	
Porthouse J	22 Northumb Fus	Pte	02/01/18	Desertion	5yrs PS	F&F	213/20	852
Basham W	New Zealand FA	Dvr	03/01/18	Desertion x2	10yrs PS		213/19	853
Deuchart JS	8/9 R Irish Rifles	Rfm	03/01/18	Desertion x2	3yrs PS	F&F	213/19	854
Riza Ali	Civilian	Alien	03/01/18	Espionage	5yrs PS		213/18	
Gunnell A	Oxon & Bucks LI	Pte	04/01/18	Desertion	5yrs PS		213/19	
Allen H	1/5 Essex	Cpl	08/01/18	Disobedience	10yrs PS	Egypt	213/20	855
Anon No 24232	Chinese Lab Corps	Coolie	08/01/18	Striking	5yrs PS	F&F	213/20	856
Hackett T	9 Sherwood Fstrs	Pte	08/01/18	Desertion	10yrs PS	F&F	213/19	
Rowe L	6 D Cornwall LI	Pte	08/01/18	Cowardice +	Not Conf	F&F	213/20	857
Thorne A	16 Canadian EF	Pte	08/01/18	Desertion	7yrs PS	F&F	213/19	
Gagan G	20 Middlesex	Pte	10/01/18	Sleeping	5yrs PS	F&F	213/19	858
Juteau F	38 Canadian EF	Pte	10/01/18	Desertion	10yrs PS	F&F	213/19	
Lajoie U	38 Canadian EF	Pte	10/01/18	Desertion	10yrs PS	F&F	213/19	
Hurd G	14 R Welsh Fus	Sgt	11/01/18	Desertion	10yrs PS	F&F	213/20	
Drysdale W	16 Highland LI	Pte	12/01/18	Desertion	5yrs PS	F&F	213/19	859
Rushworth J	1 Loyal N Lancs	Pte	12/01/18	Desertion	5yrs PS	F&F	213/19	
Seymour John	2 R Inniskilling Fus	Pte	12/01/18	Desertion	XXX 24/01/18	F&F	213/20	860
McLaughlan P	15 Highland LI	Pte	13/01/18	Desertion	10yrs PS	F&F	213/28	861
Bassett J	1/5 N Staffordshire	Pte	14/01/18	Desertion	10yrs PS	F&F	213/19	
Bolem G	2 York & Lancaster	Pte	14/01/18	Desertion	10yrs PS	F&F	213/27	
Jennings H	58 Canadian EF	Pte	14/01/18	Desertion	10yrs PS	F&F	213/20	

Name	Unit	Rank	Date	Offence	Final sentence	Location	Ref	Note
Pareezer S	21 Manchester	Pte	14/01/18	Desertion	15yrs PS	Italy	213/19	862
Leary J	8 S Staffordshire	Pte	16/01/18	Desertion	5yrs PS	F&F	213/19	
Smith A	20 Liverpool	Pte	16/01/18	Desertion	10yrs PS	F&F	213/19	
Smith C	14 Trench Mortar Bty	Dvr	16/01/18	Desertion	5yrs PS		213/19	
Clarke Wilfred	2 Durham LI	Pte	17/01/18	Desertion	XXX 09/02/18	F&F	213/20	863
McMillan R	11 Northumb Fus	Pte	17/01/18	Desertion	15yrs PS	Italy	213/19	
Rabjohn F	10 W Riding	Pte	17/01/18	Desertion	15yrs PS	Italy	213/19	
Spencer Victor M	1 New Zealand EF	Pte	17/01/18	Desertion	XXX 24/02/18		213/20	864
Carpenter P	102 Canadian EF	Pte	19/01/18	Desertion	10yrs PS	F&F	213/19	
Earle J	1 R Berkshire	Pte	19/01/18	Quitting	15yrs PS	F&F	213/20	
Hall G	2 KO Yorks LI	Pte	19/01/18	Desertion	5yrs PS	F&F	213/20	
Power J	10 R Irish Rifles	Rfm	20/01/18	Desertion	Not Conf	F&F	213/20	865
Chalmers J	107 Canadian Pnrs	Pte	21/01/18	Absence	7yrs PS	F&F	213/20	
Hannan J	13 Canadian EF	Pte	21/01/18	Desertion	10yrs PS	F&F	213/19	
Barker R	2 R Scots	Pte	23/01/18	Desertion	5yrs PS	F&F	213/24	
Clarke W	RFA	Dvr	24/01/18	Desertion	10yrs PS		213/19	
Doyle PL	2 Canadian EF	Pte	24/01/18	Desertion	10yrs PS	F&F	213/19	
Lodge E	RFA	Gnr	24/01/18	Desertion x2	10yrs PS		213/20	
Lunt E	2 Welsh	Pte	24/01/18	Desertion	5yrs PS	F&F	213/20	
Peddar A	9 W Riding	Pte	25/01/18	Desertion	5yrs PS	F&F	213/23	
Tomalin GA	116 Canadian EF	Pte	26/01/18	Desertion	5yrs PS	F&F	213/19	
Howell T	R Canadian Regt	Pte	27/01/18	Desertion	2yrs HL	F&F	213/19	
Conway A	15 R Scots	Pte	28/01/18	Desertion	5yrs PS	F&F	213/20	
Dagesse AC	22 Canadian EF	Pte	28/01/18	Desertion	Not Conf	F&F	213/20	866
Morrison JH	R Canadian Regt	Pte	28/01/18	Desertion	5yrs PS	F&F	213/19	
Wade W	1/4 York & Lancaster	Pte	28/01/18	Desertion	5yrs PS	F&F	213/21	867
Walsh J	22 Canadian EF	Pte	28/01/18	Desertion	5yrs PS	F&F	213/19	
Pearson A V	8 E Surrey	Pte	29/01/18	Desertion	10yrs PS	F&F	213/20	
Walls H	7 R W Surrey	Pte	29/01/18	Desertion	5yrs PS	F&F	213/20	
Atkinson G	2 R Scots	Pte	30/01/18	Desertion	15yrs PS	F&F	213/20	
Harley C	1 R Scots Fus	Pte	30/01/18	Desertion	5yrs PS	F&F	213/19	
Holmes Albert	8 KOR Lancaster	Pte	30/01/18	Desertion	15yrs PS	F&F	213/22	868
Horler Ernest	12 W Yorks	Pte	30/01/18	Desertion x2	XXX 17/02/18	F&F	213/20	869
Doherty JO	1 Loyal N Lancs	Pte	31/01/18	Desertion	5yrs PS	F&F	213/20	
Gerraghty F	1 R Irish Fus	Pte	31/01/18	Desertion	2yrs HL	F&F	213/20	
West J	8 R Berkshire	Pte	31/01/18	Desertion	5yrs PS	F&F	213/20	
Barrington H	2 Manchester	Pte	01/02/18	Desertion	5yrs PS	F&F	213/20	
Delande [Dalande] Hector	8 Seaforth Hdrs	Pte	04/02/18	Desertion x2	XXX 09/03/18	F&F	213/20	870
Drummond S	17 Highland LI	Pte	04/02/18	Desertion	5yrs PS	F&F	213/21	871
White C J	RFA	Gnr	04/02/18	Desertion	5yrs PS		213/20	
Wickens A	9 Rifle Bde	Cpl (L/S)	04/02/18	Murder	XXX 07/03/18	F&F	213/20	872
Clarke W	2/4 E Lancs	Pte	05/02/18	Cowardice	5yrs PS	F&F	213/20	
Barnett L	1/9 London	Rfm	07/02/18	Desertion	10yrs PS	F&F	213/20	
Fairburn E	18 Canadian EF	Pte	07/02/18	Desertion	XXX 02/03/18	F&F	213/20	873
Gibson W	1/6 W Yorks	Pte	07/02/18	Desertion	10yrs PS	F&F	213/20	
Lewis D	1/6 Cheshire	Pte	07/02/18	Desertion	5yrs PS	F&F	213/20	
Woolley F	10 R W Surrey	Pte	08/02/18	Desertion x2	15yrs PS	Italy	213/20	874
Anderson A	46 Canadian EF	Pte	09/02/18	Desertion	10yrs PS	F&F	213/20	
Jennings F	24 Canadian EF	Sgt	11/02/18	Desertion	15yrs PS	F&F	213/20	875
Melsom AJC	ASC	Dvr	11/02/18	Desertion	5yrs PS		213/20	
Carter E	6 R Irish	Pte	12/02/18	Desertion	Not Conf	F&F	213/20	
Greenwood G	14 Durham LI	Pte	12/02/18	Desertion	10yrs PS	F&F	213/23	
Welsh C	8 Canadian EF	Pte	12/02/18	Desertion	XXX 06/03/18	F&F	213/20	876
Reed G R	1 Canadian Mtd Rifles	Pte	13/02/18	Desertion	5yrs PS	F&F	213/20	
Wilson J	4 Canadian Mtd Rifles	Pte	13/02/18	Desertion	15yrs PS	F&F	213/20	
Hall E P	RFA	Dvr	14/02/18	Desertion	5yrs PS		213/20	
Brooke R	10 W Yorks	Pte	15/02/18	Desertion	5yrs PS	F&F	213/21	
Markham A	2 Suffolk	Pte	15/02/18	Desertion	5yrs PS	F&F	213/20	
Memish I	Turkish Army	POW	15/02/18	Murder	XXX	Egypt	213/20	
Ukovitch S	102 Canadian EF	Pte	16/02/18	Desertion	10yrs PS	F&F	213/20	
Graham W	22 Royal Fus	Pte	18/02/18	Desertion	5yrs PS	F&F	213/20	877
Lyons J	1 KO Yorks LI	Sgt	19/02/18	Desertion	Not Conf	Salonika	213/22	
Thickett W	8 S Staffordshire	Pte	19/02/18	Desertion	5yrs PS	F&F	213/20	
Wood L	1/6 London	Rfm	19/02/18	Desertion	5yrs PS	F&F	213/20	
Booth H	1 E Lancs	Pte	20/02/18	Desertion	15yrs PS	F&F	213/23	
Carroll T	1 Lancs Fus	Pte	20/02/18	Desertion	2yrs HL	F&F	213/20	
Paish G	12/13 Northumb Fus	Pte	20/02/18	Desertion	5yrs PS	F&F	213/20	
Adams J	9 R Welsh Fus	Pte	21/02/18	Desertion	15yrs PS	F&F	213/23	

Name	Unit	Rank	Date	Offence	Final sentence	Location	Ref	Note
Calitz [?] MC	S African Horse Arty	Gnr	22/02/18	Desertion	10yrs PS		213/20	
Hooper H	13 R Sussex	Pte	22/02/18	Desertion	5yrs PS	F&F	213/20	878
Lodge HEJ	19 Canadian EF	Pte	23/02/18	Desertion	XXX 13/03/18	F&F	213/20	
Moller AE	1 S African Infantry	Pte	25/02/18	Desertion x2	5yrs PS		213/21	
Dagesse Arthur Charles	22 Canadian EF	Pte	26/02/18	Desertion	XXX 15/03/18	F&F	213/20	879
McMullan J	2 Scottish Rifles	Pte	26/02/18	Desertion	5yrs PS	F&F	213/20	
Westaby A	1 Northumb Fus	Pte	27/02/18	Desertion	5yrs PS	F&F	213/20	
Gladman W	RFA	Dvr	01/03/18	Desertion	5yrs PS		213/20	
Jagger H	16 Middlesex	Pte	01/03/18	Desertion	5yrs PS	F&F	213/20	880
Johnson GL	121 MGC	Pte	01/03/18	Sleeping	5yrs PS		213/20	
Young J	5 Yorks	Pte	02/03/18	Desertion	3yrs PS	F&F	213/21	
Lewis W	1/22 London	Pte	05/03/18	Desertion	5yrs PS	F&F	213/20	
Hartley F	4 Royal Fus	Pte	06/03/18	Desertion x2	5yrs PS	F&F	213/20	
Holmes Albert	8 KOR Lancaster	Pte	06/03/18	Desertion	XXX 22/04/18	F&F	213/22	881
Burkett W	2 R Sussex	Pte	07/03/18	Desertion	10yrs PS	F&F	213/21	
Larsen A	Ordnance Corps	Pte	07/03/18	Desertion	10yrs PS	Italy	213/20	
Woodhouse G	7 Border	Pte	08/03/18	Desertion	5yrs PS	F&F	213/21	
Brown TMcG	158 Lab Coy	Pte	12/03/18	Desertion	10yrs PS	F&F	213/21	
Murphy P	47 MGC	Pte	12/03/18	Desertion	5yrs PS		213/23	
Vogel E	1/19 London	Pte	12/03/18	Desertion	5yrs PS	F&F	213/21	882
Mellor J	MGC	L/Cpl	13/03/18	Qitting post	10yrs PS		213/21	
Stokes T	2 KRRC	Pte	14/03/18	Quitting	2yrs HL	F&F	213/21	
Oatway R	9 KRRC	Rfm	16/03/18	Desertion	5yrs PS	F&F	213/21	
Rodway W	9 KRRC	Rfm	16/03/18	Desertion	5yrs PS	F&F	213/21	
Hughes Henry J	1/5 York & Lancaster	Pte	19/03/18	Desertion	XXX 10/04/18	F&F	213/21	883
Murray PE	4 Connaught Rangers	Lt	19/03/18	Desertion	Cashiered + 3yrs PS	S Africa	90/8	884
Vose S	17 Lancs Fus	Pte	20/03/18	Desertion	10yrs PS	F&F	213/21	885
Fox H	5 W Yorks	Pte	26/03/18	Desertion	7yrs PS	F&F	213/21	
McDonald H	1/6 Highland LI	Pte	30/03/18	Desertion	10yrs PS	Egypt	213/22	886
Wood T	2 Northumb Fus	Pte	01/04/18	Sleeping	2yrs HL	Salonika	213/21	
Massey H	MGC	Pte	02/04/18	Desertion	2yrs HL		213/21	
Meyrick LH	2 New Zealand EF	Pte	04/04/18	Desertion	5yrs PS		213/21	887
Miller S	2 KO Yorks LI	Cpl	04/04/18	Desertion	5yrs PS	F&F	213/21	
Brazier E	1/5 Bedfordshire	Pte	06/04/18	Cowardice	Not Conf	Egypt	213/22	
Cheetham H	1/5 Bedfordshire	Pte	06/04/18	Cowardice	5yrs PS	Egypt	213/22	
Darrington C	1/5 Bedfordshire	Pte	06/04/18	Cowardice	Not Conf	Egypt	213/22	
Joyce A	1/5 Bedfordshire	Pte	06/04/18	Cowardice	Not Conf	Egypt	213/22	
Webb E	1/5 Bedfordshire	Pte	06/04/18	Cowardice	Not Conf	Egypt	213/22	
Whitbread W	1/5 Bedfordshire	Pte	06/04/18	Cowardice	Not Conf	Egypt	213/22	
Craig W	RGA	Gnr	07/04/18	Desertion	5yrs PS		213/21	
Cover J	RFA	Gnr	08/04/18	Desertion	10yrs PS		213/21	
Reid James	6 Cameron Hdrs	L/Cpl	13/04/18	Desertion x2/Esc	XXX 11/05/18	F&F	213/22	888
Horton HS	1 S Staffordshire	Pte	14/04/18	Desertion	7yrs PS	Italy	213/21	
Andrew WJ	8/4 [?] Hampshire	Pte	19/04/18	Cowardice	10yrs PS		213/23	
Davey Richard	15 Hampshire	Pte	19/04/18	Desertion	10yrs PS	F&F	213/21	889
Tong F	15 Hampshire	Pte	19/04/18	Desertion	10yrs PS	F&F	213/21	890
Dale J	1 R Scots Fus	Sgt	20/04/18	Desertion	7yrs PS	F&F	213/22	
Maunders A	1 S Staffordshire	Pte	20/04/18	Quitting	1yr HL	Italy	213/21	
Mellers B	1 Leicestershire	Pte	20/04/18	Desertion	10yrs PS	F&F	213/23	
Bell R	10 Scottish Rifles	Pte	21/04/18	Desertion	5yrs PS	F&F	213/22	
Halcrow J	9 Durham LI	Pte	21/04/18	Desertion	5yrs PS		213/21	
Richmond Malcolm	1/6 Gordon	Pte	21/04/18	Desertion	XXX 26/05/18	F&F	213/22	891
Stafford W	10 Scottish Rifles	Pte	21/04/18	Desertion	5yrs PS	F&F	213/22	
Terry CE	10 Royal Fus	Pte	22/04/18	Desertion	5yrs PS	F&F	213/22	
Thompson S	10 Royal Fus	Pte	22/04/18	Desertion	5yrs PS	F&F	213/21	
Hall J	RFA	Dvr	23/04/18	Desertion	5yrs PS		213/22	
Stevens J	16 DAC	Dvr	23/04/18	Desertion	5yrs PS		213/22	
Whitchard PG	2 Welsh	Pte	24/04/18	Desertion	5yrs PS	F&F	213/22	
Armstrong W	RFA	Gnr	25/04/18	Desertion	10yrs PS		213/22	
Berry F	12 S Wales Bdrs	Pte	25/04/18	Desertion	5yrs PS	F&F	213/21	892
Topps A	7 Kings Shropshire LI	Pte	25/04/18	Desertion	7yrs PS	F&F	213/22	
Watkins A	12 S Wales Bdrs	Pte	25/04/18	Desertion	5yrs PS	F&F	213/21	893
O'Neill Frank	1 Sherwood Fstrs	Pte	26/04/18	Desertion	XXX 16/05/18	F&F	213/22	894
Spry W	2 Royal Fus	Pte	26/04/18	Des + Quitting	10yrs PS	F&F	213/21	895
Wiles W	2 Royal Fus	Pte	26/04/18	Desertion	10yrs PS	F&F	213/21	
Jelly J	RE	Pnr	27/04/18	Mutiny +	5yrs PS	Italy	213/22	896
McFarlane John	4 Liverpool	Pte	28/04/18	Desertion x3	XXX 22/05/18	F&F	213/22	897
Moran H	5 Scottish Rifles	Pte	28/04/18	Desertion	10yrs PS		213/23	898

Name	Unit	Rank	Date	Offence	Final sentence	Location	Ref	Note
Skone James	2 Welsh	Pte	28/04/18	Murder	XXX 10/05/18	F&F	213/22	899
Hoja H	Civilian	Civ	29/04/18	Desertion x2	PS Life	Salonika	213/23	
Musse M	Civilian	Civ	29/04/18	Desertion	10yrs PS	Salonika	213/23	
Sims Robert W	2 R Scots	Pte	30/04/18	Desertion x2	XXX 19/05/18	F&F	213/22	900
Delisle Leopold	22 Canadian EF	Pte	01/05/18	Desertion	XXX 21/05/18	F&F	213/22	901
Hughes J	RFA	Dvr	01/05/18	Desertion	7yrs PS	F&F	213/22	902
Cotterill W	2 Canadian EF	Pte	02/05/18	Desertion	5yrs PS	F&F	213/22	
Gallant J	1 Manchester	Pte	02/05/18	Desertion	7yrs PS	Egypt	213/22	
Hills W	8 Sherwood Fstrs	Pte	02/05/18	Desertion	5yrs PS	F&F	213/22	
Russell J	RFA	Gnr	03/05/18	Desertion	10yrs PS		213/22	
Bell R	123 Field Coy RE	Spr	04/05/18	Murder	XXX 22/05/18	F&F	213/22	903
Joseph AJ	1 S Wales Bdrs	Pte	05/05/18	Against Inhab	5yrs PS	F&F	213/22	
Leahy J	1 Gloucestershire	Cpl	05/05/18	Against Inhab	5yrs PS	F&F	213/22	
Richards T	2 Welsh	Pte	05/05/18	Against Inhab	5yrs PS	F&F	213/22	
Allen JE	RFA	Gnr	07/05/18	Desertion	5yrs PS		213/23	
O'Connor J	10/11 Highland LI	Pte	07/05/18	Desertion	10yrs PS	F&F	213/22	
Connelly D	15 Highland LI	Pte	08/05/18	Desertion	5yrs PS	F&F	213/22	904
Young R	2 R Berkshire	Cpl	08/05/18	Desertion	10yrs PS	F&F	213/23	
Close CH	1 New Zealand EF	Pte	10/05/18	Desertion	15yrs PS	F&F	213/24	905
Gordon L	31 Canadian EF	Pte	10/05/18	Desertion	5yrs PS	F&F	213/22	
Boswell A	16 R Warwickshire	Pte	11/05/18	Sleeping	3yrs PS	F&F	213/22	
Hinton A	16 R Warwickshire	Pte	11/05/18	Sleeping	3yrs PS	F&F	213/22	
Houlram D	2 R Irish	Pte	11/05/18	Desertion	5yrs PS	F&F	213/22	
Howle J T	1/6 N Staffordshire	Pte	11/05/18	Desertion	5yrs PS	F&F	213/22	
Philpott S	1 Hampshire	Pte	12/05/18	Desertion	5yrs PS	F&F	213/22	
Compton W	1 Norfolk	Pte	14/05/18	Desertion	7yrs PS	F&F	213/22	
McCormick M	12 Manchester	Pte	14/05/18	Desertion	5yrs PS	F&F	213/22	
Pendlebury A	12 Manchester	Pte	14/05/18	Desertion	5yrs PS	F&F	213/22	
Earl[e] William J	1/7 Lancs Fus	Pte	15/05/18	Desertion	XXX 27/05/18	F&F	213/22	906
Ashby W	1 Norfolk	Pte	16/05/18	Desertion	5yrs PS	F&F	213/22	907
Broadbridge FG	10 Royal Fus	Pte	16/05/18	Desertion	5yrs PS	F&F	213/22	
Butler J	13 Rifle Bde	Rfn	16/05/18	Desertion	5yrs PS	F&F	213/22	
Chapman S	9 Norfolk	Pte	16/05/18	Desertion	10yrs PS	F&F	213/22	
Green W	1 Sherwood Fstrs	Pte	17/05/18	Desertion	5yrs PS	F&F	213/22	
Warren H	46 MGC	Cpl	17/05/18	Desertion	5yrs PS		213/22	
Brigham Thomas	1/10 Manchester	Pte	18/05/18	Desertion	XXX 04/06/18	F&F	213/22	908
Dickin F	1/6 W Riding	Pte	18/05/18	Cowardice	10yrs PS	F&F	213/22	
Footner A	2 Hampshire	Pte	18/05/18	Desertion	Not Conf	F&F	213/23	909
Fowles Stephen M	44 Canadian EF	Pte	18/05/18	Desertion	XXX 19/06/18	F&F	213/23	910
Heath G	2 Royal Fus	Pte	18/05/18	Desertion	10yrs PS	F&F	213/22	
Allen W	1 Devon	Pte	19/05/18	Desertion	15yrs PS	F&F	213/23	
McFarlan A	1 Cameron Hdrs	Pte	19/05/18	Desertion	5yrs PS	F&F	213/22	
Mason J	2 R Scots Fus	Pte	20/05/18	Desertion	15yrs PS	F&F	213/22	
Duncan A	1/6 A&S Hdrs	Pte	21/05/18	Desertion	10yrs PS	F&F	213/22	911
Moran H	5 Scottish Rifles	Pte	22/05/18	Desertion	Not Conf	F&F	213/23	912
Macky J	1 Hampshire	Pte	23/05/18	Desertion	7yrs PS	F&F	213/22	
Spicer T	1/1 Hertfordshire	Pte	23/05/18	Desertion	5yrs PS	F&F	213/22	
Ashby WF	23 Middlesex	Pte	24/05/18	Desertion	15yrs PS	F&F	213/24	913
Peacock B	1/7 W Yorks	Pte	25/05/18	Desertion	10yrs PS	F&F	213/22	914
Ricketts JC	Drake Bn RNVR	A/B	25/05/18	Desertion	5yrs PS		213/22	
Foulkes HD	S African Regt	Pte	26/05/18	Desertion	10yrs PS		213/23	
Fraser R	13 R Scots	Pte	27/05/18	Desertion	7yrs PS	F&F	213/22	
Gilder H	2/20 London	Pte	27/05/18	Cowardice+	10yrs PS	F&F	213/24	915
Bond J	2 R Scots	Pte	28/05/18	Desertion	10yrs PS	F&F	213/22	
Kelly C	11 Manchester	Pte	28/05/18	Desertion	7yrs PS	F&F	213/23	
Parkin Daniel	1 Gordon Hdrs	Pte	28/05/18	Desertion	5yrs PS	F&F	213/22	
Smith J	2 R Scots	Pte	28/05/18	Desertion	10yrs PS	F&F	213/22	
Wood J	2 R Scots	Pte	28/05/18	Desertion	10yrs PS	F&F	213/22	
Pingson W	2 R Welsh Fus	Pte	29/05/18	Desertion	5yrs PS	F&F	213/22	
Brooks C	6 Yorks	Pte	30/05/18	Desertion	5yrs PS	F&F	213/22	
Edwards T	RFA	Gnr	30/05/18	Mutiny+	3yrs PS		213/22	916
Mayotte N	38 Canadian EF	Pte	30/05/18	Desertion	7yrs PS	F&F	213/22	
Nolan J	1 W Yorks	Pte	30/05/18	Desertion	10yrs PS	F&F	213/23	
Barker FW	13 London	Pte	01/06/18	Desertion	10yrs PS	F&F	213/22	917
Howell S	7 S Staffordshire	Pte	01/06/18	Sleeping	5yrs PS	F&F	213/22	
Pemberton J	1/7 W Yorks	Rfm	01/06/18	Desertion	10yrs PS	F&F	213/23	918
Scott J	2 Royal Fus	Pte	02/06/18	Desertion	15yrs PS	F&F	213/23	
Spry William	2 Royal Fus	Pte	02/06/18	Desertion	XXX 14/06/18	F&F	213/22	919

Name	Unit	Rank	Date	Offence	Final sentence	Location	Ref	Note
Millen W	1 R Inniskilling Fus	Pte	03/06/18	Desertion	10yrs PS	F&F	213/23	
Smith W	2 KO Yorks LI	Pte	03/06/18	Desertion	3yrs PS	F&F	213/22	
Hudson E	2 Leicestershire	Pte	04/06/18	Desertion	5yrs PS	Egypt	213/24	
Rose A	Hawke Bn RNVR	A/B	04/06/18	Desertion	5yrs PS		213/22	
Giles AE	9 Welsh	Pte	05/06/18	Desertion	15yrs PS	F&F	213/23	
Zorn F	78 Canadian EF	Pte	05/06/18	Desertion	10yrs PS	F&F	213/23	
Brewster LN	8 London	Pte	06/06/18	Quitting	2yrs HL	F&F	213/23	
Hannah J	18 Highland LI	Pte	06/06/18	Desertion	5yrs PS	F&F	213/23	920
Butcher Frederick Charles	7 E Kent (Buffs)	Pte	07/06/18	Desertion	5yrs PS	F&F	213/23	921
Merrills W	7 E Kent (Buffs)	Pte	07/06/18	Desertion	5yrs PS	F&F	213/23	
Affleck A	S African Regt	Pte	08/06/18	Desertion	15yrs PS		213/24	
Day J	2 R Scots Fus	Pte	08/06/18	Desertion x3	10yrs PS	F&F	213/24	
Dossett Walter	1/4 York & Lancaster	Pte	08/06/18	Desertion	XXX 25/06/18	F&F	213/23	922
Fowkes J	10 Worcestershire	Pte	08/06/18	Desertion	Not Conf	F&F	213/23	
Foster T	2/5 W Yorks	Pte	11/06/18	Desertion	5yrs PS	F&F	213/22	
Haines FG	2/4 R Berkshire	Pte	11/06/18	Desertion	15yrs PS	F&F	213/23	
Houlton W	2/5 Lancs Fus	Pte	11/06/18	Desertion	5yrs PS	F&F	213/24	
Howarth J	1/4 Loyal N Lancs	Pte	11/06/18	Desertion	5yrs PS	F&F	213/23	
Coward J	2 E Lancs	Pte	12/06/18	Cowardice	10yrs PS	F&F	213/24	
Duckworth A	2 E Lancs	Pte	12/06/18	Cowardice	10yrs PS	F&F	213/24	
Harrison S	2 E Lancs	Pte	12/06/18	Cowardice	5yrs PS	F&F	213/24	
Lane FJ	2 E Lancs	Pte	12/06/18	Cowardice	10yrs PS	F&F	213/24	
Parsons E	2 E Lancs	Pte	12/06/18	Cowardice	10yrs PS	F&F	213/24	
Spear J	5 R Berkshire	Pte	12/06/18	Desertion	5yrs PS	F&F	213/22	
Thomason TJ	2 E Lancs	Pte	12/06/18	Cowardice	5yrs PS	F&F	213/24	
Gellibrand J	1 E Lancs	Pte	13/06/18	Desertion	15yrs PS	F&F	213/23	
Willis J	2 Wiltshire	Pte	13/06/18	Desertion x2	15 yrs PS	F&F	213/23	923
McAdam A	1/7 Highland LI	Pte	14/06/18	Desertion	5yrs PS	F&F	213/23	924
McDowall F	1/7 Highland LI	Pte	14/06/18	Desertion	5yrs PS	F&F	213/23	925
Wang En Yung	Chinese Lab Corps	Coolie	14/06/18	Against Inhab	XXX 26/06/18	F&F	213/24	926
Yang Ch'ing Shan	Chinese Lab Corps	Coolie	14/06/18	Against Inhab	XXX 26/06/18	F&F	213/24	927
Lister H	49 MGC	Pte	15/06/18	Desertion	10yrs PS		213/23	
Lawrence H	5 MGC	Pte	16/06/18	Desertion	5yrs PS		213/23	
Mayne FG	1 D Cornwall LI	Pte	16/06/18	Desertion	5yrs PS	F&F	213/23	
Jackson J	8 York & Lancaster	Pte	17/06/18	Desertion	15yrs PS	Italy	213/24	
Jackson JH	1 KO Scottish Bdrs	Pte	17/06/18	Desertion	15yrs PS	F&F	213/24	
Cunnington C	16 Lancs Fus	Pte	18/06/18	Sleeping	5yrs PS	F&F	213/22	928
Anon No 70618	Chinese Lab Corps	Coolie	20/06/18	Striking +	5yrs PS	F&F	213/24	929
Potter J L	11 A&S Hdrs	Pte	25/06/18	Desertion	10yrs PS	F&F	213/23	
Richard A	22 Canadian EF	Pte	25/06/18	Desertion	Not Conf	F&F	213/25	
Betts W	2/5 Gloucestershire	Pte	26/06/18	Desertion	2yrs HL	F&F	213/24	930
Roberts E	2/5 Gloucestershire	Pte	26/06/18	Desertion	2yrs HL	F&F	213/23	931
Walker GW	8 Sherwood Fstrs	Pte	27/06/18	Desertion	Not Conf	F&F	213/24	
Vaughan W	8 N Staffordshire	Pte	28/06/18	Desertion	15yrs PS	F&F	213/24	
Rothwell J	10 Lancs Fus	Pte	29/06/18	Desertion	5yrs PS	F&F	213/23	
Burke EW	2 R Sussex	Pte	30/06/18	Desertion	10yrs PS	F&F	213/24	
Bossana Dezari	Gold Coast Regt	Pte	01/07/18	Murder	Not Conf	East Africa	213/27	932
McGrath D	1/19 London	Pte	01/07/18	Desertion	5yrs PS	F&F	213/23	933
Thompson G	1/19 London	Pte	01/07/18	Desertion	5yrs PS	F&F	213/23	934
Tseng Sung Kung	60 Chinese Lab Corps	Coolie	01/07/18	Murder	XXX 23/07/18	F&F	213/23	935
Irwin S	1 R Scots Fus	Pte	02/07/18	Desertion	10yrs PS	F&F	213/23	
Meadowcroft F	8 KOR Lancaster	Pte	02/07/18	Desertion	10yrs Ps	F&F	213/23	
Fogerty J	11 Rifle Bde	Rfm	04/07/18	Desertion	5yrs PS	F&F	213/24	
Briggs Arthur	9 Sherwood Fstrs	Pte	05/07/18	Desertion	XXX 19/07/18	F&F	213/24	936
Kane J	2 R Scots Fus	Pte	05/07/18	Desertion	10yrs PS	F&F	213/23	
Turner W	8 Seaforth Hdrs	Pte	05/07/18	Desertion	10yrs PS	Egypt	213/31	
Munro NA	6 Australian IF	Pte	06/07/18	Desertion	10yrs PS		213/23	
Scholes William	2 S Wales Bdrs	Pte	06/07/18	Desertion	XXX 10/08/18	F&F	213/24	937
Dowling J	Connaught Rangers	Pte (L/C)	08/07/18	Aiding enemy x3	PS Life	UK	92/4	938
Johnson Frederick (false)	2 Border	Pte	08/07/18	Desertion	XXX 01/08/18	F&F	213/24	939
Ling Wilson N	2 Canadian EF	Pte	08/07/18	Desertion	XXX 12/08/18	F&F	213/24	940
McClair Harry	2 Border	Pte	08/07/18	Desertion	XXX 01/08/18	F&F	213/24	941
Milligan G	Hood Bn R Naval VR	A/B	09/07/18	Desertion	5yrs PS		213/23	
Morrall AG	10 R Warwickshire	Pte	09/07/18	Quitting	10yrs PS	F&F	213/24	
Potts T	5 Durham LI	Pte	09/07/18	Desertion	5yrs PS	F&F	213/24	
Rascid S	Turkish Army	POW	10/07/18	Murder	XXX		213/24	
Daoud M	Turkish Army	POW	11/07/18	Mutiny	2yrs HL		213/24	
Ainley George	1/4 KO Yorks LI	Pte	13/07/18	Desertion x3	XXX 30/07/18	F&F	213/24	942

Name	Unit	Rank	Date	Offence	Final sentence	Location	Ref	Note
Poole RS	1/4 KO Yorks LI	Pte	13/07/18	Desertion	10yrs PS	F&F	213/23	
Malia J	RE	Spr	14/07/18	Striking +	5yrs PS		213/24	943
Richardson W	4/5 Black Watch	Pte	15/07/18	Desertion	10yrs PS	F&F	213/25	
Doyle J	1 N Staffordshire	Pte	16/07/18	Sleeping	2yrs HL	F&F	213/24	
Hale J	1 N Staffordshire	Pte	16/07/18	Sleeping	2yrs HL	F&F	213/24	
Villiers V	2 Manchester	Pte	16/07/18	Desertion	10yrs PS	F&F	213/23	
Wood T	12 E Surrey	Pte	16/07/18	Desertion	10yrs PS	F&F	213/24	944
Beal EJ	7 E Yorks	Gnr	17/07/18	Desertion	5yrs PS	F&F	213/24	
Ziff S	38 Royal Fus	Pte	17/07/18	Sleeping	10yrs PS	Egypt	213/26	
Burgess H	2 Coldstream Gds	Pte	18/07/18	Desertion x3 +	5yrs PS	F&F	213/24	945
Cunningham H	2 York & Lancaster	Pte	18/07/18	Desertion	10yrs PS	F&F	213/24	
Marshall T	29 MGC	Pte	18/07/18	Desertion	10yrs PS		213/24	
Owen JE	27 Canadian EF	Pte	18/07/18	Desertion	10yrs PS	F&F	213/25	
Bell SE	11 E Yorks	Pte	22/07/18	Desertion	10yrs PS	F&F	213/24	
Ridsdale W	6 Cheshire	Pte	22/07/18	Desertion	10yrs PS	F&F	213/24	
Butcher Frederick C	7 E Kent (Buffs)	Pte	23/07/18	Desertion	XXX 27/08/18	F&F	213/25	946
Jacobs CP	S African ASC	Dvr	23/07/18	Mutiny+	10yrs PS		213/24	947
Purkin D	1 Gordon Hdrs	Pte	23/07/18	Desertion	10yrs PS	F&F	213/24	
Barrett J	RGA	Gnr	25/07/18	Desertion	5yrs PS		213/24	
Chao Hsing I	Chinese Lab Corps	Coolie	25/07/18	Murder	XXX 09/08/18	F&F	213/24	948
Gull J	1 E Kent (Buffs)	Pte	25/07/18	Sleeping x2	5yrs PS	F&F	213/24	
May P	1/24 London	Pte	25/07/18	Sleeping	1yr HL	F&F	213/24	
O'Connell Benjamin	1 Irish Gds	Pte	25/07/18	Desertion	XXX 08/08/18	F&F	213/24	949
Baker William	26 Royal Fus	Pte	26/07/18	Desertion x2	XXX 14/08/18	F&F	213/24	950
King W	7 R Sussex	Pte	26/07/18	Desertion	5yrs PS	F&F	213/24	
Stevenson David	13 Middlesex	Pte	26/07/18	Desertion	XXX 18/07/18	F&F	213/23	951
Swain John	5 R Berkshire	Pte	26/07/18	Desertion	XXX11/08/18	F&F	213/24	952
Mahomed N	Malay States Garr Regt	Sepoy	27/07/18	Striking/AWOL	2yrs HL	Aden	90/7	953
Compton W	1 Norfolk	Pte	29/07/18	Desertion	10yrs PS	F&F	213/24	
Gazzard JC	1/11 London	Pte	30/07/18	Striking +	2yrs HL	Egypt	213/24	954
Hendricks Henry	2 Leinster	Pte	30/07/18	Desertion	XXX 23/08/18	F&F	213/24	955
Lawson W	10 A&S Hdrs	Pte	01/08/18	Desertion x2	15yrs PS	F&F	213/25	
Moore H	1/5 S Lancs	L/Cpl	01/08/18	Desertion	5yrs PS	F&F	213/24	
Wilson [?] CA	5 British West Indies	Pte	01/08/18	Striking x2	5yrs PS		213/26	956
Greenlagh JT	1 R Marines LI	Pte	02/08/18	Desertion	10yrs PS		213/24	
Andrews M	9 Northumb Fus	Pte	04/08/18	Desertion	5yrs PS		213/24	
Davies T	32 MGC	Pte	04/08/18	Desertion	5yrs PS		213/24	
Rogers R	9 Northumb Fus	Pte	04/08/18	Desertion	5yrs PS	F&F	213/24	
Cowell AF	1 Middlesex	Pte	07/08/18	Desertion	10yrs PS	F&F	213/24	
Owen T	8 R W Surrey	Pte	07/08/18	Desertion	5yrs PS	F&F	213/25	
Nesbit Joseph	1 Leicestershire	Pte	08/08/18	Desertion	XXX 23/08/18	F&F	213/24	957
Nicholson J	1 R Berkshire	Pte	08/08/18	Disobedience x2	5yrs PS	F&F	213/24	
Fielding F	1/4 York & Lancaster	Pte	10/08/18	Sleeping	10yrs PS	F&F	213/24	958
Hanlon James [Tade]	RFA	Gnr	10/08/18	Desertion	Not Conf		213/24	
Shawcross A	1/7 Manchester	Pte	10/08/18	Desertion	5yrs pS	F&F	213/24	
Tickle E	1/7 Manchester	Pte	10/08/18	Desertion	5yrs PS	F&F	213/24	
Parrott JC	13 R Inniskilling Fus	Pte	11/08/18	Desertion	5yrs PS	F&F	213/24	
Stovin E	10 E Yorks	Pte	12/08/18	Desertion	15yrs PS		213/25	959
Welsh T	10 Royal Fus	Pte	13/08/18	Desertion	5yrs PS	F&F	213/25	
Entwhistle PJ	17 Lancs Fus	Pte	14/08/18	Desertion	10yrs PS	F&F	213/24	960
Parker HP	RFA	Pte	14/08/18	Desertion	10yrs PS		213/26	
Smith T	1 R Irish	Pte	14/08/18	Murder	Not Conf	Egypt	213/29	
Thomas H	2 Hampshire	Pte	15/08/18	Desertion x2	10yrs PS	F&F	213/24	
Dunn T	RFA	Gnr	16/08/18	Sleeping	10yrs PS		213/25	
Haque S	6 York & Lancaster	Pte	16/08/18	Desertion	10yrs PS	F&F	213/25	
Burgess GF	723 Lab Corps	Pte	17/08/18	Desertion	Not Conf		213/25	
Dagless JA	1/7 W Yorks	Rfm	17/08/18	Desertion	10yrs PS	F&F	213/24	961
Jones A	1 Northumb Fus	Pte	18/08/18	Desertion	5yrs PS	F&F	213/24	
Maidment J	8 KOR Lancaster	Pte	18/08/18	Desertion	5yrs PS	F&F	213/24	
Murphy Patrick	47 MGC	Pte	19/08/18	Desertion	XXX 12/09/18	F&F	213/25	962
O'Shea T	18 Durham LI	Pte	19/08/18	Desertion	10yrs PS	F&F	213/24	963
Sibun G	1/20 London	Pte	19/08/18	Desertion	5yrs PS	F&F	213/25	964
Todd EH	1/20 London	Pte	19/08/18	Desertion	5yrs PS	F&F	213/25	965
Brookes W	25 KRRC	Rfm	20/08/18	Against Inhab +	10yrs PS	F&F	213/24	966
Lovatt C	8 N Staffordshire	Pte	20/08/18	Desertion	15yrs PS	F&F	213/25	
Caton H	4 KOR Lancaster	Pte	21/08/18	Desertion	5yrs PS		213/25	
James W	4 KOR Lancaster	Pte	21/08/18	Desertion	7yrs PS		213/25	
Martin J	1/5 KOR Lancaster	Pte	25/08/18	Desertion	5yrs PS	F&F	213/25	

Name	Unit	Rank	Date	Offence	Final sentence	Location	Ref	Note
Broughton TH	13 York and Lancaster	Pte	26/08/18	Desertion	10yrs PS	F&F	213/24	967
Brown J	18 Durham LI	Pte	26/08/18	Desertion	10yrs PS	F&F	213/25	968
Golder E	12 KRRC	Pte	26/08/18	Sleeping	3yrs PS	F&F	213/25	
Hui I He	Chinese Lab Corps	Coolie	26/08/18	Murder	XXX 12/09/18	F&F	213/25	969
Jones T	17 Manchester	Pte	26/08/18	Desertion/Esc	10yrs PS	F&F	213/26	
Long S	2 KO Yorks LI	Pte	26/08/18	Desertion	10yrs PS	F&F	213/25	
Lafond R	22 Canadian EF	Pte	28/08/18	Desertion	7yrs PS	F&F	213/25	
Mainguy O	22 Canadian EF	Pte	28/08/18	Desertion x2	7yrs PS	F&F	213/25	
Peloquin C	22 Canadian EF	Pte	28/08/18	Desertion	7yrs PS	F&F	213/25	
Covell FR	2/4 R W Surrey	Sgt	29/08/18	Desertion	10yrs PS	F&F	213/25	
Davies WR	11/2 Manchester	Pte	29/08/18	Desertion	10yrs PS		213/24	
Annison T	S African Comp Bn	Pte	30/08/18	Desertion	10yrs PS		213/27	
Bateman Frank	1/4 York & Lancaster	Pte	30/08/18	Desertion	XXX 10/09/18	F&F	213/25	970
Grainger S	3 Worcestershire	Pte	30/08/18	Desertion x3	15yrs PS	F&F	213/25	
Lochland J	13 R Scots	Pte	30/08/18	Desertion	5yrs PS	F&F	213/25	
Donaghy P	22 Northumb Fus	Pte	02/09/18	Desertion x2	10yrs PS	F&F	213/25	971
Mills T	22 Northumb Fus	Pte	02/09/18	Desertion	10yrs PS		213/25	
Hughes R	11 R Scots	Pte	03/09/18	Desertion +	10yrs PS	F&F	213/25	972
Coles GH	1/5 Suffolk	Pte	06/09/18	Violence/Esc	5yrs PS	Palestine	213/27	
Duffin M	7 Seaforth Hdrs	Pte	06/09/18	Desertion	10yrs PS	F&F	213/25	
Wilden H	1/5 Suffolk	Pte	06/09/18	Violence +	Not Conf	Egypt	213/27	973
Curnew JB	3 Canadian MGC	Pte	09/09/18	Desertion	5yrs PS	F&F	213/25	
Howe E	1 R W Surrey	Pte	09/09/18	Desertion	5yrs PS	F&F	213/25	
Knight Harry T	1 R W Surrey	Pte	09/09/18	Desertion	XXX 06/10/18	F&F	213/25	974
Short E	12 Highland LI	Pte	09/09/18	Desertion	10yrs PS	F&F	213/25	
Smith E	5 Scottish Rifles	Pte	09/09/18	Desertion	5yrs PS	F&F	213/25	
St Leger EF	RFA	Gnr	09/09/18	Desertion	10yrs PS		213/25	
Gibson David	12 R Scots	Pte	10/09/18	Desertion x2	XXX 24/09/18	F&F	213/25	975
McArthur A	12 R Scots	Pte	10/09/18	Desertion	15yrs PS	F&F	213/25	
Mound W	12 R Scots	Pte	10/09/18	Desertion x2	15yrs PS	F&F	213/25	
Schofield W	2 Lancs Fus	Pte	10/09/18	Desertion x2	10yrs PS	F&F	213/25	
Williams T	RGA	Gnr	10/09/18	Desertion	10yrs PS		213/25	
Young Robert	11 Worcestershire	Pte	10/09/18	Desertion	XXX 18/09/18	Salonika	213/25	976
Britton J	8 Canadian EF	Pte	11/09/18	Desertion	10yrs PS	F&F	213/25	
Paterson John H	1 Essex	2 Lt	11/09/18	Murder +	XXX 24/09/18	F&F	90/8	977
Greenwood DD	78 Canadian EF	Pte	12/09/18	Desertion	15yrs PS	F&F	213/25	
Harris H	1/4 KOR Lancaster	Pte	12/09/18	Against Inhab	10yrs PS	F&F	213/26	
Labrum H	4 Worcestershire	Pte	12/09/18	Desertion	10yrs PS	F&F	213/25	
McNaught M	1 R Dublin Fus	Pte	12/09/18	Desertion	10yrs PS	F&F	213/25	
Norton P	1 R Dublin Fus	Pte	12/09/18	Desertion	10yrs PS	F&F	213/25	
White J	Leinster (att 1 R Dublin)	Pte	12/09/18	Desertion	10yrs PS	F&F	213/25	
Dawson C	2 Leicestershire	Pte	13/09/18	Sleeping	10yrs PS	Egypt	213/26	
Fee J	2 R Scots	Pte	13/09/18	Desertion	15yrs PS	F&F	213/25	
Tuke H	R Marines LI	Pte	13/09/18	Desertion	5yrs PS	F&F	213/25	
Harrigan T	13 R Scots	Pte	14/09/18	Desertion	10yrs PS	F&F	213/26	
Busby H	7 R Berkshire	Pte	16/09/18	Desertion	15yrs PS	Salonika	213/26	
Elmer CH	10 Canadian FA	Dvr	16/09/18	Desertion x2	5yrs PS	F&F	213/29	
Jeffrey EAV	155 Lab Coy	Pte	16/09/18	Desertion	5yrs PS		213/28	
Campbell T	1/4 Seaforth Hdrs	Pte	20/09/18	Desertion x2	10yrs PS	F&F	213/25	978
Elford Lawrence	7/8 KO Scottish Bdrs	Pte	20/09/18	Desertion	XXX 11/10/18	F&F	213/25	979
Ottaway MW	Canadian Engrs	Pte	20/09/18	Desertion	7yrs PS	F&F	213/25	
Millar EA	1 Canadian MGC	Pte	22/09/18	Desertion	5yrs PS	F&F	213/25	
Phillips A	1 Canadian MGC	Pte	22/09/18	Desertion	5yrs PS	F&F	213/25	
Bramwell J	15 Sherwood Fstrs	Pte	23/09/18	Desertion	10yrs PS	F&F	213/25	980
Woitytzka W	German Army	POW	23/09/18	Striking +	1yr HL		213/26	981
Blenkiron William	9 Durham LI	Pte	24/09/18	Disobedience x3	90 days FP1		213/25	
O'Hare S	2 Scottish Rifles	Pte	24/09/18	Against Inhab	7yrs PS	F&F	213/25	
Sandelin HF	4 Canadian Mtd Rifles	Pte	24/09/18	Desertion	5yrs PS	F&F	213/27	
Hodgkiss G	Leinster	Pte	25/09/18	Desertion x2	10yrs PS		213/28	
Veryard Frederick G	13 Middlesex	Pte	25/09/18	Desertion	10yrs PS	F&F	213/25	
Palchett E	5 MGC	Pte	26/09/18	Desertion	5yrs PS		213/25	
Tolley J	7 Liverpool	Pte	26/09/18	Desertion	Not Conf	F&F	213/26	982
Wallace J	6 Liverpool	Pte	26/09/18	Desertion	5yrs PS		213/26	
Hornby E	11 E Lancs	Pte	27/09/18	Desertion	10yrs PS	F&F	213/25	
McKay A	Seaforth Hdrs	Pte	27/09/18	Desertion	7yrs PS		213/25	
Lowrie J	192 Lab Coy	Pte	28/09/18	Desertion	5yrs PS		213/25	
Ridding WH	2 Wiltshire	Pte	28/09/18	Desertion	1yr HL	F&F	213/26	
Walker F	7 R Sussex	Pte	28/09/18	Desertion	5yrs PS	F&F	213/25	

Name	Unit	Rank	Date	Offence	Final sentence	Location	Ref	Note
Saffer Samuel	1/18 London	Rfm	30/09/18	Desertion	5yrs PS	F&F	213/26	983
Currie R	11 R Scots Fus	Pte	02/10/18	Desertion	5yrs PS	F&F	213/26	
Robinson R	Labour Corps	Pte	02/10/18	Desertion	5yrs PS	F&F	213/27	
Underhill H	7 W Yorks	Pte	02/10/18	Desertion	5yrs PS	F&F	213/25	
Magee T	RGA	Gnr	03/10/18	Desertion	10yrs PS		213/25	
Baker J	4/5 Black Watch	Pte	04/10/18	Desertion	5yrs PS	F&F	213/26	
Phoraoh James T	2/5 York & Lancaster	Pte	06/10/18	Desertion	5yrs PS	F&F	213/25	
Frankham G	3 MGC	Pte	10/10/18	Desertion	10yrs PS		213/25	
Johnson J	1 Northumb Fus	Pte	10/10/18	Desertion	5yrs PS	F&F	213/25	
Reilly C	2 Highland LI	Pte	10/10/18	Desertion	5yrs PS	F&F	213/25	
Arme A	13 R Scots	Pte	11/10/18	Desertion	7yrs PS	F&F	213/26	
Gatley W	1/4 R Welsh Fus	Pte	12/10/18	Desertion	3yrs PS	F&F	213/26	
Smith LP	1/24 London	Pte	12/10/18	Desertion	3yrs PS	F&F	213/26	
Attridge WT	1 Northants	Pte	14/10/18	Desertion	5yrs PS	F&F	213/26	
Bennett H	7 Leicestershire	Pte	14/10/18	Mutiny	15yrs PS	F&F	213/26	
Clarke G	13 York and Lancaster	Pte	14/10/18	Desertion	10yrs PS	F&F	213/25	984
Knight F	7 Leicestershire	Pte	14/10/18	Mutiny	15yrs PS	F&F	213/26	
Barrass R	1 Northants	Pte	15/10/18	Desertion	5yrs PS	F&F	213/26	
Brown J	1 Gloucestershire	Pte	15/10/18	Desertion	5yrs PS	F&F	213/26	
McGaskell J	2 R Scots	Pte	15/10/18	Against Inhab	2yrs PS	F&F	213/26	
Jackson Ernest	24 Royal Fus	Pte	16/10/18	Desertion	XXX 07/11/18	F&F	213/26	985
Hetherington A	8 KOR Lancaster	Pte	17/10/18	Desertion	5yrs PS	F&F	213/25	
McManus P	7 Middlesex	Pte	17/10/18	Desertion	10yrs PS	F&F	213/26	
Button FH	43 Canadian EF	Pte	18/10/18	Desertion	15yrs PS	F&F	213/26	
Dick A	6 R Scots Fus	Pte	18/10/18	Desertion	10yrs PS	F&F	213/26	
Wyles C	2 Yorks	Pte	18/10/18	Desertion	10yrs PS	F&F	213/26	
Harris Louis	10 W Yorks	Pte	19/10/18	Cowardice+	XXX 07/11/18	F&F	213/26	986
McKay P	2 Highland LI	Pte	19/10/18	Desertion	5yrs PS	F&F	213/25	
Campbell JW	3 Canadian MGC	Pte	20/10/18	Desertion	15yrs PS	F&F	213/26	
Dean EC	3 Canadian MGC	Pte	20/10/18	Desertion	15yrs PS	F&F	213/26	
Melvin R [aka Haig H]	2 A & S Hdrs	Pte	20/10/18	Desertion	15yrs PS	F&F	213/27	
Murree C	3 Canadian MGC	Pte	20/10/18	Desertion	15yrs PS	F&F	213/26	
Harrington A	2 R Scots	Pte	21/10/18	Desertion	5yrs PS	F&F	213/25	
Stower E	2 S Staffordshire	Pte	22/10/18	Desertion x2	5yrs PS	F&F	213/25	
Borrana Dezari	Gold Coast Regt	Pte	23/10/18	Murder	XXX 10/11/18	F&F	213/27	987
Gould RS	1 Norfolk	Pte	23/10/18	Desertion	5yrs PS	F&F	213/25	
Williams G	4 Royal Fus	Pte	26/10/18	Desertion	5yrs PS	F&F	213/25	
Davies JT	1 Kings Shropshire LI	Pte	27/10/18	Desertion	5yrs PS	F&F	213/26	
Whyte J	2 Yorks	Pte	27/10/18	Desertion	15yrs PS	F&F	213/26	
Orr B	22 Northumb Fus	Pte	28/10/18	Desertion x2	15yrs PS	F&F	213/26	988
Exley J	6 Manchester	Pte	29/10/18	Desertion	5yrs PS	F&F	213/26	
Foster G	2 S Staffordshire	Pte	29/10/18	Desertion	15yrs PS	F&F	213/26	
Crowley W	1 Welsh Gds	Sgt	31/10/18	Cowardice	Not Conf	F&F	213/26	
Hawkins G	10 E Yorks	Pte	01/11/18	Desertion	10yrs PS		213/26	
Moore H	1 Middlesex	Pte	01/11/18	Desertion x2	Quashed	F&F	213/27	
Stewart W	3 Middlesex	Pte	01/11/18	Desertion	PS Life	Salonika	213/28	
George AH	1 Manchester	Rfm	02/11/18	Desertion	5yrs PS	Palestine	213/27	
Lyddy P	2 Leinster	Pte	02/11/18	Desertion x4	15yrs PS	Salonika	213/28	
Murphy T	2 Leinster	Pte	02/11/18	Desertion x2	10yrs PS	F&F	213/28	
Walsh [?] J	1 R Inniskilling Fus	Pte	03/11/18	Against Inhab	15yrs PS		213/26	989
Goldie W	17 R Scots	Pte	04/11/18	Desertion	5yrs PS	F&F	213/27	990
Smith A	19 Durham LI	Pte	04/11/18	Desertion	10yrs PS	F&F	213/26	991
King AW	11 Essex	Pte	05/11/18	Desertion	15yrs PS	F&F	213/25	
Marvin A	20 Middlesex	Pte	06/11/18	Desertion	5yrs PS	F&F	213/26	992
Taylor W	6 R W Surrey	Pte	06/11/18	Desertion	10yrs PS	F&F	213/27	
Betts W	13 R Inniskilling Fus	Pte	07/11/18	Desertion	5yrs PS	F&F	213/26	
Cotter D	1 R Munster Fus	Pte	07/11/18	Desertion	2yrs HL	F&F	213/27	
Ealing S	1 R Warwickshire	Pte	07/11/18	Desertion	5yrs PS	F&F	213/27	
Hughes W	1 R Munster Fus	Pte	07/11/18	Desertion	2yrs HL	F&F	213/27	
Lloyd W	1 R Munster Fus	Pte	07/11/18	Desertion	2yrs HL	F&F	213/27	
Blenkin S	7 E Yorks	Pte	08/11/18	Desertion x2	5yrs PS	F&F	213/26	
Green AG	4 Royal Fus	Pte	08/11/18	Desertion	5yrs PS	F&F	213/27	
Groves WL	4 Royal Fus	Pte	08/11/18	Desertion x2	15yrs PS	F&F	213/27	
Jamieson N	7 E Lancs	Pte	08/11/18	Desertion x2/Esc	5yrs PS	F&F	213/26	
Butcher J	4 Grenadier Gds	Pte	09/11/18	Desertion	Not Conf	F&F	213/26	
Higgins W	11 R Scots	Pte	10/11/18	Desertion	3yrs PS	F&F	213/26	
Bentley W	15 Durham LI	Pte	11/11/18	Desertion x2	5yrs PS	F&F	213/26	
Nelson A	2 R Scots Fus	Pte	12/11/18	Desertion	10yrs PS	F&F	213/26	

Name	Unit	Rank	Date	Offence	Final sentence	Location	Ref	Note
Bolton J	2/7 Liverpool	Pte	14/11/18	Desertion	5yrs PS	F&F	213/27	
McGhee D	1 KOR Lancaster	Pte	14/11/18	Desertion	5yrs PS	F&F	213/27	
Murphy D	1 KOR Lancaster	Pte	14/11/18	Desertion	7yrs PS	F&F	213/27	
Milligan J	2 R Scots	Pte	15/11/18	Desertion	5yrs PS	F&F	213/27	
Herbert F	4 S African Infantry	Pte	16/11/18	Desertion	5yrs PS		213/27	
Parkin J	4 S African Infantry	Pte	16/11/18	Desertion x2	5yrs PS		213/27	
Hodges J	2 S Wales Bdrs	Pte	17/11/18	Desertion	10yrs PS	F&F	213/27	
Vaughan W	8 N Staffordshire	Pte	17/11/18	Desertion	15yrs PS	F&F	213/27	
Compton D	1 R W Kent	Pte	18/11/18	Desertion	5yrs PS	F&F	213/27	
Pitchford J	1 Northumb Fus	Pte	18/11/18	Desertion	5yrs PS	F&F	213/27	
Walker W	7 E Yorks	Pte	18/11/18	Desertion	15yrs PS		213/26	
Davies J	15 Welsh	Pte (L/C)	19/11/18	Desertion	5yrs PS	F&F	213/26	993
Smith R	1 R W Surrey	Pte	19/11/18	Desertion	5yrs PS	F&F	213/26	
McEwan JA	1 Lincolnshire	Pte	21/11/18	Desertion	5yrs PS	F&F	213/26	
Lidster A	2 York & Lancaster	Pte	22/11/18	Desertion	10yrs PS	F&F	213/27	
Frew J	2/10 R Scots	Pte	23/11/18	Civil Offence	5yrs PS	N Russia	213/28	
Richmond J	2/10 R Scots	Pte	23/11/18	Civil Offence	5yrs PS	N Russia	213/28	
Turner C	RFA	Dvr	23/11/18	Desertion	5yrs PS		213/26	
Wilson A	1 R Irish Rifles	Pte	26/11/18	Desertion x2	10yrs PS	F&F	213/27	
Collis W	9 Royal Fus	Pte	27/11/18	Disobedience	5yrs PS	F&F	213/28	
Denny Albert	8 British West Indies	Pte	03/12/18	Murder	XXX 20/01/19	Italy	90/8	994
Williams J	2/4 Oxon & Bucks LI	Pte	04/12/18	Desertion	5yrs PS	F&F	213/26	
Bazinett E	10 R Warwickshire	Pte	07/12/18	Desertion	5yrs PS	F&F	213/27	
Bettney E	10 R Warwickshire	Pte	07/12/18	Desertion	10yrs PS	F&F	213/27	
Duchart J	1 R Irish Rifles	Pte	10/12/18	Desertion	10yrs PS	F&F	213/29	
Johnson A	2 Canadian Const Coy	Pte	10/12/18	Murder	15yrs PS	F&F	213/28	
Khan M	RGA	Gnr	13/12/18	Murder	PS Life		213/29	
Dewar JW	10/11 Highland LI	Pte	14/12/18	Against Inhab x2+	20yrs PS	F&F	213/27	995
Flanagan J	1 Liverpool	Pte	14/12/18	Against Inhab x2+	20yrs PS	F&F	213/27	996
Pound F	2 R Berkshire	Pte	23/12/18	Desertion	2yrs HL	F&F	213/27	
Labrum H	4 Worcestershire	Pte	24/12/18	Desertion	10yrs PS	F&F	213/27	
Laverock R	11 Rifle Bde	Rfm	26/12/18	Desertion x3	15yrs PS	F&F	213/27	
Sanches A	9 British West Indies	Pte	27/12/18	Mutiny	20yrs PS	Italy	213/27	
Anon No 4976	Chinese Lab Corps	Coolie	28/12/18	Against Inhab x2+	To be XXX	F&F	213/28	997
Wan Fa Yu	Chinese Lab Corps	Coolie	28/12/18	Against Inhab x2+	XXX 15/01/19	F&F	213/28	998
Ashby W	1 Norfolk	Pte	29/12/18	Desertion	5yrs PS	F&F	213/27	999
Atkins P	18 KRRC	Rfm	30/12/18	Desertion	10yrs PS	F&F	213/29	1000
Haithwaite C	8 W Yorks	Rfm	30/12/18	Desertion x2	10yrs PS	F&F	213/27	
Newton WE	RFA	Pte	31/12/18	Desertion x2	10yrs PS		213/27	
Scarffe A	9 R Inniskilling Fus	Pte	31/12/18	Desertion	5yrs PS	F&F	213/29	1001
Lochland J	13 R Scots	Pte	08/01/19	Desertion	5yrs PS	F&F	213/28	
Boyce J	8 Black Watch	Pte	09/01/19	Desertion	10yrs PS	F&F	213/27	
Coleman J	1 R Warwickshire	Pte	09/01/19	Desertion	15yrs PS	F&F	213/28	
Knight WE	1/5 London	Rfm	21/01/19	Desertion	5yrs PS	F&F	213/28	1002
Sumner J	1 Middlesex	Pte	21/01/19	Desertion	2yrs HL	F&F	213/28	
Unwin J	8 N Staffordshire	Pte	22/01/19	Desertion	5yrs PS	F&F	213/27	
Smith W	4 Seaforth Hdrs	Pte	24/01/19	Desertion	5yrs PS	F&F	213/28	
Walklate GF	1 KOR Lancaster	L/Cpl	06/02/19	Desertion	5yrs PS	F&F	213/28	
Alli Checkmamid O	Civilian		17/02/19	Murder	XXX (Hanged)	T'caucasia	213/34	
Mayne FG	1 D Cornwall LI	Pte	18/02/19	Desertion	10yrs PS	F&F	213/28	
Emm A	13 Northumb Fus	Pte	19/02/19	Desertion	10yrs PS	F&F	213/28	
Lamude WT	1 S African Infantry	Pte	19/02/19	Desertion	5yrs PS		213/28	
Mohammedoff Meshadie AO	Civilian		21/02/19	Robbery	10yrs PS	Baku	213/34	
Dahashev Mohammed	Civilian		24/02/19	Murder	Not Conf	Baku	213/34	
Riddle J	11 Scottish Rifles	Pte (L/C)	24/02/19	Desertion	10yrs PS	Macedonia	213/28	
Curnew JB	3 Canadian MGC	Pte	24/03/19	Mutiny	PS Life	F&F	213/29	
McDonnell C	3 Canadian MGC	Pte	24/03/19	Mutiny	PS Life	F&F	213/29	
Pritchard SP	6 Kings Shropshire LI	Pte	24/03/19	Mutiny	PS Life	F&F	213/29	
Fensome R	2 Rifle Bde	Rfm	26/03/19	Desertion	5yrs PS	F&F	213/30	
Ramazan Bairam O	Civilian		27/03/19	Aiding Enemy	PS Life	T'caucasia	213/34	1003
Anon No 39237	Chinese Lab Corps	Coolie	03/04/19	Murder	Not Conf	F&F	213/29	
Wang Ch'un Ch'ih	Chinese Lab Corps	Coolie	14/04/19	Murder	XXX 08/05/19	F&F	213/29	1004
Illin Andrew	Civilian		20/04/19	Murder	3yrs PS	Turkey	213/34	1005
Chang Ju Chih	Chinese Lab Corps	Coolie	05/05/19	Murder x4	XXX 14/02/20	F&F	213/31	1006
Hamdi Mehmed	3 Turkish Army	POW	09/05/19	Murder	XXX	Egypt	213/29	1007
Khalil Mehmed H	7 Turkish Army	POW	09/05/19	Murder	XXX	Egypt	213/29	1008
Moussa Ahmed	7 Turkish Army	POW	09/05/19	Murder	XXX	Egypt	213/29	1009
Melkoniantz Gregorieff	Civilian		16/05/19	Murder	Not Conf	S Russia	213/34	1010

Name	Unit	Rank	Date	Offence	Final sentence	Location	Ref	Note
Willis Frank	RFA	Gnr	17/05/19	Murder	XXX 27/05/19	F&F	213/29	1011
Gamal RE	Civilian		19/05/19	Treason	10yrs Det	Egypt	213/31	
Hetatah A	Civilian		19/05/19	Treason	15yrs Det	Egypt	213/31	
Chandler Joseph	Lincolnshire	Pte	28/05/19	Murder	XXX 11/08/19	F&F	213/30	1012
Anon No 75891	Chinese Lab Corps	Coolie	30/05/19	Murder	PS Life	F&F	213/29	1013
Sukkar M (Dahan)	Civilian		01/06/19	Murder/Riot	XXX (Hanged)	Egypt	213/34	
Osman Ismail	Civilian		03/06/19	Hostile Act	XXX	S Russia	213/34	
Ashmawi M	Civilian		19/06/19	Murder+Riot	PS Life	Egypt	213/32	1014
Salah AH [Gadalla Rageb]	Civilian		19/06/19	Murder+Riot	XXX (Hanged)	Egypt	213/32	1015
Adams J	RASC	Pte	23/06/19	Murder	15yrs PS		213/30	
Kozienko Alexander T	Civilian		01/07/19	Murder	Life HL	S Russia	213/34	
Deriagin I	1 Slavo-British Legion	Pte	13/07/19	Mutiny	XXX 00/07/19	N Russia	213/32	
Pesochnikoff J	1 Slavo-British Legion	Sgt	13/07/19	Mutiny	XXX 00/07/19	N Russia	213/32	
Sakharoff F	1 Slavo-British Legion	Pte	13/07/19	Mutiny	XXX 00/07/19	N Russia	213/32	
Shouliatieff T	1 Slavo-British Legion	Pte	13/07/19	Mutiny	10yrs PS	N Russia	213/32	
Bitel S	1 Slavo-British Legion	Pte	14/07/19	Mutiny	XXX 00/07/19	N Russia	213/32	
Cherbukin F	1 Slavo-British Legion	Pte	14/07/19	Mutiny	XXX 00/07/19	N Russia	213/32	
Elisaieff I	1 Slavo-British Legion	Pte	14/07/19	Mutiny	XXX 00/07/19	N Russia	213/32	
Kanieff P	1 Slavo-British Legion	Cpl	14/07/19	Mutiny	XXX 00/07/19	N Russia	213/32	
Lashkoff V	1 Slavo-British Legion	Pte	14/07/19	Mutiny	XXX 00/07/19	N Russia	213/32	
Petonhoff M	1 Slavo-British Legion	Pte	14/07/19	Mutiny	10yrs PS	N Russia	213/32	
Posdjeef N	1 Slavo-British Legion	Pte	14/07/19	Mutiny	XXX 00/07/19	N Russia	213/32	
Taratin P	1 Slavo-British Legion	Pte	14/07/19	Mutiny	XXX 00/07/19	N Russia	213/32	
Volkoff P	1 Slavo-British Legion	Pte	14/07/19	Mutiny	XXX 00/07/19	N Russia	213/32	
Babourkin P	1 Slavo-British Legion	Pte	17/07/19	Sedition	10yrs PS	N Russia	213/32	
Bykoff V	1 Slavo-British Legion	Pte	17/07/19	Mutiny	10yrs PS	N Russia	213/32	
Evstraloff P	1 Slavo-British Legion	Pte	17/07/19	Mutiny	10yrs PS	N Russia	213/32	
Kosmitcheef A	1 Slavo-British Legion	Pte	17/07/19	AWOL	10yrs PS	N Russia	213/32	
Miand G	1 Slavo-British Legion	Pte	17/07/19	Mutiny	10yrs PS	N Russia	213/32	
Sharoff V	1 Slavo-British Legion	Pte	17/07/19	Mutiny	10yrs PS	N Russia	213/32	
Tonkikh V	1 Slavo-British Legion	Pte	17/07/19	Mutiny	10yrs PS	N Russia	213/32	
Davids Abraham	1 Cape Col Lab Coy	Pte	05/08/19	Murder	XXX 26/08/19	F&F	213/30	1016
Harris Peter (Willie)	1 Cape Col Lab Coy	Pte	05/08/19	Murder	XXX 26/08/19	F&F	213/30	1017
Nigeradze Konstantin	Civilian		08/08/19	Robbery	XXX	S Russia	213/34	1018
Crisp W	45 Royal Fus	Pte	21/08/19	Not specified	2yrs HL	N Russia	213/31	
Enright W	45 Royal Fus	Pte	21/08/19	Not specified	2yrs HL	N Russia	213/31	
Nash FC	Labour Corps	Pte	03/09/19	Murder	PS Life	Turkey	90/8	1019
Hussein H	Turkish Army	POW	18/09/19	Murder x2	2yrs HL	Mesopotamia	90/7	1020
Kirkor B	Turkish Army	POW	20/09/19	Murder	15yrs PS	Mesopotamia	213/31	1021
Markalitdze Arsen	Civilian		21/09/19	Armed Robbery	XXX	S Russia	213/34	1022
Sinsadze Elany	Civilian		21/09/19	Armed Robbery	XXX	S Russia	213/34	1023
Vasadze Isak	Civilian		21/09/19	Armed Robbery	XXX	S Russia	213/34	1024
Alberts F (aka Boos)	1 Cape Col Lab Coy	Pte	29/09/19	Desertion	XXX 15/10/19	F&F	213/31	1025
Ackhurst S	6 R Marines	Pte	04/10/19	Disobedience	5yrs PS	N Russia	213/30	
Allinson W	6 R Marines	Pte	04/10/19	Disobedience	5yrs PS	N Russia	213/30	
Barnard JD	6 R Marines	Pte	04/10/19	Disobedience	5yrs PS	N Russia	213/30	
Blackbourne EC	6 R Marines	Pte	04/10/19	Disobedience	5yrs PS	N Russia	213/30	
Cheeseman L	6 R Marines	Pte	04/10/19	Disobedience	5yrs PS	N Russia	213/30	
Deane WG	6 R Marines	Pte	04/10/19	Disobedience	5yrs PS	N Russia	213/30	
Felgate M	6 R Marines	Pte	04/10/19	Disobedience	5yrs PS	N Russia	213/30	
Flint G	6 R Marines	Pte	04/10/19	Disobedience	5yrs PS	N Russia	213/30	
Holden AT	6 R Marines	Pte	04/10/19	Disobedience	5yrs PS	N Russia	213/30	
Knight RV	6 R Marines	Pte	04/10/19	Disobedience	5yrs PS	N Russia	213/30	
Robe A	6 R Marines	Pte	04/10/19	Disobedience	5yrs PS	N Russia	213/30	
Todd JW	6 R Marines	L/Cpl	04/10/19	Disobedience	5yrs PS	N Russia	213/30	
Wright H	6 R Marines	Pte	04/10/19	Disobedience	5yrs PS	N Russia	213/30	
Antonio Y	Macedonian Mule Coy	Muleteer	08/10/19	Murder x3	XXX 31/10/19	Turkey	213/31	1026
Kalli K	Macedonian Mule Coy	Muleteer	08/10/19	Murder x3	XXX 31/10/19	Turkey	213/31	1027
Louka YH	Macedonian Mule Coy	Muleteer	08/10/19	Murder x3	XXX 31/10/19	Turkey	213/31	1028
Simeoni G	Macedonian Mule Coy	Muleteer	08/10/19	Murder x3	XXX 31/10/19	Turkey	213/31	1029
Dgintcharadze Gerondi D	Civilian		07/11/19	Murder	XXX	S Russia	213/34	1030
Djianshia Alexis P	Civilian		07/11/19	Murder	Not Conf	S Russia	213/34	1031
Michalaichvili Ilya	Civilian		07/11/19	Murder	XXX	S Russia	213/34	1032
Tavarlkiladze Gerasin	Civilian		07/11/19	Murder	Not Conf	S Russia	213/34	1033
Tchelidze Kondrat C	Civilian		07/11/19	Murder	Not Conf	S Russia	213/34	1034
Avny H	39 Turkish Army	POW	14/11/19	Murder	XXX	Mesopotamia	213/31	1035
Aslett J	Ordnance Corps	Cpl (Sgt)	24/11/19	Murder	PS Life		213/31	
Fehmi Hassan	Civilian (Turkish Police)		15/01/20	Murder	10yrs PS	Turkey	213/34	1036

Name	Unit	Rank	Date	Offence	Final sentence	Location	Ref	Note
Hei Chi Ming	Chinese Lab Corps	Coolie	30/01/20	Murder	XXX 21/02/30	F&F	213/31	1037
Hennessy P	21 Hampshire	Pte	30/01/20	Murder	10yrs PS		213/31	
K'ung Ch'ing Hsing	Chinese Lab Corps	Coolie	30/01/20	Murder	XXX 21/02/30	F&F	213/31	1038
Beridze Ilia	Civilian		09/03/20	Murder	XXX	S Russia	213/34	1039
Gualia Pallady	Civilian		09/03/20	Murder	XXX	S Russia	213/34	1040
Kutchvah Silevan	Civilian		09/03/20	Murder	XXX	S Russia	213/34	1041
Sanikidze Kerial	Civilian		09/03/20	Murder	XXX	S Russia	213/34	1042
Tsangonria Philip	Civilian		09/03/20	Murder	XXX	S Russia	213/34	1043
Ogly Omer K	Civilian		06/04/20	Murder	XXX	S Russia	213/34	1044
Mamoulashvilli David N	Civilian		15/04/20	Murder	XXX	S Russia	213/34	1045
Mskladze Arkaki	Civilian		15/04/20	Murder	XXX	S Russia	213/34	1046
Ilfstaty J	Black Sea Lab Bn	Lbr	30/04/20	Murder	XXX	S Russia	213/31	1047
Ackreledies Panagiot	Civilian		17/05/20	Murder	10yrs HL	S Russia	213/34	1048
Sarafede Demetre	Civilian		17/05/20	Murder	Not Conf	S Russia	213/34	1049
Hasan Hussein	Civilian		06/07/20	Hostile Act	10yrs HL	Turkey	213/34	1050
Jafir Hamdi	Civilian		06/07/20	Hostile Act	10yrs HL	Turkey	213/34	1051
Mehmet Zaccharia	Civilian		06/07/20	Hostile Act	10yrs HL	Turkey	213/34	1052
Osman Ahmed	Civilian		06/07/20	Hostile Act	10yrs HL	Turkey	213/34	1053
Salih Ali	Civilian		06/07/20	Hostile Act	10yrs HL	Turkey	213/34	1054
Mahmoud Laz	Civilian		22/07/20	Hostile Act	10yrs HL	Turkey	213/34	1055
Mehmed Hafouz	Civilian		22/07/20	Hostile Act	10yrs HL	Turkey	213/34	1056
Edham Aziz	Civilian		27/07/20	Murder	PS Life	Egypt	213/34	1057
Riza Mehmet N A [?]	Civilian		05/08/20	Poss firearms	PS Life		213/34	
Verpe Shakir [?] O	Civilian		17/08/20	Aiding Enemy	XXX		213/34	
Ahmed	Egyptian Army	Lt	19/08/20	Treason	2yrs PS	Egypt	213/34	1058
Djelal	Egyptian Army	Sub Lt	19/08/20	Treason	2yrs PS	Egypt	213/34	1059
Kemal Mehmet	Civilian		19/08/20	Rebellion	1yr HL	Egypt	213/34	1060
Kiemal	Egyptian Army	Sub Lt	19/08/20	Treason	5yrs PS	Egypt	213/34	1061
Shamssedin	Egyptian Army	Colonel	19/08/20	Treason	5yrs PS	Egypt	213/34	1062
Sulieman Khalil O	Civilian		23/08/20	Aiding Enemy	PS Life		213/34	1063
Sadik Mashuk [?]	Civilian		28/08/20	Murder	XXX		213/34	
Delaney V	1 Connaught Rangers	Pte	03/09/20	Mutiny	PS Life	India		1064
Flannery J	1 Connaught Rangers	Pte (L/C)	03/09/20	Mutiny	PS Life	India		1065
Gogarty PJ	1 Connaught Rangers	Pte	03/09/20	Mutiny	PS Life	India		1066
Hawes J	1 Connaught Rangers	Pte	03/09/20	Mutiny	PS Life	India		1067
Moran T	1 Connaught Rangers	Pte	03/09/20	Mutiny	PS Life	India		1068
Daly JJ	1 Connaught Rangers	Pte	04/09/20	Mutiny	XXX 02/11/20	India		1069
Devine T	1 Connaught Rangers	Pte	04/09/20	Mutiny	PS Life	India		1070
Egan E	1 Connaught Rangers	Pte	04/09/20	Mutiny	PS Life	India		1071
Fitzgerald M	1 Connaught Rangers	Pte	04/09/20	Mutiny	PS Life	India		1072
Gleeson JJ	1 Connaught Rangers	Pte	04/09/20	Mutiny	PS Life	India		1073
Hynes P	1 Connaught Rangers	Pte	04/09/20	Mutiny	PS Life	India		1074
Kelly J	1 Connaught Rangers	Pte	04/09/20	Mutiny	PS Life	India		1075
Oliver J	1 Connaught Rangers	Pte	04/09/20	Mutiny	PS Life	India		1076
Salih Ibrahim O	Civilian		07/09/20	Murder	XXX	Egypt	213/34	1077
Moustafa Emin O	Civilian		08/09/20	Aiding Enemy	PS Life	Egypt	213/34	1078
Abdi Hussein O	Civilian		13/09/20	Rebellion	2yrs HL	Egypt	213/34	1079
Arif Ali O	Civilian		13/09/20	Rebellion	2yrs HL	Egypt	213/34	1080
Mehmed Salih C	Civilian		13/09/20	Rebellion	2yrs HL	Egypt	213/34	1081
Ahmet Arif O	Civilian		14/09/20	Aiding Enemy	XXX	Egypt	213/34	1082
Faizi Ibrahim [?] O	Civilian		20/09/20	Murder +	XXX		213/34	
Hassan Veli [?] O	Civilian		20/09/20	Murder +	XXX		213/34	
Rizeli Elias	Civilian		22/09/20	Hostile Act+	XXX		213/34	1083
Kalayi Georgio DO	Civilian		23/09/20	Murder+	PS Life	Egypt	213/34	1084
Moustafa Mehmed O	Civilian		27/09/20	Rebellion	PS Life	Egypt	213/34	1085
Flynn R	2 R Dublin Fus	Pte	11/10/20	Murder	XXX 06/11/20	Turkey	90/8	1086
Hardy F	2 R Dublin Fus	Pte	11/10/20	Murder x2	PS Life	Turkey	90/8	1087
Ahmed AAG	Civilian		22/11/20	Murder	Quashed	Egypt	213/32	
Ahmed MA	Civilian		22/11/20	Murder	Quashed	Egypt	213/32	
Ali MJ	Civilian		22/11/20	Murder	Quashed	Egypt	213/32	
Ali MS	Civilian		22/11/20	Murder	Quashed	Egypt	213/32	
Bedan SD	Civilian		22/11/20	Murder	10yrs PS	Egypt	213/32	
El Arabi HM	Civilian		22/11/20	Murder	XXX	Egypt	213/32	
Hassan MA	Civilian		22/11/20	Murder	XXX	Egypt	213/32	1088
Ibrahim MA	Civilian		22/11/20	Murder	Quashed	Egypt	213/32	
Helmore CGR	R Marine LI	Pte	11/02/21	Murder	PS Life	Ireland	213/32	1089
Gomma [Beisi] Saied	Civilian		12/06/21	Hostile Act	XXX (Hanged)	Egypt	213/34	1090
El Dib AMSA	Egyptian Lab Corps	Pte	04/07/21	Murder	Quashed	Egypt	213/32	1091

Name	Unit	Rank	Date	Offence	Final sentence	Location	Ref	Note
Zahab Salama MAE	Civilian		25/08/21	Murder	20yrs PS	Egypt	213/34	1092
Ali MH	Civilian		01/09/21	Murder	XXX (Hanged)	Egypt	213/32	1093
Naga I I	Civilian		01/09/21	Murder	XXX (Hanged)	Egypt	213/32	1094
Hadl AS	38 Egyptian Lab Corps	Rais	10/04/22	Murder	10yrs PS	Egypt	213/34	
Ledan AO	38 Egyptian Lab Corps	Rais	10/04/22	Murder	10yrs PS	Egypt	213/34	
Morad MH	38 Egyptian Lab Corps	Rais	10/04/22	Murder	10yrs PS	Egypt	213/34	
El Bassil Hamad Pasha	Civilian		09/08/22	Sedition	7yrs PS	Egypt	213/34	1095
El Ghazzar Elwi	Civilian		09/08/22	Sedition	7yrs PS	Egypt	213/34	1096
El Sheria Murad	Civilian		09/08/22	Sedition	7yrs PS	Egypt	213/34	1097
Ghali Wassif	Civilian		09/08/22	Sedition	7yrs PS	Egypt	213/34	1098
Hanna Morcos	Civilian		09/08/22	Sedition	7yrs PS	Egypt	213/34	1099
Khayat George	Civilian		09/08/22	Sedition	7yrs PS	Egypt	213/34	1100
Wassef Wissa	Civilian		09/08/22	Sedition	7yrs PS	Egypt	213/34	1101
Ali Hafez H	Civilian		31/08/22	Att Murder/Arms	XXX (Hanged)	Egypt	213/34	
Ali Youssef	Civilian		31/08/22	Att Murder/Arms	15yrs PS	Egypt	213/34	
Azab Tewfik A	Civilian		31/08/22	Att Murder+	XXX (Hanged)	Egypt	213/34	1102
Rushdi Ahmed	Civilian		31/08/22	Att Murder/Arms	XXX (Hanged)	Egypt	213/34	
El Khalik Mohammed Ali	Civilian		09/07/23	Conspiracy	XXX (Hanged)	Egypt	213/34	1103
Nazir Ibrahim Khalil	Civilian		09/07/23	Conspiracy	XXX (Hanged)	Egypt	213/34	1104
Sadik Arif O	Civilian		07/08/23	Pillage	XXX	Egypt	213/34	1105
Osman Hafiz	Civilian		11/08/23	Treason	PS Life	Egypt	213/34	1106
Fayis Bey	Civilian		07/09/23	Hostile Act	PS Life	Egypt	213/34	1107

Death sentences in alphabetical order

Name	Unit	Rank	Date	Offence	Final sentence	Location	Ref	Note
Abdallah Mohamed Bin	Civilian		05/11/15	Espionage	14yrs Imp	East Africa	213/34	125
Abdi Hussein O	Civilian		13/09/20	Rebellion	2yrs HL	Egypt	213/34	1079
Abdul Rahim	Civilian		13/09/15	Martial Law	XXX	Egypt	213/3	111
Abigail John Henry	8 Norfolk	Pte	24/08/17	Desertion	XXX 12/09/17	F&F	213/17	733
Abuary Abdulla	Civilian (Enemy officer?)		07/12/14	Espionage	PS Life	Port Sudan	90/6	
Ackhurst S	6 R Marines	Pte	04/10/19	Disobedience	5yrs PS	N Russia	213/30	
Ackreledies Panagiot	Civilian		17/05/20	Murder	10yrs HL	S Russia	213/34	1048
Adams H	1 Newfdland Canadian EF	Pte	23/05/17	Desertion	10yrs PS	F&F	213/15	
Adams J	20 Liverpool	Pte	26/02/16	Sleeping	3yrs PS	F&F	213/8	
Adams J	9 R Welsh Fus	Pte	21/02/18	Desertion	15yrs PS	F&F	213/23	
Adams J	RASC	Pte	23/06/19	Murder	15yrs PS		213/30	
Adams N	1/5 KO Yorks LI	Pte	13/10/15	Sleeping	5yrs PS	F&F	213/6	
Adams T	8 R W Kent	Pte	25/08/16	Sleeping	5yrs PS	F&F	213/11	
Adamson JS	7 Cameron Hdrs	Pte	31/10/17	Cowardice	XXX 23/11/17	F&F	213/18	817
Adshead A	1/9 Manchester	Pte	09/09/15	Sleeping	10yrs PS	Gallipoli	213/5	
Affleck A	S African Regt	Pte	08/06/18	Desertion	15yrs PS		213/24	
Affleck C	1 E Lancs	Pte	05/12/14	Cowardice	2yrs HL	F&F	213/3	
Agon DW	42 Canadian EF	Pte	15/12/17	Desertion	15yrs PS	F&F	213/19	
Ahmed	Egyptian Army	Lt	19/08/20	Treason	2yrs PS	Egypt	213/34	1058
Ahmed AAG	Civilian		22/11/20	Murder	Quashed	Egypt	213/32	
Ahmed MA	Civilian		22/11/20	Murder	Quashed	Egypt	213/32	
Ahmed MM	Egyptian Lab Corps	Lbr	28/09/17	Violence	XXX 10/10/17	F&F	213/17	777
Ahmet Arif O	Civilian		14/09/20	Aiding Enemy	XXX	Egypt	213/34	1082
Ainley George	1/4 KO Yorks LI	Pte	13/07/18	Desertion x3	XXX 30/07/18	F&F	213/24	942
Aitchison B	66 RFA	Gnr	11/01/17	Disobedience	5yrs PS	Mesopotamia	90/7	573
Alberts F (aka Boos)	1 Cape Col Lab Coy	Pte	29/09/19	Desertion	XXX 15/10/19	F&F	213/31	1025
Aldridge H	5 Wiltshire	Pte	19/12/16	Sleeping	5yrs PS	Mesopotamia	90/7	534
Aldridge W	7 KRRC	Rfm	26/07/15	Cowardice	10yrs PS	F&F	213/4	
Alexander William	10 Canadian EF	CQMSgt	29/09/17	Desertion	XXX 18/10/17	F&F	213/17	780
Ali Hafez H	Civilian		31/08/22	Att Murder/Arms	XXX (Hanged)	Egypt	213/34	
Ali MH	Civilian		01/09/21	Murder	XXX (Hanged)	Egypt	213/32	1093
Ali MJ	Civilian		22/11/20	Murder	Quashed	Egypt	213/32	
Ali MS	Civilian		22/11/20	Murder	Quashed	Egypt	213/32	
Ali Youssef	Civilian		31/08/22	Att Murder/Arms	15yrs PS	Egypt	213/34	
Allen B	2/6 Gloucestershire	Pte	04/11/16	Sleeping	10yrs PS	F&F	213/12	
Allen H	1/5 Essex	Cpl	08/01/18	Disobedience	10yrs PS	Egypt	213/20	855
Allen J	2 R Dublin Fus	Pte	16/09/15	Desertion	2yrs HL	F&F	213/5	
Allen J	Canadian EF	Pte	05/09/17	Against Inhab	PS Life	F&F	213/17	
Allen JE	RFA	Gnr	07/05/18	Desertion	5yrs PS		213/23	
Allen TF	2 Leicestershire	Pte	01/09/16	Sleeping	2yrs HL	Mesopotamia	90/7	439
Allen W	1 KO Yorks LI	Pte	29/12/16	Sleeping	2yrs HL	Salonika	213/13	
Allen W	1 Devon	Pte	19/05/18	Desertion	15yrs PS	F&F	213/23	
Allender J	2 York & Lancaster	Pte	19/07/17	Desertion	15yrs PS	F&F	213/16	
Alli Checkmamid O	Civilian		17/02/19	Murder	XXX (Hanged)	T'caucasia	213/34	
Allinson W	6 R Marines	Pte	04/10/19	Disobedience	5yrs PS	N Russia	213/30	
Allison A	7 Norfolk	Pte (L/C)	12/09/16	Sleeping	5yrs PS	F&F	213/11	
Allison CF	20 Middlesex	Pte	07/08/16	Desertion	Not Conf	F&F	213/10	418
Allison J	4 Canadian EF	Pte	03/07/16	Desertion	5yrs PS	F&F	213/10	
Allsop Arthur E	12 KRRC	Rfm	13/03/17	Desertion	5 yrs PS	F&F	213/14	607
Allsop Arthur E	12 KRRC	Rfm	31/05/17	Desertion	XXX 15/06/17	F&F	213/15	664
Allsopp G	705 Lab Coy	Pnr	19/12/17	Desertion	5yrs PS		213/19	
Ames S	4 Liverpool	Pte (L/C)	12/01/17	Desertion	5yrs PS	F&F	213/13	
Ammon J	1/5 Sherwood Fstrs	Pte	19/10/17	Quitting	5yrs PS	F&F	213/18	
Anderberg Anton	8 Rifle Bde	Pte	01/11/15	Disobedience+	2yrs HL	F&F	213/6	124
Anderson A	7 Yorks	Pte	22/11/15	Desertion	Not Conf	F&F	213/7	
Anderson A	7 Yorks	Pte	14/12/15	Desertion	10yrs PS	F&F	213/7	

Name	Unit	Rank	Date	Offence	Final sentence	Location	Ref	Note
Anderson A	5 Yorks	Pte	28/12/17	Desertion	5yrs PS	F&F	213/19	
Anderson A	46 Canadian EF	Pte	09/02/18	Desertion	10yrs PS	F&F	213/20	
Anderson J	4 W Riding	Pte	12/06/16	Disobedience	2yrs HL	F&F	213/10	
Anderson J	19 Durham LI	Pte	30/12/16	Cowardice	10yrs PS	F&F	213/13	548
Anderson James	12 Liverpool	Pte	03/09/16	Cowardice	XXX 12/09/16	F&F	213/10	441
Anderson R	1 Highland LI	Pte	08/02/16	Sleeping	5yrs PS	Mesopotamia	90/7	169
Anderson T	22 Northumb Fus	Pte	05/10/17	Desertion	10yrs PS	F&F	213/18	786
Anderson W	1 R Irish Rifles	Rfm	14/04/15	Sleeping	3mos FP1	F&F	213/3	
Anderson W	10 KO Yorks LI	Pte	05/01/16	Sleeping	5yrs PS	F&F	213/7	
Anderson William E	5 Dorset	Pte	09/03/17	Desertion	XXX 31/03/17	F&F	213/14	603
Anderton	1 Manchester	Pte	21/11/14	Cowardice	2yrs HL	F&F	213/2	
Andrew WJ	8/4 [?] Hampshire	Pte	19/04/18	Cowardice	10yrs PS		213/23	
Andrews A	11 R W Surrey	Pte	04/06/16	Striking	5yrs PS	F&F	213/9	
Andrews C	1 R Irish Rifles	Rfm	01/05/17	Desertion x2	5yrs PS	F&F	213/15	
Andrews M	9 Northumb Fus	Pte	04/08/18	Desertion	5yrs PS	F&F	213/24	
Annison T	S African Comp Bn	Pte	30/08/18	Desertion	10yrs PS		213/27	
Anon No 24232	Chinese Lab Corps	Coolie	08/01/18	Striking	5yrs PS	F&F	213/20	856
Anon No 39237	Chinese Lab Corps	Coolie	03/04/19	Murder	Not Conf	F&F	213/29	
Anon No 4976	Chinese Lab Corps	Coolie	28/12/18	Against Inhab x2+	To be XXX	F&F	213/28	997
Anon No 70618	Chinese Lab Corps	Coolie	20/06/18	Striking +	5yrs PS	F&F	213/24	929
Anon No 75891	Chinese Lab Corps	Coolie	30/05/19	Murder	PS Life	F&F	213/29	1013
Anstead [?] Alfred Thomas	4 Royal Fus	Pte	05/11/16	Desertion	XXX 15/11/16	F&F	213/12	497
Antonio Y	Macedonian Mule Coy	Muleteer	08/10/19	Murder x3	XXX 31/10/19	Turkey	213/31	1026
Appleby A	1 D Cornwall LI	Pte	22/06/15	Striking	3yrs PS	F&F	213/4	
Archer J	8 R Berkshire	Pte	13/12/15	Sleeping	6 Mos HL	F&F	213/6	
Archer J	20 Durham LI	Pte	02/11/16	Desertion	Not Conf	F&F	213/12	492
Archibald James	17 R Scots	Pte	23/05/16	Desertion	XXX 04/06/16	F&F	213/9	315
Argyle A	2 Leicestershire	Pte	07/12/14	Sleeping	5yrs PS	Mesopotamia	213/1	
Arif Ali O	Civilian		13/09/20	Rebellion	2yrs HL	Egypt	213/34	1080
Arkinson W	11 A&S Hdrs	Pte	14/01/17	Desertion	5yrs PS	F&F	213/13	
Arme A	13 R Scots	Pte	11/10/18	Desertion	7yrs PS	F&F	213/26	
Armes WH	9 R Warwickshire	Pte	01/01/16	Sleeping	5yrs PS	Mesopotamia	90/7	143
Armstrong R	11 Manchester	Pte	27/09/15	Striking+	2yrs HL	Gallipoli	213/5	118
Armstrong W	RFA	Gnr	25/04/18	Desertion	10yrs PS		213/22	
Arnold Frederick S	Canadian FA	Dvr	05/07/16	Desertion	XXX 25/07/16	F&F	213/10	393
Ashby H	1 Grenadier Gds	Pte	21/08/16	Desertion	5yrs PS	F&F	213/11	
Ashby W	1 Norfolk	Pte	16/05/18	Desertion	5yrs PS	F&F	213/22	907
Ashby W	1 Norfolk	Pte	29/12/18	Desertion	5yrs PS	F&F	213/27	999
Ashby WF	23 Middlesex	Pte	24/05/18	Desertion	15yrs PS	F&F	213/24	913
Ashe Thomas	Civilian	Sinn Fein	08/05/16	Rebellion	PS Life	Dublin	213/8	292
Ashmawi M	Civilian		19/06/19	Murder + Riot	PS Life	Egypt	213/32	1014
Ashton Harry	11 Scottish Rifles	L/Sgt	21/05/17	Desertion	Not Conf	Salonika	213/16	657
Ashton Harry	11 Scottish Rifles	L/Sgt	30/06/17	Desertion	XXX 08/07/17	Salonika	213/16	687
Ashwood W	2 KO Scottish Bdrs	Pte	21/09/15	Sleeping	10yrs PS	F&F	213/5	
Ashworth E	6 KOR Lancaster	Pte	25/09/17	Desertion/Drunk	5yrs PS	Mesopotamia	90/7	
Aslett J	Ordnance Corps	Cpl (Sgt)	24/11/19	Murder	PS Life		213/31	
Assister WJ	8 E Kent (Buffs)	Pte	18/08/17	Desertion	2yrs HL	F&F	213/16	730
Atkins P	18 KRRC	Rfm	30/12/18	Desertion	10yrs PS	F&F	213/29	1000
Atkinson Alfred	1 W Yorks	L/Cpl	20/02/15	Desertion	XXX 02/03/15	F&F	213/3	46
Atkinson F	1/7 W Riding	Pte	26/12/16	Sleeping	2yrs HL	F&F	213/13	
Atkinson G	2 R Scots	Pte	12/10/16	Desertion	3yrs PS	F&F	213/12	
Atkinson G	2 R Scots	Pte	30/01/18	Desertion	15yrs PS	F&F	213/20	
Attridge WT	1 Northants	Pte	14/10/18	Desertion	5yrs PS	F&F	213/26	
Attwell AG	5 Wiltshire	Pte	02/10/15	Sleeping	5yrs PS	Gallipoli	213/6	
Attwell FN	7 Wiltshire	Pte	25/08/16	Sleeping	1yr HL	Salonika	213/11	
Atwell G	12 Northumb Fus	Pte	16/05/17	Desertion	2yrs HL	F&F	213/15	
Auckland A	7 KRRC	Rfm	29/07/17	Violence	10yrs PS	F&F	213/16	
Auger Fortunat	14 Canadian EF	Pte	15/03/16	Desertion	XXX 26/03/16	F&F	213/8	191
Avny H	39 Turkish Army	POW	14/11/19	Murder	XXX	Mesopotamia	213/31	1035
Ayre JA	1 Middlesex	Pte	25/03/16	Striking	3yrs PS	F&F	213/8	
Azab Tewfik A	Civilian		31/08/22	Att Murder +	XXX (Hanged)	Egypt	213/34	1102
Babourkin P	1 Slavo-British Legion	Pte	17/07/19	Sedition	10yrs PS	N Russia	213/32	
Bacon A	10 Essex	Pte	12/07/16	Desertion	Not Conf	F&F	213/11	
Bacon GV	Civilian	Alien	26/02/17	Espionage	PS Life	UK	92/3	596
Bacon MA	88 Coy RGA	Sgt	25/06/15	Desertion	XXX [?]	Hong Kong	213/4	
Badawi SAL	Civilian		27/09/15	Martial Law	XXX (Hanged)	Egypt	213/3	119
Badger W	1/5 S Staffordshire	Pte	19/09/16	Sleeping	2yrs HL	F&F	213/11	
Bagnell J	36 Australian IF	Pte	01/11/17	Desertion	10yrs PS		213/18	

Name	Unit	Rank	Date	Offence	Final sentence	Location	Ref	Note
Bailey J	6 KOR Lancaster	Pte	13/09/15	Mutiny	2yrs HL	Gallipoli	213/5	
Bailey L	1 Liverpool	Pte	30/11/16	Desertion	5yrs PS	F&F	213/12	
Bailey Thomas	1 Life Gds	Tpr	11/11/14	Sleeping	2yrs HL	F&F	213/2	
Baker Benjamin	2 Grenadier Gds	Pte	25/09/14	Sleeping	5yrs PS	F&F	213/2	
Baker EC	2/20 London	Pte	21/09/16	Sleeping	10yrs PS	F&F	213/11	
Baker FJ	1 New Zealand EF	Pte	04/07/17	Desertion	15yrs PS		213/16	696
Baker H	3 Coldstream Gds	Pte	08/11/17	Desertion	5yrs PS	F&F	213/18	
Baker J	4/5 Black Watch	Pte	04/10/18	Desertion	5yrs PS	F&F	213/26	
Baker T	12 York & Lancaster	Pte	25/06/17	Desertion	5yrs PS	F&F	213/16	684
Baker W	1/5 E Lancs	Pte	01/09/15	Sleeping	5yrs PS	Gallipoli	213/5	
Baker W	2 Durham LI	Pte	04/06/17	Cowardice	10yrs PS	F&F	213/15	
Baker William	26 Royal Fus	Pte	26/07/18	Desertion x2	XXX 14/08/18	F&F	213/24	950
Bakewell A	RFA	Dvr	26/09/17	Desertion	5yrs PS		213/17	
Baldwin F	3 Middlesex	Pte	10/07/15	Sleeping	3yrs PS	F&F	213/4	
Balfour J	4 (att 2) A&S Hdrs	Pte	26/03/16	Desertion	3yrs PS	UK	213/8	196
Ball G	9 Sherwood Fstrs	Pte	31/07/15	Sleeping	2yrs HL	Egypt	213/5	
Ball JH	66 Bde RFA	Gnr	26/09/17	Sleeping	3yrs HL	Mesopotamia	90/7	773
Ball Joseph	2 Middlesex	Pte	30/12/14	Desertion	XXX 12/01/15	F&F	213/3	16
Ballinger H	6 R Berkshire	Pte	11/06/17	Desertion	5yrs PS	F&F	213/15	
Ballock J	R Scots Fus	Pte	15/12/16	Desertion x2	5yrs PS		213/12	
Balmbro C	8 KO Yorks LI	Pte	25/03/17	Desertion	10yrs PS	F&F	213/15	
Banks G	1 N Staffordshire	Pte	31/03/15	Sleeping	2yrs HL	F&F	213/3	
Banks L	7 KOR Lancaster	Pte	28/11/17	Desertion	5yrs PS	F&F	213/18	
Bannister H	7 Rifle Bde	Rfm	01/07/16	Sleeping	2yrs HL	F&F	213/9	
Barber G	2 E Surrey	Pte	09/05/17	Sleeping	3yrs PS	Salonika	213/15	
Barfoot F	14 Australian IF	Pte	08/08/17	Desertion	10yrs PS		213/17	
Barker F	1 Norfolk	Pte	12/08/15	Sleeping	10yrs PS	F&F	213/4	
Barker FW	13 London	Pte	01/06/18	Desertion	10yrs PS	F&F	213/22	917
Barker J	2 KO Yorks LI	Pte	19/02/16	Desertion	3 Mos FP1	F&F	213/7	
Barker R	6 London	Rfm	08/06/16	Desertion	5yrs PS	F&F	213/9	
Barker R	2 R Scots	Pte	23/01/18	Desertion	5yrs PS	F&F	213/24	
Barker Robert Loveless	6 Royal Fus (London)	Rfm	28/09/16	Desertion	XXX 04/11/16	F&F	213/11	461
Barker T	1/7 Black Watch	Pte	26/09/15	Sleeping	6mos HL	F&F	213/5	117
Barker W	7 N Staffordshire	Pte	31/01/16	Sleeping	1yr HL	Egypt	213/7	
Barkley P	8 R Irish Fus	Pte	16/05/16	Disobedience	Not Conf	F&F	213/9	
Barlow C	1 Hampshire	Pte	26/12/14	Sleeping	5yrs PS	F&F	213/3	
Barnaby A	148 RFA	Gnr	08/11/16	Desertion	5yrs PS		213/12	
Barnard A	1/4 Norfolk	Pte	31/10/15	Sleeping	5yrs PS	Gallipoli	213/6	
Barnard JD	6 R Marines	Pte	04/10/19	Disobedience	5yrs PS	N Russia	213/30	
Barnes H	2 KO Yorks LI	Pte	28/03/15	Desertion	15yrs PS	F&F	213/3	
Barnes John E	7 R Sussex	Pte	10/06/17	Desertion	XXX 04/07/17	F&F	213/15	674
Barnes T	6 S Lancs	Pte (L/C)	18/09/16	Desertion	5yrs PS	Mesopotamia	90/7	450
Barnett L	1/9 London	Rfm	07/02/18	Desertion	10yrs PS	F&F	213/20	
Barnett W	1 New Zealand EF	Pte	12/08/16	Desertion	5yrs PS		213/10	422
Barr CA	59 Australian IF	Pte	27/12/16	Desertion	5yrs PS		213/13	
Barr J	2 Seaforth Hdrs	Pte	28/09/15	Sleeping	10yrs PS	F&F	213/5	
Barr N	10 R Irish Rifles	Rfm	11/03/17	Desertion	10yrs PS	F&F	213/14	606
Barrass R	1 Northants	Pte	15/10/18	Desertion	5yrs PS	F&F	213/26	
Barratt Frederick Martin	7 KRRC	Rfm	21/06/17	Desertion	XXX 10/07/17	F&F	213/16	681
Barre N	4 Canadian EF	Pte	01/10/17	Desertion+	5yrs PS	F&F	213/17	781
Barrett F	4 KRRC	Rfm	14/08/15	Desertion	10yrs PS	F&F	213/5	
Barrett FA	5 Australian IF	Pte	26/12/16	Desertion	2yrs HL		213/13	
Barrett H	2 Leinster	Dmr	02/11/14	Cowardice	2 HL	F&F	213/2	
Barrett J	RGA	Gnr	25/07/18	Desertion	5yrs PS		213/24	
Barrington A	2 Manchester	Pte	17/11/17	Desertion	5yrs PS	F&F	213/18	
Barrington H	2 Manchester	Pte	01/02/18	Desertion	5yrs PS	F&F	213/20	
Barritt C	East Non Combat Corps	Pte	10/06/16	Disobedience	10yrs PS	F&F	213/9	341
Barron H	55 MGC	Pte	12/06/17	Quitting	10yrs PS		213/15	
Barrowclough N	4 Bedfordshire	Pte	16/06/17	Desertion	Not Conf	F&F	213/16	
Barry J	4 R Munster Fus	Pte	03/07/16	Desertion	3yrs PS		213/10	
Bartholemew H	25 Australian IF	Pte	01/12/16	Desertion	10yrs PS		213/13	
Bartle H	1 Coldstream Gds	Pte	20/12/15	Desertion	3yrs PS	F&F	213/6	
Barton Granville W	1 R Irish Rifles	Rfm	21/08/16	Desertion	3yrs PS	F&F	213/10	
Barton GW	13 Middlesex	Sgt	13/09/16	Desertion	Not Conf	F&F	213/11	
Bartrum G	7 Norfolk	Pte	24/03/17	Disobedience	1yr HL	F&F	213/8	
Basham W	New Zealand FA	Dvr	03/01/18	Desertion x2	10yrs PS		213/19	853
Bass GA	13 Essex	Pte	30/10/16	Desertion	5yrs PS	F&F	213/12	491
Bassett J	12 Royal Fus	Pte	17/07/16	Desertion	10 yrs PS	F&F	213/10	

Name	Unit	Rank	Date	Offence	Final sentence	Location	Ref	Note
Bassett J	1/5 N Staffordshire	Pte	14/01/18	Desertion	10yrs PS	F&F	213/19	
Bate W	9 Cheshire	Pte	22/04/16	Disobedience	15yrs PS	F&F	213/8	
Bateman F	1/4 York & Lancaster	Pte	21/05/17	Desertion	15yrs PS	F&F	213/15	658
Bateman Frank	1/4 York & Lancaster	Pte	30/08/18	Desertion	XXX 10/09/18	F&F	213/25	970
Bateman Joseph	2 S Staffordshire	Pte	04/11/17	Desertion	XXX 03/12/17	F&F	213/18	819
Bates W	19 Durham LI	Pte	30/12/16	Cowardice	10yrs PS	F&F	213/13	549
Battersby WR	1/5 Liverpool	Rfm	05/05/15	Sleeping	2yrs HL	F&F	213/4	
Baxter HJ	9 Suffolk	Pte	10/09/16	Striking	5yrs PS	F&F	213/11	
Baxter W	3 Middlesex	Pte	28/11/16	Sleeping	3yrs PS	Salonika	213/13	
Bayliss C	42 RFA	Dvr	25/10/16	Desertion	5yrs PS		213/12	
Bazinett E	10 R Warwickshire	Pte	07/12/18	Desertion	5yrs PS	F&F	213/27	
Beadle E	8 R W Kent	Pte	07/04/16	Sleeping	5yrs PS	F&F	213/8	
Beadle F	2 Royal Fus	Pte	12/10/17	Desertion	15yrs PS	F&F	213/17	
Beal EJ	7 E Yorks	Pte	31/01/17	Desertion	5yrs PS	F&F	213/13	
Beal EJ	7 E Yorks	Gnr	17/07/18	Desertion	5yrs PS	F&F	213/24	
Bearman W	3 Middlesex	Pte	10/07/15	Sleeping	3yrs PS	F&F	213/4	
Beattie A	15 R Irish Rifles	Rfm	27/02/16	Desertion	5yrs PS	F&F	213/7	182
Beaudoin C	14 Canadian EF	Pte	14/01/16	Desertion	10yrs PS	F&F	213/7	
Beaumont Ernest Alfred	2 Leicestershire	Pte	11/06/15	Desertion	XXX 24/06/15	F&F	213/4	74
Beaumont K	1 KO Yorks LI	Pte	02/07/15	Sleeping	5yrs PS	F&F	213/4	
Beavis GHS	3 East Non Combat Corps	Pte	13/06/16	Disobedience	10yrs PS	F&F	213/9	360
Beck C	6 R Munster Fus	Pte	18/12/15	Sleeping	Not Conf	Salonika	213/7	
Beck JE	8 Norfolk	Pte	24/08/17	Desertion	Not Conf	F&F	213/17	
Bedan SD	Civilian		22/11/20	Murder	10yrs PS	Egypt	213/32	
Bedford A	1/7 W Yorks	Rfm	29/10/17	Desertion	10yrs PS	F&F	213/18	813
Bedford G	4 Bedfordshire	Pte	28/11/16	Cowardice	Not Conf	F&F	213/12	525
Beeby Ernest	212 RE	Pnr	15/11/16	Desertion	XXX 09/12/16		213/12	511
Beere G	2 E Surrey	Pte	09/05/17	Sleeping	3yrs PS	Salonika	213/15	
Begg C	1 Highland L I	Pte	29/03/15	Desertion	5yrs PS	F&F	213/3	
Bell AA	2/20 London	Pte	20/07/16	Sleeping	5yrs PS	F&F	213/10	
Bell John	57 Bty RFA	Dvr	16/04/15	Desertion x3	XXX 25/04/15	F&F	213/3	63
Bell P	1 R Scots Fus	Pte	10/03/15	Desertion	10yrs PS	F&F	213/3	
Bell R	10 Scottish Rifles	Pte	21/04/18	Desertion	5yrs PS	F&F	213/22	
Bell R	123 Field Coy RE	Spr	04/05/18	Murder	XXX 22/05/18	F&F	213/22	903
Bell SE	11 E Yorks	Pte	22/07/18	Desertion	10yrs PS	F&F	213/24	
Bell W	1/7 Highland LI	Pte	17/09/17	Drunk	5yrs PS	Egypt	213/18	762
Bellamy E	1 KRRC	Rfm	19/01/17	Desertion	10yrs PS	F&F	213/13	
Bellamy W	1 KRRC	Rfm	02/07/15	Cowardice	XXX 16/07/15	F&F	213/4	80
Bellet J	1 R Berkshire	Pte	05/10/16	Desertion	10yrs PS	F&F	213/12	
Benard B	22 Canadian EF	Pte	28/03/17	Desertion x2	15yrs PS	F&F	213/14	
Benham William	1/3 London	Pte	29/06/17	Desertion	XXX 12/07/17	F&F	213/16	686
Benians A	14 Highland LI	Pte	05/11/16	Sleeping	2yrs HL	F&F	213/12	498
Benn E	41 MGC	Pte	12/07/17	Desertion	10yrs PS		213/17	
Bennett FW	8 R W Surrey	Pte	13/03/16	Desertion	10yrs PS	F&F	213/8	
Bennett G	2 KO Yorks LI	Pte	15/12/17	Desertion	5yrs PS	F&F	213/19	
Bennett H	7 Leicestershire	Pte	14/10/18	Mutiny	15yrs PS	F&F	213/26	
Bennett John	1 Hampshire	Pte	16/08/16	Cowardice	XXX 28/08/16	F&F	213/10	426
Bentley W	15 Durham LI	Pte	11/11/18	Desertion x2	5yrs PS	F&F	213/26	
Beridze Ilia	Civilian		09/03/20	Murder	XXX	S Russia	213/34	1039
Bernard A	11 Essex	Pte	06/10/16	Desertion	5yrs PS	F&F	213/12	
Bernier G	14 Canadian EF	Pte	27/07/17	Desertion	2yrs HL	F&F	213/16	
Berrington C	7 E Yorks	Pte	28/02/16	Cowardice	5yrs PS	F&F	213/8	
Berry	2 Manchester	Pte	20/08/15	Cowardice	10yrs PS	F&F	213/5	
Berry F	6 E Kent (Buffs)	Pte	11/09/16	Sleeping	5yrs PS	F&F	213/11	
Berry F	12 S Wales Bdrs	Pte	25/04/18	Desertion	5yrs PS	F&F	213/21	892
Best J	1/4 R Scots Fus	Pte	19/09/17	Disobedience x2	10yrs PS	Egypt	213/18	
Best J	2 Lincolnshire	Sgt	31/10/17	Cowardice	10yrs PS	F&F	213/18	
Best T	6 Northants	Pte	24/08/17	Desertion	10yrs PS	F&F	213/17	
Bettney E	10 R Warwickshire	Pte	07/12/18	Desertion	10yrs PS	F&F	213/27	
Betts W	2/5 Gloucestershire	Pte	26/06/18	Desertion	2yrs HL	F&F	213/24	930
Betts W	13 R Inniskilling Fus	Pte	07/11/18	Desertion	5yrs PS	F&F	213/26	
Bevan Charles	Civilian	Sinn Fein	04/05/16	Rebellion	3yrs PS	Dublin	213/8	243
Bevan Thomas	Civilian	Sinn Fein	03/05/16	Rebellion	10yrs PS	Dublin	213/8	224
Beveridge A	24 DAC	Dvr	30/06/16	Striking	2yrs HL		213/9	
Bickers F	3 Canadian EF	Pte	11/02/16	Desertion	5yrs PS	F&F	213/8	
Bilton S	1 E Kent (Buffs)	Pte	29/01/16	Desertion	10yrs PS	F&F	213/7	
Birch A	11 Worcestershire	Pte	13/10/17	Sleeping	5yrs PS	Salonika	213/18	
Birch E	7 N Staffordshire	Pte	18/10/15	Sleeping	5yrs PS	Gallipoli	213/6	

Name	Unit	Rank	Date	Offence	Final sentence	Location	Ref	Note
Birch F	1 Worcestershire	Pte	08/10/16	Desertion	5yrs PS	F&F	213/12	
Birch P	10 Essex	Pte	16/12/17	Desertion	5yrs PS	F&F	213/19	
Bird JE	11 Sherwood Fstrs	Pte	01/10/15	Sleeping	2yrs HL	F&F	213/6	
Bird W	1 KOR Lancaster	Pte	13/11/15	Sleeping	1yr HL	F&F	213/6	
Bird William G	1/5 S Staffordshire	Pte	18/05/15	Sleeping	2yrs HL	F&F	213/4	
Birtle A	2 W Riding	Pte	21/05/16	Desertion	2yrs HL	F&F	213/10	
Bishop CB	2 R Sussex	Pte	16/11/16	Desertion	5yrs PS	F&F	213/12	
Bishop TA	7 Canadian EF	Pte	31/10/16	Desertion	5yrs PS	F&F	213/12	
Bitel S	1 Slavo-British Legion	Pte	14/07/19	Mutiny	XXX 00/07/19	N Russia	213/32	
Black A	49 Australian IF	Pte	30/04/17	Desertion	5yrs PS		213/15	
Black JW	1 New Zealand EF	Pte	12/04/17	Desertion	10yrs PS		213/14	631
Black P	1/4 Black Watch	Pte	27/11/15	Desertion	3yrs PS	F&F	213/6	134
Black Peter	1/4 (att 1/7) Black Watch	Pte	03/09/16	Desertion	XXX 18/09/16	F&F	213/11	442
Black W	2 New Zealand EF	Pte	02/09/17	Desertion	10yrs PS		213/17	742
Blackbarrow James	2 E Surrey	Pte	24/07/15	Desertion	10yrs PS	F&F	213/4	
Blackbourne EC	6 R Marines	Pte	04/10/19	Disobedience	5yrs PS	N Russia	213/30	
Blackman E	1 E Kent (Buffs)	Pte	20/01/16	Desertion	10yrs PS	F&F	213/7	
Blackwell J	3 Middlesex	Pte	25/09/15	Sleeping	3yrs PS	F&F	213/5	
Bladen Charles FH	10 York & Lancaster	Pte	08/03/16	Desertion	XXX 23/03/16	F&F	213/8	189
Blakemore D	8 N Staffordshire	Pte	26/05/17	Desertion	15yrs PS	F&F	213/15	
Blakemore Denis	8 N Staffordshire	Pte	28/06/17	Desertion	XXX 09/07/17	F&F	213/16	685
Blanch AJ	4 Australian IF	Pte	20/02/17	Desertion	10yrs PS		213/14	
Blanchette G	22 Canadian EF	Pte	07/06/17	Desertion	15yrs PS	F&F	213/16	
Bleasedale W	116 Canadian EF	Pte	10/12/17	Desertion	Not Conf	F&F	213/20	
Blenkin S	7 E Yorks	Pte	08/11/18	Desertion x2	5yrs PS	F&F	213/26	
Blenkiron William	9 Durham LI	Pte	24/09/18	Disobedience x3	90 days FP1		213/25	
Blewitt J	10 D Cornwall LI	Pte	23/01/17	Desertion	10yrs PS	F&F	213/13	579
Bly GH	9 Liverpool	Pte	27/03/16	Sleeping	10yrs PS		213/9	
Blyth F	148 RFA	Gnr	08/11/16	Desertion	5yrs PS		213/12	
Boag E	6 KO Scottish Bdrs	Pte	26/06/16	Desertion	Not Conf	F&F	213/11	
Boak G	1 Seaforth Hdrs	Pte	07/10/16	Insubordination	3yrs PS	Mesopotamia	213/12	
Boakes A	11 Suffolk	Pte	17/05/17	Cowardice	15yrs PS	F&F	213/15	
Bodnarchuk B	1 Canadian EF	Pte	31/10/16	Desertion	5yrs PS	F&F	213/12	
Bogdanov V	2 Canadian Pnr Bn	Pte	04/09/17	Desertion	5yrs PS	F&F	213/17	
Bold R	3 Canadian EF	Pte	21/07/16	Desertion	10yrs PS	F&F	213/10	
Bolem G	2 York & Lancaster	Pte	14/01/18	Desertion	10yrs PS	F&F	213/27	
Bolton E	1 Cheshire	Pte	11/08/15	Desertion	10yrs PS	F&F	213/5	
Bolton J	17 Liverpool	Pte	22/08/17	Desertion	Not Conf	F&F	213/17	
Bolton J	2/7 Liverpool	Pte	14/11/18	Desertion	5yrs PS	F&F	213/27	
Bolton J Edward	1 Cheshire	Pte	24/03/16	Desertion	XXX 14/04/16	F&F	213/8	194
Bond J	2 R Scots	Pte	28/05/18	Desertion	10yrs PS	F&F	213/22	
Bond JW	13 York and Lancaster	Pte	04/04/17	Desertion	10yrs PS	F&F	213/14	619
Bone JW	7 East Yorks	Pte	06/12/15	Desertion	5yrs PS	F&F	213/6	
Bonner B	East Non Combat Corps	Pte	10/06/16	Disobedience	10yrs PS	F&F	213/9	342
Bonsey R	1 R Dragoons	Pte	10/02/16	Quitting	1yr HL	F&F	213/8	
Boot E	1 S Staffordshire	Pte	05/03/17	Desertion	5yrs PS	F&F	213/14	
Booth H	1 E Lancs	Pte	20/02/18	Desertion	15yrs PS	F&F	213/23	
Borrana Dezari	Gold Coast Regt	Pte	23/10/18	Murder	XXX 10/11/18	F&F	213/27	987
Bossana Dezari	Gold Coast Regt	Pte	01/07/18	Murder	Not Conf	East Africa	213/27	932
Bostock J	2 Cheshire	Pte	25/09/15	Sleeping	2yrs HL	F&F	213/5	
Boswell A	16 R Warwickshire	Pte	11/05/18	Sleeping	3yrs PS	F&F	213/22	
Botfield Albert	9 S Staffordshire	Pte	01/10/16	Cowardice +	XXX 18/10/16	F&F	213/12	462
Boulton RO	1 Canadian MGC	Cpl	17/06/16	Desertion	5yrs PS	F&F	213/10	
Bowen J	11 Sherwood Fstrs	Pte	23/06/17	Desertion	10yrs PS	F&F	213/15	
Bowerman William	1 E Surrey	Pte	08/03/17	Desertion	XXX 24/03/17	F&F	213/14	601
Bowran Joseph	2 Lancs Fus	Pte	24/02/16	Desertion	5yrs PS	F&F	213/7	
Bowsher A	8 E Kent (Buffs)	Pte	20/05/16	Desertion	10yrs PS	F&F	213/9	
Bowsher A	8 E Kent (Buffs)	Pte	06/12/16	Desertion	10yrs PS	F&F	213/13	
Bowyer E	1 Welsh	Pte	13/07/15	Sleeping	3yrs PS	F&F	213/4	
Boyce J	8 Black Watch	Pte	09/01/19	Desertion	10yrs PS	F&F	213/27	
Boylan P	2 Leinster	Pte	15/10/17	Desertion	5yrs PS	F&F	213/17	
Boyle W	8 Bedfordshire	Pte	10/02/16	Desertion	10yrs PS	F&F	213/7	
Bozan K	85 Canadian EF	Pte	13/06/17	Desertion	10yrs PS	F&F	213/16	
Bradford F	2 Durham LI	Pte	15/03/15	Disobedience	15yrs PS	F&F	213/3	
Bradford S	2 York & Lancaster	Pte	15/01/17	Sleeping	2yrs HL	F&F	213/13	
Bradley J	7 Kings Shropshire LI	Pte	01/12/17	Desertion	5yrs PS	F&F	213/18	
Bradshaw P	6 Dragoons	Tpr	25/11/14	Desertion	5yrs PS	F&F	213/1	12
Brady	2 Lancs Fus	Pte	30/06/15	Desertion	5yrs PS	F&F	213/4	

Name	Unit	Rank	Date	Offence	Final sentence	Location	Ref	Note
Brady D	2 R Scots Fus	Pte	14/08/17	Desertion	15yrs PS	F&F	213/16	
Brady JE	4 Australian Pnr Bn	Pte	29/08/17	Desertion	PS Life		213/17	
Brady Michael	Civilian	Sinn Fein	08/05/16	Rebellion	3yrs PS	Dublin	213/8	293
Braithwaite A	7 Liverpool	Pte	08/07/15	Sleeping+	6 Mos HL	F&F	213/4	86
Braithwaite John	New Zealand Rifle Bde	Pte	11/10/16	Mutiny	XXX 29/10/16	F&F	90/6	474
Bramwell J	15 Sherwood Fstrs	Pte	23/09/18	Desertion	10yrs PS	F&F	213/25	980
Bramwell PJ	2 Bedfordshire	Pte	05/01/15	Sleeping	2yrs HL	F&F	213/3	
Brand J	1 Northumb Fus	Pte	08/02/15	Disobedience+	10yrs PS	F&F	213/3	37
Brannigan J	6 DAC	Gnr	29/09/15	Desertion	Quashed		213/5	
Brannigan P	4 (att 2) A&S Hdrs	Pte	26/03/16	Desertion	5yrs PS	UK	213/8	197
Brannon JT	11 Sherwood Fstrs	Pte	27/12/16	Sleeping	5yrs PS	F&F	213/13	
Bray Walter W	6 Dragoon Gds	Pte	02/06/15	Sleeping	5yrs PS	F&F	213/4	
Brazier E	1/5 Bedfordshire	Pte	06/04/18	Cowardice	Not Conf	Egypt	213/22	
Brazier R	1 Norfolk	Pte	12/08/15	Sleeping	15yrs PS	F&F	213/4	
Brazier W	104 DAC RFA	Cpl	26/04/17	Against Inhab	10yrs PS		213/15	
Bremmer A	D Cornwall LI	Pte	02/10/15	Desertion	10yrs PS	F&F	213/6	
Brennan G	1 Leinster	Pte	14/06/15	Sleeping	3yrs PS	F&F	213/4	
Brennan J	Civilian	Sinn Fein	04/05/16	Rebellion	3yrs PS	Dublin	213/8	244
Brennan Joseph	1/8 Liverpool	Pte	30/06/16	Desertion	XXX 16/07/16	F&F	213/9	390
Brennan M	Civilian	Sinn Fein	05/05/16	Rebellion	3yrs PS	Dublin	213/8	276
Brennan Robert	Civilian	Sinn Fein	10/05/16	Rebellion	5yrs PS	Dublin	213/8	301
Brennan W	RAMC	Pte	13/12/16	Desertion	5yrs PS		213/13	
Brewin H	6 Leicestershire	Pte	25/10/15	Sleeping	5yrs PS	F&F	213/6	
Brewster A	2 Essex	Pte	06/05/16	Sleeping	5yrs PS	F&F	213/10	
Brewster HF	East Non Combat Corps	Pte	10/06/16	Disobedience	10yrs PS	F&F	213/9	343
Brewster J	2 R Irish Rifles	Rfm	08/04/15	Desertion	Quashed	F&F	213/3	
Brewster LN	8 London	Pte	06/06/18	Quitting	2yrs HL	F&F	213/23	
Bridges F	2 R Sussex	Pte	26/07/17	Sleeping	2yrs HL	F&F	213/16	
Bridges W	1/10 London	Pte	09/09/15	Sleeping	2yrs HL	Gallipoli	213/5	106
Bridle W	2 E Surrey	Pte	14/02/15	Desertion	2yrs HL	F&F	213/3	
Briggs Arthur	9 Sherwood Fstrs	Pte	05/07/18	Desertion	XXX 19/07/18	F&F	213/24	936
Briggs James	2 Border	Pte	19/02/15	Desertion	XXX 06/03/15	F&F	213/3	45
Brigham T	1/10 Manchester	Pte	08/11/17	Desertion	15yrs PS	F&F	213/18	825
Brigham Thomas	1/10 Manchester	Pte	18/05/18	Desertion	XXX 04/06/18	F&F	213/22	908
Bright B	9 R Irish Rifles	Rfm	25/11/16	Desertion	15yrs PS	F&F	213/12	522
Briscoe T	1/5 S Lancs	Cpl	01/10/15	Cowardice	Not Conf	F&F	213/6	
Bristow W	2 Rifle Bde	Rfm	21/05/15	Striking	3mos FP1	F&F	213/4	
Britton Charles	1/5 R Warwickshire	Pte	31/08/17	Desertion	XXX 12/09/17	F&F	213/17	740
Britton D	1 Welsh Gds	Pte	11/02/16	Quitting	3yrs PS	F&F	213/7	
Britton J	8 Canadian EF	Pte	11/09/18	Desertion	10yrs PS	F&F	213/25	
Broad P	4 Australian Pnr Bn	Pte	05/07/17	Desertion	10yrs PS		213/16	
Broad T	2 E Surrey	Pte	03/04/15	Desertion	3mos FP1	F&F	213/4	
Broadbridge FG	10 Royal Fus	Pte	16/05/18	Desertion	5yrs PS	F&F	213/22	
Broaderick Frederick	11 R Warwickshire	Pte	20/07/17	Desertion	XXX 01/08/17	F&F	213/16	702
Broadrick F	11 R Warwickshire	Pte	02/02/17	Desertion	10yrs PS	F&F	213/13	
Brocklesby JH	2 North Non Combat Corps	Pte	13/06/16	Disobedience	10yrs PS	F&F	213/9	361
Brogan J	2 R Munster Fus	Pte	02/04/17	Desertion	5yrs PS	F&F	213/14	
Brompton J	5 R Irish Rifles	Rfm	04/02/16	Desertion	5yrs PS	Ireland	213/8	167
Brompton J	1 R Irish Fus	Pte	26/06/17	Desertion	15yrs PS	F&F	213/16	
Brook C	1/6 W Yorks	Pte	03/03/16	Disobedience	2yrs HL	F&F	213/8	
Brook T	9 W Riding	Pte	04/12/15	Quitting	3 mos FP1	F&F	213/7	
Brooke R	4 Rifle Bde	Rfm	13/03/15	Sleeping	Not Conf	F&F	213/3	
Brooke R	10 W Yorks	Pte	15/02/18	Desertion	5yrs PS	F&F	213/21	
Brookes R	3/5 Lancs Fus	Pte	30/10/17	Desertion	15yrs PS	F&F	213/18	
Brookes W	8 KRRC	Sgt	04/01/17	Desertion	5yrs PS	F&F	213/13	
Brookes W	25 KRRC	Rfm	20/08/18	Against Inhab +	10yrs PS	F&F	213/24	966
Brookfield N	12 S Staffordshire	Pte	10/03/17	Desertion	2yrs HL	F&F	213/14	605
Brooks A	9 Durham LI	Pte	01/12/17	Desertion	5yrs PS		213/19	
Brooks C	5 Wiltshire	Pte	07/09/15	Disobedience	7yrs PS	Gallipoli	213/5	
Brooks C	6 Wiltshire	Pte	18/11/16	Desertion	15yrs PS	F&F	213/12	
Brooks C	6 Yorks	Pte	30/05/18	Desertion	5yrs PS	F&F	213/22	
Brooks F	Civilian	Sinn Fein	04/05/16	Rebellion	3yrs PS	Dublin	213/8	245
Brooks T	1 Essex	Pte	22/10/15	Disobedience	5yrs PS	Gallipoli	213/6	
Broomfield E	7 Lincolnshire	L/Cpl	07/09/17	Desertion x2	15yrs PS	F&F	213/17	
Broughton TH	13 York and Lancaster	Pte	26/08/18	Desertion	10yrs PS	F&F	213/24	967
Brown A	2 KOR Lancaster	Pte	19/03/15	Sleeping	2yrs HL	F&F	213/3	
Brown A	1 E Yorks	Pte	27/03/15	Sleeping	2yrs HL	F&F	213/3	
Brown A	7 N Staffordshire	Pte	18/01/16	Cowardice	7yrs PS	Gallipoli [?]	213/7	155

Name	Unit	Rank	Date	Offence	Final sentence	Location	Ref	Note
Brown A	ASC	Dvr	25/06/16	Desertion	5yrs PS		213/10	
Brown Archibald	10 Black Watch	Pte	20/05/17	Desertion	XXX 01/06/17	Salonika	213/15	656
Brown C	2 Scots Gds	Pte	05/01/16	Sleeping	3yrs PS	F&F	213/7	
Brown F	1/5 Bedfordshire	Pte	09/09/15	Sleeping	2yrs HL	Gallipoli	213/5	
Brown G	2 KO Yorks LI	Pte	14/05/15	Desertion	15yrs PS	F&F	213/4	
Brown H	ASC	Dvr	04/09/14	Sleeping	2yrs HL		213/2	
Brown H	8 Rifle Bde	Cpl	26/10/15	Desertion	10yrs PS	F&F	213/6	
Brown J	10 W Riding	Pte	18/04/17	Desertion	10yrs PS	F&F	213/15	
Brown J	24 Northumb Fus	Dvr	05/05/17	Desertion	5yrs PS	F&F	213/15	647
Brown J	18 Durham LI	Pte	26/08/18	Desertion	10yrs PS	F&F	213/25	968
Brown J	1 Gloucestershire	Pte	15/10/18	Desertion	5yrs PS	F&F	213/26	
Brown P	1 R Warwickshire	Pte	25/09/15	Desertion	10yrs PS	F&F	213/5	
Brown R	9 Worcestershire	Pte	19/04/16	Sleeping	5yrs PS	Mesopotamia	90/7	208
Brown R	13 R Scots	Pte	20/09/17	Desertion	5yrs PS	F&F	213/17	
Brown T	1/5 Sherwood Fstrs	Pte	19/10/17	Quitting	5yrs PS	F&F	213/18	
Brown TMcG	158 Lab Coy	Pte	12/03/18	Desertion	10yrs PS	F&F	213/21	
Brown W	ASC	Pte	29/04/17	Desertion	15yrs PS		213/15	
Browne Archibald	2 Essex	Pte	09/12/14	Desertion	XXX 19/12/14	F&F	213/1	15
Bruce AE	9 E Surrey	Pte	30/04/17	Desertion	3yrs PS	F&F	213/15	
Bryan H	13 York and Lancaster	Pte	18/12/17	Desertion x2	10yrs PS	F&F	213/20	847
Bryan WH	7 Northants	Pte	29/02/16	Desertion	10yrs PS	F&F	213/8	
Bryant C	3 Middlesex	Pte	10/07/15	Sleeping	3yrs PS	F&F	213/4	
Bryant Ernest	10 Cheshire	Pte	23/09/17	Desertion x2	XXX 27/10/17	F&F	213/18	769
Bryant WJ	42 Canadian EF	Pte	15/12/17	Desertion	15yrs PS	F&F	213/19	
Buchanan A	4 Canadian EF	Pte	02/07/16	Desertion +	10yrs PS	F&F	213/10	392
Buchanan J	1/6 Black Watch	Pte	26/01/17	Desertion	10yrs PS	F&F	213/13	582
Buckle J	4 Yorks	Pte	15/11/17	Desertion	5yrs PS	F&F	213/18	
Buckley M	2 R Irish Rifles	Rfm	14/02/15	Desertion	Quashed	F&F	213/3	
Buckley WJ	1 Australian IF	Pte	24/02/17	Desertion	10yrs PS		213/14	
Budworth JT	2 KRRC	Rfm	13/01/17	Desertion	5yrs PS	F&F	213/13	
Bullas J	1/7 Worcestershire	Pte	03/09/17	Cowardice	Not Conf	F&F	213/17	
Bulman T	4 (att 2) R Munster Fus	Pte	03/07/16	Desertion	3yrs PS	F&F	213/10	
Bunn L	2/7 Worcestershire	Pte	08/06/16	Sleeping	5yrs PS	F&F	213/9	
Buntin J	1/7 Highland LI	Pte	02/01/18	Desertion	Not Conf	Egypt	213/20	
Burch HE	5 MGC	Pte	29/03/16	Sleeping+	3yrs PS	F&F	213/8	199
Burden Herbert	1 Northumb Fus	Pte	02/07/15	Desertion	XXX 21/07/15	F&F	213/4	81
Burford GH	2 KO Yorks LI	Pte	28/03/15	Desertion	15yrs PS	F&F	213/3	
Burgess C	10 KRRC	Rfm	26/08/17	Desertion	5yrs PS	F&F	213/16	
Burgess GF	723 Lab Corps	Pte	17/08/18	Desertion	Not Conf		213/25	
Burgess H	2 Coldstream Gds	Pte	18/07/18	Desertion x3 +	5yrs PS	F&F	213/24	945
Burgess William	1 Lincolnshire	Pte	08/05/16	Desertion	10yrs PS	F&F	213/10	
Burgoyne A	7 E Surrey	Pte	01/06/17	Desertion	10yrs PS	F&F	213/15	
Burke EW	2 R Sussex	Pte	30/06/18	Desertion	10yrs PS	F&F	213/24	
Burke James	Civilian	Sinn Fein	05/05/16	Rebellion	3yrs PS	Dublin	213/8	277
Burke P	1 Gloucestershire	Pte	30/05/16	Disobedience	1yr HL	F&F	213/9	
Burke W	2 R Inniskilling Fus	Pte	10/04/15	Desertion+	15yrs PS	F&F	213/4	61
Burke W	6 R Dublin Fus	Pte	03/02/16	Quitting	3yrs PS	Salonika	213/7	
Burke W	1 Liverpool	Pte	30/11/16	Desertion	5yrs PS	F&F	213/12	
Burkett W	2 R Sussex	Pte	07/03/18	Desertion	10yrs PS	F&F	213/21	
Burns E	2/7 Manchester	Pte	29/06/17	Sleeping	2yrs HL	F&F	213/16	
Burns J	8 KO Scottish Bdrs	Gnr	26/03/16	Desertion	15yrs PS	F&F	213/8	
Burns W	1 Gordon Hdrs	Pte	20/08/17	Desertion	5yrs PS	F&F	213/16	
Burrell FG	2 R Warwickshire	Pte	23/01/15	Desertion	2yrs HL	F&F	213/3	
Burrell William Henry	2 R Sussex	Pte	30/04/15	Desertion	5yrs PS	F&F	213/4	66
Burrell William Henry	2 R Sussex	Pte	05/05/16	Desertion	XXX 22/05/16	F&F	213/9	278
Burrows EW	6 Northumb Fus	Pte	22/06/17	Desertion	5yrs PS	F&F	213/16	
Burt A	4 Royal Fus	Pte	13/03/17	Desertion	10yrs PS	F&F	213/14	
Burt John	2 New Zealand Rifle Bde	Pte	01/12/16	Desertion	10yrs PS		213/12	
Burtch JA	38 Canadian EF	Pte	13/09/17	Desertion	5yrs PS	F&F	213/17	
Burton G	2 E Kent (Buffs)	Pte	29/12/17	Sleeping	2yrs HL	Salonika	213/13	
Burton J	1 Northumb Fus	Pte	09/04/15	Desertion	10yrs PS	F&F	213/4	
Burton R	9 Sherwood Fstrs	Pte	31/07/15	Sleeping	2yrs HL	Egypt	213/5	
Burton Robert	6 S Lancs	Pte	07/02/17	Sleeping	XXX 19/02/17	Mesopotamia	90/7	587
Burugi S	Civilian		28/05/16	Treason	10yrs PS	Macedonia	213/12	321
Busby H	7 R Berkshire	Pte	16/09/18	Desertion	15yrs PS	Salonika	213/26	
Buschman Fernando	Civilian	Alien	29/08/14	Espionage	XXX 19/10/14	UK	92/3	3
Bush James	1 W Yorks	Pte	14/04/16	Desertion	5yrs PS	F&F	213/8	
Bushnell V	8 York & Lancaster	Pte	08/10/17	Desertion	10yrs PS	F&F	213/18	

Name	Unit	Rank	Date	Offence	Final sentence	Location	Ref	Note
Butcher Frederick C	7 E Kent (Buffs)	Pte	23/07/18	Desertion	XXX 27/08/18	F&F	213/25	946
Butcher Frederick Charles	7 E Kent (Buffs)	Pte	07/06/18	Desertion	5yrs PS	F&F	213/23	921
Butcher J	4 Grenadier Gds	Pte	13/08/17	Desertion	5yrs PS	F&F	213/16	
Butcher J	4 Grenadier Gds	Pte	09/11/18	Desertion	Not Conf	F&F	213/26	
Butler	R Scots Fus	Pte	28/09/14	Desertion	Not Conf		213/2	
Butler Alexander	R Canadian Dragoons	Tpr	24/06/16	Murder	XXX 02/07/16	F&F	90/6	383
Butler J	8 Cheshire	Pte	20/09/16	Quitting	3yrs PS	Mesopotamia	90/7	454
Butler J	13 Rifle Bde	Rfn	16/05/18	Desertion	5yrs PS	F&F	213/22	
Butterley B	25 Northumb Fus	Pte	16/03/17	Desertion	5yrs PS	F&F	213/14	608
Buttle AE	2 KO Yorks LI	Pte	25/07/16	Desertion	10yrs PS	F&F	213/10	
Button FH	43 Canadian EF	Pte	18/10/18	Desertion	15yrs PS	F&F	213/26	
Byers Joseph	1 R Scots Fus	Pte	30/01/15	Desertion	XXX 06/02/15	F&F	213/3	26
Bykoff V	1 Slavo-British Legion	Pte	17/07/19	Mutiny	10yrs PS	N Russia	213/32	
Byrne H	6 Northumb Fus	Pte	19/06/17	Desertion x2	5yrs PS	F&F	213/15	
Byrne J	Civilian	Sinn Fein	04/05/16	Rebellion	3yrs PS	Dublin	213/8	246
Byrnes AJ	25 Australian IF	Pte	15/07/16	Violence	10yrs PS		213/10	
Cadby J	8 R Welsh Fus	Pte	24/09/15	Sleeping	6 Mos HL	Gallipoli	213/5	
Cairnie Peter W	1 R Scots Fus	Pte	15/12/16	Desertion	XXX 28/12/16	F&F	213/12	529
Calderwood W	5 R Irish	Pte	15/08/16	Striking	3yrs PS	Salonika	213/11	424
Calitz [?] MC	S African Horse Arty	Gnr	22/02/18	Desertion	10yrs PS		213/20	
Callaghan J	8 Seaforth Hdrs	Pte	21/12/17	Desertion	5yrs PS	F&F	213/19	
Caller A	2 RW Surrey	Pte	03/02/15	AWOL+	3mos FP1	F&F	213/3	29
Callow H	1 E Surrey	Pte	14/06/15	Sleeping	2yrs HL	F&F	213/4	
Cameron John	1/5 Northumb Fus	Pte	24/11/16	Desertion	XXX 04/12/16	F&F	213/12	518
Cameron W	1/8 Lancs Fus	Pte	12/08/15	Cowardice	Commuted	Gallipoli	213/5	
Cameron W	27 Canadian EF	Pte	18/11/17	Desertion	10yrs PS	F&F	213/18	
Campbell GH	1 Canadian FA	Gnr	31/05/16	Desertion	10yrs PS	F&F	213/9	
Campbell J	RFA	Dvr	08/03/16	Desertion	10yrs PS		213/8	
Campbell JW	3 Canadian MGC	Pte	20/10/18	Desertion	15yrs PS	F&F	213/26	
Campbell S	2 York & Lancaster	Pte	07/10/17	Desertion	5yrs PS	F&F	213/18	
Campbell T	1/4 Seaforth Hdrs	Pte	20/09/18	Desertion x2	10yrs PS	F&F	213/25	978
Canavan WJ	6 R Irish Rifles	Rfm	06/12/15	Sleeping	3yrs PS	Salonika	213/7	
Canning A	8 R W Kent	Pte	07/04/16	Sleeping	5yrs PS	F&F	213/8	
Capel T	2 E Surrey	Pte	24/03/15	Sleeping	3mos FP1	F&F	213/3	
Capener A	9 Worcestershire	Pte	19/08/16	Sleeping	3yrs PS	Mesopotamia	90/7	427
Carabine E	8 R Inniskilling Fus	Pte	03/03/17	Desertion	10yrs PS	F&F	213/16	
Carberry J	2 S Lancs	Pte	09/06/16	Cowardice+	10yrs PS	F&F	213/9	336
Carberry M	6 R Irish Rifles	Rfm	29/06/16	Violence	18mos HL	Salonika	213/10	
Card Edward A	20 KRRC	Rfm	09/09/16	Desertion	XXX 22/09/16	F&F	213/11	446
Carden H	22 Manchester	Pte	03/08/16	Desertion	3yrs PS	F&F	213/11	
Carey A	MGC	Pte	29/05/16	Cowardice	15yrs PS		213/9	
Carey Joseph	7 R Irish Fus	Pte	22/08/16	Desertion x2	XXX 15/09/16	F&F	213/11	433
Carleton J	38 Canadian EF	L/Cpl	10/05/17	Desertion	10yrs PS	F&F	213/15	
Carlton F	6 Cameron Hdrs	Pte	20/03/16	Desertion	5yrs PS	F&F	213/8	
Carolan G	2/5 Lancs Fus	Pte	24/12/17	Desertion x2	10yrs PS		213/19	
Carpenter AE	18 Liverpool	Pte	19/10/17	Quitting	10yrs PS	F&F	213/18	
Carpenter P	102 Canadian EF	Pte	19/01/18	Desertion	10yrs PS	F&F	213/19	
Carr James G	2 Welsh	Pte	22/01/16	Desertion/Esc	XXX 07/02/16	F&F	213/7	160
Carr T	2 Bedfordshire	Pte	26/02/16	Sleeping	3yrs PS	F&F	213/8	
Carrington H	7 R Munster Fus	Pte	23/12/15	Misc	Not Conf	Salonika	213/7	
Carroll T	1 Lancs Fus	Pte	20/02/18	Desertion	2yrs HL	F&F	213/20	
Carson A	9 R Irish Rifles	Rfm	21/01/16	Desertion	2yrs HL	F&F	213/7	159
Carter AE	2 Bedfordshire	Pte	15/12/14	Quitting/Sleeping	2yrs HL	F&F	213/3	
Carter E	6 R Irish	Pte	12/02/18	Desertion	Not Conf	F&F	213/20	
Carter GL	14 Welsh	Pte	19/01/16	Sleeping	3mos FP1	Egypt	213/7	
Carter Harold George	73 Canadian EF	Pte	05/04/17	Desertion	XXX 20/04/17	F&F	213/14	627
Carter Henry	11 Middlesex	Pte	12/04/16	Desertion	XXX 26/04/16	F&F	213/8	204
Cartwright A	1 Cheshire	Sgt	11/08/15	Desertion	10yrs PS	F&F	213/5	
Cartwright C	2 North Non Combat Corps	Pte	12/06/16	Disobedience	10yrs PS	F&F	213/9	349
Cartwright L	9 Worcestershire	Pte	04/09/16	Sleeping	3yrs PS	Mesopotamia	90/7	443
Casey E	1 R Scots Fus	Pte	10/03/15	Desertion	10yrs PS	F&F	213/3	
Cassidy F	2 R Inniskilling Fus	Pte	30/05/17	Desertion x2	Not Conf	F&F	213/19	
Cassidy James	1 R Inniskilling Fus	Pte	15/07/16	Desertion	XXX 23/07/16	F&F	213/10	398
Castonguay OA	22 Canadian EF	Pte	07/07/17	Desertion	15yrs PS	F&F	213/16	
Caton H	4 KOR Lancaster	Pte	21/08/18	Desertion	5yrs PS		213/25	
Caulfield J	13 Highland LI	Pte	09/07/17	Desertion	Not Conf	UK	213/16	697
Chadwick	1 KO Yorks LI	Pte	22/09/14	Cowardice	Quashed	Singapore	213/2	
Chadwick JW	1/7 W Yorks	Rfm	01/08/15	Quitting	5yrs PS	F&F	213/4	95

Name	Unit	Rank	Date	Offence	Final sentence	Location	Ref	Note
Chalk C	3 Rifle Bde	Rfm	10/09/17	Desertion	10yrs PS	F&F	213/17	
Chalk T	8 Bedfordshire	Pte	04/10/17	Desertion	10yrs PS	F&F	213/18	
Chalmers J	107 Canadian Pnrs	Pte	21/01/18	Absence	7yrs PS	F&F	213/20	
Chandler Joseph	Lincolnshire	Pte	28/05/19	Murder	XXX 11/08/19	F&F	213/30	1012
Chandler SE	42 Canadian EF	Pte	11/07/16	Desertion	10yrs PS	F&F	213/10	
Chandler W	11 Essex	Pte	03/09/17	Desertion	5yrs PS	F&F	213/17	
Chang Ju Chih	Chinese Lab Corps	Coolie	05/05/19	Murder x4	XXX 14/02/20	F&F	213/31	1006
Chant T	7 R Sussex	Pte	03/06/17	Desertion	10yrs PS	F&F	213/15	
Chao Hsing I	Chinese Lab Corps	Coolie	25/07/18	Murder	XXX 09/08/18	F&F	213/24	948
Chapman JW	1 Devon	Pte	21/08/15	Sleeping	10yrs PS	F&F	213/5	
Chapman S	HQ 1 Canadian DT	Pte	06/10/16	Disobedience	3yrs PS	F&F	213/12	
Chapman S	9 Norfolk	Pte	16/05/18	Desertion	10yrs PS	F&F	213/22	
Chapman T	2 Lincolnshire	Pte	26/04/15	Desertion	5yrs PS	F&F	213/4	
Chapman V	3 Middlesex	L/Cpl	16/06/15	Desertion	15yrs PS	F&F	213/4	
Chapman W	1 N Staffordshire	Pte	20/01/15	Desertion	10yrs PS	F&F	213/3	
Charnock W	8 KOR Lancaster	Pte	11/09/16	Desertion	5yrs PS	F&F	213/11	
Chase Herbert	2 Lancs Fus	Pte	29/05/15	Cowardice	XXX 12/06/15	F&F	213/4	72
Cheeney RL	24 Canadian EF	Pte	12/08/17	Desertion	15yrs PS	F&F	213/16	
Cheeseman Frank William	18 KRRC	Rfm	03/10/17	Desertion	XXX 20/10/17	F&F	213/17	782
Cheeseman L	6 R Marines	Pte	04/10/19	Disobedience	5yrs PS	N Russia	213/30	
Cheetham H	1/5 Bedfordshire	Pte	06/04/18	Cowardice	5yrs PS	Egypt	213/22	
Chemmings J	1 R Marine LI	Pte	20/11/17	Desertion	5yrs PS		213/18	
Cherbukin F	1 Slavo-British Legion	Pte	14/07/19	Mutiny	XXX 00/07/19	N Russia	213/32	
Cherry J	59 Australian IF	Pte	23/06/17	Desertion	90 days FP1		213/16	
Chisholm Alexander	20 Army Troop Coy RE	Cpl	10/05/15	Murder	XXX 17/05/15	F&F	90/6	68
Christie T	6 R Munster Fus	Pte	04/04/17	Cowardice+	10yrs PS	Salonika	213/15	620
Clancy Peter	Civilian	Sinn Fein	03/05/16	Rebellion	10yrs PS	Dublin	213/8	225
Clark F	1 Northants	Pte	26/01/17	Desertion	5yrs PS	F&F	213/13	
Clark G	1/7 Black Watch	Pte	07/11/15	Sleeping	2yrs HL	F&F	213/6	129
Clark HFG	2 Bedfordshire	Pte	15/12/14	Quitting/Sleeping	2yrs HL	F&F	213/3	
Clark T	1 Royal Fus	Pte	29/04/16	Desertion	5yrs PS	F&F	213/9	
Clarke A	2 Worcestershire	Pte	09/08/16	Desertion	5yrs PS	F&F	213/11	
Clarke AG	13 Essex	Sgt	22/09/17	Desertion	5yrs PS	F&F	213/17	768
Clarke C	1 Border	Pte	04/09/17	Desertion	5yrs PS	F&F	213/17	
Clarke F	46 Australian	Pte	05/09/17	Desertion	PS Life		213/18	
Clarke F	225 MGC	Pte	17/12/17	Not recorded	5yrs PS		213/21	
Clarke FH	46 Australian IF	Pte	28/06/17	Desertion	10yrs PS		213/16	
Clarke FH	46 Australian IF	Pte	28/06/17	Desertion	10yrs PS		213/16	
Clarke G	RGA	Gnr	19/04/16	Desertion	10yrs PS		213/9	
Clarke G	13 York and Lancaster	Pte	14/10/18	Desertion	10yrs PS	F&F	213/25	984
Clarke Hubert A	2 British West Indies	Pte	07/08/17	Striking +	XXX 11/08/17	Egypt	213/17	720
Clarke J	Civilian	Sinn Fein	04/05/16	Rebellion	3yrs PS	Dublin	213/8	247
Clarke J	15 R Irish Rifles	Rfm	05/09/17	Quitting	5yrs PS	F&F	213/17	748
Clarke JW	6 KO Scottish Bdrs	Pte	06/12/15	Sleeping	6 Mos HL	F&F	213/6	
Clarke T	1 R Berkshire	Pte	28/04/16	Desertion	10yrs PS	F&F	213/9	
Clarke Thomas J	Civilian	Sinn Fein	01/05/16	Rebellion	XXX 03/05/16	Dublin	213/8	217
Clarke W	8 Devon	Pte	19/12/16	Desertion	15yrs PS	F&F	213/13	
Clarke W	84 RFA	Dvr	17/05/17	Desertion	15yrs PS		213/15	
Clarke W	RFA	Dvr	24/01/18	Desertion	10yrs PS		213/19	
Clarke W	2/4 E Lancs	Pte	05/02/18	Cowardice	5yrs PS	F&F	213/20	
Clarke Wilfred	2 Durham LI	Pte	08/11/16	Desertion	10yrs PS	F&F	213/12	501
Clarke Wilfred	2 Durham LI	Pte	17/01/18	Desertion	XXX 09/02/18	F&F	213/20	863
Clarke WP	7/8 KO Scottish Bdrs	Pte	05/12/16	Desertion	2yrs HL	F&F	213/13	
Cleasby T	9 Lancs Fus	Pte	23/08/16	Sleeping	2yrs HL	F&F	213/10	
Clee R	9 S Staffordshire	Pte	28/08/16	Desertion	10yrs PS	F&F	213/11	
Clements W	2 Essex	Pte	01/10/15	Sleeping	Not Conf	F&F	213/6	
Cliffe J	1 S Staffordshire	Pte	05/03/17	Desertion	5yrs PS	F&F	213/14	
Clifton J	2 York & Lancaster	Pte	30/06/16	Desertion	10yrs PS	F&F	213/10	
Clinch EW	2 Wiltshire	Pte	09/06/16	Disobedience	Not Conf	F&F	213/10	
Close CH	1 New Zealand EF	Pte	10/05/18	Desertion	15yrs PS	F&F	213/24	905
Coates G	1/4 York & Lancaster	Pte	19/11/17	Desertion	10yrs PS	F&F	213/18	831
Coffey Denis	2 R Munster Fus	Pte	30/01/16	Desertion	5yrs PS	F&F	213/7	
Cogdell E	1 E Surrey	Pte	27/10/15	Sleeping	10yrs PS	F&F	213/6	
Coghlan T	1 R Irish Rifles	Rfm	21/05/15	Desertion	5yrs PS	F&F	213/4	
Colaluca A	8 E Kent (Buffs)	Pte	02/12/15	Sleeping	Quashed	Salonika	213/6	
Colbeck F	10 W Riding	Pte	16/10/15	Sleeping	2yrs HL	F&F	213/6	
Cole AAJ	1/8 Liverpool	Pte	19/07/17	Desertion	15yrs PS	F&F	213/16	701
Cole J	1 D Cornwall LI	Pte	16/05/16	Sleeping	2yrs HL	F&F	213/9	

Name	Unit	Rank	Date	Offence	Final sentence	Location	Ref	Note
Coleman J	1 Scottish Rifles	Pte	06/03/16	Desertion	5yrs PS	F&F	213/8	
Coleman J	1 R Warwickshire	Pte	09/01/19	Desertion	15yrs PS	F&F	213/28	
Coleman John	2 Sherwood Fstrs	Pte	02/07/15	Desertion	10yrs PS	F&F	213/4	
Coleman M	2 Leinster	Pte	28/03/17	Striking	5yrs PS	F&F	213/16	
Coleman R	Civilian	Sinn Fein	04/05/16	Rebellion	3yrs PS	Dublin	213/8	248
Coles F	1 Grenadier Gds	Cpl	24/12/14	Sleeping/Quitting	2yrs HL	F&F	213/3	
Coles GH	1/5 Suffolk	Pte	06/09/18	Violence/Esc	5yrs PS	Palestine	213/27	
Coley J	1 S Staffordshire	Pte	01/11/16	Desertion	Quashed	F&F	213/12	
Collins A	7 Canadian EF	Pte	10/02/16	Desertion	10yrs PS	F&F	213/8	
Collins C	8 R Berkshire	Pte	13/12/15	Sleeping	1yr HL	F&F	213/6	
Collins E	1/4 Gloucestershire	Pte	03/09/17	Desertion	10yrs PS	F&F	213/17	744
Collins George E	1 Lincolnshire	Pte	07/02/15	Desertion	XXX 15/02/15	F&F	213/3	34
Collins H	2 R Warwickshire	Pte	18/01/15	Desertion	5yrs PS	F&F	213/3	21
Collins JA	2 S Lancs	Pte	26/06/16	Desertion	5yrs PS	F&F	213/10	
Collins T	5 Northumb Fus	Pte	08/08/16	Desertion	5yrs PS	F&F	213/11	
Collis W	9 Royal Fus	Pte	27/11/18	Disobedience	5yrs PS	F&F	213/28	
Compton D	1 R W Kent	Pte	18/11/18	Desertion	5yrs PS	F&F	213/27	
Compton W	1 Norfolk	Pte	14/05/18	Desertion	7yrs PS	F&F	213/22	
Compton W	1 Norfolk	Pte	29/07/18	Desertion	10yrs PS	F&F	213/24	
Comte Gustave	22 Canadian EF	Pte	06/06/17	Desertion	XXX 03/07/17	F&F	213/15	670
Condon S	52 Australian IF	Pte	01/02/17	Desertion	10yrs PS		213/14	
Connell	2 Lancs Fus	Pte	19/10/15	Sleeping	5yrs PS	F&F	213/6	
Connell H	12 KRRC	Pte	10/01/16	Sleeping	2yrs HL	F&F	213/7	
Connell P	6 R Munster Fus	Pte	04/04/17	Cowardice+	10yrs PS	Salonika	213/15	621
Connelly D	15 Highland LI	Pte	08/05/18	Desertion	5yrs PS	F&F	213/22	904
Connelly P	7 Gloucestershire	Pte	16/01/16	Quitting	Not Conf	Gallipoli [?]	213/8	149
Connolly	2 Lancs Fus	Pte	24/02/16	Desertion	5yrs PS	F&F	213/7	
Connolly James	Civilian	Sinn Fein	09/05/16	Rebellion	XXX 12/05/16	Dublin	213/8	299
Connor J	1 R Irish Fus	Pte	04/08/16	Desertion	10yrs PS	F&F	213/10	
Connor J	1 R Irish Fus	Pte	11/01/17	Desertion	15yrs PS	F&F	213/14	
Connor P	22 Northumb Fus	Pte	05/11/17	Desertion	3yrs PS	F&F	213/18	820
Connors M	6 R Munster Fus	Pte	04/04/17	Cowardice+	10yrs PS	Salonika	213/15	622
Conroy P	RFA	Dvr	31/10/17	Desertion	10yrs PS		213/18	
Conway A	15 R Scots	Pte	28/01/18	Desertion	5yrs PS	F&F	213/20	
Cook A	9 W Yorks	Pte	12/12/15	Sleeping	3mos FP1	Gallipoli	213/7	
Cook M	3 Bty RFA	Dvr	25/09/17	Desertion +	5yrs PS	Mesopotamia	90/7	772
Cook PH	51 Australian IF	Pte	27/04/17	Desertion	2yrs HL		213/15	
Cook T	7 Yorks	Pte	22/11/15	Desertion	Not Conf	F&F	213/7	
Cook T	7 Yorks	Pte	14/12/15	Desertion	10yrs PS	F&F	213/7	
Cooper A	2 Essex	Pte	20/09/14	Cowardice	3yrs PS	F&F	213/2	
Cooper T	3 Rifle Bde	Pte	30/01/15	Striking	5yrs PS	F&F	213/3	
Corbett J	3 Rifle Bde	Rfm	20/11/14	Sleeping	Quashed	F&F	213/2	
Corbett SE	14 Welsh	Pte	18/12/17	Cowardice	5yrs PS	F&F	213/19	848
Corcoran JW	2 S Wales Bdrs	Pte	24/10/15	Sleeping	5yrs PS	Gallipoli	213/6	
Cork WJ	1/1 Monmouth	Rfm	16/03/17	Desertion	15yrs PS	F&F	213/14	
Cornell GJ	38 Canadian EF	Pte	12/07/17	Desertion	15yrs PS	F&F	213/16	
Correy Frederick De B	2 Canadian Tunnelling Coy	Spr	24/07/16	Desertion	10yrs PS	F&F	213/10	
Corrigan William	Civilian	Sinn Fein	05/05/16	Rebellion	5yrs PS	Dublin	213/8	279
Cosgrave Phillip B	Civilian	Sinn Fein	04/05/16	Rebellion	5yrs PS	Dublin	213/8	249
Cosgrave William	Civilian	Sinn Fein	04/05/16	Rebellion	PS Life	Dublin	213/8	250
Cossman CE	13 Canadian EF	Pte	26/01/16	Desertion	Quashed GOA	F&F	213/7	
Coster J	1/5 D Cornwall LI	Pte	15/06/16	Desertion	5yrs PS	F&F	213/9	373
Costin W	6 Liverpool	Rfm	27/07/16	Sleeping	6mos HL		213/11	
Cottam A	10 Loyal North Lancs	Sgt	18/10/15	Cowardice	10yrs PS	F&F	213/6	
Cotter D	1 R Munster Fus	Pte	07/11/18	Desertion	2yrs HL	F&F	213/27	
Cotterill J	2 Oxon & Bucks LI	Pte	08/10/14	Sleeping	2yrs HL	F&F	213/1	
Cotterill W	2 Canadian EF	Pte	02/05/18	Desertion	5yrs PS	F&F	213/22	
Cottier SJ	ASC	Dvr	15/04/16	Desertion x2	10yrs PS		213/8	
Cottingham J	6 E Kent (Buffs)	Pte	18/08/16	Sleeping	5yrs PS	F&F	213/10	
Coulby F	38 Canadian EF	Pte	03/10/17	Desertion	5yrs PS	F&F	213/17	
Course SG	1/13 London	Pte	14/10/16	Cowardice	Not Conf	F&F	213/12	481
Court RS	48 Australian IF	Pte	11/09/17	Desertion	PS Life		213/17	
Couzens A	4 Royal Fus	Sgt	25/03/15	Cowardice	3yrs PS	F&F	213/3	
Covell FR	2/4 R W Surrey	Sgt	29/08/18	Desertion	10yrs PS	F&F	213/25	
Cover J	RFA	Gnr	08/04/18	Desertion	10yrs PS		213/21	
Coward J	1/5 S Lancs	Pte	18/10/17	Striking x2	5yrs PS	F&F	213/17	
Coward J	2 E Lancs	Pte	12/06/18	Cowardice	10yrs PS	F&F	213/24	
Cowell AF	1 Middlesex	Pte	07/08/18	Desertion	10yrs PS	F&F	213/24	

Name	Unit	Rank	Date	Offence	Final sentence	Location	Ref	Note
Cowell J	1 Devon	Pte	07/04/15	Desertion	10yrs PS	F&F	213/4	
Cowley R	11 Sherwood Fstrs	Pte	16/07/17	Desertion	Not Conf	F&F	213/16	
Cowls A	36 Australian IF	Pte	31/10/17	Desertion	10yrs PS		213/18	
Cox A	2 Essex	Pte	04/10/15	Sleeping	2yrs HL	F&F	213/6	
Cox W	2 Gloucestershire	Pte	07/06/15	Sleeping	3yrs PS	F&F	213/4	
Cox W	2 R Sussex	Pte	16/09/15	Sleeping	2yrs HL	F&F	213/5	
Coyle F	4 (att 2) A&S Hdrs	Pte	24/04/16	Desertion	6 Mos HL	F&F	213/9	
Cozens A	1 E Surrey	Pte	14/06/15	Sleeping	2yrs HL	F&F	213/4	
Craig T	3 E Lancs	Pte	23/12/16	Desertion	18 Mos HL	UK	213/13	535
Craig W	RAMC	Pte	22/06/16	Desertion	10yrs PS		213/9	
Craig W	RGA	Gnr	07/04/18	Desertion	5yrs PS		213/21	
Crane J	10 R W Surrey	Pte	29/03/17	Desertion	10yrs PS	F&F	213/14	
Craven F	2 Grenadier Gds	Pte	04/01/16	Desertion	PS Life	F&F	213/8	
Crawford ER	New Zealand Engineers	Spr	03/07/17	Desertion	5yrs PS		213/16	692
Crawford SH	16 Australian IF	Pte	28/07/17	Desertion	10yrs PS		213/16	
Crawshaw C	9 Loyal North Lancs	Pte	18/10/15	Sleeping	5yrs PS	F&F	213/6	
Cray H	15 Cheshire	Sgt	31/12/16	Desertion	10yrs PS	F&F	213/13	566
Creegan J	6 Leinster	Pte	20/12/15	Insubordination	10yrs PS	Salonika	213/7	
Creighton H	RFA	Pte	22/08/16	Desertion	5yrs PS		213/11	
Crichton J	32 MGC	Pte	27/11/16	Desertion	3yrs PS		213/12	
Crimmins Herbert	18 W Yorks	Pte	21/08/16	Desertion	XXX 05/09/16	F&F	213/10	429
Crisp W	45 Royal Fus	Pte	21/08/19	Not specified	2yrs HL	N Russia	213/31	
Cronin J	6 Loyal N Lancs	Pte	04/05/16	Desertion	10yrs PS	Mesopotamia	90/7	251
Crook R	1/6 W Riding	Pte	28/08/15	Sleeping	5yrs PS	F&F	213/5	
Cross C	11 Liverpool	Pte	03/06/17	Desertion	10yrs PS	F&F	213/15	
Cross F	13 York and Lancaster	Pte	04/04/17	Desertion	10yrs PS	F&F	213/14	623
Cross F	13 York and Lancaster	Pte	24/06/17	Desertion	Not Conf	F&F	213/16	683
Cross F	13 York and Lancaster	Pte	18/12/17	Desertion	10yrs Ps	F&F	213/20	849
Crowhurst J	8 R W Surrey	Pte	13/08/17	Cowardice x2	15yrs PS	F&F	213/17	
Crowley W	1 Welsh Gds	Sgt	31/10/18	Cowardice	Not Conf	F&F	213/26	
Crowther FE	1 KO Yorks LI	Pte	15/07/15	Sleeping	3yrs PS	F&F	213/4	
Crozier James	9 R Irish Rifles	Rfm	14/02/16	Desertion	XXX 27/02/16	F&F	213/7	175
Crump F	2 London	Pte	23/06/16	Desertion	5yrs PS	F&F	213/9	382
Cruse HS	ASC	Pte	02/09/16	Desertion	10yrs PS		213/11	
Crute C	1 Loyal N Lancs	Pte	18/03/16	Desertion	15yrs PS	F&F	213/8	
Cryer CE	2 North Non Combat Corps	Pte	12/06/16	Disobedience	10yrs PS	F&F	213/9	350
Cullen John F	Civilian	Sinn Fein	04/05/16	Rebellion	3yrs PS	Dublin	213/8	252
Cummings J	1 Liverpool	Pte	16/03/16	Desertion	2yrs HL	F&F	213/8	
Cummings Thomas	1 Irish Gds	Pte	19/01/15	Desertion	XXX 28/01/15	F&F	213/3	23
Cummings William H	2/20 London	Pte	20/07/16	Sleeping	5yrs PS	F&F	213/10	
Cunliffe J	8 W Riding	Pte	03/02/17	Desertion	5yrs PS	F&F	213/13	
Cunningham D	2 Essex	Pte	11/01/15	Quitting x2	10 yrs PS	F&F	213/3	
Cunningham F	1 Lincolnshire	Pte	31/12/14	Cowardice	10yrs PS	F&F	213/3	
Cunningham H	2 York & Lancaster	Pte	18/07/18	Desertion	10yrs PS	F&F	213/24	
Cunningham T	11 S Lancs	Pte	11/09/16	Desertion x2	Not Conf	F&F	213/11	447
Cunnington C	16 Lancs Fus	Pte	18/06/18	Sleeping	5yrs PS	F&F	213/22	928
Cunnington Samuel H	2 R Warwickshire	Pte	29/04/17	Desertion	XXX 19/05/17	F&F	213/15	641
Curnew JB	3 Canadian MGC	Pte	09/09/18	Desertion	5yrs PS	F&F	213/25	
Curnew JB	3 Canadian MGC	Pte	24/03/19	Mutiny	PS Life	F&F	213/29	
Currie Adam	9 Seaforth Hdrs	Pte	16/02/16	Desertion	10yrs PS	F&F	213/7	176
Currie G	2 R Scots Fus	Pte	17/04/17	Desertion	10yrs PS	F&F	213/15	
Currie R	11 R Scots Fus	Pte	02/10/18	Desertion	5yrs PS	F&F	213/26	
Currington C	2 Essex	Pte	01/07/15	Desertion	3yrs PS	F&F	213/4	
Curtis F	10 Cheshire	Pte	19/04/17	Desertion	10yrs PS	F&F	213/14	
Cuthbert J	9 Cheshire	Pte	22/04/16	Disobedience	XXX 06/05/16	F&F	213/8	209
Cuthbertson J	5 Northumb Fus	Pte	24/11/16	Desertion	15yrs PS	F&F	213/12	
Cutmore George	2 Black Watch	Pte	02/07/17	Desertion	XXX 25/07/17	Mesopotamia	90/7	690
Daganli D	Gold Coast Regt	Cpl	13/10/17	Cowardice	14yrs PS	East Africa	213/22	
Dagesse AC	22 Canadian EF	Pte	28/01/18	Desertion	Not Conf	F&F	213/20	866
Dagesse Arthur Charles	22 Canadian EF	Pte	26/02/18	Desertion	XXX 15/03/18	F&F	213/20	879
Dagless JA	1/7 W Yorks	Rfm	17/08/18	Desertion	10yrs PS	F&F	213/24	961
Dagomba A	Gold Coast Regt	Pte	26/10/17	Sleeping	14yrs PS		213/19	
Dahashev Mohammed	Civilian		24/02/19	Murder	Not Conf	Baku	213/34	
Daikee HO	1 New Zealand EF	Pte	20/10/17	Desertion	Not Conf	F&F	213/18	806
Dale Arthur	13 R Scots	Pte	20/02/16	Murder	XXX 03/02/16	F&F	213/7	179
Dale G	10 Lincolnshire	Pte	17/10/17	Desertion x2	15yrs PS	F&F	213/18	800
Dale J	1 R Scots Fus	Sgt	20/04/18	Desertion	7yrs PS	F&F	213/22	
Dale W	6 Loyal North Lancs	Pte	04/11/15	Sleeping	10yrs Ps	Gallipoli	213/6	

Name	Unit	Rank	Date	Offence	Final sentence	Location	Ref	Note
Daley A	4 Canadian Mtd Rifles	Pte	15/09/17	Desertion	15yrs PS	F&F	213/17	
Daley Edward	Civilian	Sinn Fein	03/05/16	Rebellion	XXX 04/05/16	Dublin	213/8	226
Dalgetty G	2 Highland LI	Pte	08/02/15	Cowardice +	Not Conf	F&F	213/3	38
Dalgetty G	2 Highland LI	Pte	10/02/15	Cowardice +	1yr HL	F&F	213/3	40
Dalton H	2 Yorks	Pte	23/01/16	Desertion	5yrs PS	F&F	213/7	
Daly D	4 R Munster Fus	Pte	30/12/15	Desertion	10yrs PS		213/7	
Daly JJ	1 Connaught Rangers	Pte	04/09/20	Mutiny	XXX 02/11/20	India		1069
Dalziel J	1 Highland LI	Pte	10/04/15	Sleeping	2yrs HL	F&F	213/3	
Daniels William T	18 MGC	Pte	18/08/16	Sleeping	3yrs PS		213/10	
Daoud M	Turkish Army	POW	11/07/18	Mutiny	2yrs HL		213/24	
Darby A	1 Border	Pte	08/05/16	Quitting	Not Conf	Gallipoli	213/10	
Darkiya	2/2 King's African Rifles	Pte	09/08/17	Sleeping	2yrs HL	Egypt	213/17	
Darlington J	2/8 Liverpool	Pte	16/12/17	Desertion	5yrs PS	F&F	213/18	846
Darrington C	1/5 Bedfordshire	Pte	06/04/18	Cowardice	Not Conf	Egypt	213/22	
Davenport W	2 Lancs Fus	Pte	24/02/16	Desertion	5yrs PS	F&F	213/7	
Davey Richard	15 Hampshire	Pte	19/04/18	Desertion	10yrs PS	F&F	213/21	889
Davey W	11 R W Surrey	Pte	05/09/17	Desertion	10yrs PS	F&F	213/17	
Davids Abraham	1 Cape Col Lab Coy	Pte	05/08/19	Murder	XXX 26/08/19	F&F	213/30	1016
Davidson D	5 Highland LI	Pte	28/05/17	Sleeping	2yrs HL		213/16	
Davidson H	(Hawke) R Naval Div	S'man	12/11/16	Desertion	3yrs PS		213/12	
Davidson J	Lab Corps	Pte	09/11/17	Desertion	2yrs HL		213/18	
Davidson JC	5 Dragoon Gds	Pte	11/01/16	Sleeping	2yrs HL	F&F	213/7	147
Davies A	19 Durham LI	Pte	28/12/16	Quitting	15yrs PS	F&F	213/13	540
Davies A	RAMC	Pte	11/08/17	Desertion	5yrs PS		213/18	
Davies F	13 Welsh	Pte	09/02/16	Sleeping	3yrs PS	F&F	213/7	170
Davies G	7 Gloucestershire	Pte	08/10/15	Sleeping	5yrs PS	Gallipoli	213/6	
Davies J	18 Welsh	Pte	20/07/16	Sleeping	3yrs PS	F&F	213/10	404
Davies J	15 Welsh	Pte (L/C)	19/11/18	Desertion	5yrs PS	F&F	213/26	993
Davies JT	1 Kings Shropshire LI	Pte	27/10/18	Desertion	5yrs PS	F&F	213/26	
Davies Richard M	11 Sherwood Fstrs	Pte	13/07/17	Desertion	3yrs PS	F&F	213/16	698
Davies T	32 MGC	Pte	04/08/18	Desertion	5yrs PS		213/24	
Davies W	7 Kings Shropshire LI	Pte	01/12/17	Desertion	5yrs PS	F&F	213/18	
Davies WJ	1 Manchester	Pte	07/02/15	Desertion	5yrs PS	F&F	213/3	
Davies WR	11/2 Manchester	Pte	29/08/18	Desertion	10yrs PS		213/24	
Davis E	Australian IF	Pte	05/04/16	Violence +	2yrs HL		213/8	202
Davis F	KOR Lancaster	Pte	24/11/14	Cowardice	2yrs HL		213/1	
Davis G	2 Leicestershire	Pte	13/12/14	Sleeping	5yrs PS	Mesopotamia	213/1	
Davis John	Follower	Carrier	15/11/15	Murder	10yrs PS		213/4	
Davis P	1 R Munster Fus	Pte	04/07/15	Cowardice	10yrs PS	Mesopotamia	213/4	
Davis R	7 N Staffordshire	Pte	18/01/16	Cowardice	7yrs PS	Gallipoli [?]	213/7	156
Davis Richard M	11 Sherwood Fstrs	Pte	25/10/17	Desertion	XXX 15/11/17	F&F	213/18	809
Davis Thomas	1 R Munster Fus	Pte	22/06/15	Quitting	XXX 02/07/15	Gallipoli	213/4	79
Davison F	2 KO Yorks LI	Pte	17/05/15	Desertion	15yrs PS	F&F	213/4	
Davys Richard	Civilian	Sinn Fein	01/05/16	Rebellion	10yrs PS	Dublin	213/8	218
Dawes J	1 N Staffordshire	Pte	14/01/17	Quitting	5yrs PS	F&F	213/13	
Dawson A	6 R Munster Fus	Pte	04/04/17	Cowardice +	10yrs PS	Salonika	213/15	624
Dawson C	2 Leicestershire	Pte	13/09/18	Sleeping	10yrs PS	Egypt	213/26	
Dawson E	9 KO Yorks LI	Pte	14/09/17	Desertion	10yrs PS	F&F	213/17	
Dawson J	1 Gordon Hdrs	Pte	28/12/15	Sleeping	3yrs PS	F&F	213/7	
Dawson W	1 Loyal N Lancs	Pte	24/04/16	Desertion	5yrs PS	F&F	213/8	
Day J	2 R Scots Fus	Pte	08/06/18	Desertion x3	10yrs PS	F&F	213/24	
Day W	1/5 S Lancs	Rfm	20/05/15	Sleeping	5yrs PS	F&F	213/4	
Day W	7 Rifle Bde	Rfm	08/09/17	Desertion	10yrs PS	F&F	213/17	
Days J	7 S Lancs	Pte	27/10/17	Desertion	10yrs PS	F&F	213/18	
de Fehr B	1 Canadian Reserve Park	Dvr	22/08/16	Murder	XXX 25/08/16	F&F	213/10	
De Fontenay GA	37 Australian IF	Pte	01/09/17	Desertion	10yrs PS		213/18	
de Valera Edward	Civilian	Sinn Fein	08/05/16	Rebellion	PS Life	Dublin	213/8	294
Deacons M	2 Irish Gds	Pte	28/02/16	Striking x2	2yrs HL	F&F	213/8	
Dean A	1 KRRC	Pte	02/02/16	Sleeping	3yrs PS	F&F	213/7	
Dean EC	3 Canadian MGC	Pte	20/10/16	Desertion	15yrs PS	F&F	213/26	
Dean V	7 R W Surrey	Pte	07/11/17	Desertion	5yrs PS	F&F	213/18	
Deane WG	6 R Marines	Pte	04/10/19	Disobedience	5yrs PS	N Russia	213/30	
Deboi C	RAMC	Pte	22/06/16	Desertion	10yrs PS		213/9	
Debuse G	4 Royal Fus	Pte	25/05/15	Sleeping	3yrs PS	F&F	213/4	
Deehy Edward	2 R Irish	Pte	02/03/16	Desertion	5yrs PS	F&F	213/8	
Delande [Dalande] Hector	8 Seaforth Hdrs	Pte	04/02/18	Desertion x2	XXX 09/03/18	F&F	213/20	870
Delaney James	2 A&S Hdrs	Pte	05/10/16	Mutiny	2yrs HL	F&F	90/6	464
Delaney V	1 Connaught Rangers	Pte	03/09/20	Mutiny	PS Life	India		1064

Name	Unit	Rank	Date	Offence	Final sentence	Location	Ref	Note
Delargey Edward	1/8 R Scots	Pte	24/08/17	Desertion	XXX 06/09/17	F&F	213/17	734
Delisle Leopold	22 Canadian EF	Pte	01/05/18	Desertion	XXX 21/05/18	F&F	213/22	901
Dempsey J	Civilian	Sinn Fein	05/05/16	Rebellion	3yrs PS	Dublin	213/8	280
Dempsey M	19 Durham LI	L/Cpl	30/12/16	Cowardice	10yrs PS	F&F	213/13	550
Dennington AF	12 E Surrey	Pte	16/04/17	Sleeping	10yrs PS	F&F	213/14	633
Dennis John James	1 Northants	Pte	03/12/15	Desertion	XXX 30/01/16	F&F	213/7	136
Dennis T	5 Leicestershire	Pte	17/07/16	Desertion	10yrs PS	F&F	213/10	
Denny Albert	8 British West Indies	Pte	03/12/18	Murder	XXX 20/01/19	Italy	90/8	994
Denzell W	3 Australian IF	Pte	15/03/17	Desertion	10yrs PS		213/14	
Depper Charles	1/4 R Berkshire	Pte	02/09/16	Desertion	XXX 13/09/16	F&F	213/11	440
Deriagin I	1 Slavo-British Legion	Pte	13/07/19	Mutiny	XXX 00/07/19	N Russia	213/32	
Derritt G	42 Canadian EF	Pte	27/11/17	Desertion	5yrs PS	F&F	213/18	
Desborough W	2 E Surrey	Pte	11/02/15	Sleeping	84days FP1	F&F	213/3	
Deuchart JS	8/9 R Irish Rifles	Rfm	03/01/18	Desertion x2	3yrs PS	F&F	213/19	854
Devine T	1 Connaught Rangers	Pte	04/09/20	Mutiny	PS Life	India		1070
Dewar JW	10/11 Highland LI	Pte	14/12/18	Against Inhab x2+	20yrs PS	F&F	213/27	995
Dgintcharadze Gerondi D	Civilian		07/11/19	Murder	XXX	S Russia	213/34	1030
Dick A	6 R Scots Fus	Pte	18/10/18	Desertion	10yrs PS	F&F	213/26	
Dickenson F	18 MGC	Pte	16/07/16	Striking	10yrs PS		213/10	
Dickin F	1/6 W Riding	Pte	18/05/18	Cowardice	10yrs PS	F&F	213/22	
Dickinson GH	1 Northants	Pte	06/04/16	Sleeping	5yrs PS	F&F	213/8	
Dickson A	2 R Scots	Pte	24/05/17	Desertion	5yrs PS	F&F	213/16	
Dickson W	10 Black Watch	Pte	13/05/17	Sleeping	2yrs HL	Salonika	213/16	
Dimes Frank	181 Bde RFA	Dvr	30/09/16	Disobedience	10yrs PS		213/11	
Dineen J	9 Cheshire	Pte	22/04/16	Disobedience	15yrs PS	F&F	213/8	
Dionne C	15 Canadian EF	Pte	17/10/17	Desertion	5yrs PS	F&F	213/17	
Djelal	Egyptian Army	Sub Lt	19/08/20	Treason	2yrs PS	Egypt	213/34	1059
Djianshia Alexis P	Civilian		07/11/19	Murder	Not Conf	S Russia	213/34	1031
Docherty J	1/4 Seaforth Hdrs	Pte	21/07/16	Desertion	5yrs PS	F&F	213/16	405
Docherty John	9 Black Watch	Pte	30/12/15	Desertion+	5yrs PS	F&F	213/7	142
Docherty John	9 Black Watch	Pte	03/02/16	Desertion	XXX 15/02/16	F&F	213/7	166
Docherty Thomas	2 KO Scottish Bdrs	Pte	04/07/15	Desertion	XXX 16/07/15	F&F	213/4	82
Doe J	2 Middlesex	Pte	06/10/17	Desertion	10yrs PS	F&F	213/19	
Doeltz W	German Army	POW	29/10/17	Insubordinaion	168 days HL	Egypt	213/18	
Doherty J	10/11 Highland LI	Pte	08/03/17	Desertion+	15yrs PS	F&F	213/14	602
Doherty JO	1 Loyal N Lancs	Pte	31/01/18	Desertion	5yrs PS	F&F	213/20	
Donaghy P	22 Northumb Fus	Pte	02/09/18	Desertion x2	10yrs PS	F&F	213/25	971
Donaldson H	9 Yorks	Pte	16/06/17	Desertion	10yrs PS	F&F	213/15	
Donnelly J	1 Irish Gds	Pte	25/10/17	Desertion	2yrs HL	F&F	213/18	
Donnelly JG	13 R Scots	Pte	22/03/16	Desertion	10yrs PS	F&F	213/8	
Donnelly M	1/7 Highland LI	Pte	02/01/18	Desertion	Not Conf	Egypt	213/20	
Donnelly Thomas	1 W Yorks	Pte	31/08/16	Desertion	5yrs PS	F&F	213/11	
Donohue M	6 Leinster	Cpl	12/05/16	Violence+	3yrs PS	Salonika	213/9	307
Donovan HJ	11 E Yorks	Pte	27/06/16	Quitting	5yrs PS		213/10	
Donovan Thomas	16 KRRC	Rfm	17/10/17	Desertion x3	XXX 31/10/17	F&F	213/18	801
Doolan J	26 Australian IF	Pte	24/06/17	Desertion	5yrs PS		213/16	
Doran J	19 Liverpool	Pte	22/05/16	Desertion	2yrs HL	F&F	213/10	
Dorr C	38 Australian IF	Pte	26/10/17	Desertion x2	10yrs PS		213/18	
Dorrington J	Civilian	Sinn Fein	04/05/16	Rebellion	3yrs PS	Dublin	213/8	253
Dossett Walter	1/4 York & Lancaster	Pte	08/06/18	Desertion	XXX 25/06/18	F&F	213/23	922
Dougherty John	Civilian	Sinn Fein	03/05/16	Rebellion	10yrs PS	Dublin	213/8	227
Dowling A	2 Yorks	Pte	25/08/16	Sleeping	3yrs PS	F&F	213/10	
Dowling J	Connaught Rangers	Pte (L/C)	08/07/18	Aiding enemy x3	PS Life	UK	92/4	938
Downey J	8 R Inniskilling Fus	Pte	11/05/16	Disobedience	Quashed	F&F	213/9	
Downey John	Civilian	Sinn Fein	05/05/16	Rebellion	3yrs PS	Dublin	213/8	281
Downey Patrick Joseph	6 Leinster	Pte	01/12/15	Disobedience	XXX 27/12/15	Salonika	213/7	135
Downing Thomas	6 S Lancs	Pte	07/02/17	Sleeping	XXX 19/02/17	Mesopotamia	90/7	588
Dowsey H	19 Durham LI	Pte	28/12/16	Quitting	15yrs PS	F&F	213/13	541
Dowswell A	6 Leicestershire	Pte	25/10/15	Sleeping	5yrs PS	F&F	213/6	
Doyle F	44 Canadian EF	Pte	15/07/17	Desertion	3yrs PS	F&F	213/16	
Doyle Gerald	Civilian	Sinn Fein	05/05/16	Rebellion	3yrs PS	Dublin	213/8	282
Doyle J	1 N Staffordshire	Pte	16/07/18	Sleeping	2yrs HL	F&F	213/24	
Doyle James	Civilian	Sinn Fein	10/05/16	Rebellion	5yrs PS	Dublin	213/8	302
Doyle P	9 R Dublin Fus	Pte	23/05/16	Desertion	10yrs PS	F&F	213/9	
Doyle PL	2 Canadian EF	Pte	24/01/18	Desertion	10yrs PS	F&F	213/19	
Doyle T	2 Manchester	Pte	27/03/15	Desertion	Not Conf	F&F	213/3	
Draper A	1 R W Kent	Pte	11/04/15	Sleeping	Remitted	F&F	213/4	
Drennan A	2 R Irish Rifles	Rfm	08/03/15	Desertion	10yrs PS	F&F	213/3	

Name	Unit	Rank	Date	Offence	Final sentence	Location	Ref	Note
Dring T	1 E Yorks	Pte	19/10/17	Desertion	10yrs PS		213/18	
Driver F	2 E Surrey	L/Cpl	23/03/15	Quitting	5yrs PS	F&F	213/3	52
Driver T	RE	Spr	26/06/16	Desertion	5yrs PS		213/9	
Drummond A	2 A&S Hdrs	Pte	03/07/16	Desertion	10yrs PS	F&F	213/10	
Drummond S	17 Highland LI	Pte	04/02/18	Desertion	5yrs PS	F&F	213/21	871
Drysdale W	16 Highland LI	Pte	12/01/18	Desertion	5yrs PS	F&F	213/19	859
Dubue E	52 Canadian EF	Pte	29/11/17	Desertion	10yrs PS	F&F	213/19	835
Duce J	9 KO Yorks LI	Pte	30/11/17	Desertion	5yrs PS	F&F	213/18	
Duchart J	1 R Irish Rifles	Pte	10/12/18	Desertion	10yrs PS	F&F	213/29	
Duckworth A	2 E Lancs	Pte	12/06/18	Cowardice	10yrs PS	F&F	213/24	
Dudley J	7 Rifle Bde	Rfm	25/10/15	Desertion	10yrs PS	F&F	213/6	
Duffin M	7 Seaforth Hdrs	Pte	06/09/18	Desertion	10yrs PS	F&F	213/25	
Dukes S	16 R Welsh Fus	Pte	30/11/17	Desertion x2	5yrs PS	F&F	213/19	
Dumesnil A	22 Canadian EF	Pte	15/09/17	Desertion	15yrs PS	F&F	213/17	
Dunbar R	2 KOR Lancaster	Pte	11/03/15	Desertion	Quashed	F&F	213/3	
Dunbavin J	4 Liverpool	Sgt	20/11/16	Cowardice	5yrs PS	F&F	213/13	
Duncan A	1/6 A&S Hdrs	Pte	21/05/18	Desertion	10yrs PS	F&F	213/22	911
Duncan John	1 Cameron Hdrs	Pte	18/02/15	Desertion	XXX 07/03/15	F&F	213/3	44
Duncombe S	2 Royal Fus	Pte	04/09/17	Desertion	10yrs PS	F&F	213/17	
Dunford S	RFA	Dvr	15/02/15	Desertion	2yrs HL		213/3	
Dunk J	2 E Surrey	Pte	24/03/15	Sleeping	42days FP1	F&F	213/3	
Dunn J	New Zealand EF	Pte	18/07/15	Sleeping	Commuted		213/5	94
Dunn J	2/8 Liverpool	Pte	04/09/17	Desertion	10yrs PS	F&F	213/17	746
Dunn JS	19 Durham LI	Pte	30/12/16	Cowardice	10yrs PS	F&F	213/13	551
Dunn T	RFA	Gnr	16/08/18	Sleeping	10yrs PS		213/25	
Durston TW	8 S Wales Bdrs	Pte	07/10/15	Sleeping	2yrs HL	F&F	213/6	
Dutton F	7 N Staffordshire	Pte	18/01/16	Cowardice	7yrs PS	Gallipoli [?]	213/7	157
Dwyer E	1 York & Lancaster	Pte	26/08/15	Sleeping	5yrs PS	F&F	213/5	
Dwyer Percy	6 Dragoon Gds	Pte	04/11/14	Sleeping	2yrs HL	F&F	213/2	
Dyckhoff J	2/24 London	Pte	07/10/16	Sleeping	15yrs PS	F&F	213/12	
Dyett Edwin LA	2 Nelson Bn R Naval Div	Sub Lt	02/12/16	Desertion	XXX 05/01/17	F&F	90/6	527
Dyson P	2 Manchester	Pte	02/08/15	Cowardice	Quashed	F&F	213/5	
Eakimchuk M	85 Canadian EF	Pte	03/10/17	Desertion	10yrs PS	F&F	213/18	
Ealing S	1 R Warwickshire	Pte	07/11/18	Desertion	5yrs PS	F&F	213/27	
Earl[e] William J	1/7 Lancs Fus	Pte	15/05/18	Desertion	XXX 27/05/18	F&F	213/22	906
Earle J	1 R Berkshire	Pte	19/01/18	Quitting	15yrs PS	F&F	213/20	
Earp Arthur Grove	1/5 R Warwickshire	Pte	10/07/16	Desertion	XXX 22/07/16	F&F	213/10	395
Eaton J	7 N Staffordshire	Pte	11/07/16	Casting Arms	10yrs PS	Mesopotamia	90/7	396
Eckman A	119 DAC	Gnr	04/10/17	Desertion	10yrs PS		213/17	783
Edham Aziz	Civilian		27/07/20	Murder	PS Life	Egypt	213/34	1057
Edmondstone R	17 R Scots	Pte	05/12/17	Desertion	5yrs PS	F&F	213/19	838
Edwards A	3 Middlesex	Pte	10/07/15	Sleeping	6mos HL	F&F	213/4	
Edwards EG	1/8 Manchester	Pte	30/07/17	Desertion	5yrs PS	F&F	213/16	711
Edwards F	53 Bty RFA	Saddler	08/03/16	Desertion	10yrs PS		213/8	
Edwards HR	50 Australian IF	Pte	26/04/17	Desertion +	5yrs PS		213/15	637
Edwards M	1/4 York & Lancaster	Pte	17/11/16	Desertion	10yrs PS	F&F	213/12	
Edwards T	RFA	Gnr	30/05/18	Mutiny +	3yrs PS		213/22	916
Egan E	1 Connaught Rangers	Pte	04/09/20	Mutiny	PS Life	India		1071
El Arabi HM	Civilian		22/11/20	Murder	XXX	Egypt	213/32	
El Bassil Hamad Pasha	Civilian		09/08/22	Sedition	7yrs PS	Egypt	213/34	1095
El Dib AMSA	Egyptian Lab Corps	Pte	04/07/21	Murder	Quashed	Egypt	213/32	1091
El Ghazzar Elwi	Civilian		09/08/22	Sedition	7yrs PS	Egypt	213/34	1096
El Khalik Mohammed Ali	Civilian		09/07/23	Conspiracy	XXX (Hanged)	Egypt	213/34	1103
El Sheria Murad	Civilian		09/08/22	Sedition	7yrs PS	Egypt	213/34	1097
Elford Lawrence	7/8 KO Scottish Bdrs	Pte	20/09/18	Desertion	XXX 11/10/18	F&F	213/25	979
Elisaieff I	1 Slavo-British Legion	Pte	14/07/19	Mutiny	XXX 00/07/19	N Russia	213/32	
Elley Patrick	2 R Irish Rifles	Rfm	17/02/16	Desertion +	10yrs PS	F&F	213/7	177
Elliot L	2 KO Scottish Bdrs	Sgt	24/02/17	Desertion	15yrs PS	F&F	213/14	
Ellis C	7 N Staffordshire	Pte	16/10/15	Sleeping	5yrs PS	Gallipoli	213/6	
Ellis T	9 Rifle Bde	Rfm	04/04/16	Sleeping	7yrs PS	F&F	213/8	
Ellison J	18 Canadian EF	Pte	13/08/16	Desertion	5yrs PS	F&F	213/10	
Ellwood J	2 Leinster	Pte	14/12/17	Desertion	Not Conf	F&F	213/20	
Elmer CH	10 Canadian FA	Dvr	16/09/18	Desertion x2	5yrs PS	F&F	213/29	
Elsdon J	2 R Warwickshire	Pte	24/01/15	Desertion	5yrs PS	F&F	213/3	
Elson RE	7 N Staffordshire	Pte	02/02/16	Cowardice	7yrs PS	Egypt	213/7	
Elvin JE	23 Northumb Fus	CSM	02/07/17	Desertion	5yrs PS	F&F	213/16	691
Emeny CA	1/3 London	Pte	27/02/17	Desertion	10yrs PS	F&F	213/14	
Emm A	13 Northumb Fus	Pte	19/02/19	Desertion	10yrs PS	F&F	213/28	

Name	Unit	Rank	Date	Offence	Final sentence	Location	Ref	Note
Enright W	45 Royal Fus	Pte	21/08/19	Not specified	2yrs HL	N Russia	213/31	
Entwhistle PJ	17 Lancs Fus	Pte	14/08/18	Desertion	10yrs PS	F&F	213/24	960
Etchingham John R	Civilian	Sinn Fein	10/05/16	Rebellion	5yrs PS	Dublin	213/8	303
Evans A	6 Cameron Hdrs	Pte	14/01/17	Desertion	10yrs PS	F&F	213/13	
Evans AJ	46 Australian IF	Pte	27/06/17	Desertion	10yrs PS		213/16	
Evans Andrew	1 R Scots Fus	Pte	30/01/15	Desertion	XXX 06/02/15	F&F	213/3	27
Evans AW	2 East Non Combat Corps	Pte	24/06/16	Disobedience	10yrs PS	F&F	213/9	
Evans D	2 Welsh	Pte	13/08/16	Desertion	5yrs PS	F&F	213/11	
Evans DL	1 R Munster Fus	Sgt	03/05/15	Cowardice	10yrs PS	Gallipoli	213/4	
Evans DW	1 Welsh Gds	Pte	15/06/16	Sleeping	Not Conf	F&F	213/9	
Evans E	RE	Spr	05/07/15	Desertion	Not Conf		213/4	
Evans EE	9 York & Lancaster	Pte	16/02/16	Sleeping	5yrs PS	F&F	213/7	
Evans G	1 Devon	Pte	27/10/15	Sleeping	5yrs PS	F&F	213/6	
Evans W	1 KRRC	Pte	12/11/15	Desertion	3yrs PS	F&F	213/6	
Evans W	13 Essex	Pte	28/04/16	Desertion	5yrs PS	F&F	213/9	214
Eveleigh Alfred	1 E Kent (Buffs)	Pte	05/01/16	Desertion	10yrs PS	F&F	213/7	145
Eveleigh Alfred	1 E Kent (Buffs)	Pte	13/02/16	Desertion	XXX 24/02/16	F&F	213/7	174
Everill George	1 N Staffordshire	Pte	03/09/17	Desertion	XXX 14/09/17	F&F	213/17	745
Evstraloff P	1 Slavo-British Legion	Pte	17/07/19	Mutiny	10yrs PS	N Russia	213/32	
Exley J	6 Manchester	Pte	29/10/18	Desertion	5yrs PS	F&F	213/26	
Fagan A	10 Cheshire	Pte	25/07/17	Desertion	5yrs PS	F&F	213/16	
Fagan G	2 Leicestershire	Pte	28/03/17	Cowardice	3yrs PS	Mesopotamia	213/14	
Fagence P	2 Middlesex	Pte	19/11/14	Sleeping	1yr HL	F&F	213/2	
Fairburn E	18 Canadian EF	Pte	07/02/18	Desertion	XXX 02/03/18	F&F	213/20	873
Fairhead S	7 Norfolk	Cpl	31/07/16	Cowardice	5yrs PS	F&F	213/11	
Faizi Ibrahim [?] O	Civilian		20/09/20	Murder +	XXX		213/34	
Farey H	2 Middlesex	Pte	31/01/15	Sleeping	2yrs HL	F&F	213/3	
Farr Harry	1 W Yorks	Pte	02/10/16	Cowardice	XXX 18/10/16	F&F	213/12	463
Farrell J	1 Northumb Fus	Pte	16/12/16	Desertion	10yrs PS	F&F	213/13	
Farrell J	2/5 Northumb Fus	Pte	26/12/16	Desertion	Not Conf	UK	213/13	
Farrow AW	1/2 London	Pte	12/09/17	Desertion	5yrs PS	F&F	213/17	758
Fathers E	8 Canadian EF	Pte	30/09/17	Desertion	10yrs PS	F&F	213/19	
Fatoma	W African Regt	Pte	05/07/15	Cowardice	XXX 19/07/15	Cameroon	213/4	83
Faulkner J	Civilian	Sinn Fein	06/05/16	Rebellion	3yrs PS	Dublin	213/8	288
Fay M	1 Leinster	Pte	14/06/15	Sleeping	3yrs PS	F&F	213/4	
Fayis Bey	Civilian		07/09/23	Hostile Act	PS Life	Egypt	213/34	1107
Featherstone C	14 York & Lancaster	Pte	12/07/16	Desertion	15yrs PS	F&F	213/10	397
Fedrick G	49 Australian IF	Pte	17/09/17	Desertion	PS Life		213/17	
Fee J	2 R Scots	Pte	13/09/18	Desertion	15yrs PS	F&F	213/25	
Fehmi Hassan	Civilian (Turkish Police)		15/01/20	Murder	10yrs PS	Turkey	213/34	1036
Felgate M	6 R Marines	Pte	04/10/19	Disobedience	5yrs PS	N Russia	213/30	
Fellows Ernest	3 Worcestershire	Pte	14/07/15	Desertion	XXX 26/07/15	F&F	213/4	88
Fenn T	9 Royal Fus	Pte	28/12/16	Sleeping	5yrs PS	F&F	213/13	
Fensome R	2 Rifle Bde	Rfm	26/03/19	Desertion	5yrs PS	F&F	213/30	
Ferguson	1 R Scots Fus	Pte	07/10/15	Desertion	10yrs PS	F&F	213/6	
Ferguson Joseph	1 R Scots Fus (att RE)	Pte	24/03/17	Desertion	XXX 20/04/17	F&F	213/14	611
Fermoy RH	7 Norfolk	Pte	24/03/16	Disobedience	18mos HL	F&F	213/8	
Fetterley P	38 Canadian EF	Pte	14/06/17	Desertion x2	15yrs PS	F&F	213/16	
Feuillade G	8 Rifle Bde	Rfm	26/10/15	Desertion	10yrs PS	F&F	213/6	
Fewins G	13 Middlesex	Pte	27/07/17	Cowardice +	15 yrs PS	F&F	213/16	709
Fewins G	13 Middlesex	Pte	14/12/17	Desertion	10yrs PS	F&F	213/19	
Field A	20 Royal Fus	Pte	20/11/16	Desertion	5yrs PS	F&F	213/12	515
Field AB	9 Royal Fus	Pte	14/12/15	Desertion	2yrs HL	F&F	213/6	
Field T	1 R W Surrey	Pte	17/10/15	Cowardice	Quashed	F&F	213/6	
Fielding F	1/4 York & Lancaster	Pte	10/08/18	Sleeping	10yrs PS	F&F	213/24	958
Fields JT	2 York & Lancaster	Pte	09/09/16	Desertion	Not Conf	F&F	213/11	
Fillingham A	2 Lancs Fus	Sgt	04/06/15	Cowardice	Quashed	F&F	213/4	
Findlay W	2 R Scots Fus	Pte	14/08/17	Desertion	15yrs PS	F&F	213/16	
Findler JF	8 N Staffordshire	Pte	07/12/16	Disobedience	15yrs PS	F&F	213/12	
Findley T	1 Loyal N Lancs	Pte	20/05/15	Desertion +	5yrs PS	F&F	213/4	69
Fineboy	W African Regt	Pte	01/11/15	Quitting	3yrs PS		213/4	
Finney W	7 N Staffordshire	Pte	31/10/15	Sleeping	5yrs PS	Gallipoli	213/6	
Fisher-Jones D	3 Canadian EF	Pte	17/08/17	Desertion	10yrs PS	F&F	213/17	
Fitchford S	2 S Staffordshire	Pte	12/05/17	Desertion	10yrs PS	F&F	213/15	
FitzGerald A	2 R Irish	Pte	27/04/15	Sleeping	5yrs PS	F&F	213/4	
Fitzgerald E	4 (att 21) R Munster Fus	Pte	07/01/16	Desertion	5yrs PS		213/7	
Fitzgerald F	7 Gloucestershire	Pte	08/12/15	Striking +	3yrs PS	Gallipoli	213/7	137
Fitzgerald M	1 Connaught Rangers	Pte	04/09/20	Mutiny	PS Life	India		1072

Name	Unit	Rank	Date	Offence	Final sentence	Location	Ref	Note
Fitzgerald P	2 Highland LI	Pte	08/02/15	Cowardice	Not Conf	F&F	213/3	39
Fitzgerald P	2 Highland LI	Pte	10/02/15	Cowardice +	1yr HL	F&F	213/3	41
FitzGerald P	2 Black Watch	L/Cpl	25/04/16	Disobedience	Not Conf	Mesopotamia	90/7	211
Fitzhenry M	7/8 R Irish Fus	Pte	27/04/17	Desertion+	10yrs PS	F&F	213/15	639
Fitzjohn C	11 Lincolnshire	Pte	30/08/17	Desertion	5yrs PS	F&F	213/17	
Fitzpatrick J	2 R Inniskilling Fus	Pte	24/12/17	Desertion	5yrs PS	F&F	213/19	
Flanagan J	1 Liverpool	Pte	14/12/18	Against Inhab x2 +	20yrs PS	F&F	213/27	996
Flannagan R	1 R Welsh Fus	Pte	20/01/15	Desertion	2yrs HL	F&F	213/3	
Flannery J	1 Connaught Rangers	Pte (L/C)	03/09/20	Mutiny	PS Life	India		1065
Fleet F	RAMC	Pte	22/03/16	Desertion	15yrs PS		213/9	
Fletcher F	88 MGC	Pte	13/02/17	Desertion	5yrs PS		213/13	
Fletcher WJ	29 Canadian EF	Pte	24/09/17	Desertion	5yrs PS	F&F	213/17	
Flint G	6 R Marines	Pte	04/10/19	Disobedience	5yrs PS	N Russia	213/30	
Florence JR	48 Australian IF	Pte	02/07/16	Desertion	10yrs PS	F&F	213/16	
Flynn Hugh	18 Highland LI	Pte	27/10/16	Desertion	XXX 15/11/16	F&F	213/12	489
Flynn M	1/8 Liverpool	Pte	22/05/17	Desertion	10yrs PS	F&F	213/15	660
Flynn R	2 R Dublin Fus	Pte	11/10/20	Murder	XXX 06/11/20	Turkey	90/8	1086
Fogarty P	Civilian	Sinn Fein	06/05/16	Rebellion	3yrs PS	Dublin	213/8	289
Fogerty J	11 Rifle Bde	Rfm	04/07/18	Desertion	5yrs PS	F&F	213/24	
Foister J	East Non Combat Corps	Pte	02/06/16	Disobedience x2	Not Conf	F&F	213/10	324
Foister J	East Non Combat Corps	Pte	07/06/16	Disobedience	10yrs PS	F&F	213/9	332
Fone MH	RFA	Gnr	29/03/15	Sleeping	3mos FP		213/4	
Footner A	2 Hampshire	Pte	18/05/18	Desertion	Not Conf	F&F	213/23	909
Footner AE	2 Hampshire	Pte	05/11/16	Desertion	5yrs PS	F&F	213/12	
Ford H	7 Gloucestershire	Pte	16/01/16	Quitting	Not Conf	Gallipoli [?]	213/8	150
Forrest D	19 Durham LI	Pte	28/12/16	Quitting	15yrs PS	F&F	213/13	542
Forrest J	2 A&S Hdrs	Pte	09/03/15	Desertion	10yrs PS	F&F	213/3	
Foster C	2 R Sussex	Pte	30/10/15	Casting Arms	Quashed	F&F	213/6	
Foster CW	19 Manchester	Pte	13/11/16	Cowardice	10yrs PS	F&F	213/12	506
Foster G	2 S Staffordshire	Pte	11/07/17	Desertion x2	2yrs HL	F&F	213/17	
Foster G	2 S Staffordshire	Pte	29/10/18	Desertion	15yrs PS	F&F	213/26	
Foster H	6 Dorset	Pte	23/06/17	Desertion	5yrs PS	F&F	213/15	
Foster J	1/8 Manchester	Pte	15/08/15	Cowardice	Not Conf	Gallipoli	213/5	100
Foster JA	59 Australian IF	Pte	23/01/17	Cowardice	Not Conf		213/14	
Foster JA	51 Australian IF	Pte	07/05/17	Desertion x2	10yrs PS		213/15	
Foster T	2/5 W Yorks	Pte	11/06/18	Desertion	5yrs PS	F&F	213/22	
Foulkes HD	S African Regt	Pte	26/05/18	Desertion	10yrs PS		213/23	
Foulkes Thomas	1/10 Manchester	Pte	01/11/17	Desertion	XXX 21/11/17	F&F	213/18	818
Fouracres S	8 Leicestershire	Pte	19/09/15	Sleeping	Not Conf	F&F	213/5	
Fowkes J	10 Worcestershire	Pte	08/06/18	Desertion	Not Conf	F&F	213/23	
Fowles SM	44 Canadian EF	Pte	12/12/17	Desertion	15yrs PS	F&F	213/19	842
Fowles Stephen M	44 Canadian EF	Pte	18/05/18	Desertion	XXX 19/06/18	F&F	213/23	910
Fox H	2 KOR Lancaster	L/Cpl	20/09/16	Desertion	2yrs HL	Salonika	213/11	
Fox H	9 Sherwood Fstrs	Pte	29/12/17	Desertion	10yrs PS	F&F	213/19	
Fox H	5 W Yorks	Pte	26/03/18	Desertion	7yrs PS	F&F	213/21	
Fox J	2 Highland LI	Pte	14/04/16	Striking x2	XXX 12/05/16	F&F	213/8	205
Fox Joseph Stanley Victor	1 Wiltshire	L/Cpl	06/04/15	Desertion	XXX 20/04/15	F&F	213/3	57
Frafra A	Gold Coast Regt	Pte	12/10/17	Cowardice	14yrs PS		213/19	
Frafra Aziberi	Gold Coast Regt	Pte	19/09/16	Casting Arms +	XXX 28/09/16	East Africa	213/11	453
Francis J	13 R Scots	Pte	14/01/17	Desertion	5yrs PS	F&F	213/13	
Frankham G	3 MGC	Pte	10/10/18	Desertion	10yrs PS		213/25	
Frankhan G	76 MGC	Pte	09/06/17	Desertion	10yrs PS		213/15	
Fraser Evan	2 R Scots	Pte	09/05/15	Desertion x3	XXX 02/08/15	F&F	213/4	67
Fraser G	2 R Scots	Pte	21/04/15	Desertion	Quashed	F&F	213/4	
Fraser J	1 Canadian EF	Pte	30/10/16	Desertion	Not Conf	F&F	213/12	
Fraser J	2 A&S Hdrs	Pte	17/03/17	Desertion	2yrs HL	F&F	213/14	
Fraser R	13 R Scots	Pte	27/05/18	Desertion	7yrs PS	F&F	213/22	
Frear WT	3 East Non Combat Corps	Pte	13/06/16	Disobedience	10yrs PS	F&F	213/9	362
Frederick OR	49 Australian IF	Pte	29/08/17	Desertion	15yrs PS		213/17	
Fredrick OR	49 Australian IF	Pte	29/08/17	Desertion	15yrs PS		213/17	
Freeman H	1 Rifle Bde	Rfm	10/02/15	Sleeping	10yrs PS	F&F	213/3	
Freer J	2 Lancs Fus	Pte	02/08/16	Desertion	10yrs PS	F&F	213/10	
Freestone B	2 Middlesex	Pte	08/12/14	Sleeping	Quashed		213/1	
French J	8 R Inniskilling Fus	Pte	16/10/16	Desertion	5yrs PS	F&F	213/12	
French J	8 R Inniskilling Fus	Pte	10/01/17	Desertion	10yrs PS	F&F	213/13	
Frew J	1/4 R Scots Fus	Pte	19/09/17	Disobedience	10yrs PS	Egypt	213/18	
Frew J	2/10 R Scots	Pte	23/11/18	Civil Offence	5yrs PS	N Russia	213/28	
Friel J	2 Highland LI	Pte	29/08/15	Desertion	5yrs PS	F&F	213/5	

Name	Unit	Rank	Date	Offence	Final sentence	Location	Ref	Note
Friend FG	2 S Staffordshire	Pte	23/03/16	Desertion	15yrs PS	F&F	213/8	
Frith H	3 Australian IF	Pte	11/12/16	Desertion	10yrs PS		213/13	
Frost E	13 Cheshire	Pte	06/03/17	Desertion	10yrs PS	F&F	213/14	
Fryer John	12 E Surrey	Pte	10/06/17	Desertion	XXX 24/06/17	F&F		675
Fullard T	8 R Dublin Fus	Pte	01/06/17	Desertion	10yrs PS	F&F	213/15	
Fuller J	2 R Sussex	Pte	13/12/17	Absence	5yrs PS	F&F	213/19	
Fuller R	2 E Surrey	Cpl	20/03/15	Desertion	5yrs PS	F&F	213/3	
Gadsby A	1 Northants	Pte	08/02/15	Desertion	Not Conf	F&F	213/3	
Gagan G	20 Middlesex	Pte	10/01/18	Sleeping	5yrs PS	F&F	213/19	858
Galfin E	1 Liverpool	Pte	17/09/16	Desertion	3yrs PS	F&F	213/11	
Gallagher A	4 Liverpool	Pte	29/11/17	Desertion	2yrs HL	F&F	213/19	
Gallagher D	1 R Inniskilling Fus	Pte	01/01/16	Sleeping	5yrs PS	Gallipoli	213/7	
Gallagher J	13 Canadian EF	Pte	17/02/16	Desertion	Quashed GOA	F&F	213/7	
Gallant J	1 Manchester	Pte	02/05/18	Desertion	7yrs PS	Egypt	213/22	
Gallighan Peter	Civilian	Sinn Fein	16/05/16	Rebellion	5yrs PS	Dublin	213/8	310
Gamal RE	Civilian		19/05/19	Treason	10yrs Det	Egypt	213/31	
Gamble J	2 R Inniskilling Fus	Pte	31/05/17	Desertion	10yrs PS	F&F	213/15	
Ganley M	1 KO Yorks LI	Pte	22/09/17	Sleeping	2yrs HL	Salonika	213/17	
Gant J	2 Essex	Pte	06/05/16	Sleeping	5yrs PS	F&F	213/10	
Garden James	1 Highland LI	Pte	05/10/16	Mutiny	15yrs PS	F&F	90/6	465
Gardiner C	1/20 London	Pte	08/10/17	Desertion	15yrs PS	F&F	213/19	790
Gardiner William	1/13 London	Pte	14/10/16	Cowardice	5yrs PS	F&F	213/12	482
Gardner J	2 Border	Pte	19/02/15	Desertion	5yrs PS	F&F	213/3	
Garfoot G	Sherwood Fstrs	Pte	04/11/17	Desertion	Not Conf		213/18	
Garmory W	12 Manchester	Pte	22/08/15	Desertion	2yrs HL	F&F	213/5	102
Garner WW	1/4 London	Pte	22/05/17	Desertion	10yrs PS	F&F	213/15	661
Garnhum C	2 Canadian Heavy Bty	Gnr	09/10/17	Desertion	Not Conf	F&F	213/18	
Garrett D	9 R Warwickshire	Pte	26/11/15	Sleeping	5yrs PS	Gallipoli	213/7	
Garrity TA	19 Durham LI	Pte	30/12/16	Cowardice	10yrs PS	F&F	213/13	552
Garswood G	2/5 Lancs Fus	Pte	24/05/17	Desertion	10yrs PS	F&F	213/15	
Gatercole W	6 R Dublin Fus	Pte	14/09/15	Sleeping	10yrs PS	Gallipoli	213/5	
Gates W	1 Leicestershire	Pte	26/10/16	Desertion	5yrs PS	F&F	213/12	
Gatley W	1/4 R Welsh Fus	Pte	12/10/18	Desertion	3yrs PS	F&F	213/26	
Gaudie N	2 North Non Combat Corps	Pte	13/06/16	Disobedience	10yrs PS	F&F	213/9	363
Gaudy A	22 Canadian EF	Pte	06/06/17	Desertion	15yrs PS	F&F	213/16	
Gault A	1/6 A&S Hdrs	Pte	08/10/15	Sleeping	3yrs PS	F&F	213/6	121
Gawler Robert	1 E Kent (Buffs)	Pte	10/02/16	Desertion x 2	XXX 24/02/16	F&F	213/7	171
Gaylard P	1/15 London	Cpl	25/10/17	Desertion	10yrs PS	F&F	213/18	810
Gayson WE	6 Dragoons	Pte	25/11/14	Desertion	5yrs PS	F&F	213/1	13
Gazzard JC	1/11 London	Pte	30/07/18	Striking +	2yrs HL	Egypt	213/24	954
Gellibrand J	1 E Lancs	Pte	13/06/18	Desertion	15yrs PS	F&F	213/23	
Gentry WA	12 E Surrey	Pte	16/04/17	Quitting	10yrs PS	F&F	213/14	634
Geoghegan T	7 R Irish Fus	Pte	22/08/16	Disobedience+	3yrs PS	F&F	213/11	434
George AH	1 Manchester	Rfm	02/11/18	Desertion	5yrs PS	Palestine	213/27	
George TE	7 Northumb Fus	Pte	30/03/17	Insubordinaion	Not Conf	F&F	213/15	
Gerraghty F	1 R Irish Fus	Pte	31/01/18	Desertion	2yrs HL	F&F	213/20	
Gerrard WJ	1/4 Norfolk	Pte	27/12/17	Cowardice	10yrs PS	Egypt	213/20	851
Ghali Wassif	Civilian		09/08/22	Sedition	7yrs PS	Egypt	213/34	1098
Gibbin A	1 Loyal N Lancs	Pte	26/02/15	Desertion	2yrs HL	F&F	213/3	
Gibbon L	1 E Yorks	Pte	19/10/17	Desertion	10yrs PS		213/20	
Gibbons J	6 R Irish Rifles	Rfn	23/11/16	Desertion	15yrs PS	Salonika	213/13	
Gibbons J	1 R Irish Rifles	Rfm	28/11/17	Desertion	15yrs PS	F&F	213/19	
Gibbons M	8 Yorks	Pte	09/03/17	Desertion	10yrs PS	F&F	213/14	
Gibbs T	3 Essex	Pte	16/06/15	Desertion	15yrs PS	UK	213/4	77
Gibson David	12 R Scots	Pte	10/09/18	Desertion x2	XXX 24/09/18	F&F	213/25	975
Gibson H	RFA	Gnr	09/11/17	Desertion	5yrs PS		213/18	
Gibson T	7 R Irish Rifles	Rfm	09/11/17	Desertion	5yrs PS		213/18	
Gibson W	1/6 W Yorks	Pte	07/02/18	Desertion	10yrs PS	F&F	213/20	
Giggins GW	19 Durham LI	Pte	30/12/16	Cowardice	10yrs PS	F&F	213/13	553
Gilbert W	3 Middlesex	Pte	27/08/15	Sleeping	5yrs PS	F&F	213/5	
Gilder H	2/20 London	Pte	27/05/18	Cowardice+	10yrs PS	F&F	213/24	915
Giles AE	9 Welsh	Pte	05/06/18	Desertion	15yrs PS	F&F	213/23	
Giles G	1/6 S Staffordshire	Pte	08/04/17	Desertion	5yrs PS	F&F	213/14	
Giles G	1/6 S Staffordshire	Pte	19/11/17	Desertion	10yrs PS	F&F	213/18	
Giles H	1/5 R Warwickshire	Pte	11/06/16	Quitting	2yrs HL	F&F	213/10	
Giles H	11 Worcestershire	Pte	13/10/17	Sleeping	5yrs PS	Salonika	213/18	
Giles Peter	14 Northumb Fus	Pte	15/08/16	Desertion	XXX 24/08/16		213/10	425
Gilham Harry	1 E Kent (Buffs)	Pte	04/11/16	Desertion	Not Conf	F&F	213/12	

Name	Unit	Rank	Date	Offence	Final sentence	Location	Ref	Note
Gill E	52 RFA	Gnr	04/08/17	Desertion	5 yrs PS		213/16	
Gill W	9 Black Watch	Pte	30/11/15	Desertion	2yrs HL	F&F	213/6	
Gill William J	8 Sherwood Fstrs	Pte	17/07/16	Desertion	10yrs PS	F&F	213/10	
Gillam A	40 Australian IF	Pte	26/10/17	Desertion	10yrs PS		213/18	
Gillman A	8 Royal Fus	Pte	12/04/16	Desertion	10yrs PS	F&F	213/8	
Gilmore A	6/7 R Scots Fus	Pte	27/09/17	Desertion	15yrs PS	F&F	213/18	
Gilmore Patrick	2 Durham LI	Pte	16/07/15	Desertion	10yrs PS	F&F	213/4	
Gilmour A	6/7 R Scots Fus	Pte	27/09/17	Desertion	15yrs PS	F&F	213/17	
Ginn AA	45 Australian IF	Pte	04/09/17	Desertion	PS Life		213/17	
Girling A	1/4 Suffolk	Pte	12/10/16	Desertion	10yrs PS	F&F	213/12	
Gisbourne S	1 D Cornwall LI	Pte	27/09/15	Sleeping	10yrs PS	F&F	213/5	
Gladman W	RFA	Dvr	01/03/18	Desertion	5yrs PS		213/20	
Gleadow George E	1 W Yorks	Sgt	01/03/17	Desertion	XXX 06/04/17	F&F	213/14	597
Gleeson JJ	1 Connaught Rangers	Pte	04/09/20	Mutiny	PS Life	India		1073
Glover TL	1/11 London	Rfm	15/05/17	Sleeping	2yrs HL	Egypt	213/15	650
Godfree C	2 Middlesex	Pte	26/01/16	Desertion	10yrs PS	F&F	213/7	
Godfrey A	1 E Surrey	Pte	17/10/15	Sleeping	3mos FP1	F&F	213/6	
Godfrey Albert	1 R W Surrey	Pte	04/10/14	Sleeping	2yrs HL		213/2	
Godfrey E	9 KRRC	Rfm	27/12/15	Desertion	10yrs PS	F&F	213/7	
Godfrey R	6 S Lancs	Pte	25/07/15	Sleeping	2yrs HL	Gallipoli	213/5	
Godson C	12 E Yorks	Pte	26/07/16	Desertion	10yrs PS		213/10	
Godwin J	2 KRRC	Rfm	18/01/15	Quitting	2yrs HL	F&F	213/3	
Goff E	9 Devon	Pte	07/11/17	Desertion	5yrs PS	F&F (?)	213/19	821
Gogarty PJ	1 Connaught Rangers	Pte	03/09/20	Mutiny	PS Life	India		1066
Goggins Peter	19 Durham LI	L/Cpl	28/12/16	Quitting	XXX 18/01/17	F&F	213/13	543
Golder E	12 KRRC	Pte	26/08/18	Sleeping	3yrs PS	F&F	213/25	
Goldie W	17 R Scots	Pte	04/11/18	Desertion	5yrs PS	F&F	213/27	990
Gomma [Beisi] Saied	Civilian		12/06/21	Hostile Act	XXX (Hanged)	Egypt	213/34	1090
Gonsalves SF	30 Australian IF	Pte	21/02/17	Desertion	5yrs PS		213/14	
Gooch Robert W	1/4 Suffolk	Pte	06/02/17	Desertion	10yrs PS	F&F	213/13	
Goodall TW	1 R Warwickshire	Cpl	03/04/16	Desertion	10yrs PS	F&F	213/8	
Goodchild FW	1 R Munster Fus	Pte	12/10/15	Sleeping	5yrs Ps	Gallipoli	213/6	
Goodfellow T	7 N Staffordshire	Pte	16/10/15	Sleeping	5ysr PS	Gallipoli	213/6	
Goodhead A	11 KRRC	Rfm	15/04/16	Desertion	5yrs PS	F&F	213/8	
Goody WT	1 Rifle Bde	Pte	30/07/17	Desertion	Not Conf	F&F	213/16	
Gordon E	8 R W Surrey	L/Cpl	23/10/16	Striking	2yrs HL	F&F	213/12	
Gordon J	1 Scottish Rifles	Pte	06/04/15	Desertion	10yrs PS	F&F	213/3	
Gordon L	31 Canadian EF	Pte	10/05/18	Desertion	5yrs PS	F&F	213/22	
Gore Frederick C	7 E Kent (Buffs)	Pte	08/09/17	Desertion	XXX 16/10/17	F&F	213/17	756
Gormley J	2 Worcestershire	Pte	06/06/16	Desertion	2yrs PS	F&F	213/9	
Gosheff P	Civilian		20/05/16	Treason	XXX	Macedonia	213/12	313
Goten L	Civilian	Alien	24/09/17	Espionage	PS Life	UK	92/4	770
Gould M	2 R Warwickshire	Pte	24/01/15	Desertion	5yrs PS	F&F	213/3	
Gould RS	1 Norfolk	Pte	23/10/18	Desertion	5yrs PS	F&F	213/25	
Gould W	2 R Irish Fus	Pte	03/05/17	Plundering	1yr HL	Salonika	213/15	
Gracey A	1 N Staffordshire	Pte	31/03/15	Sleeping	Quashed	F&F	213/3	
Grady W	2 Manchester	Pte	20/08/15	Cowardice	10yrs PS	F&F	213/5	
Graham H	7 Essex	Pte	21/07/17	Sleeping	5yrs PS	F&F	213/17	
Graham J	2 KO Yorks LI	Pte	14/05/15	Desertion	15yrs PS	F&F	213/4	
Graham J	2 R Munster Fus	Pte	09/12/15	Desertion	XXX 21/12/15	F&F	213/6	140
Graham J	11 Border	Pte	27/04/17	Desertion	5yrs PS	F&F	213/15	640
Graham W	2 Lancs Fus	Pte	24/02/16	Desertion	5yrs Ps	F&F	213/7	
Graham W	22 Royal Fus	Pte	18/02/18	Desertion	5yrs PS	F&F	213/20	877
Grainger S	1 Worcestershire	Pte	02/08/16	Desertion	10yrs PS	F&F	213/10	
Grainger S	3 Worcestershire	Pte	30/08/18	Desertion x3	15yrs PS	F&F	213/25	
Grampton James	9 York & Lancaster	Pte	23/01/17	Desertion	XXX 04/02/17	F&F	213/13	580
Granderson W	79 RFA	Gnr	05/02/17	Desertion	5yrs PS		213/13	
Graner J	9 KRRC	Rfm	07/01/16	Desertion	10yrs PS	F&F	213/7	
Grannon J	7 E Yorks	Pte	10/12/17	Desertion	5yrs PS		213/18	
Grant J	1/5 Gordon Hdrs	Pte	01/06/17	Desertion	10yrs PS	F&F	213/15	
Graves H	11 Liverpool	Pte	03/06/17	Desertion+	5yrs PS	F&F	213/15	667
Graves H	11 Liverpool	Pte	12/08/17	Desertion	10yrs PS	F&F	213/16	
Gray T	14 Canadian EF	Pte	21/03/16	Desertion	5yrs PS	F&F	213/8	
Greaves H	19 Durham LI	Pte	30/12/16	Cowardice	10yrs PS	F&F	213/13	554
Greaves S	1 R Warwickshire	Pte	11/01/15	Sleeping	3yrs PS	F&F	213/3	
Green A	1 N Staffordshire	Pte	20/02/15	Desertion	5yrs PS	F&F	213/3	
Green AG	4 Royal Fus	Pte	08/11/18	Desertion	5yrs PS	F&F	213/27	
Green C	Kings Shropshire LI	L/Cpl	07/10/16	Desertion	7yrs PS		213/12	

Name	Unit	Rank	Date	Offence	Final sentence	Location	Ref	Note
Green C	7 Kings Shropshire LI	Pte	18/03/17	Desertion	Quashed	F&F	213/15	
Green W	1/4 York & Lancaster	Pte	09/08/17	Desertion	5yrs PS	F&F	213/16	722
Green W	1 Sherwood Fstrs	Pte	17/05/18	Desertion	5yrs PS	F&F	213/22	
Greenhalgh H	2 Manchester	Pte	27/03/15	Desertion	10yrs PS	F&F	213/3	
Greenlagh JT	1 R Marines LI	Pte	02/08/18	Desertion	10yrs PS		213/24	
Greenwood DD	78 Canadian EF	Pte	12/09/18	Desertion	15yrs PS	F&F	213/25	
Greenwood G	14 Durham LI	Pte	12/02/18	Desertion	10yrs PS	F&F	213/23	
Gregory T	4 Canadian EF	Pte	04/08/16	Desertion	10yrs PS	F&F	213/10	
Gregson J	1 E Lancs	Pte	05/12/14	Cowardice	2yrs HL	F&F	213/3	
Greig J	58 Canadian EF	Pte	28/11/17	Desertion	5yrs PS	F&F	213/19	
Gribben J	1 R Irish Rifles	Rfm	20/04/16	Cowardice	15yrs PS	F&F	213/9	
Grice S	7 Border	Pte	13/01/17	Desertion	5yrs PS	F&F	213/13	
Griffin A	197 MGC	Pte	11/11/17	Desertion	15yrs PS		213/18	
Griffin W	2 KOR Lancaster	Pte	19/03/15	Sleeping	2yrs HL	F&F	213/3	
Griffiths B	18 MGC	Pte	16/07/16	Striking	10yrs PS		213/10	
Griffiths S	2 KO Yorks LI	Pte	25/11/16	Desertion	10yrs PS	F&F	213/12	
Grimes A	1 R W Surrey	Pte (L/C)	27/07/16	Desertion	5yrs PS	F&F	213/11	
Grist JP	14 Australian IF	Pte	13/09/17	Desertion	10yrs PS		213/17	
Groates G	7 East Yorks	Pte	06/12/15	Desertion	5yrs PS		213/6	
Groves Henry	4 Hussars	Pte	24/09/14	Cowardice	2yrs HL	F&F	213/2	
Groves WL	4 Royal Fus	Pte	08/11/18	Desertion x2	15yrs PS	F&F	213/27	
Grozier AE	1 E Yorks	Cpl	14/09/17	Desertion	10yrs PS		213/17	
Grundy F	8 N Staffordshire	Pte	07/12/16	Disobedience	15yrs PS	F&F	213/12	
Gualia Pallady	Civilian		09/03/20	Murder	XXX	S Russia	213/34	1040
Gull J	1 E Kent (Buffs)	Pte	25/07/18	Sleeping x2	5yrs PS	F&F	213/24	
Gunn P	1 Gordon Hdrs	Pte	28/12/15	Sleeping	3yrs PS	F&F	213/7	
Gunnell A	Oxon & Bucks LI	Pte	04/01/18	Desertion	5yrs PS		213/19	
Gunston CA	7 Gloucestershire	Pte	16/01/16	Quitting	Not Conf	Gallipoli [?]	213/8	151
Hackett J	7 Leicestershire	Pte	05/07/17	Desertion	5yrs PS	F&F	213/16	
Hackett J	7 Leicestershire	Pte	23/11/17	Disobedience	Not Conf	F&F	213/19	
Hackett T	9 Sherwood Fstrs	Pte	08/01/18	Desertion	10yrs PS	F&F	213/19	
Hackney D	7 N Staffordshire	Pte	16/10/15	Sleeping	5yrs PS	Gallipoli	213/6	
Haddock James A	12 York & Lancaster	Pte	24/08/16	Desertion	XXX 16/09/16	F&F	213/11	435
Haddon W	1 (Garr) Northants	Cpl	15/01/16	Disobedience	Not Conf	Egypt	213/7	
Hadl AS	38 Egyptian Lab Corps	Rais	10/04/22	Murder	10yrs PS	Egypt	213/34	
Haggar CW	1 Devon	Pte	21/08/15	Sleeping	10yrs PS	F&F	213/5	
Haggett J	1 Wiltshire	Pte	10/04/17	Desertion	2 yrs HL	F&F	213/14	
Hagn A	Civilian	Alien	27/08/17	Espionage	PS Life	UK	92/4	738
Hailwood E	2 Border	Pte	07/05/16	Desertion	5yrs PS	F&F	213/10	
Haines FG	2/4 R Berkshire	Pte	11/06/18	Desertion	15yrs PS	F&F	213/23	
Haithwaite C	8 W Yorks	Rfm	30/12/18	Desertion x2	10yrs PS	F&F	213/27	
Halcrow J	9 Durham LI	Pte	21/04/18	Desertion	5yrs PS		213/21	
Hale A	2 R Inniskilling Fus	Pte	29/12/16	Desertion x2	5yrs PS	F&F	213/13	
Hale J	1 N Staffordshire	Pte	16/07/18	Sleeping	2yrs HL	F&F	213/24	
Hall C	2 North Non Combat Corps	Pte	13/06/16	Disobedience	10yrs PS	F&F	213/9	364
Hall E	25 RFA	Dvr	15/08/16	Desertion	10yrs PS		213/11	
Hall E P	RFA	Dvr	14/02/18	Desertion	5yrs PS		213/20	
Hall G	2 E Lancs	Pte	08/09/16	Cowardice	15yrs PS	F&F	213/11	
Hall G	2 KO Yorks LI	Pte	19/01/18	Desertion	5yrs PS	F&F	213/20	
Hall H	25 Northumb Fus	Pte	10/02/17	Sleeping	10yrs PS	F&F	213/13	591
Hall J	RFA	Dvr	23/04/18	Desertion	5yrs PS		213/22	
Hall S	2 North Non Combat Corps	Pte	12/06/16	Disobedience	10yrs PS	F&F	213/9	351
Hall V	2 West Indies	Pte	14/09/16	Sleeping	10yrs PS		213/11	
Hallam T	9 Worcestershire	Pte	19/08/16	Sleeping	3yrs PS	Mesopotamia	90/7	
Hallett G	8 S Lancs	Pte	12/12/16	Cowardice	3yrs PS	F&F	213/13	
Halliday E	10 Loyal N Lancs	Pte	17/05/17	Desertion	10yrs PS	F&F	213/15	
Halligan J	14 Canadian EF	Cpl	26/04/16	Desertion	Not Conf	F&F	213/9	
Halsall J	7 Liverpool	Pte	17/07/16	Sleeping	2yrs HL	Salonika	213/11	400
Halsall W	1 Lancs Fus	Pte	18/09/15	Disobedience	10yrs PS	Gallipoli	213/5	
Halstead E	1 KO Yorks LI	Pte	10/08/15	Sleeping	5yrs PS	F&F	213/4	
Hamdi Mehmed	3 Turkish Army	POW	09/05/19	Murder	XXX	Egypt	213/29	1007
Hamilton A	1 Scottish Rifles	Pte	16/06/16	Desertion	Not Conf	F&F	213/9	
Hamilton Arthur	14 Durham LI	Pte	15/02/17	Desertion	XXX 27/03/17	F&F	213/14	593
Hamilton D	8 R Irish Fus	Pte	09/06/16	Desertion	5yrs PS	F&F	213/9	
Hamilton J	15 Highland LI	Pte	23/07/17	Desertion	5yrs PS	F&F	213/16	705
Hamilton L	1/6 A&S Hdrs	Pte	19/08/15	Sleeping	10yrs PS	F&F	213/4	101
Hamilton Thomas Grant	38 RFA	Dvr	20/09/16	Striking	XXX 03/10/16	F&F	213/11	455
Hamilton W	93 MGC	Pte	31/03/17	Desertion	5yrs PS		213/14	

Name	Unit	Rank	Date	Offence	Final sentence	Location	Ref	Note
Hamling J	45 Australian IF	Pte	22/12/16	Desertion	10yrs PS		213/13	
Hammond A	1 E Surrey	Pte	05/10/15	Desertion	Quashed	F&F	213/6	
Hammond A	4 Australian Pnr Bn	Pte	05/07/17	Desertion	10yrs PS		213/16	
Hammond W	2 E Surrey	Pte	14/02/15	Desertion	3yrs HL	F&F	213/3	
Hampden A	1 New Zealand EF	Pte	30/08/16	Desertion	Not Conf		213/11	438
Hampsey J	2 A&S Hdrs	Pte	17/06/16	Striking	10yrs PS	F&F	213/9	
Hampshire F	2/5 W Riding	Pte	07/06/17	Desertion	15yrs PS	F&F	213/15	
Hancock E	12 Suffolk	Pte	21/08/16	Desertion	10yrs PS	F&F	213/10	430
Hancock H	2 S Wales Bdrs	Pte	24/10/15	Sleeping	5yrs PS	Gallipoli	213/6	
Hancock J	8 E Yorks	Pte	24/05/17	Desertion	10yrs PS	F&F	213/15	
Hand J	2 Gloucestershire	Pte	21/07/15	Sleeping	5yrs PS	F&F	213/4	
Hanifin T	6 Leinster	Pte	06/12/15	Insubordination	2yrs HL	Salonika	213/7	
Hanlon James [Tade]	RFA	Gnr	10/08/18	Desertion	Not Conf		213/24	
Hanna George	2 R Irish Fus	Pte	15/12/16	Desertion	7yrs PS	F&F	213/13	530
Hanna George	1 R Irish Fus	Pte	19/10/17	Desertion	XXX 06/11/17	F&F	213/18	804
Hanna Morcos	Civilian		09/08/22	Sedition	7yrs PS	Egypt	213/34	1099
Hanna S	6 R Irish Fus	Pte	04/10/15	Desertion	10yrs PS	India	213/6	
Hanna S	6 R Irish Rifles	Pte	04/10/15	Desertion	10yrs PS	Egypt	213/7	
Hannah J	18 Highland LI	Pte	06/06/18	Desertion	5yrs PS	F&F	213/23	920
Hannan J	13 Canadian EF	Pte	21/01/18	Desertion	10yrs PS	F&F	213/19	
Hannon W	7 R Dublin Fus	Pte	09/11/16	Sleeping	5yrs PS	Salonika	213/12	
Hanson	6 R Irish Fus	Pte	04/10/15	Desertion	10 yrs PS	Gallipoli	213/7	
Hanson E	4 E Yorks	Pte	27/12/17	Desertion	5yrs PS	F&F	213/19	
Hapted E	2 Rifle Bde	Rfm	09/01/15	Sleeping	2yrs HL	F&F	213/3	
Haque S	6 York & Lancaster	Pte	16/08/18	Desertion	10yrs PS	F&F	213/25	
Hardaker W	2 R Warwickshire	Pte	07/09/17	Desertion	10yrs PS	F&F	213/17	
Hardie JN	52 Canadian EF	Pte	30/11/17	Desertion	5yrs PS	F&F	213/19	836
Harding E	46 Australian IF	Pte	05/09/17	Desertion	20yrs PS		213/17	
Harding Frederick	1 KRRC	Rfm	15/06/16	Desertion	XXX 29/06/16	F&F	213/9	374
Hardy F	2 R Dublin Fus	Pte	11/10/20	Murder x2	PS Life	Turkey	90/8	1087
Hargraves J	2 D Cornwall LI	Pte	25/01/15	Against inhab	20yrs PS	F&F	213/3	
Hargreaves F	2 R Warwickshire	Pte	14/12/14	Desertion	2yrs HL	F&F	213/3	
Harley C	1 R Scots Fus	Pte	30/01/18	Desertion	5yrs PS	F&F	213/19	
Harley WM	9 Essex	Sgt	24/08/16	Desertion	Not Conf	F&F	213/11	
Harries WM	R Monmouth	Spr	14/01/16	Desertion	10yrs PS		213/7	
Harrigan LJ	34 Australian IF	Pte	21/03/17	Disobedience x2	Not Conf		213/14	
Harrigan T	13 R Scots	Pte	14/09/18	Desertion	10yrs PS	F&F	213/26	
Harrington A	2 R Scots	Pte	21/10/18	Desertion	5yrs PS	F&F	213/25	
Harris (Beverstein) Abraham	11 Middlesex	Pte	04/03/16	Desertion	XXX 20/03/16	F&F	213/7	186
Harris B	9 W Yorks	Pte	17/12/15	Sleeping	2mos FP1	Gallipoli	213/7	
Harris E	2 S Staffordshire	Pte	04/11/17	Desertion	15yrs PS	F&F	213/18	
Harris Ernest Walter [Jack]	10 Lancs Fus	Pte	23/01/17	Desertion	XXX 03/02/17	F&F	213/13	581
Harris G	3 Rifle Bde	Rfm	23/05/16	Desertion	3yrs PS	F&F	213/9	
Harris H	Lab Coy		17/09/17	Desertion	Not Conf		213/17	
Harris H	1/4 KOR Lancaster	Pte	12/09/18	Against Inhab	10yrs PS	F&F	213/26	
Harris J	7 Gloucestershire	Pte	05/10/15	Sleeping	5yrs PS	Gallipoli	213/6	
Harris J	10 Lancs Fus	Pte	01/10/16	Desertion	5yrs PS	F&F	213/12	
Harris J	9 Welsh	Pte	21/02/17	Desertion	10yrs PS	F&F	213/15	
Harris Louis	10 W Yorks	Pte	19/10/18	Cowardice+	XXX 07/11/18	F&F	213/26	986
Harris Peter (Willie)	1 Cape Col Lab Coy	Pte	05/08/19	Murder	XXX 26/08/19	F&F	213/30	1017
Harris T	1/9 London	Pte	27/09/17	Desertion	15yrs PS	F&F	213/17	
Harris Thomas	1 R W Kent	Pte	12/06/15	Desertion	XXX 21/06/15	F&F	213/4	75
Harrison P	2 R Warwickshire	Pte	23/01/15	Desertion	5yrs PS	F&F	213/3	
Harrison S	2 E Lancs	Pte	12/06/18	Cowardice	5yrs PS	F&F	213/24	
Hart A	1/22 London	Pte	27/07/17	Desertion	10yrs PS	F&F	213/17	
Hart Benjamin Albert	1/4 Suffolk	Pte	28/01/17	Desertion	XXX 06/02/17	F&F	213/13	583
Hart H	2 British West Indies	Pte	27/08/17	Striking	10yrs PS		213/17	
Hartells Bert	3 Worcestershire	Pte	14/07/15	Desertion	XXX 26/07/15	F&F	213/4	89
Hartfield HJ	RGA	Gnr	29/07/16	Desertion	10yrs PS		213/10	
Hartley F	4 Royal Fus	Pte	06/03/18	Desertion x2	5yrs PS	F&F	213/20	
Hartley S	1/5 York & Lancaster	Pte	17/11/16	Desertion	10yrs PS	F&F	213/12	
Harvey JC	1 KOR Lancaster	Cpl	20/09/14	Cowardice	3yrs PS	F&F	213/2	
Harvey T	19 Manchester	Pte	23/09/16	Sleeping	Not Conf	F&F	213/11	457
Harvey W	1 Sherwood Fstrs	Pte	05/02/15	Desertion	2yrs HL	F&F	213/3	
Harvey W	2 R Berkshire	Pte	09/08/17	Desertion	10yrs PS	F&F	213/16	
Harwood R	2 KOR Lancaster	Pte	19/03/15	Sleeping	Quashed	F&F	213/3	
Hasan Hussein	Civilian		06/07/20	Hostile Act	10yrs HL	Turkey	213/34	1050
Hasemere John William	RFA	Dvr	30/04/16	Threatening	XXX 12/05/16	F&F	213/8	216

Name	Unit	Rank	Date	Offence	Final sentence	Location	Ref	Note
Haslam GE	6 East Lancs	Pte	22/11/15	Desertion	5yrs PS	Gallipoli	213/6	
Hassan MA	Civilian		22/11/20	Murder	XXX	Egypt	213/32	1088
Hassan Veli [?] O	Civilian		20/09/20	Murder +	XXX		213/34	
Hastie C	2 Welsh	Pte	12/02/15	Desertion	2yrs HL	F&F	213/3	
Hastings G	8 E Kent (Buffs)	Pte	30/08/17	Desertion	10yrs PS	F&F	213/17	
Hatcher G	2 S Wales Bdrs	Pte	06/01/17	Desertion	2yrs HL	F&F	213/13	
Hatherill J	1 Essex	Pte	10/10/15	Sleeping	5yrs PS	Gallipoli	213/6	
Hatton A	1/5 R Warwckshire	Pte	11/06/16	Quitting	2yrs HL		213/10	
Hatton C	60 Australian IF	Pte	10/06/17	Desertion	5yrs PS		213/16	
Hauptman KG	German Army	POW	05/07/16	Hostile Act	Not Conf		213/9	394
Havelin W	14 Canadian EF	Pte	26/04/16	Desertion	Not Conf	F&F	213/9	
Hawes J	1 Connaught Rangers	Pte	03/09/20	Mutiny	PS Life	India		1067
Hawker F	ASC	Pte	07/01/16	Desertion	Not Conf		213/7	
Hawkins CH	1 N Staffordshire	Pte	20/01/15	Desertion	10yrs PS	F&F	213/3	
Hawkins CH	1 N Staffordshire	Pte	12/05/16	Desertion/Esc	10yrs PS	F&F	213/9	
Hawkins G	46 Australian IF	Pte	27/06/17	Desertion	10yrs PS		213/16	
Hawkins G	10 E Yorks	Pte	01/11/18	Desertion	10yrs PS		213/26	
Hawkins J	25 Australian IF	Pte	15/07/16	Striking	10yrs PS		213/10	
Hawkins T	7 R W Surrey	Pte	03/01/17	Desertion	10yrs PS	F&F	213/13	568
Hawkins T	7 R W Surrey	Pte	12/06/17	Desertion	10yrs PS	F&F	213/15	
Hawkins Thomas	2 R W Surrey	Pte	07/11/17	Desertion	XXX 22/11/17	F&F	213/18	822
Hawthorne Frederick	1/5 S Staffordshire	Pte (L/C)	31/07/16	Cowardice	XXX 11/08/16	F&F	213/10	410
Hayden G	6 R Irish Rifles	Rfm	06/12/15	Sleeping	3yrs PS	Salonika	213/7	
Hayes JH	8 London	Rfm	01/08/17	Desertion	10yrs PS	F&F	213/16	712
Hayes R	1 Liverpool	Rfm	08/07/15	Striking x2	6mos HL	F&F	213/4	
Hayes T	1 Cheshire	Pte	01/03/15	Sleeping	10yrs PS	F&F	213/3	
Haynes A	1/6 Essex	Pte	25/09/15	Sleeping	2yrs HL	Gallipoli	213/5	
Haynes W	6 R Irish Rifles	Rfm	29/06/16	Striking+	5yrs PS	Salonika	213/10	385
Hayward H	1 R Irish Fus	Pte	06/05/17	Desertion	10yrs PS	F&F	213/15	
Hazelden F	4 Canadian EF	Pte	01/10/17	Desertion	10yrs PS	F&F	213/18	
Hearnden A	2 E Surrey	Pte	20/03/15	Desertion	Quashed	F&F	213/4	
Heath G	2 Royal Fus	Pte	18/05/18	Desertion	10yrs PS	F&F	213/22	
Heathcote H	2 E Lancs	Pte	02/09/17	Desertion +	10yrs PS	F&F	213/17	743
Heathcote W	8 S Staffordshire	Pte	12/03/17	Desertion x2	10yrs PS	F&F	213/14	
Hedger Frederick	18 KRRC	Rfm	06/10/17	Desertion	5yrs PS	F&F	213/17	788
Hedges L	1 R Scots Fus	Pte	31/05/16	Desertion	10yrs PS	F&F	213/9	
Hei Chi Ming	Chinese Lab Corps	Coolie	30/01/20	Murder	XXX 21/02/30	F&F	213/31	1037
Helmore CGR	R Marine LI	Pte	11/02/21	Murder	PS Life	Ireland	213/32	1089
Henderson N	78 Canadian EF	Pte	15/12/17	Desertion	10yrs PS	F&F	213/19	
Hendricks Henry	2 Leinster	Pte	30/07/18	Desertion	XXX 23/08/18	F&F	213/24	955
Hennelbury M	14 Australian IF	Pte	08/08/17	Desertion	10yrs PS		213/17	
Hennessy P	21 Hampshire	Pte	30/01/20	Murder	10yrs PS		213/31	
Henshall	2 Lancs Fus	Pte	30/06/15	Desertion	5yrs PS	F&F	213/4	
Henshaw T	1 Northumb Fus	Pte	02/10/15	Sleeping	5yrs PS	F&F	213/6	
Hepple [Hope] Robert	1 R Inniskilling Fus	Pte	09/06/17	Desertion	XXX 05/07/17	F&F	213/16	673
Herbert F	4 S African Infantry	Pte	16/11/18	Desertion	5yrs PS		213/27	
Herbert J	2 E Kent (Buffs)	Pte	29/12/16	Sleeping	2yrs HL	Salonika	213/13	
Heron S	3 Dragoons	Pte	25/11/14	Desertion	5yrs PS	F&F	213/1	14
Heslop G	4 Northumberalnd Fus	Pte	08/04/17	Desertion	10yrs PS		213/15	
Hetatah A	Civilian		19/05/19	Treason	15yrs Det	Egypt	213/31	
Hetherington A	8 KOR Lancaster	Pte	17/10/18	Desertion	5yrs PS	F&F	213/25	
Hewitt BB	19 Durham LI	Pte	30/12/16	Cowardice	10yrs PS	F&F	213/13	555
Hewitt GH	2 KO Yorks LI	Pte	15/05/16	Violence/striking	1yr HL	F&F	213/10	
Hewitt W	1 DAC	Dvr	10/07/16	Desertion	2yrs HL		213/10	
Hewston JJ	Civilian	Sinn Fein	04/05/16	Rebellion	XXX 08/05/16	Dublin	213/8	254
Heyes A	5 S Lancs	Rfm	21/04/15	Sleeping	3yrs PS	F&F	213/4	
Hickey J	8 R Inniskilling Fus	Pte	06/05/16	Sleeping	2yrs HL	F&F	213/9	
Hicks GE	East Non Combat Corps	Pte	10/06/16	Disobedience	10yrs PS	F&F	213/9	344
Hickton W	7 N Staffordshire	Pte	08/10/15	Sleeping	5yrs PS	Gallipoli	213/6	
Higgins J	1/9 A&S Hdrs	Pte	19/08/16	Desertion	XXX 26/08/16	F&F	213/10	428
Higgins John Morris	1 Canadian EF	Pte	26/11/16	Desertion	XXX 07/12/16	F&F	213/12	524
Higgins W	11 R Scots	Pte	10/11/18	Desertion	3yrs PS	F&F	213/26	
Highgate Thomas	R W Kent	Pte	06/09/14	Desertion	XXX 08/09/14	F&F	213/2	5
Highway E	20 Lancs Fus	Pte	12/05/16	Indiscipline	5yrs PS	F&F	213/9	308
Hill G	2 Manchester	Pte	20/08/15	Cowardice	10yrs PS	F&F	213/5	
Hill W	9 E Surrey	Pte	03/06/16	Threatening+	5yrs PS	F&F	213/9	330
Hill W	7 D Cornwall LI	Pte	21/09/17	Desertion	10yrs PS	F&F	213/17	
Hills W	8 Sherwood Fstrs	Pte	02/05/18	Desertion	5yrs PS	F&F	213/22	

Name	Unit	Rank	Date	Offence	Final sentence	Location	Ref	Note
Hilton AJ	7 Liverpool	Pte	10/07/15	Sleeping+	1yr HL	F&F	213/4	87
Hinchem J	2 KO Yorks LI	Pte	20/10/16	Desertion	1yr HL	F&F	213/12	
Hinton A	2 Manchester	Pte	27/04/15	Desertion	15yrs PS	F&F	213/4	
Hinton A	16 R Warwickshire	Pte	11/05/18	Sleeping	3yrs PS	F&F	213/22	
Hiscoke W	1 Rifle Bde	Cpl	23/03/16	Desertion	10yrs PS	F&F	213/8	
Hiskey E	9 Suffolk	Pte	26/10/16	Desertion	5yrs PS	F&F	213/12	
Hobbs RF	3 Royal Fus	Pte	20/04/15	Desertion	10yrs PS	F&F	213/4	
Hobday A	9 Worcestershire	Pte	06/01/16	Quitting+	2mos FP1	Gallipoli	213/7	146
Hocking J	RFA	Dvr	10/01/16	Desertion	10yrs PS		213/7	
Hodges AG	7 Gloucestershire	Pte	16/01/16	Quitting	Not Conf	Gallipoli [?]	213/8	152
Hodges J	2 S Wales Bdrs	Pte	05/09/17	Desertion	15yrs PS	F&F	213/17	
Hodges J	2 S Wales Bdrs	Pte	17/11/18	Desertion	10yrs PS	F&F	213/27	
Hodges WJ	English Civilian	N/A	11/08/17	Espionage	5yrs PS		213/20	
Hodgetts Oliver	1 Worcestershire	Pte	22/05/15	Cowardice	XXX 04/06/15	F&F	213/4	70
Hodgetts W	3 Worcestershire	Pte	19/06/15	Desertion	10yrs PS	F&F	213/4	
Hodgkiss G	2 Leinster	Pte	25/03/17	Desertion	15yrs PS	F&F	213/14	
Hodgkiss G	Leinster	Pte	25/09/18	Desertion x2	10yrs PS		213/28	
Hodgson A	2 KO Yorks LI	Pte	24/06/15	Desertion	5yrs PS	F&F	213/4	
Hodgson WJ	28 Canadian EF	Pte	20/06/17	Desertion	10yrs PS	F&F	213/16	
Hoey R	2 Yorks	Pte	19/09/15	Sleeping	Quashed	F&F	213/5	112
Hogan P	49 MGC	Pte	28/06/16	Desertion	5yrs PS		213/9	
Hogg E	110 MGC	Pte	01/04/16	Desertion	Not Conf		213/9	
Hoja H	Civilian	Civ	29/04/18	Desertion x2	PS LIfe	Salonika	213/23	
Holdcroft C	10 Sherwood Fstrs	Pte	27/02/16	Desertion	10yrs PS	F&F	213/9	
Holden AT	6 R Marines	Pte	04/10/19	Disobedience	5yrs PS	N Russia	213/30	
Holden J	12 Manchester	Pte	09/10/17	Desertion	10yrs PS	F&F	213/17	
Holderness HA	1/5 Bedfordshire	Pte	26/10/17	Disobedience	5yrs PS	Egypt	213/19	
Holderness W	11 Royal Fus	Pte	27/02/17	Desertion	Not Conf	F&F	213/14	
Holderness William	11 Royal Fus	Pte	19/08/16	Desertion	10yrs PS	F&F	213/10	
Holien MT	46 Australian IF	Pte	09/07/17	Desertion	10yrs PS		213/16	
Holland James	10 Cheshire	Pte (L/C)	18/05/16	Cowardice+	XXX 30/05/16	F&F	213/9	312
Holliday G	RFA	Dvr	24/12/17	Desertion	5yrs PS		213/19	
Hollingsworth W	2 Essex	Pte	14/07/15	Desertion	Not Conf	F&F	213/4	
Hollins W	7 N Staffordshire	Pte	07/12/15	Sleeping	5yrs PS	Gallipoli	213/7	
Holloway Albert	2 R W Surrey	Pte	11/07/16	Cowardice	Not Conf	F&F	213/10	
Holmes Albert	8 KOR Lancaster	Pte	30/01/18	Desertion	15yrs PS	F&F	213/22	868
Holmes Albert	8 KOR Lancaster	Pte	06/03/18	Desertion	XXX 22/04/18	F&F	213/22	881
Holmes J	2 KO Yorks LI	Pte	14/05/15	Desertion	15yrs PS	F&F	213/4	
Holmes Samuel	2 Grenadier Gds	Pte	09/10/14	Sleeping	2yrs HL	F&F	213/2	
Holmes T	2 Durham LI	Pte	26/01/16	Desertion	10yrs PS	F&F	213/7	
Holmes W	44 Canadian EF	Pte	20/09/17	Desertion	2yrs HL	F&F	213/17	
Holmes W	44 Canadian EF	Pte	13/12/17	Desertion	15yrs PS (n/s)	F&F	213/19	
Holt Ellis	19 Manchester	Pte	05/02/17	Desertion x2	XXX 04/03/17	F&F	213/13	586
Holywood T	1 Cheshire	Pte	10/11/14	Quitting	2yrs HL	F&F	213/1	
Honeysett GR	6 R Irish	Pte	20/04/17	Cowardice	10yrs PS	F&F	213/14	
Hont Frederick	1 Liverpool	Pte	12/07/16	Desertion	3yrs PS	F&F	213/11	
Hood A	11 R Warwickshire	Pte	20/07/17	Desertion	15yrs PS	F&F	213/16	
Hood T	2 E Surrey	Pte	20/03/15	Sleeping	5yrs PS	F&F	213/3	
Hookins A	1 E Surrey	Pte	14/06/15	Sleeping	2yrs HL	F&F	213/4	
Hooper G	1 R Welsh Fus	Pte	18/01/15	Desertion	2yrs HL	F&F	213/3	
Hooper H	13 R Sussex	Pte	22/02/18	Desertion	5yrs PS	F&F	213/20	878
Hope Thomas	2 Leinster	Pte	04/02/15	Desertion	XXX 02/03/15	F&F	213/3	32
Hopkins JT	2 York & Lancaster	Pte	19/08/16	Desertion	2yrs HL	F&F	213/10	
Hopkins T	1 Irish Gds	Pte	25/10/17	Desertion	2yrs HL	F&F	213/18	
Hopkins Thomas	1/8 Lancs Fus	Pte	05/12/17	Quitting+Esc	XXX 13/02/18	F&F	213/20	839
Hopkinson E	19 Durham LI	L/Cpl	24/12/16	Quitting	15yrs PS	F&F	213/13	536
Hopley JW	11 KRRC	Pte	01/10/16	Desertion	Not Conf	F&F	213/12	
Hopper JR	20 Durham LI	Pte	02/11/16	Desertion	Not Conf	F&F	213/12	493
Horgan Dennis	4 R Munster Fus	Pte	22/01/16	Desertion	2yrs HL	F&F	213/7	
Horler Ernest	12 W Yorks	Pte	30/01/18	Desertion x2	XXX 17/02/18	F&F	213/20	869
Hornby E	11 E Lancs	Pte	27/09/18	Desertion	10yrs PS	F&F	213/25	
Hornick E	2/11 London	Rfm	02/05/17	Desertion	5yrs PS	F&F	213/15	644
Horsfall R	2 Manchester	Pte	20/08/15	Cowardice	10yrs PS	F&F	213/5	
Horsley J	22 Northumb Fus	Cpl	19/06/17	Desertion x2	5yrs PS	F&F	213/15	680
Horton HS	1 S Staffordshire	Pte	14/04/18	Desertion	7yrs PS	Italy	213/21	
Houlram D	2 R Irish	Pte	11/05/18	Desertion+	5yrs PS	F&F	213/22	
Houlton W	2/5 Lancs Fus	Pte	11/06/18	Desertion	5yrs PS	F&F	213/24	
Howard J	1/7 W Riding	Pte	23/08/16	Sleeping	2yrs HL	F&F	213/10	

Name	Unit	Rank	Date	Offence	Final sentence	Location	Ref	Note
Howarth J	1/4 Loyal N Lancs	Pte	11/06/18	Desertion	5yrs PS	F&F	213/23	
Howe E	1 R W Surrey	Pte	09/09/18	Desertion	5yrs PS	F&F	213/25	
Howell FL	8 Lincolnshire	Pte	12/02/16	Desertion	10yrs PS	F&F	213/7	
Howell S	7 S Staffordshire	Pte	01/06/18	Sleeping	5yrs PS	F&F	213/22	
Howell T	R Canadian Regt	Pte	27/01/18	Desertion	2yrs HL	F&F	213/19	
Howle J T	1/6 N Staffordshire	Pte	11/05/18	Desertion	5yrs PS	F&F	213/22	
Hozier WG	5 R Berkshire	Pte	06/08/17	Desertion	15yrs PS	F&F	213/17	
Hubbard W	2 Leicestershire	Pte	17/06/16	Sleeping	2yrs HL	Mesopotamia	90/7	375
Hudson E	2 Leicestershire	Pte	04/06/18	Desertion	5yrs PS	Egypt	213/24	
Hudson F	2 Bedfordshire	Pte	02/02/15	Sleeping	3mos FP1	F&F	213/3	
Hudson J	1 Norfolk	Pte	12/08/15	Sleeping	15yrs PS	F&F	213/4	
Hudson W	42 Canadian EF	Pte	28/11/17	Desertion	5yrs PS	F&F	213/19	
Hughes E	1 York & Lancaster	Pte	21/09/15	Sleeping	5yrs PS	F&F	213/5	
Hughes Frank	2 New Zealand EF	Pte	12/08/16	Desertion	XXX 25/08/16		213/10	423
Hughes George E	7 KOR Lancaster	L/Cpl	09/11/16	Desertion	XXX 23/11/16	F&F	213/12	503
Hughes Henry J	1/5 York & Lancaster	Pte	19/03/18	Desertion	XXX 10/04/18	F&F	213/21	883
Hughes J	1/5 A&S Hdrs	Pte	20/08/17	Casting Arms	10yrs PS	Egypt	213/17	731
Hughes J	1/5 York & Lancaster	Pte	10/12/17	Desertion	10yrs PS	F&F	213/19	
Hughes J	RFA	Dvr	01/05/18	Desertion	7yrs PS	F&F	213/22	902
Hughes P	10/11 Highland LI	Pte	27/03/17	Desertion	15yrs PS	F&F	213/14	
Hughes R	11 R Scots	Pte	03/09/18	Desertion +	10yrs PS	F&F	213/25	972
Hughes W	4 Royal Fus	Pte	09/03/15	Sleeping	10yrs PS	F&F	213/3	
Hughes W	2 Welsh	Pte	22/01/16	Desertion	5yrs PS	F&F	213/7	
Hughes W	1 R Munster Fus	Pte	07/11/18	Desertion	2yrs HL	F&F	213/27	
Hui I He	Chinese Lab Corps	Coolie	26/08/18	Murder	XXX 12/09/18	F&F	213/25	969
Hunt R	3 Worcestershire	Pte	23/08/15	Sleeping	5yrs PS	F&F	213/5	
Hunt William G	18 Manchester	Pte	02/11/16	Desertion	XXX 14/11/16	F&F	213/12	494
Hunter George	2 Durham LI	Pte	22/06/16	Desertion	XXX 02/07/16	F&F	213/9	381
Hunter GW	7 E Yorks	Pte	25/03/16	Desertion	10yrs PS		213/8	
Hunter GW	2 Coldstream Gds	Pte	03/08/16	Desertion	2yrs HL	F&F	213/10	
Hunter M	1 Cameronians	Pte	09/10/15	Desertion	3yrs PS	F&F	213/6	
Hunter Thomas	Civilian	Sinn Fein	04/05/16	Rebellion	PS Life	Dublin	213/8	255
Hunter William	1 Loyal N Lancs	Pte	05/02/16	Desertion/Esc	XXX 21/02/16	F&F	213/7	168
Hurd A	9 Essex	Pte	15/12/16	Sleeping	5yrs PS	F&F	213/13	
Hurd G	14 R Welsh Fus	Sgt	11/01/18	Desertion	10yrs PS	F&F	213/20	
Hurwitz-y-Zender Ludovico	Civilian	Alien	20/03/16	Espionage	XXX 11/4/16	UK	92/3	193
Hussein H	Turkish Army	POW	18/09/19	Murder x2	2yrs HL	Mesopotamia	90/7	1020
Hussein MS	Civilian		03/09/16	War treason	Acquitted		213/12	
Hutchins C	1 D Cornwall LI	Pte	27/09/15	Sleeping	10yrs PS	F&F	213/5	
Hutchinson FH	13 Canadian EF	Pte	26/01/16	Desertion	Quashed GOA	F&F	213/7	
Hutson H	1/4 Norfolk	Pte	17/10/15	Sleeping	5yrs PS	Gallipoli	213/6	
Hyde B	9 R Warwickshire	Pte	17/01/16	Desertion	10yrs PS	Gallipoli [?]	213/8	154
Hyde John J	10 KRRC	Rfm	26/08/17	Desertion	XXX 05/09/17	F&F	213/17	735
Hynes P	1 Connaught Rangers	Pte	04/09/20	Mutiny	PS Life	India		1074
Ibadan A	4 Nigerian Regt	Pte (L/C)	29/10/17	Cowardice x2	14yrs PS	East Africa	213/21	
Ibrahim MA	Civilian		22/11/20	Murder	Quashed	Egypt	213/32	
Iles W	7 Gloucestershire	Pte	16/01/16	Quitting	Not Conf	Gallipoli [?]	213/8	153
Ilfstaty J	Black Sea Lab Bn	Lbr	30/04/20	Murder	XXX	S Russia	213/31	1047
Illin Andrew	Civilian		20/04/19	Murder	3yrs PS	Turkey	213/34	1005
Ingersoll RA	24 Canadian EF	Pte	06/08/17	Desertion	10yrs PS	F&F	213/16	
Ingham Albert	18 Manchester	Pte	20/11/16	Desertion	XXX 01/12/16	F&F	213/12	516
Inglis R	2 Black Watch	Pte	21/07/17	Sleeping	5yrs PS	Mesopotamia	90/7	703
Inglis W	1 Gordon Hdrs	Pte	21/03/16	Desertion	10yrs PS	F&F	213/8	
Ingram AA	7 S Lancs	Pte	27/02/17	Desertion	10yrs PS	F&F	213/14	
Insley J	7 KRRC	Rfm	10/10/16	Desertion	Not Conf	F&F	213/12	
Irvine A	11 A&S Hdrs	Pte	06/11/17	Desertion	5yrs PS	F&F	213/18	
Irvine F	5 Northumb Fus	Pte	09/05/17	Desertion	10yrs PS	F&F	213/15	
Irvine G	Civilian	Sinn Fein	01/05/16	Rebellion	10yrs PS	Dublin	213/8	219
Irvine G	49 Australian IF	Pte	30/04/17	Desertion	10yrs PS		213/15	
Irvine William J	KOR Lancaster	L/Cpl	05/04/15	Desertion x2	XXX 20/04/15	F&F	213/3	56
Irving W	2 Scottish Rifles	Pte	04/10/15	Sleeping	1yr HL	F&F	213/6	
Irwin S	2 R Scots Fus	Pte	14/08/17	Desertion	15yrs PS	F&F	213/16	
Irwin S	1 R Scots Fus	Pte	02/07/18	Desertion	10yrs PS	F&F	213/23	
Isbister G	52 Canadian EF	Pte	19/10/17	Desertion	10yrs PS	F&F	213/18	805
Itko CD	Civilian		23/05/16	Treason	XXX	Macedonia	213/12	316
Ives Frederick	3 Worcestershire	Cpl	07/07/15	Desertion	XXX 26/07/15	F&F	213/4	85
Iveson H	2 KO Yorks LI	Pte	14/05/15	Desertion	15yrs PS	F&F	213/4	
Izatt William	9 Essex	Pte	25/09/16	Sleeping	5yrs PS	F&F	213/11	

Name	Unit	Rank	Date	Offence	Final sentence	Location	Ref	Note
Jackson A	2 S Lancs	Pte	10/02/15	Cowardice	3yrs PS	F&F	213/3	
Jackson CR	2 North Non Combat Corps	Pte	13/06/16	Disobedience	10yrs PS	F&F	213/9	365
Jackson E	55 DAC RFA	Gnr	26/08/16	Desertion	5yrs PS		213/11	
Jackson EE	1/8 Liverpool	Pte	22/05/17	Desertion	10yrs PS	F&F	213/15	662
Jackson Ernest	24 Royal Fus	Pte	16/10/18	Desertion	XXX 07/11/18	F&F	213/26	985
Jackson G	2 E Yorks	Pte	14/01/16	Striking+	5yrs PS		213/7	
Jackson J	2 Coldstream Gds	Pte	25/10/17	Desertion	5yrs PS	F&F	213/18	
Jackson J	8 York & Lancaster	Pte	17/06/18	Desertion	15yrs PS	Italy	213/24	
Jackson JH	1 KO Scottish Bdrs	Pte	17/06/18	Desertion	15yrs PS	F&F	213/24	
Jacobs CP	S African ASC	Dvr	23/07/18	Mutiny+	10yrs PS		213/24	947
Jacobs J	7 D Cornwall LI	L/Cpl	24/07/16	Desertion	2yrs HL	F&F	213/10	
Jacques J	18 Canadian EF	Sgt	25/09/17	Desertion	10yrs PS	F&F	213/17	
Jafir Hamdi	Civilian		06/07/20	Hostile Act	10yrs HL	Turkey	213/34	1051
Jagger H	16 Middlesex	Pte	01/03/18	Desertion	5yrs PS	F&F	213/20	880
James A	2 R Warwickshire	Pte	18/10/17	Desertion	10yrs PS	F&F	213/18	
James M	5 Munster Fus	Pte	05/04/16	Desertion	5yrs PS		213/8	
James W	13 Welsh	Pte	15/10/16	Cowardice	15yrs PS	F&F	213/12	484
James W	4 KOR Lancaster	Pte	21/08/18	Desertion	7yrs PS		213/25	
Jamieson N	7 E Lancs	Pte	08/11/18	Desertion x2/Esc	5yrs PS	F&F	213/26	
Janssen Haicke MP	Civilian	Alien	15/07/15	Espionage	XXX 29/07/15	UK	92/3	92
Jardine C	15 R Irish Rifles	Rfm	05/09/17	Quitting	5yrs PS	F&F	213/17	749
Jarman G	2 KOR Lancaster	L/Cpl	19/03/15	Sleeping	5yrs PS	F&F	213/3	
Jarry D	14 Canadian EF	Pte	02/02/16	Desertion	10yrs PS	F&F	213/8	
Jarvis WE	1/8 Worcestershire	Pte	19/12/16	Desertion	5yrs PS	F&F	213/13	
Jefferies Alfred Leonard	6 Somerset LI	Pte	09/10/16	Desertion	XXX 01/11/16	F&F	213/12	472
Jefferson H	7 Suffolk	Pte	09/04/16	Insubordination+	2yrs HL	F&F	213/9	203
Jeffrey EAV	155 Lab Coy	Pte	16/09/18	Desertion	5yrs PS		213/28	
Jeffries William	12 Middlesex	Pte	11/07/16	Desertion	5yrs PS	F&F	213/11	
Jelly J	RE	Pnr	27/04/18	Mutiny+	5yrs PS	Italy	213/22	896
Jenkins M	4 Australian Pnr Bn	Pte	05/07/17	Desertion	10yrs PS		213/16	
Jenkins P	14 R Warwickshire	Cpl	10/07/17	Desertion	5yrs PS	F&F	213/16	
Jenkinson C	1 York & Lancaster	Pte	25/02/15	Desertion	10yrs PS	F&F	213/3	
Jenning C	1/8 Worcestershire	Pte	25/09/17	Cowardice	15yrs PS	F&F	213/19	
Jennings F	24 Canadian EF	Sgt	11/02/18	Desertion	15yrs PS	F&F	213/20	875
Jennings H	58 Canadian EF	Pte	14/01/18	Desertion	10yrs PS	F&F	213/20	
Jennings John	2 S Lancs	Pte	20/06/16	Desertion	XXX 26/06/16	F&F	213/9	378
John E	10 Australian IF	Pte	17/08/15	Sleeping	2yrs HL		213/5	
Johnson A	1 Liverpool	Pte	08/12/14	Desertion	2yrs HL	F&F	213/1	
Johnson A	1 Liverpool	Pte	09/02/16	Desertion	10yrs Ps	F&F	213/7	
Johnson A	1 Liverpool	Pte	03/04/17	Desertion	2yrs PS	F&F	213/14	
Johnson A	2 Canadian Const Coy	Pte	10/12/18	Murder	15yrs PS	F&F	213/28	
Johnson Frederick (false)	2 Border	Pte	08/07/18	Desertion	XXX 01/08/18	F&F	213/24	939
Johnson GL	121 MGC	Pte	01/03/18	Sleeping	5yrs PS		213/20	
Johnson H	7 Durham LI	Pte	24/02/17	Desertion	5yrs PS		213/14	
Johnson J	8 York & Lancaster	Pte	17/08/17	Desertion	15yrs PS	F&F	213/17	
Johnson J	1 Northumb Fus	Pte	10/10/18	Desertion	5yrs PS	F&F	213/25	
Johnson LE	10 Essex	Pte	14/03/17	Desertion	10yrs PS	F&F	213/14	
Johnson LE	10 Essex	Pte	17/09/17	Desertion	Not Conf	F&F	213/17	
Johnson O	Canadian EF	Pte	05/09/17	Against Inhab	PS Life	F&F	213/17	
Johnson W	1 Welsh	Pte	01/07/15	Sleeping	5yrs PS	F&F	213/4	
Johnson W	2 S Staffordshire	Pte	23/03/16	Desertion	2yrs HL	F&F	213/8	
Johnston A	1 R Irish Rifles	Rfm	13/08/15	Sleeping	2yrs Imp	F&F	213/4	
Johnston J	1/6 Gordon Hdrs	Pte	08/12/17	Desertion	5yrs PS	F&F	213/18	841
Jones A	2 R Welsh Fus	Pte	24/12/15	Desertion	3 yrs PS	F&F	213/7	
Jones A	4 Royal Fus	Pte	15/09/17	Desertion	15yrs PS	F&F	213/21	
Jones A	7 R Welsh Fus	Pte	24/09/17	Desertion	5yrs PS	Egypt	213/17	
Jones A	1 Northumb Fus	Pte	18/08/18	Desertion	5yrs PS	F&F	213/24	
Jones DG	1 S Wales Bdrs	Pte	01/05/16	Desertion	5yrs PS	F&F	213/9	
Jones J	17 R Welsh Fus	Pte	27/01/16	Sleeping	3yrs PS	F&F	213/7	164
Jones J	7 N Staffordshire	Pte	02/02/16	Cowardice	7yrs PS	Egypt	213/7	
Jones J	6 Kings Shropshire LI	Pte	20/04/16	Desertion	15yrs PS	F&F	213/8	
Jones JA	7 Rifle Bde	Pte	16/07/17	Desertion	10yrs PS	F&F	213/16	
Jones John	1 Northants	Pte	10/02/16	Desertion/Esc	XXX 24/02/16	F&F	213/7	172
Jones L	22 Northumb Fus	Pte	04/10/17	Cowardice	5yrs PS	F&F	213/18	784
Jones R	2 R Warwickshire	Pte	14/12/14	Desertion	2yrs HL	F&F	213/3	
Jones R	2 R Warwickshire	Pte	25/02/15	Desertion	2yrs HL	F&F	213/3	
Jones Richard M	6 S Lancs	Pte	07/02/17	Desertion	XXX 21/02/17	Mesopotamia	90/7	589
Jones T	1 Cheshire	Pte	12/08/15	Sleeping	Commuted	F&F	213/5	

Name	Unit	Rank	Date	Offence	Final sentence	Location	Ref	Note
Jones T	17 Manchester	Pte	26/08/18	Desertion/Esc	10yrs PS	F&F	213/26	
Jones W	1 N Staffordshire	Pte	18/03/15	Cowardice	10yrs PS	F&F	213/3	
Jones W	9 R Welsh Fus	Pte	02/04/17	Desertion	10yrs PS	F&F	213/14	617
Jones William	43 Bty RFA	Gnr	06/04/15	Desertion +	XXX 20/04/15		213/3	58
Jones William	9 R Welsh Fus	Pte	28/09/17	Desertion	XXX 25/10/17	F&F	213/17	778
Jordan PB	3 East Non Combat Corps	Pte	13/06/16	Disobedience	10yrs PS	F&F	213/9	366
Jordon TH	7 R W Kent	Pte	05/12/17	Desertion	5yrs PS	F&F	213/19	
Joseph AJ	1 S Wales Bdrs	Pte	05/05/18	Against Inhab	5yrs PS	F&F	213/22	
Joseph J	2 Northumb Fus	Pte	11/08/15	Sleeping	3yrs PS	F&F	213/4	
Joyce A	1/5 Bedfordshire	Pte	06/04/18	Cowardice	Not Conf	Egypt	213/22	
Joyce J	2 R Warwickshire	Pte	07/02/15	Desertion	3mos FP1	F&F	213/3	
Jude A	1 R W Kent	Pte	01/03/15	Desertion	Quashed	F&F	213/3	
Jumbo	Camp Follower	Carrier	13/01/16	Theft	3mos FP1	Cameroon	213/8	
Jung J	66 MGC	Pte	09/10/16	Sleeping	3yrs PS		213/12	
Juteau F	38 Canadian EF	Pte	10/01/18	Desertion	10yrs PS	F&F	213/19	
Kalayi Georgio DO	Civilian		23/09/20	Murder+	PS Life	Egypt	213/34	1084
Kalli K	Macedonian Mule Coy	Muleteer	08/10/19	Murder x3	XXX 31/10/19	Turkey	213/31	1027
Kane J	1 R Irish Rifles	Rfm	20/04/16	Cowardice	15yrs PS	F&F	213/9	
Kane J	2 R Scots Fus	Pte	05/07/18	Desertion	10yrs PS	F&F	213/23	
Kane Thomas	2 R Irish Rifles	Rfm	06/08/16	Desertion	1yr HL	F&F	213/10	
Kanieff P	1 Slavo-British Legion	Cpl	14/07/19	Mutiny	XXX 00/07/19	N Russia	213/32	
Kay H	2 Yorks	Pte	19/09/15	Sleeping	Quashed	F&F	213/5	113
Kay L	13 Hussars	Tpr	24/11/14	Desertion	5yrs PS	F&F	213/1	
Kay W	2 Lancs Fus	Pte	13/12/14	Quitting	2yrs HL	F&F	213/1	
Keeble EG	R Marines LI	Pte	05/03/17	Desertion	10yrs PS		213/14	
Keegan J	2 S Wales Bdrs	Pte	22/06/17	Desertion	5yrs PS	F&F	213/16	
Keeling E	11 Sherwood Fstrs	Pte	13/07/17	Desertion	3yrs PS	F&F	213/16	
Keen William	7 R W Surrey	Pte	29/08/17	Desertion	10yrs PS	F&F	213/17	
Keeson WH	1 E Surrey	Pte	28/10/16	Desertion	15yrs PS	F&F	213/13	
Keightley S	7/8 R Irish Fus	Cpl	22/05/17	Desertion	10yrs PS	F&F	213/15	
Keiller P	MGC	Pte	29/05/16	Cowardice	15yrs PS		213/9	
Kelleher T	4 R Munster Fus	Pte	03/07/16	Desertion	3yrs PS		213/10	
Kelly C	11 Manchester	Pte	28/05/18	Desertion	7yrs PS	F&F	213/23	
Kelly G	2 Scottish Rifles	Pte	05/03/15	Sleeping	3mos FP1	F&F	213/3	
Kelly J	2 Manchester	Pte	26/06/16	Disobedience	15yrs PS	F&F	213/11	
Kelly J	2 (Gn) R Irish Fus	Pte	29/09/16	Quitting	2yrs HL	Salonika	213/11	
Kelly J	3 Bty RFA	Dvr	25/09/17	Desertion/Drunk	5yrs PS	Mesopotamia	90/7	
Kelly J	1 Connaught Rangers	Pte	04/09/20	Mutiny	PS Life	India		1075
Kelly P	Civilian	Sinn Fein	04/05/16	Rebellion	3yrs PS	Dublin	213/8	256
Kelly R	Civilian	Sinn Fein	04/05/16	Rebellion	3yrs PS	Dublin	213/8	257
Kelly T	3 R Inniskilling Fus	Pte	12/02/15	Desertion x2	2yrs PS	Ireland	213/3	42
Kemal Mehmet	Civilian		19/08/20	Rebellion	1yr HL	Egypt	213/34	1060
Kemp T	1 KOR Lancaster	Pte	19/05/17	Desertion	10yrs PS	F&F	213/15	
Kempson HG	10 Rifle Bde	Rfm	23/03/17	Disobedience	5yrs PS	F&F	213/14	
Kempton H	148 RFA	Gnr	10/11/16	Desertion	5yrs PS		213/13	
Kendall H	1 York & Lancaster	Pte	21/09/15	Sleeping	5yrs PS	F&F	213/5	
Kendrick EG	6 Lincolnshire	Pte	06/01/17	Desertion	10yrs PS	F&F	213/13	
Kennedy J	104 RFA	Dvr	06/11/16	Desertion	10yrs PS		213/12	
Kennedy J	RFA	Dvr	20/11/16	Desertion	5yrs PS		213/12	
Kennedy P	7 Yorks	Pte	22/11/15	Desertion	Not Conf	F&F	213/7	
Kent Edmund	Civilian	Sinn Fein	01/05/16	Rebellion	XXX 08/05/16	Dublin	213/8	220
Kent Thomas	Civilian	Sinn Fein	04/05/16	Rebellion	XXX	Dublin	213/8	258
Kent W	Civilian		14/06/16	Poss firearms	5yrs PS	Dublin	92/3	372
Kerr Henry H	7 Canadian EF	Pte	07/11/16	Desertion	XXX 21/11/16	F&F	213/12	499
Kerr WA	2 New Zealand EF	Pte	04/09/17	Desertion	10yrs PS		213/17	747
Kerridge J	RAMC	Pte	04/07/15	Desertion	10yrs PS		213/4	
Kershaw H	10 Lincolnshire	Cpl	19/05/17	Desertion	10yrs PS	F&F	213/15	654
Kershaw James	KOR Lancaster	Pte	14/04/15	Desertion	XXX 26/04/15	F&F	213/3	62
Khalil Mehmed H	7 Turkish Army	POW	09/05/19	Murder	XXX	Egypt	213/29	1008
Khan M	RGA	Gnr	13/12/18	Murder	PS Life		213/29	
Khayat George	Civilian		09/08/22	Sedition	7yrs PS	Egypt	213/34	1100
Kidman E	4 Canadian EF	Pte	28/02/16	Desertion	2yrs HL	F&F	213/8	
Kiemal	Egyptian Army	Sub Lt	19/08/20	Treason	5yrs PS	Egypt	213/34	1061
Kimber E	24 Royal Fus	Pte	25/07/17	Cowardice	7yrs PS	F&F	213/16	708
King AE	2 Leicestershire	Pte	02/12/14	Sleeping	2yrs HL	Mesopotamia	213/2	
King AW	11 Essex	Pte	05/11/18	Desertion	15yrs PS	F&F	213/25	
King H	2 E Surrey	L/Cpl	20/03/15	Sleeping	5yrs PS	F&F	213/3	
King H	Tank Corps	Cpl (Sgt)	03/08/17	Desertion	5yrs PS	F&F	213/17	717

Name	Unit	Rank	Date	Offence	Final sentence	Location	Ref	Note
King J	5 Northumb Fus	Pte	19/06/17	Desertion	10yrs PS	F&F	213/15	
King JH	13 Rifle Bde	Rfm	30/08/17	Desertion	10yrs PS	F&F	213/18	
King John	1 New Zealand EF	Pte	05/08/17	Desertion	XXX 19/08/17		213/16	719
King R	2 Durham LI	Pte	28/02/16	Desertion	15yrs PS	F&F	213/7	
King R	1/7 Black Watch	Pte	25/04/16	Quitting	2yrs HL	F&F	213/8	212
King Richard F	Civilian	Sinn Fein	10/05/16	Rebellion	5yrs PS	Dublin	213/8	304
King T	1/4 Dragoon Gds	Pte	10/06/16	Disobedience	2yrs HL		213/9	
King W	1 R Scots Fus	Pte	10/03/15	Desertion	10yrs PS	F&F	213/3	
King W	7 R Sussex	Pte	26/07/18	Desertion	5yrs PS	F&F	213/24	
Kinsey F	21 Manchester	Pte	20/10/17	Desertion	10yrs PS	F&F	213/18	807
Kirk A	6 KO Yorks LI	Pte	14/09/15	Civil	20yrs PS	F&F	213/5	
Kirk E	10 W Yorks	Pte	26/11/17	Desertion	5yrs PS	F&F	213/19	
Kirk Ernest	1 W Yorks	Pte	26/02/15	Desertion	XXX 06/03/15	F&F	213/3	47
Kirkor B	Turkish Army	POW	20/09/19	Murder	15yrs PS	Mesopotamia	213/31	1021
Kirkpatrick R	5 Durham LI	Pte	22/05/17	Desertion	5yrs PS	F&F	213/15	
Kirman Charles Henry	7 Lincolnshire	Pte	07/09/17	Desertion x2	XXX 23/09/17	F&F	213/17	754
Kitchen J	1 Loyal N Lancs	Pte	24/05/16	Sleeping	2yrs HL	F&F	213/9	
Knight AF	14 Hampshire	Pte	03/01/17	Desertion	Not Conf	F&F	213/13	
Knight Charles W	10 R Welsh Fus	Pte	06/11/15	Murder	XXX 15/11/15	F&F	213/6	128
Knight E	9 KRRC	Rfm	10/10/16	Quitting	5yrs PS	F&F	213/12	
Knight F	7 Leicestershire	Pte	14/10/18	Mutiny	15yrs PS	F&F	213/26	
Knight Harry T	1 R W Surrey	Pte	09/09/18	Desertion	XXX 06/10/18	F&F	213/25	974
Knight M	2 Middlesex	Pte	06/02/15	Sleeping	3mos FP1	F&F	213/3	
Knight RV	6 R Marines	Pte	04/10/19	Disobedience	5yrs PS	N Russia	213/30	
Knight WE	9 York & Lancaster	Pte	04/10/17	Desertion	15yrs PS	F&F	213/17	
Knight WE	1/5 London	Rfm	21/01/19	Desertion	5yrs PS	F&F	213/28	1002
Knightly R	2 KO Yorks LI	Pte	02/08/16	Desertion	2yrs HL	F&F	213/11	
Knighton W	1 Northants	Pte	17/06/16	Desertion	5yrs PS	F&F	213/9	
Kosmitcheef A	1 Slavo-British Legion	Pte	17/07/19	AWOL	10yrs PS	N Russia	213/32	
Kozienko Alexander T	Civilian		01/07/19	Murder	Life HL	S Russia	213/34	
Krebs A	78 Canadian EF	Pte	11/11/17	Desertion	15yrs PS	F&F	213/18	
Kremers C	78 Canadian EF	Pte	10/05/17	Desertion x2	15yrs PS	F&F	213/15	
Krivetsky A	2 Canadian Pnr Bn	Pte	04/09/17	Desertion	5yrs PS	F&F	213/17	
Kucer A	4 S African Infantry	Pte	27/12/16	Desertion	15yrs PS		213/13	
Kudatski S	2 Canadian Pnr Bn	Pte	04/09/17	Desertion	5yrs PS		213/17	
K'ung Ch'ing Hsing	Chinese Lab Corps	Coolie	30/01/20	Murder	XXX 21/02/30	F&F	213/31	1038
Kusasi Allasan	Gold Coast Regt	Pte	30/08/17	Sleeping	5yrs PS		213/19	
Kutchvah Silevan	Civilian		09/03/20	Murder	XXX	S Russia	213/34	1041
Labor John	Camp Follower	Carrier	13/01/16	Theft	3mos FP1	Cameroon	213/8	
Labrum H	4 Worcestershire	Pte	12/09/18	Desertion	10yrs PS	F&F	213/25	
Labrum H	4 Worcestershire	Pte	24/12/18	Desertion	10yrs PS	F&F	213/27	
Lacey F	2 Grenadier Gds	Pte	23/04/15	Sleeping	2yrs HL	F&F	213/3	
Lack JB	1 Norfolk	Pte	12/08/15	Sleeping	10yrs PS	F&F	213/4	
Lacy Michael	Civilian	Sinn Fein	10/05/16	Rebellion	5yrs PS	Dublin	213/8	305
Lafond R	22 Canadian EF	Pte	28/08/18	Desertion	7yrs PS	F&F	213/25	
Lajoie U	38 Canadian EF	Pte	10/01/18	Desertion	10yrs PS	F&F	213/19	
LaLancette Joseph	22 Canadian EF	Pte	07/06/17	Desertion	XXX 03/07/17	F&F	213/15	672
LaLiberte Come	3 Canadian EF	Pte	25/07/16	Desertion	XXX 04/08/16	F&F	213/10	407
Lally James	Civilian		09/06/16	Poss firearms	10yrs PS	Dublin	92/3	337
Lamb Alexander	RFA	Dvr	19/09/15	Desertion	XXX 02/10/15		213/5	114
Lamb W	6 R Dublin Fus	Pte	05/06/17	Sleeping	5yrs PS	Salonika	213/16	
Lambert W	22 Manchester	Pte (L/C)	20/03/17	Desertion	Not Conf	F&F	213/15	609
Lamude WT	1 S African Infantry	Pte	19/02/19	Desertion	5yrs PS		213/28	
Lane F	4 Canadian EF	Pte	03/07/16	Desertion	10yrs PS	F&F	213/10	
Lane FJ	2 E Lancs	Pte	12/06/18	Cowardice	10yrs PS	F&F	213/24	
Lane J	35 DAC	Gnr	11/04/17	Desertion	2yrs HL		213/14	
Lane JH	5 S Lancs	Rfm	26/10/16	Disobedience	10yrs PS	F&F	213/12	
Langridge A	2 R Sussex	Pte	25/08/16	Desertion+	Not Conf	F&F	213/11	437
Larginson S	1/8 Liverpool	Pte	17/10/16	Desertion	15yrs PS	F&F	213/12	485
Larsen A	Ordnance Corps	Pte	07/03/18	Desertion	10yrs PS	Italy	213/20	
Lashkoff V	1 Slavo-British Legion	Pte	14/07/19	Mutiny	XXX 00/07/19	N Russia	213/32	
Latham George	2 Lancs Fus	Cpl	11/01/15	Desertion	XXX 22/01/15	F&F	213/3	19
Latimer G	1 Border	Pte	20/10/15	Cowardice	10yrs PS	Gallipoli	213/6	
Latour T	22 Canadian EF	Pte	14/07/17	Desertion	15yrs PS	F&F	213/16	
Latta W	1/4 R Scots Fus	Pte	19/09/17	Disobedience	10yrs PS	Egypt	213/18	
Latto GS	51 Australian IF	Pte	12/08/17	Desertion	15yrs PS		213/17	
Latto M	13 Canadian EF	Pte	16/01/16	Desertion	15yrs PS	F&F	213/7	
Laurie W	2 Rifle Bde	Rfm	21/06/17	Desertion	5yrs PS	F&F	213/15	

Name	Unit	Rank	Date	Offence	Final sentence	Location	Ref	Note
Lavender G	4 Australian IF	L/Cpl	06/08/16	Desertion	15yrs PS		213/10	
Laverock R	11 Rifle Bde	Rfm	26/12/18	Desertion x3	15yrs PS	F&F	213/27	
Law A	13 Canadian EF	Pte	22/01/16	Desertion +	10yrs PS	F&F	213/7	161
Law HG	2 North Non Combat Corps	Pte	12/06/16	Disobedience	10yrs PS		213/9	352
Law J	1/19 London	Pte	03/07/17	Desertion	3 Mos FP1	F&F	213/16	693
Law W	1/19 London	Pte	11/11/16	Desertion	5yrs PS	F&F	213/12	504
Law William E	2 North Non Combat Corps	Pte	12/06/16	Disobedience	10yrs PS	F&F	213/9	353
Lawler F	2 York & Lancaster	Pte (L/C)	22/05/16	Desertion	10yrs PS	F&F	213/9	
Lawler T	1 KRRC	Pte	09/01/15	Sleeping	2yrs HL	F&F	213/3	
Lawless Frank	Civilian	Sinn Fein	08/05/16	Rebellion	10yrs PS	Dublin	213/8	295
Lawless James	Civilian	Sinn Fein	08/05/16	Rebellion	10yrs PS	Dublin	213/8	296
Lawrence Ernest	2 Devon	Pte	07/11/17	Desertion x3	XXX 22/11/17	F&F	213/20	823
Lawrence H	5 MGC	Pte	16/06/18	Desertion	5yrs PS		213/23	
Lawrence R	8 E Surrey	Pte	11/04/17	Desertion	Not Conf	F&F	213/15	
Lawrence W	10 Highland LI	Pte	15/03/16	Cowardice	10yrs PS	F&F	213/8	
Lawson W	10 A&S Hdrs	Pte	01/08/18	Desertion x2	15yrs PS	F&F	213/25	
Le Guier Bertie	14 Australian IF	Pte	11/10/16	Mutiny	2yrs HL	F&F	90/6	475
Leader FM	72 Canadian EF	Lt	29/11/16	Disobedience	10yrs PS + Cash'd	F&F	90/6	526
Leahy Denis	Civilian		09/06/16	Poss firearms	10yrs PS	Dublin	92/3	338
Leahy F	6 R Munster Fus	Pte	04/04/17	Cowardice +	10yrs PS	Salonika	213/15	625
Leahy J	1 Gloucestershire	Cpl	05/05/18	Against Inhab	5yrs PS	F&F	213/22	
Leary J	9 Scottish Rifles	Pte	30/07/16	Desertion	10yrs PS	F&F	213/10	408
Leary J	8 S Staffordshire	Pte	16/01/18	Desertion	5yrs PS	F&F	213/19	
Leatherbarrow C	1/7 Lancs Fus	Pte	13/09/15	Sleeping	10yrs PS	Gallipoli	213/5	
Leavey E	6 R Irish Rifles	Rfm	12/05/17	Desertion	7yrs PS	Salonika	213/15	
Ledan AO	38 Egyptian Lab Corps	Rais	10/04/22	Murder	10yrs PS	Egypt	213/34	
LeDoux L	58 Canadian EF	Pte	19/09/17	Desertion	10yrs PS	F&F	213/17	
Lee (Irish) George	2 Rifle Bde	Rfm	21/09/15	Desertion	XXX 03/10/15	F&F	213/5	115
Lee J	1/10 London	Pte	30/10/17	Striking	10yrs PS	Egypt	213/19	815
Lefebure J E	14 Canadian EF	Pte	02/02/16	Desertion	5yrs PS	F&F	213/8	
Legg H	2 DAC	Dvr	06/07/16	Desertion	5yrs PS		213/9	
Leicester JW	1/15 London	Pte	08/09/17	Desertion	10yrs PS	F&F	213/17	757
Leins J	Employment Coy	Pte	24/11/17	Desertion	5yrs PS		213/19	
Lemay A	22 Canadian EF	Pte	24/02/17	Desertion	5yrs PS	F&F	213/14	595
Lemay A	22 Canadian EF	Pte	27/03/17	Desertion x2	5yrs PS	F&F	213/14	
Lepley JE	48 Australian IF	Pte	28/06/17	Desertion	10yrs PS		213/16	
Leslie A	35 Australian IF	Pte	13/08/17	Desertion +	10yrs PS		213/17	726
Lester R	19 Australian IF	Pte	19/12/16	Desertion	10yrs PS		213/13	
Letten S	RFA	Gnr	26/08/16	Desertion	10yrs PS		213/11	
Lever S	Scottish Rifles	Pte	09/09/17	Desertion	10yrs PS		213/17	
Levins G	Civilian	Sinn Fein	04/05/16	Rebellion	3yrs PS	Dublin	213/8	259
Lewin F	11 Sherwood Fstrs	Pte	01/11/16	Cowardice	Not Conf	F&F	213/12	
Lewis C	12 Highland LI	Cpl	25/02/16	Desertion	XXX 11/03/16	F&F	213/7	181
Lewis D	6 Cheshire	Pte	08/11/17	Desertion	5yrs PS	F&F	213/18	
Lewis D	1/6 Cheshire	Pte	07/02/18	Desertion	5yrs PS	F&F	213/20	
Lewis Griffith	2 S Lancs	Pte	20/06/16	Desertion	XXX 26/06/16	F&F	213/9	379
Lewis J	2/20 London	Pte	22/08/16	Sleeping	5yrs PS	F&F	213/11	
Lewis John	5 Dorset	Pte	09/03/17	Desertion	Not Conf	F&F	213/14	604
Lewis John	5 Dorset	Pte	06/04/17	Desertion	XXX 19/04/17	F&F	213/14	628
Lewis LA	4 Canadian Mtd Rifles	Pte	15/09/17	Desertion	15yrs PS	F&F	213/17	
Lewis T	44 Canadian EF	Pte	11/11/17	Desertion x2	10yrs PS	F&F	213/18	
Lewis W	1/22 London	Pte	05/03/18	Desertion	5yrs PS	F&F	213/20	
Lewis William E	124 RFA	Gnr	05/10/16	Mutiny	XXX 29/10/16	F&F	90/6	466
Lidster A	2 York & Lancaster	Pte	22/11/18	Desertion	10yrs PS	F&F	213/27	
Liggett J	1/35 Trench Mtr Bty	Gnr	12/04/17	Desertion	2yrs HL		213/14	
Light F	8 R W Surrey	Pte	25/10/17	Cowardice	Not Conf	F&F	213/18	
Lillystone J	6 Wiltshire	Pte	12/04/16	Sleeping	3yrs PS	F&F	213/8	
Lindridge R	20 KRRC	Rfm	10/08/16	Desertion	5yrs PS		213/11	420
Lindsay G	12 A&S Hdrs	Pte	16/10/17	Desertion	5yrs PS	Salonika	213/18	
Ling Wilson N	2 Canadian EF	Pte	29/12/16	Desertion	2yrs HL	F&F	213/13	546
Ling Wilson N	2 Canadian EF	Pte	08/07/18	Desertion	XXX 12/08/18	F&F	213/24	940
Lingard J	6 Northumb Fus	Pte	11/10/16	Desertion	5yrs PS	F&F	213/12	
Lingard J	6 Northumb Fus	Pte	28/11/16	Desertion	15yrs PS	F&F	213/13	
Linnett F	2 R Warwickshire	Pte	18/01/15	Desertion +	5yrs PS	F&F	213/3	22
Lipowich J	8 Canadian EF	Pte	24/12/17	Desertion	5yrs PS	F&F	213/19	
Lisney G	1 KRRC	Pte	02/02/16	Sleeping	3yrs PS	F&F	213/7	
Lister H	49 MGC	Pte	15/06/18	Desertion	10yrs PS		213/23	
Lister R	13 R Scots	Pte	25/01/17	Desertion	5yrs PS	F&F	213/13	

Name	Unit	Rank	Date	Offence	Final sentence	Location	Ref	Note
Liston C	9 R Dublin Fus	Pte	12/05/16	Desertion	7yrs PS	F&F	213/9	
Litters HJ	48 Australian IF	Pte	19/10/16	Disobedience x2	5yrs PS		213/12	
Little Alexander	10 Australian IF	Pte	05/10/16	Striking	2yrs HL	F&F	90/6	467
Liversidge PH	2 KRRC	Rfm	26/01/17	Desertion	5yrs PS	F&F	213/13	
Livesay R	5 R Irish	Pte	12/08/15	AWOL	2yrs HL		213/5	99
Livingstone C	1/6 Highland LI	Pte	02/08/17	Sleeping	3yrs PS	Egypt	213/17	714
Livingstone John	RFA	Gnr	04/11/14	Sleeping	2yrs HL		213/2	
Llewellyn TJ	4 S Wales Bdrs (att RFA)	Pte	26/09/17	Sleeping	3yrs HL	Mesopotamia	90/7	774
Lloyd H	2 KO Scottish Bdrs	Pte	12/02/15	Desertion	5yrs PS	F&F	213/3	
Lloyd J	RE	Spr	08/11/17	Desertion	Not Conf		213/18	
Lloyd W	1 R Munster Fus	Pte	07/11/18	Desertion	2yrs HL	F&F	213/27	
Loader Frederick	1/22 London	Pte	03/07/17	Desertion	10yrs PS	F&F	213/16	694
Loader Frederick	1/22 London	Pte	02/08/17	Desertion	XXX 19/08/17	F&F	213/16	715
Lochland J	13 R Scots	Pte	30/08/18	Desertion	5yrs PS	F&F	213/25	
Lochland J	13 R Scots	Pte	08/01/19	Desertion	5yrs PS	F&F	213/28	
Lochrie J	10 A&S Hdrs	Pte	13/04/16	Desertion	5yrs PS	F&F	213/8	
Lock J	2 E Surrey	Pte	20/02/15	Desertion	84days	F&F	213/3	
Lock TW	2 E Surrey	Pte	11/01/15	Desertion+	2yrs HL	F&F	213/3	20
Locke EJ	57 Australian IF	Pte	15/03/17	Desertion	10yrs PS		213/14	
Locke G	25 Australian IF	Pte	29/01/17	Desertion	5yrs PS		213/13	
Locke H	11 Manchester	L/Cpl	24/09/15	Cowardice	Quashed	Gallipoli	213/5	
Lockwood A	10 W Yorks	Pte	09/08/15	Striking	5yrs PS	F&F	213/4	
Locky A	2 Durham LI	Pte (L/C)	04/06/17	Cowardice	15yrs PS	F&F	213/15	
Lodge E	RFA	Gnr	24/01/18	Desertion x2	10yrs PS		213/20	
Lodge HEJ	19 Canadian EF	Pte	23/02/18	Desertion	XXX 13/03/18	F&F	213/20	
Lody Carl Hans	Civilian	Alien	02/11/14	Espionage	XXX 06/11/14	UK	92/3	10
Logan J	7 Highland LI	Pte	28/05/17	Desertion	5yrs PS	F&F	213/16	
Logan J	7 Highland LI	Pte	02/01/18	Cowardice	10yrs PS	Egypt	213/21	
Long D	8 R Irish Fus	Pte	22/08/16	Sleeping	3yrs PS	F&F	213/11	
Long JD	1/17 London	Pte	12/10/17	Desertion	5yrs PS	F&F	213/17	796
Long S	2 KO Yorks LI	Pte	26/08/18	Desertion	10yrs PS	F&F	213/25	
Longman M	1 Rifle Bde	Rfm	28/12/14	Sleeping	3mos FP1	F&F	213/3	
Longshaw Alfred	18 Manchester	Pte	20/11/16	Desertion	XXX 01/12/16	F&F	213/12	517
Looker H	2 Suffolk	Pte	06/07/17	Desertion	5yrs PS	F&F	213/16	
Lord H	9 Worcestershire	Pte	14/12/15	Sleeping	2mos FP1	Gallipoli	213/7	
Lothian D	48 Australian IF	Pte	27/07/17	Cowardice+	10yrs PS		213/16	710
Louka YH	Macedonian Mule Coy	Muleteer	08/10/19	Murder x3	XXX 31/10/19	Turkey	213/31	1028
Lovatt C	8 N Staffordshire	Pte	20/08/18	Desertion	15yrs PS	F&F	213/25	
Lovitt E	2 R Berkshire	Pte	22/07/17	Desertion	5yrs PS	F&F	213/16	
Lowen Albert	1 Rifle Bde	Rfm	10/09/17	Desertion	10yrs PS	F&F	213/17	
Lown RA	2 North Non Combat Corps	Pte	12/06/16	Disobedience	10yrs PS	F&F	213/9	354
Lowrie J	192 Lab Coy	Pte	28/09/18	Desertion	5yrs PS		213/25	
Lowry T	2 New Zealand EF	Pte	26/12/16	Desertion	15yrs PS		213/13	538
Lowton G	17 Sherwood Fstrs	Pte	19/07/16	Desertion	XXX 30/07/16	F&F	213/10	402
Lucas J	1/7 London	Rfm	28/08/17	Desertion	15yrs PS	F&F	213/17	
Lumley JG	19 Durham LI	Pte	30/12/16	Cowardice	10yrs PS	F&F	213/13	556
Lunny	2 Lancs Fus	Pte	04/06/15	Cowardice	Quashed	F&F	213/4	
Lunt E	2 Welsh	Pte	24/01/18	Desertion	5yrs PS	F&F	213/20	
Lyddy P	2 Leinster	Pte	02/11/18	Desertion x4	15yrs PS	Salonika	213/28	
Lynch Finian	Civilian	Sinn Fein	03/05/16	Rebellion	10yrs PS	Dublin	213/8	228
Lynch FN	9 KRRC	Rfm	05/06/17	Desertion	10yrs PS	F&F	213/15	
Lynch H	26 Australian IF	Pte	28/09/16	Desertion/Esc	Not Conf		213/11	
Lynch J	2 R Inniskilling Fus	Pte	01/07/17	Drunk/AWOL	2yrs HL	F&F	213/16	
Lynch J	1 R Irish Rifles	Rfm	06/10/17	Cowardice	15yrs PS	F&F	213/17	
Lynch Jeremiah C	Civilian	Sinn Fein	17/05/16	Rebellion	10yrs PS	Dublin	213/8	311
Lynch P	1 R Munster Fus	Pte	12/10/15	Sleeping	5yrs PS	Gallipoli	213/6	
Lyons J	1 KO Yorks LI	Sgt	19/02/18	Desertion	Not Conf	Salonika	213/22	
Lyons P	1 KRRC	Pte	15/02/15	Sleeping	2yrs HL	F&F	213/3	
Lyons W	4 E Yorks	Pte	27/11/17	Desertion	5yrs PS		213/19	
MacAuley W	17 Manchester	Pte	24/03/16	Sleeping	Not Conf	F&F	213/9	195
MacDonagh Thomas	Civilian	Sinn Fein	01/05/16	Rebellion	XXX 03/05/16	Dublin	213/8	221
MacDonald Henry [Harry]	12 W Yorks	Pte	24/10/16	Desertion	XXX 04/11/16	F&F	213/12	488
MacDonald John	19 Durham LI	L/Cpl	28/12/16	Quitting	XXX 18/01/17	F&F	213/13	544
MacKenzie J	7 Seaforth Hdrs	Pte	05/08/15	Desertion	2yrs HL	F&F	213/4	
Mackie Alexander	2 Highland LI	Pte	01/10/14	AWOL	2yrs HL	F&F	213/2	
Mackness Ernest	1 Scottish Rifles	Pte	09/10/15	Desertion	10yrs PS	F&F	213/6	122
Mackness Ernest	1 Scottish Rifles	Pte	14/09/17	Desertion	XXX 01/10/17	F&F	213/17	761
Macky J	1 Hampshire	Pte	23/05/18	Desertion	7yrs PS	F&F	213/22	

Name	Unit	Rank	Date	Offence	Final sentence	Location	Ref	Note
MacMillan J	RAMC	Pte	09/11/16	Desertion	15yrs PS		213/7	
MacPherson Nicol	1/8 A&S Hdrs	Pte	05/11/15	Sleeping	2yrs HL	F&F	213/6	126
Maddison G	9 Durham LI	Pte	11/02/17	Desertion	5yrs PS		213/14	
Maddison T	2 W Yorks	Pte	21/02/15	Sleeping	3mos FP1	F&F	213/3	
Magee T	RGA	Gnr	03/10/18	Desertion	10yrs PS		213/25	
Magill J	R Irish Rifles	L/Cpl	31/12/17	Desertion	3yrs PS		213/19	
Maguire J	2 R Dublin Fus	Pte	03/11/16	Disobedience	5yrs PS	F&F	213/12	
Mahmoud Laz	Civilian		22/07/20	Hostile Act	10yrs HL	Turkey	213/34	1055
Mahomed N	Malay States Garr Regt	Sepoy	27/07/18	Striking/AWOL	2yrs HL	Aden	90/7	953
Mahoney T	2 R Munster Fus	Pte	04/04/16	Desertion	5yrs PS	F&F	213/8	
Maidment J	8 KOR Lancaster	Pte	27/09/16	Desertion	6mos HL	F&F	213/11	
Maidment J	8 KOR Lancaster	Pte	18/08/18	Desertion	5yrs PS	F&F	213/24	
Mailey T	1/4 R Scots Fus	Pte	13/07/17	Disobedience	5yrs PS	Egypt	213/16	
Mainguy O	22 Canadian EF	Pte	28/08/18	Desertion x2	7yrs PS	F&F	213/25	
Major JP	1 R Scots Fus	Pte	01/10/16	Desertion	3yrs PS	F&F	213/12	
Makin R	8 Border	Pte	27/08/17	Desertion	5yrs PS	F&F	213/17	
Malia J	RE	Spr	14/07/18	Striking +	5yrs PS		213/24	943
Mallin Michael	Civilian	Sinn Fein	05/05/16	Rebellion	XXX 08/05/16	Dublin	213/8	283
Maloney J	1 Loyal N Lancs	Pte	24/08/15	Sleeping	1yr HL	F&F	213/4	
Malyon Frederick	12 RE (att RFA)	Spr	21/03/17	Desertion	XXX 04/04/17		213/14	610
Mamoulashvilli David N	Civilian		15/04/20	Murder	XXX	S Russia	213/34	1045
Mamprusi A	Gold Coast Regt	Pte (L/C)	25/04/17	Desertion +	XXX 28/04/17	East Africa	213/16	636
Mangham M	3 Canadian EF	Pte	24/07/16	Desertion	10yrs PS	F&F	213/10	
Mann JG	19 Durham LI	Pte	30/12/16	Cowardice	10yrs PS	F&F	213/13	557
Mann RC	1/5 Gloucestershire	Pte	26/08/16	Cowardice	5yrs PS	F&F	213/10	
Mann TW	ASC	Pte	23/09/16	Striking x2	10yrs PS		213/11	
March J	2 E Surrey	Pte	14/02/15	Sleeping	84days FP1	F&F	213/3	
Marchuk M	47 Canadian EF	Pte	06/09/17	Cowardice	10yrs PS		213/17	
Marflitt JB	1/4 KO Yorks LI	Pte	01/04/17	Desertion	5yrs PS	F&F	213/14	
Marienfeld	German Infantry	POW	17/03/15	Hostile Act	Not Conf		213/3	51
Marineau G	22 Canadian EF	Pte	13/09/17	Desertion	10yrs PS	F&F	213/17	
Mark F	2 W Yorks	Pte	18/11/16	Desertion	5yrs PS	F&F	213/12	
Markalitdze Arsen	Civilian		21/09/19	Armed Robbery	XXX	S Russia	213/34	1022
Markham A	2 Suffolk	Pte	15/02/18	Desertion	5yrs PS	F&F	213/20	
Markievicz Constance G	Civilian	Sinn Fein	04/05/16	Rebellion	PS Life	Dublin	213/8	260
Marks J	Civilian	Sinn Fein	04/05/16	Rebellion	3yrs PS	Dublin	213/8	261
Marlow CJ	68 Bty RFA	Gnr	27/03/15	Striking	5yrs PS		213/3	
Marples T	2 Coldstream Gds	Pte	06/10/16	Desertion	5yrs PS	F&F	213/12	
Marriott F	24 Northumb Fus	Pte	19/04/17	Desertion x2	10yrs PS	F&F	213/15	635
Marsh EA	2/4 R Berkshire	Pte	04/08/16	Desertion	5yrs PS	F&F	213/10	
Marshall D	32 MGC	Pte	20/06/17	Desertion	10yrs PS		213/15	
Marshall T	29 MGC	Pte	18/07/18	Desertion	10yrs PS		213/24	
Marshall W	4 Grenadier Gds	L/Cpl	29/05/16	Cowardice x2	10yrs PS	F&F	213/9	
Marshall W	17 Australian IF	Pte	12/09/17	Desertion	5yrs PS		213/18	
Marston E	12 Northumb Fus	Pte	16/05/17	Desertion	Not Conf	F&F	213/15	
Marten H	East Non Combat Corps	Pte	02/06/16	Disobedience x2	Not Conf	F&F	213/10	325
Marten H	East Non Combat Corps	Pte	07/06/16	Disobedience	10yrs PS	F&F	213/9	333
Martin C	11 W Yorks	Pte	22/05/17	Desertion	10yrs PS	F&F	213/15	
Martin CEJ	1 Bedfordshire	Pte	30/12/14	Sleeping	2yrs HL	F&F	213/3	
Martin Frank	Civilian		09/06/16	Poss firearms	10yrs PS	Dublin	92/3	339
Martin Harry	9 Essex	Pte	04/03/16	Desertion	XXX 20/03/16	F&F	213/7	187
Martin J	1/5 KOR Lancaster	Pte	25/08/18	Desertion	5yrs PS	F&F	213/25	
Martin R	115 MGC	Pte	15/11/17	Sleeping	Not Conf		213/18	
Martin S	1 Lincolnshire	Pte	12/12/14	AWOL	Quashed	F&F	213/3	
Martlew A	2 North Non Combat Corps	Pte	12/06/16	Disobedience	10yrs PS	F&F	213/9	355
Marvin A	20 Middlesex	Pte	06/11/18	Desertion	5yrs PS	F&F	213/26	992
Mason J	2 R Scots Fus	Pte	14/08/17	Desertion	15yrs PS	F&F	213/16	
Mason J	2 R Scots Fus	Pte	20/05/18	Desertion	15yrs PS	F&F	213/22	
Mason JT	7 Leicestershire	Pte	04/12/15	Sleeping	5yrs PS	F&F	213/6	
Mason W	3 Middlesex	Pte	10/07/15	Sleeping	3yrs PS	F&F	213/4	
Mason WE	10 Hussars	Pte	10/02/16	Sleeping	5yrs PS		213/7	
Massey H	MGC	Pte	02/04/18	Desertion	2yrs HL		213/21	
Massey L	8 York & Lancaster	Pte	08/10/17	Desertion	15yrs PS	F&F	213/17	
Massey T	2 R Irish	Pte	27/04/15	Sleeping	5yrs PS	F&F	213/4	
Massiter J	1/5 York & Lancaster	Pte	11/06/17	Desertion	5yrs PS	F&F	213/15	
Masters A	2 R Berkshire	Pte	22/07/17	Cowardice	15yrs PS	F&F	213/16	
Masterson M	5 Connaught Rangers	Pte	20/12/15	Desertion +	10yrs PS	Salonika	213/7	141
Masterson R	2 Canadian EF	Pte	01/10/17	Desertion	10yrs PS	F&F	213/18	

Name	Unit	Rank	Date	Offence	Final sentence	Location	Ref	Note
Mather A	2 Manchester	Pte	20/08/15	Cowardice	10yrs PS	F&F	213/5	
Matheson J	R Scots Fus	Cpl	28/12/14	Cowardice	2yrs HL		213/3	
Mathews N	3 S African Infantry	Pte	08/03/16	Murder	XXX 03/04/16	Egypt	90/6	190
Mathieson A	1/8 A&S Hdrs	Pte	15/12/17	Desertion	5yrs PS	F&F	213/18	844
Mathieson J	9 Black Watch	Pte	14/07/17	Desertion	5yrs PS	F&F	213/16	
Maude G	1/6 W Riding	Pte	28/08/15	Sleeping	5yrs PS	F&F	213/5	
Maunders A	1 S Staffordshire	Pte	20/04/18	Quitting	1yr HL	Italy	213/21	
Maw J	2 Durham LI	Pte	05/11/17	Desertion	5yrs PS	F&F	213/18	
Mawdsley JH	20 Lancs Fus	Pte	26/12/17	Desertion	5yrs PS	F&F	213/19	850
May P	1/24 London	Pte	25/07/18	Sleeping	1yr HL	F&F	213/24	
May W	RFA	Gnr	09/12/14	Desertion	2yrs HL		213/1	
Mayberry C	8 Welsh	Pte	09/09/15	Sleeping	1yr HL		213/5	107
Mayers James	1/13 London	Pte	01/03/17	Quitting x2	5yrs PS	F&F	213/14	598
Mayers James	1/13 Royal Fus	Pte	22/05/17	Desertion +	XXX 16/06/17	F&F	213/15	663
Mayes J	1/4 E Lancs	Pte	12/12/17	Desertion	5yrs PS	F&F	213/19	
Maynard EA	8 Bedfordshire	Pte	03/03/17	Sleeping	5yrs PS	F&F	213/14	
Mayne FG	1 D Cornwall LI	Pte	16/06/18	Desertion	5yrs PS	F&F	213/23	
Mayne FG	1 D Cornwall LI	Pte	18/02/19	Desertion	10yrs PS	F&F	213/28	
Mayo A	2 E Surrey	Pte	21/02/15	Sleeping	84days FP1	F&F	213/3	
Mayotte N	38 Canadian EF	Pte	30/05/18	Desertion	7yrs PS	F&F	213/22	
McAdam A	1/7 Highland LI	Pte	14/06/18	Desertion	5yrs PS	F&F	213/23	924
McAlinder J	8 R Inniskilling Fus	Pte	05/05/17	Desertion	10yrs PS	F&F	213/15	
McArdle J	Civilian	Sinn Fein	08/05/16	Rebellion	3yrs PS	Dublin	213/8	297
McArthur A	12 R Scots	Pte	10/09/18	Desertion	15yrs PS	F&F	213/25	
McAteer W	1 A&S Hdrs	Pte	19/07/15	Sleeping	5yrs PS	F&F	213/4	
McAuley J	2 Highland LI	Pte	18/04/15	Desertion	5yrs PS	F&F	213/4	
McBride John	Civilian	Sinn Fein	01/05/16	Rebellion	XXX 05/05/16	Dublin	213/8	222
McBride S	2 R Irish Rifles	Rfm	25/11/16	Desertion	XXX 07/12/16	F&F	213/12	523
McCaffery V	8 R Irish Fus	Pte	05/10/16	Cowardice	Not Conf	F&F	213/12	
McCall F	1 Scottish Rifles	Pte	25/07/15	Desertion	5yrs PS	F&F	213/4	
McCarthy J	1 R Irish Rifles	Rfm	05/06/15	Desertion	2yrs HL	F&F	213/4	
McCarthy S	MGC	Pte	29/10/17	Desertion	XXX [?]	F&F	213/18	814
McClair Harry	2 Border	Pte	08/07/18	Desertion	XXX 01/08/18	F&F	213/24	941
McClarnon H	1 R Irish Rifles	Rfm	05/03/15	Desertion	2yrs HL	F&F	213/3	
McCloy R	7/8 R Irish Fus	Pte	21/02/17	Desertion	10yrs PS	F&F	213/14	
McColl Charles F	4 E Yorks	Pte	27/11/17	Desertion	XXX 28/12/17	F&F	213/19	834
McConnell W	8 R Irish Rifles	Rfm	08/12/15	Sleeping	1yr HL	F&F	213/6	138
McConville J	2 R Irish Rifles	Pte	20/02/15	Sleeping	2yrs HL	F&F	213/3	
McConville N	1 A&S Hdrs	Pte	16/09/15	Sleeping	10yrs PS	F&F	213/5	
McCorkindale Daniel	11 R Scots	Pte	05/10/16	Mutiny	15yrs PS	F&F	90/6	468
McCormick J	51 Australian IF	Pte	01/05/17	Desertion	10yrs PS		213/15	
McCormick M	12 Manchester	Pte	14/05/18	Desertion	5yrs PS	F&F	213/22	
McCracken JF	15 R Irish Rifles	Rfm	27/02/16	Desertion	XXX 19/03/16	F&F	213/7	183
McCrae A	54 Canadian EF	Pte	17/09/17	Desertion	10yrs PS		213/17	
McCubbin Bertie	17 Sherwood Fstrs	Pte	19/07/16	Desertion	XXX 30/07/16	F&F	213/10	403
McCulloch D	9 Scottish Rifles	Pte	27/05/17	Desertion	5yrs PS	F&F	213/15	
McCulloch J	1 R Scots Fus	Pte	24/05/17	Desertion	10yrs PS	F&F	213/15	
McDermott J	12 Australian IF	Pte	09/07/15	Sleeping	5yrs PS		213/5	
McDermott J	Civilian	Sinn Fein	09/05/16	Rebellion	XXX 12/05/16	Dublin	213/8	300
McDermott JF	20 Manchester	Pte	17/06/16	Sleeping	2yrs PS	F&F	213/10	376
McDonald H	1/6 Highland LI	Pte	30/03/18	Desertion	10yrs PS	Egypt	213/22	886
McDonald J	2 Highland LI	Pte	08/04/15	Desertion x2	10yrs PS	F&F	213/3	
McDonald J	8/10 Gordon Hdrs	Pte	24/01/17	Desertion x2	5yrs PS	F&F	213/13	
McDonald J	RFA	Gnr	08/09/17	Desertion	10yrs PS		213/17	
McDonnell C	3 Canadian MGC	Pte	24/03/19	Mutiny	PS Life	F&F	213/29	
McDonnell H	4 Canadian EF	Pte	19/03/17	Desertion	2yrs HL	F&F	213/14	
McDougall A	2 A&S Hdrs	Pte	15/11/16	Desertion	5yrs PS	F&F	213/12	
McDowall F	1/7 Highland LI	Pte	14/06/18	Desertion	5yrs PS	F&F	213/23	925
McEntee John (Sean)	Civilian		09/06/16	Poss firearms	PS Life	Dublin	92/3	340
McEwan JA	1 Lincolnshire	Pte	21/11/18	Desertion	5yrs PS	F&F	213/26	
McFarlan A	1 Cameron Hdrs	Pte	19/05/18	Desertion	5yrs PS	F&F	213/22	
McFarland W J	9 R Irish Rifles	Rfm	27/02/16	Quitting	2yrs HL	F&F	213/8	184
McFarlane John	4 Liverpool	Pte	28/04/18	Desertion x3	XXX 22/05/18	F&F	213/22	897
McGarry J	9 Rifle Bde	Cpl	08/10/15	Cowardice	Quashed	F&F	213/6	
McGarry John	Civilian	Sinn Fein	03/05/16	Rebellion	8yrs PS	Dublin	213/8	229
McGaskell J	2 R Scots	Pte	15/10/18	Against Inhab	2yrs PS	F&F	213/26	
McGee P	9 Yorks	Pte	29/10/17	Desertion	15yrs PS	F&F	213/18	
McGeehan Bernard	1/8 Liverpool	Pte	21/10/16	Desertion	XXX 02/11/16	F&F	213/12	487

Name	Unit	Rank	Date	Offence	Final sentence	Location	Ref	Note
McGhee D	1 KOR Lancaster	Pte	14/11/18	Desertion	5yrs PS	F&F	213/27	
McGhee H	1/5 Highland LI	Pte	14/10/16	Sleeping	2yrs HL	Egypt	213/13	483
McGoldrick GM	10 Scottish Rifles	Pte	19/04/17	Desertion	10yrs PS	F&F	213/15	
McGovern T	2 A & S Hdrs	Pte	27/03/15	Desertion	10yrs PS	F&F	213/3	
McGowan James	2 Cameron Hdrs	Pte	18/09/15	Sleeping	15yrs PS	F&F	213/5	
McGrath D	1/19 London	Pte	01/07/18	Desertion	5yrs PS	F&F	213/23	933
McGrath J	9 Liverpool	Sgt	13/08/17	Cowardice	2yrs HL		213/16	
McGrath JP	1 Australian IF	Pte	12/03/17	Desertion	10yrs PS		213/14	
McGrath M	12 Manchester	Pte	24/12/17	Desertion	5yrs PS	F&F	213/19	
McGregor W	1/4 Black Watch	Pte	05/05/16	Desertion	3yrs PS	F&F	213/9	284
McGrory J	4 (att 2) Argyle & Sutherland	Pte	15/06/16	Desertion	2yrs HL	F&F	213/9	
McGuill J	1/4 E Lancs	Pte	01/01/16	Cowardice	2yrs HL	Gallipoli	213/8	
McGuire JH	4 Australian IF	Pte	15/03/17	Desertion	10yrs PS		213/14	
McIntyre D	9 Black Watch	Pte	14/03/16	Desertion	5yrs PS	F&F	213/8	
McIntyre J	12 A&S Hdrs	Pte	17/11/17	Sleeping	3yrs PS	Salonika	213/18	
McKay A	11 R Scots	Pte	30/07/16	Cowardice	Not Conf	F&F	213/10	
McKay A	Seaforth Hdrs	Pte	27/09/18	Desertion	7yrs PS		213/25	
McKay P	2 Highland LI	Pte	19/10/18	Desertion	5yrs PS	F&F	213/25	
McKie S	2 R Irish Rifles	Pte	04/02/15	Cowardice	Quashed	F&F	213/3	
McLaren J	6 Cameron Hdrs	Pte	29/09/16	Desertion	5yrs PS	F&F	213/11	
McLaughlan P	15 Highland LI	Pte	13/01/18	Desertion	10yrs PS	F&F	213/28	861
McLaughlin J	8 KO Scottish Bdrs	Pte	23/04/16	Desertion	5yrs PS	F&F	213/9	
McLean C	7 Highland LI	Pte	17/09/17	Casting Arms	4yrs PS	F&F	213/18	
McLelland C	7 R Scottish Rifles	Pte	22/03/16	Desertion	10yrs PS		213/8	
McLelland S	1/4 Seaforth Hdrs	Pte	19/09/17	Desertion	5yrs PS	F&F	213/17	764
McLennan JT	49 Australian IF	Pte	01/05/17	Desertion	10yrs PS		213/15	
McLeod DF	13 Canadian EF	Pte	29/05/16	Desertion	5yrs PS	F&F	213/9	
McLuskie J	1 Cameron Hdrs	Pte	28/01/15	Quitting x2	5yrs PS	F&F	213/3	
McManus H	3 Worcestershire	Pte	25/07/17	Desertion	2yrs HL	F&F	213/16	
McManus P	7 Middlesex	Pte	17/10/18	Desertion	10yrs PS	F&F	213/26	
McMillan A	2 Highland LI	Pte	24/02/16	Desertion	10yrs PS	F&F	213/8	
McMillan J	58 Australian IF	Pte	27/12/16	Striking	2yrs HL		213/13	
McMillan R	11 Northumb Fus	Pte	17/01/18	Desertion	15yrs PS	Italy	213/19	
McMullan J	2 Scottish Rifles	Pte	26/02/18	Desertion	5yrs PS	F&F	213/20	
McMurdie J	1 R Inniskilling Fus	Pte	15/07/16	Desertion	3yrs PS	F&F	213/10	
McNamara J	1 E Lancs	Pte	20/02/15	Desertion	10yrs PS	F&F	213/3	
McNaught M	1 R Dublin Fus	Pte	12/09/18	Desertion	10yrs PS	F&F	213/25	
McNeilly G	85 Canadian EF	Pte	26/09/17	Desertion x2	10yrs PS	F&F	213/17	
McNella James	RFA	Dvr	21/11/14	Rape	Quashed		213/2	
McNestry Patrick	Civilian	Sinn Fein	03/05/16	Rebellion	10yrs PS	Dublin	213/8	230
McPhee W	85 Canadian EF	Pte	26/09/17	Desertion	5yrs PS	F&F	213/17	
McPherson J	16 R Scots	Pte	03/08/17	Desertion	5yrs PS	F&F	213/16	
McQuade John	18 Highland LI	Pte	10/10/16	Desertion x2	XXX 06/11/16	F&F	213/12	473
McSally William	3 Worcestershire	Pte	19/06/15	Desertion	10yrs PS	F&F	213/4	
Meadowcroft F	8 KOR Lancaster	Pte	02/07/18	Desertion	10yrs Ps	F&F	213/23	
Meeguane [?] M	14 Australian IF	Pte	08/08/17	Desertion	10yrs PS		213/17	
Meehan W	Civilian	Sinn Fein	04/05/16	Rebellion	3yrs PS	Dublin	213/8	262
Mehmed Hafouz	Civilian		22/07/20	Hostile Act	10yrs HL	Turkey	213/34	1056
Mehmed Salih C	Civilian		13/09/20	Rebellion	2yrs HL	Egypt	213/34	1081
Mehmet Zaccharia	Civilian		06/07/20	Hostile Act	10yrs HL	Turkey	213/34	1052
Melin Ernest W	Civilian	Alien	20/08/14	Espionage	XXX 18/9/15	UK	92/3	1
Melinn James	Civilian	Sinn Fein	03/05/16	Rebellion	10yrs PS	Dublin	213/8	231
Melkoniantz Gregorieff	Civilian		16/05/19	Murder	Not Conf	S Russia	213/34	1010
Mellers B	1 Leicestershire	Pte	20/04/18	Desertion	10yrs PS	F&F	213/23	
Mellor J	MGC	L/Cpl	13/03/18	Qitting post	10yrs PS		213/21	
Melsom AJC	ASC	Dvr	11/02/18	Desertion	5yrs PS		213/20	
Melvin R [aka Haig H]	2 A & S Hdrs	Pte	20/10/18	Desertion	15yrs PS	F&F	213/27	
Memish I	Turkish Army	POW	15/02/18	Murder	XXX	Egypt	213/20	
Meredith J	2 Highland LI	Pte	15/11/17	Desertion	10yrs PS	F&F	213/18	
Merrills W	7 E Kent (Buffs)	Pte	07/06/18	Desertion	5yrs PS	F&F	213/23	
Mervyn Michael	Civilian	Sinn Fein	03/05/16	Rebellion	10yrs PS	Dublin	213/8	232
Metcalfe H	22 Northumb Fus	Pte	23/07/17	Desertion	5yrs PS	F&F	213/17	706
Metcalfe WE	12 Northumb Fus	Cpl	16/05/17	Desertion	10yrs PS	F&F	213/15	
Methven J	1/6 Gordon Hdrs	Pte	23/07/17	Desertion	5yrs PS	F&F	213/16	707
Meyer Albert	Civilian	Alien	05/11/15	Espionage	XXX 2/12/15	UK	92/3	127
Meyrick J	1/6 Welsh	Pte	17/04/16	Desertion	3yrs PS	F&F	213/8	
Meyrick LH	2 New Zealand EF	Pte	04/04/18	Desertion	5yrs PS		213/21	887
Miand G	1 Slavo-British Legion	Pte	17/07/19	Mutiny	10yrs PS	N Russia	213/32	

Name	Unit	Rank	Date	Offence	Final sentence	Location	Ref	Note
Michael James S	10 Scottish Rifles	Pte	01/06/17	Desertion	XXX 24/08/17	F&F	213/16	666
Michalaichvili Ilya	Civilian		07/11/19	Murder	XXX	S Russia	213/34	1032
Middleton A	2 R Scots Fus	Pte	20/07/15	Desertion	2yrs HL	F&F	213/4	
Middleton A	2 R Scots Fus	Pte	15/03/16	Striking+	10yrs PS	F&F	213/8	192
Middleton H	5 DAC	Dvr	20/06/16	Desertion	10yrs PS		213/9	
Middleton J	1 KO Yorks LI	Pte	02/07/15	Sleeping	5yrs PS	F&F	213/4	
Middleton J	1 Northumb Fus	Pte	08/09/16	Cowardice	10yrs PS		213/11	
Middleton JE	RE	Cpl	03/06/16	Desertion	10yrs PS		213/9	
Midley S	6 E Lancs	Pte	17/04/16	Sleeping	5yrs PS	Mesopotamia	90/7	206
Milbourne W	2 Suffolk	Pte	27/12/16	Desertion	10yrs PS	F&F	213/13	
Miles EJ	2 E Surrey	Pte	24/03/15	Sleeping	3mos FP1	F&F	213/3	
Millar EA	1 Canadian MGC	Pte	22/09/18	Desertion	5yrs PS	F&F	213/25	
Millar J	9 Black Watch	Pte	14/07/17	Desertion	5yrs PS	F&F	213/16	
Millar WH	13 Welsh	Pte	26/03/17	Desertion+	Not Conf	F&F	213/14	614
Millard P	4 R Munster Fus	Pte	03/07/16	Desertion	3yrs PS		213/10	
Millburn John B	24 Northumb Fus	Pte	06/10/17	Desertion	XXX 08/11/17	F&F	213/18	789
Millen W	1 R Inniskilling Fus	Pte	03/06/18	Desertion	10yrs PS	F&F	213/23	
Miller C	1(Pioneer) Australian IF	Sgt	17/05/16	Desertion	5yrs PS/Red in rank	F&F	213/9	
Miller G	2 A & S Hdrs	Pte	27/03/15	Desertion	10yrs PS	F&F	213/3	
Miller J	2 KO Scottish Bdrs	Pte	29/07/16	Desertion	5yrs PS	F&F	213/11	
Miller P	147 MGC	Pte	16/07/17	Desertion	5yrs PS		213/16	
Miller R	2 KO Scottish Bdrs	Pte	18/07/17	Desertion	10yrs PS	F&F	213/16	
Miller RL	14 Canadian EF	Pte	11/08/15	Desertion	10yrs PS	F&F	213/4	
Miller S	2 KO Yorks LI	Cpl	04/04/18	Desertion	5yrs PS	F&F	213/21	
Milligan Charles M	10 Scottish Rifles	Pte	05/05/17	Desertion	XXX 03/06/17	F&F	213/15	648
Milligan G	Hood Bn R Naval VR	A/B	09/07/18	Desertion	5yrs PS		213/23	
Milligan J	2 R Scots	Pte	15/11/18	Desertion	5yrs PS	F&F	213/27	
Milligan M	9 Durham LI	Pte	24/11/17	Desertion	5yrs PS		213/19	
Milloy J	4 Liverpool	L/Cpl	29/03/15	Desertion	5yrs PS	F&F	213/3	
Mills F	1 KRRC	Pte	28/03/15	Sleeping	3mos FP1	F&F	213/3	
Mills F	1 R Warwickshire	Pte	29/04/17	Desertion	10yrs PS	F&F	213/15	
Mills F	RAMC	Pte	28/10/17	Desertion	10yrs PS		213/18	
Mills George	2 D Cornwall LI	Pte	10/09/15	Desertion+	XXX 29/09/15	F&F	213/5	110
Mills T	22 Northumb Fus	Pte	02/09/18	Desertion	10yrs PS		213/25	
Mills W	1/10 Manchester	Pte	29/05/15	Cowardice	5yrs PS	Mesopotamia	213/4	
Mills WE	2 Durham LI	Pte	09/02/16	Desertion	10yrs PS	F&F	213/8	
Mitchell Arthur	1/6 Lancs	Pte	02/08/17	Desertion	XXX 20/08/17	F&F	213/16	716
Mitchell David	2 R Scots	Pte	07/07/15	Desertion	5yrs PS	F&F	213/4	
Mitchell Frederick W	57 Australian IF	Pte	11/10/16	Mutiny	2yrs HL	F&F	90/6	476
Mitchell James A	1 British West Indies	Pte	15/12/17	Murder	XXX 22/12/17	Palestine	213/20	845
Mitchell L	8 York & Lancaster	Pte	16/07/17	Desertion	10yrs PS	F&F	213/16	699
Mitchell Leonard	8 York & Lancaster	Pte	05/09/17	Desertion	XXX 19/09/17	F&F	213/17	750
Mitchell R	10 Loyal N Lancs	Pte	15/10/17	Desertion	10yrs PS	F&F	213/18	
Mitchell W	1 R Scots Fus	Pte	15/01/15	Cowardice	15yrs PS	F&F	213/4	
Mitchell W	2 Highland LI	L/Cpl	30/03/16	Desertion	Quashed	F&F	213/8	
Mobbs R	1 KO Yorks LI	Pte	10/08/15	Sleeping	5yrs PS	F&F	213/4	
Moffit J	15 Sherwood Fstrs	Pte	02/08/16	Quitting	5yrs PS	F&F	213/11	412
Mohamad Ahmed El Sufi	Civilian		10/04/15	Murder	XXX	Egypt	213/3	
Mohammed Khalil	Civilian		19/04/15	Att Murder	XXX	Egypt	213/3	65
Mohammedoff Meshadie AO	Civilian		21/02/19	Robbery	10yrs PS	Baku	213/34	
Moles Thomas	54 Canadian EF	Pte	04/10/17	Desertion	XXX 22/10/17	F&F	213/17	785
Moller AE	1 S African Infantry	Pte	25/02/18	Desertion x2	5yrs PS		213/21	
Molloy Bryan	Civilian	Sinn Fein	12/05/16	Rebellion	10yrs PS	Dublin	213/8	309
Molyneaux J	1 Loyal N Lancs	Pte	06/06/15	Desertion	5yrs PS	F&F	213/4	
Molyneaux James	1 Loyal N Lancs	Pte	05/06/16	Desertion	XXX 15/06/16	F&F	213/9	331
Monaghan J	9 Black Watch	Pte	13/03/16	Desertion	5yrs PS	F&F	213/8	
Monaghan M [Byrne S]	1 R Dublin Fus	Pte	12/10/17	Desertion	XXX 28/10/17	F&F	213/18	797
Monroe J	1 Canadian EF	Pte	29/06/16	Desertion	5yrs PS	F&F	213/10	
Montgomery F	1 Canadian R'way Troops	Spr	28/10/17	Insub+	5yrs PS	F&F	213/18	812
Montgomery P	10 W Riding	Pte	12/12/17	Desertion	15yrs PS	Italy	213/19	
Moon William Alfred	11 Cheshire	Pte (L/C)	11/11/16	Desertion	XXX 21/11/16	F&F	213/12	505
Mooney E	11 S Lancs	Pte	23/06/17	Desertion	10yrs PS		213/15	682
Mooney J	2 R Irish Rifles	Pte	29/03/15	Desertion	Quashed	F&F	213/3	
Mooney JA	1 Manchester	Pte	21/05/17	Sleeping	5yrs PS	Mesopotamia	90/7	659
Moorcroft S	1 N Staffordshire	Pte	06/10/15	Sleeping	1yr HL	F&F	213/6	
Moore A	6 Lincolnshire	Pte	20/09/15	Cowardice	5yrs PS	Gallipoli	213/5	
Moore H	1 Middlesex	Pte	22/10/17	Desertion	10yrs PS	F&F	213/18	
Moore H	1/5 S Lancs	L/Cpl	01/08/18	Desertion	5yrs PS	F&F	213/24	

Name	Unit	Rank	Date	Offence	Final sentence	Location	Ref	Note
Moore H	1 Middlesex	Pte	01/11/18	Desertion x2	Quashed	F&F	213/27	
Moore Thomas	ASC	Dvr	18/02/16	Murder	XXX 26/02/16	F&F	213/7	178
Moore W	2 R Warwickshire	Pte	23/01/15	Desertion	2yrs HL	F&F	213/3	
Moorhouse C	2 W Riding	Pte	09/11/16	Desertion	5yrs PS	F&F	213/12	
Moorhouse J	2 R Irish	Pte	15/09/17	Desertion	5yrs PS	F&F	213/18	
Morad MH	38 Egyptian Lab Corps	Rais	10/04/22	Murder	10yrs PS	Egypt	213/34	
Moran H	5 Scottish Rifles	Pte	28/04/18	Desertion	10yrs PS		213/23	898
Moran H	5 Scottish Rifles	Pte	22/05/18	Desertion	Not Conf	F&F	213/23	912
Moran J	1 Irish Gds	Pte	04/02/15	Desertion	2yrs HL	F&F	213/3	
Moran J	45 Australian IF	Pte	22/12/16	Desertion	10yrs PS		213/13	
Moran T	1 Connaught Rangers	Pte	03/09/20	Mutiny	PS Life	India		1068
Morgan A	4 Royal Fus	Pte	25/05/15	Sleeping	3yrs PS	F&F	213/4	
Morgan A	D1 Tank Corps	Pte	24/12/17	Desertion	15yrs PS	F&F	213/20	
Morgan TG	1/8 Middlesex	Pte	26/05/17	Desertion	2yrs HL	F&F	213/15	
Morin G	52 Canadian EF	Pte	05/09/16	Desertion	5yrs PS	F&F	213/11	444
Morley LH	12 Royal Fus	Pte	07/03/17	Sleeping/Quitting	5yrs PS	F&F	213/14	
Morrall AG	10 R Warwickshire	Pte	09/07/18	Quitting	10yrs PS	F&F	213/24	
Morris Herbert	British West Indies	Pte	07/09/17	Desertion	XXX 20/09/17	F&F	213/17	755
Morris M	2 Leinster	Pte	18/09/16	Desertion	10yrs PS	F&F	213/11	
Morris M	2 Leinster	Pte	20/08/17	Desertion x2	10yrs PS	F&F	213/16	
Morris N	12 S Wales Bdrs	Pte	29/06/16	Desertion	10yrs PS	F&F	213/9	386
Morris R	18 Australian IF	Pte	01/10/16	Desertion	2yrs HL		213/13	
Morris T	106 Bty RFA	Gnr	25/01/15	Desertion	5yrs PS		213/3	
Morris T	1 KOR Lancaster	Sgt	09/08/15	Desertion x2	10yrs PS	F&F	213/5	
Morrison D	Dragoon Gds	Pte	22/10/17	Desertion	5yrs PS		213/18	
Morrison J	9 Yorks	Pte	26/10/17	Desertion	10yrs PS	F&F	213/18	
Morrison JH	R Canadian Regt	Pte	28/01/18	Desertion	5yrs PS	F&F	213/19	
Morrison TC	2 New Zealand EF	Pte	04/08/16	Quitting+	5yrs PS		213/10	415
Morrissy James	Civilian	Sinn Fein	05/05/16	Rebellion	3yrs PS	Dublin	213/8	285
Mosey W	7 R Dublin Fus	Pte	04/04/17	Cowardice	10yrs PS	Salonika	213/15	
Mosey W	7 R Dublin Fus	Pte	18/09/17	Disobedience	Not Conf	Salonika	213/18	
Moshi M	Gold Coast Regt	Pte	13/10/17	Cowardice	7yrs PS	East Africa	213/22	
Mound W	12 R Scots	Pte	10/09/18	Desertion x2	15yrs PS	F&F	213/25	
Moussa Ahmed	7 Turkish Army	POW	09/05/19	Murder	XXX	Egypt	213/29	1009
Moustafa Emin O	Civilian		08/09/20	Aiding Enemy	PS Life	Egypt	213/34	1078
Moustafa Mehmed O	Civilian		27/09/20	Rebellion	PS Life	Egypt	213/34	1085
Mskladze Arkaki	Civilian		15/04/20	Murder	XXX	S Russia	213/34	1046
Muir C	27 Canadian EF	Pte	02/01/18	Desertion	7yrs PS	F&F	213/19	
Mulgrew E	2 Highland LI	Pte	16/09/17	Desertion	15yrs PS	F&F	213/17	
Mulgrew Edward	2 RHA	Dvr	28/10/16	Desertion	10yrs PS		213/12	
Mullany James	RFA	Dvr	20/09/16	Striking	XXX 03/10/16		213/11	456
Mullins J	8 MGC	Pte	23/05/16	Cowardice	5yrs PS		213/9	
Mullins M	1 Leinster	Pte	14/06/15	Sleeping+	3yrs PS	F&F	213/4	76
Mulvey M	2 R Irish Rifles	Pte	28/07/15	Desertion	3yrs PS	F&F	213/4	
Mulvey M	1 Australian IF	Pte	03/11/16	Desertion	Not Conf		213/13	
Mulvihill J	4 Liverpool	Pte	24/06/15	Quitting	5yrs PS	F&F	213/4	
Mumun R	Civilian		26/05/16	Treason	XXX	Macedonia	213/12	320
Munro NA	6 Australian IF	Pte	06/07/18	Desertion	10yrs PS		213/23	
Murfin FJ	3 East Non Combat Corps	Pte	13/06/16	Disobedience	10yrs PS	F&F	213/9	367
Murphy Allan	9 Scottish Rifles	Pte	30/07/16	Desertion	XXX 17/08/16	F&F	213/10	409
Murphy D	1 KOR Lancaster	Pte	14/11/18	Desertion	7yrs PS	F&F	213/27	
Murphy J	4 (att 21) R Munster Fus	Pte	07/01/16	Desertion	5yrs PS		213/7	
Murphy J	1/5 Seaforth Hdrs	Pte	26/09/17	Desertion	5yrs PS	F&F	213/18	775
Murphy JC	49 Australian IF	Pte	13/05/17	Desertion	10yrs PS		213/15	
Murphy M	2 KRRC	Rfm	01/04/16	Desertion	2yrs HL	F&F	213/8	
Murphy Michael J	6 Connaught Rangers	Pte	05/10/16	Mutiny	10yrs PS	F&F	90/6	469
Murphy P	1 R Irish Fus	Pte	21/12/14	Disob + Inhab	5yrs PS	F&F	213/3	
Murphy P	47 MGC	Pte	12/03/18	Desertion	5yrs PS		213/23	
Murphy Patrick	47 MGC	Pte	19/08/18	Desertion	XXX 12/09/18	F&F	213/25	962
Murphy R	1 R Scots	Drummer	18/10/15	Sleeping	3yrs PS		213/6	
Murphy T	2 Leinster	Pte	02/11/18	Desertion x2	10yrs PS	F&F	213/28	
Murphy Thomas	9 R Inniskilling Fus	Pte	30/04/17	Desertion	XXX 14/05/17	F&F	213/14	643
Murphy William	5/6 R Scots	Pte	28/01/17	Desertion	XXX 07/02/17	F&F	213/13	584
Murray A	1 R W Surrey	Pte	16/10/16	Striking	5yrs PS	F&F	213/12	
Murray E	1/5 Lincolnshire	Pte	07/12/17	Desertion	5yrs PS	F&F	213/19	
Murray Francis	9 Gordon Hdrs (att RE)	Pte	24/09/16	Murder x2	XXX 01/10/16		213/11	458
Murray J	1 Scottish Rifles	Pte	20/11/16	Cowardice	10yrs PS	F&F	213/12	
Murray JG	3 Canadian EF	Cpl	07/04/16	Desertion	5yrs PS	F&F	213/8	

Name	Unit	Rank	Date	Offence	Final sentence	Location	Ref	Note
Murray PE	4 Connaught Rangers	Lt	19/03/18	Desertion	Cashiered + 3yrs PS	S Africa	90/8	884
Murray Robert	81 RFA	Gnr	19/01/17	Desertion	XXX 03/02/17	F&F	213/13	577
Murree C	3 Canadian MGC	Pte	20/10/18	Desertion	15yrs PS	F&F	213/26	
Musa Abdurehman Bin	Civilian		09/11/15	Aiding enemy	XXX	East Africa	213/34	130
Musa Suliman Bin	Civilian		09/11/15	Aiding enemy	XXX	East Africa	213/34	131
Musse M	Civilian	Civ	29/04/18	Desertion	10yrs PS	Salonika	213/23	
Myers A	2 North Non Combat Corps	Pte	12/06/16	Disobedience	10yrs PS		213/9	356
Naga I I	Civilian		01/09/21	Murder	XXX (Hanged)	Egypt	213/32	1094
Nash FC	Labour Corps	Pte	03/09/19	Murder	PS Life	Turkey	90/8	1019
Nazir Ibrahim Khalil	Civilian		09/07/23	Conspiracy	XXX (Hanged)	Egypt	213/34	1104
Neal E	Border	Pte	08/01/15	Insubordination	2yrs HL		213/3	18
Neave Walter	10 W Yorks	Pte	09/05/17	Desertion	15yrs PS	F&F	213/15	649
Neave Walter	10 W Yorks	Pte	26/08/17	Desertion	XXX 30/08/17	F&F	213/17	736
Neil W	1 Black Watch	Pte	21/01/16	Sleeping	Not Conf	F&F	213/7	
Neill Gordon	6 Dragoon Gds	Pte	24/10/14	Sleeping	2yrs HL	F&F	213/2	8
Nelson A	2 R Scots Fus	Pte	12/11/18	Desertion	10yrs PS	F&F	213/26	
Nelson William Barry	14 Durham LI	Pte	01/08/16	Desertion	XXX 11/08/16	F&F	213/10	411
Nesbit Joseph	1 Leicestershire	Pte	08/08/18	Desertion	XXX 23/08/18	F&F	213/24	957
Newall J	18 MGC	Pte	16/07/16	Striking	10yrs PS		213/10	
Newell A	57 Australian IF	Pte	06/03/17	Desertion	5yrs PS		213/14	
Newey E	7 KRRC	Rfm	21/06/17	Desertion	10yrs PS	F&F	213/15	
Newman JD	1 Canadian EF	Pte	22/04/17	Desertion	10yrs PS	F&F	213/15	
Newsome H	6 Durham LI	Pte	21/01/17	Desertion	5yrs PS		213/14	
Newton W	9 Lancs Fus	Pte	12/08/16	Sleeping	5yrs PS	F&F	213/11	
Newton WE	RFA	Pte	31/12/18	Desertion x2	10yrs PS		213/27	
Nicholson Charles Bain	8 York & Lancaster	Pte	08/10/17	Desertion	XXX 27/10/17	F&F	213/18	791
Nicholson D	11 RFA	Gnr	21/10/16	Desertion	Not Conf		213/12	
Nicholson J	1 R Berkshire	Pte	08/08/18	Disobedience x2	5yrs PS	F&F	213/24	
Nicol J	2 Scottish Rifles	Pte	26/12/14	Sleeping	2yrs HL	F&F	213/3	
Nicol LP	4 Australian Pnr Bn	Pte	05/07/17	Desertion	10yrs PS		213/16	
Nigeradze Konstantin	Civilian		08/08/19	Robbery	XXX	S Russia	213/34	1018
Nisbet J	8 Leicestershire	Pte	11/05/16	Disobedience x3	10yrs PS	F&F	213/9	
Noble W	1 R Dragoons	Pte	09/08/15	Striking +	2yrs HL	F&F	213/4	97
Nolan J	9 R Dublin Fus	Pte	06/07/16	Desertion	5yrs PS	F&F	213/10	
Nolan J	1 W Yorks	Pte	30/05/18	Desertion	10yrs PS	F&F	213/23	
Nolan M	6 R Dublin Fus	Pte	30/10/16	Desertion	15yrs PS	Salonika	213/12	
Nolan T	7 R Dublin Fus	Pte	21/05/17	Desertion	2yrs HL	Salonika	213/15	
Norman F	2 KO Yorks LI	Pte	25/07/16	Desertion	15yrs PS	F&F	213/10	
Norris HG	57 Australian IF	Pte	09/06/17	Desertion	2yrs HL		213/16	
North H	3/5 Lancs Fus	Pte	30/10/17	Desertion	15yrs PS	F&F	213/18	
Norton J	Civilian	Sinn Fein	04/05/16	Rebellion	3yrs PS	Dublin	213/8	263
Norton P	1 R Dublin Fus	Pte	12/09/18	Desertion	10yrs PS	F&F	213/25	
Oatway R	9 KRRC	Rfm	16/03/18	Desertion	5yrs PS	F&F	213/21	
O'Brien D	1 Middlesex	Pte	13/09/16	Desertion	10yrs PS	F&F	213/11	
O'Brien J	14 Canadian EF	Pte	24/03/16	Desertion	10yrs PS	F&F	213/8	
O'Brien John	Civilian	Sinn Fein	04/05/16	Rebellion	3yrs PS	Dublin	213/8	264
O'Callaghan Denis	Civilian	Sinn Fein	03/05/16	Rebellion	10yrs PS	Dublin	213/8	233
O'Colbaird Concabar	Civilian	Sinn Fein	04/05/16	Rebellion	XXX 08/05/16	Dublin	213/8	265
O'Connell Benjamin	1 Irish Gds	Pte	25/07/18	Desertion	XXX 08/08/18	F&F	213/24	949
O'Connell C	R Canadian HA (RFA)	Gnr	18/10/15	Against Inhab	5yrs PS	F&F	213/6	
O'Conner F	7 D Cornwall LI	Pte	14/10/16	Cowardice	Not Conf	F&F	213/12	
O'Connor C	2 Leinster	Pte	02/01/18	Desertion	5yrs PS	F&F	213/19	
O'Connor J	10/11 Highland LI	Pte	07/05/18	Desertion	10yrs PS	F&F	213/22	
Oddy FW	17 Lancs Fus	Pte	15/12/16	Quitting	15yrs PS	F&F	213/13	531
O'Dea W	Civilian	Sinn Fein	04/05/16	Rebellion	3yrs PS	Dublin	213/8	266
O'Donovan C	Civilian	Sinn Fein	06/05/16	Rebellion	5yrs PS	Dublin	213/8	290
O'Gara John	Manchester	Pte	04/09/14	Housebreaking	Quashed		213/2	
Ogden T	1/5 Lancs Fus	Pte	17/09/15	Sleeping	10yrs PS	Gallipoli	213/5	
Ogly Omer K	Civilian		06/04/20	Murder	XXX	S Russia	213/34	1044
Ogorodnick J	47 Canadian EF	Pte	05/09/17	Cowardice +	10yrs PS	F&F	213/17	751
O'Hagan JT	1 W Yorks	Pte	31/08/16	Desertion	5yrs PS	F&F	213/11	
O'Hanrahan H	Civilian	Sinn Fein	04/05/16	Rebellion	PS Life	Dublin	213/8	267
O'Hanrahan Michael	Civilian	Sinn Fein	03/05/16	Rebellion	XXX 04/05/16	Dublin	213/8	234
O'Hare S	2 Scottish Rifles	Pte	24/09/18	Against Inhab	7yrs PS	F&F	213/25	
O'Keefe D	2 Essex	Pte	06/10/14	Sleeping	2yrs HL	F&F	213/2	
O'Kelly T	Civilian	Sinn Fein	04/05/16	Rebellion	3yrs PS	Dublin	213/8	268
Old G	58 DAC	Dvr	19/12/17	Desertion	10yrs PS		213/19	
Oldfield J	8 KOR Lancaster	Pte	18/04/17	Desertion	10yrs PS	F&F	213/15	

Name	Unit	Rank	Date	Offence	Final sentence	Location	Ref	Note
Oldknow J	19 Durham LI	Pte	30/12/16	Cowardice	10yrs PS	F&F	213/13	558
O'Leary	1 R Munster Fus	Pte	04/07/15	Cowardice	10yrs PS	Mesopotamia	213/4	
O'Leary AJ	52 Australian IF	Pte	05/03/17	Desertion	10yrs PS		213/14	
Oleinik N	38 Canadian EF	Pte	06/09/17	Desertion	5yrs PS	F&F	213/17	
Oliver J	1 Connaught Rangers	Pte	04/09/20	Mutiny	PS Life	India		1076
Ollerenshaw N	5 S Lancs	Rfm	26/10/16	Disobedience	2yrs HL	F&F	213/12	
Ollerton G	1/5 S Lancs	Rfm	03/07/17	Murder	3yrs PS	F&F	213/16	
O'Mahoney C	1 R Munster Fus	Cpl	03/05/15	Cowardice	10yrs PS	Mesopotamia	213/4	
O'Neill A	1 S Wales Bdrs	Pte	04/04/16	Desertion	XXX 30/04/16	F&F	213/8	200
O'Neill CC	2 Australian IF	Pte	04/06/17	Desertion	15yrs PS		213/17	
O'Neill Frank	1 Sherwood Fstrs	Pte	26/04/18	Desertion	XXX 16/05/18	F&F	213/22	894
O'Neill J	1/4 Black Watch	Pte	15/09/16	Disobedience	5yrs PS	F&F	213/11	449
O'Neill P	2 Durham LI	Pte	29/04/16	Desertion	15yrs PS	F&F	213/9	
Oram TG	46 Australian IF	Pte	23/04/17	Desertion	10yrs PS		213/15	
Orme CE	2 Sherwood Fstrs	Pte	05/02/17	Desertion	15yrs PS	F&F	213/14	
Orme H	1 Leicestershire	Pte	24/12/14	Quitting/Sleeping	3mos FP1	F&F	213/3	
Orr B	22 Northumb Fus	Pte	17/08/17	Desertion	5yrs PS	F&F	213/16	
Orr B	22 Northumb Fus	Pte	26/11/17	Desertion	5yrs PS	F&F	213/19	832
Orr B	22 Northumb Fus	Pte	28/10/18	Desertion x2	15yrs PS	F&F	213/26	988
Orr M	2 Canadian EF	Pte	02/10/17	Desertion	10yrs PS	F&F	213/18	
Osborne P	19 Manchester	Pte	13/11/16	Cowardice	10yrs PS	F&F	213/12	507
O'Shea J	RGA	Cpl	03/08/16	Murder	10yrs PS		213/10	
O'Shea T	18 Durham LI	Pte	19/08/18	Desertion	10yrs PS	F&F	213/24	963
Osman Ahmed	Civilian		06/07/20	Hostile Act	10yrs HL	Turkey	213/34	1053
Osman Hafiz	Civilian		11/08/23	Treason	PS Life	Egypt	213/34	1106
Osman Ismail	Civilian		03/06/19	Hostile Act	XXX	S Russia	213/34	
O'Sullivan J	2 R Irish Rifles	Bugler	10/03/15	Desertion	Qyashed	F&F	213/3	
O'Sullivan J	8/10 Gordon Hdrs (att RE)	Pte	28/08/16	Mutiny	5yrs PS	F&F	213/11	
O'Sullivan James	Civilian	Sinn Fein	05/05/16	Rebellion	8yrs PS	Dublin	213/8	286
Ottaway MW	Canadian Engrs	Pte	20/09/18	Desertion	7yrs PS	F&F	213/25	
Owen JE	27 Canadian EF	Pte	18/07/18	Desertion	10yrs PS	F&F	213/25	
Owen S	2 KRRC	Rfm	18/04/16	Desertion	5yrs PS	F&F	213/9	
Owen T	8 R W Surrey	Pte	07/08/18	Desertion	5yrs PS	F&F	213/25	
Owens J	8 R Welsh Fus	Pte	09/12/15	Sleeping	2yrs HL	Gallipoli	213/7	
Oyns Arthur Philip	RE (Field Search Lt Coy)	Spr	08/10/17	Murder	XXX 20/10/17	F&F	213/17	792
Packer HA	1/9 London	Rfm	09/12/16	Sleeping	5yrs PS	F&F	213/13	
Page F	2 Worcestershire	Pte	10/11/14	Desertion	Not Conf	F&F	213/1	
Paget J	3 Australian IF	Pte	15/03/17	Desertion	10yrs PS		213/14	
Pain Frederick	1/7 Essex	Pte	11/10/15	Sleeping	5yrs PS	Gallipoli	213/6	
Paish G	12/13 Northumb Fus	Pte	20/02/18	Desertion	5yrs PS	F&F	213/20	
Palchett E	5 MGC	Pte	26/09/18	Desertion	5yrs PS		213/25	
Paley A	2 Welsh	Pte	03/06/15	Desertion	5yrs PS	F&F	213/4	
Palmer Henry	5 Northumb Fus	Pte	11/10/16	Desertion	XXX 27/10/16	F&F	213/12	477
Pannell C	2 R Warwickshire	Pte	14/12/14	Desertion	2yrs HL	F&F	213/3	
Parchiskin E	2 Canadian Pioneers	Pnr	14/08/17	Desertion	2yrs HL	F&F	213/17	728
Pareezer S	21 Manchester	Pte	13/04/17	Desertion	15yrs PS	F&F	213/15	632
Pareezer S	21 Manchester	Pte	14/01/18	Desertion	15yrs PS	Italy	213/19	862
Parish W	1/10 London	Pte	13/11/17	Disobedience x2	15yrs PS	Egypt	213/19	827
Parker A	13 Rifle Bde	Rfm	02/07/16	Sleeping	2yrs HL	F&F	213/10	
Parker Albert Edward	7 KRRC	Rfm	04/05/16	Desertion	XXX 15/05/16	F&F	213/8	269
Parker G	7 R W Surrey	Pte	07/11/17	Desertion	10yrs PS	F&F	213/18	
Parker H	1/8 Manchester	Pte	30/08/15	Sleeping	1yr HL	Gallipoli	213/5	104
Parker HP	RFA	Pte	14/08/18	Desertion	10yrs PS		213/26	
Parker J	1 R Scots Fus	Pte	23/12/17	Att Desertion	15yrs PS	F&F	213/19	
Parker SA	6 R W Kent	Cpl	28/03/16	Desertion	5yrs PS	F&F	213/8	
Parkes E	36 Australian IF	Pte	14/08/17	Desertion	10yrs PS		213/17	
Parkin Daniel	1 Gordon Hdrs	Pte	28/05/18	Desertion	5yrs PS	F&F	213/22	
Parkin J	4 S African Infantry	Pte	16/11/18	Desertion x2	5yrs PS		213/27	
Parrott JC	13 R Inniskilling Fus	Pte	11/08/18	Desertion	5yrs PS	F&F	213/24	
Parry Albert	2 W Yorks	Pte	10/08/17	Desertion	XXX 30/08/17	F&F	213/17	723
Parry C	1 Loyal N Lancs	Pte	24/04/16	Desertion	10yrs PS	F&F	213/9	
Parsons E	2 E Lancs	Pte	12/06/18	Cowardice	10yrs PS	F&F	213/24	
Parsons JA	RFA	Dvr	04/09/14	Sleeping	2yrs HL		213/2	
Partridge R	6 Loyal North Lancs	Pte	20/10/15	Sleeping	5yrs PS	Gallipoli	213/6	
Paterson John H	1 Essex	2 Lt	11/09/18	Murder+	XXX 24/09/18	F&F	90/8	977
Patrick W	1 R Berkshire	Pte	16/03/15	Desertion	2yrs HL	F&F	213/3	
Patterson Robert Gillis	7 E Surrey	Pte	06/06/17	Desertion	XXX 04/07/17	F&F	213/15	671
Pattison J	19 Durham LI	Pte	30/12/16	Cowardice	10yrs PS	F&F	213/13	559

Name	Unit	Rank	Date	Offence	Final sentence	Location	Ref	Note
Payne A	7 N Staffordshire	Pte	22/10/15	Sleeping	10yrs PS	Gallipoli	213/6	
Payne FJ	5 Dorset	Pte (L/C)	08/02/17	Desertion	10yrs PS	F&F	213/13	
Payne S	87 Canadian EF	Pte	01/12/17	Desertion x2	3yrs PS	F&F	213/19	
Payne T	2 Leicestershire	Pte	07/12/14	Sleeping	5yrs PS	Mesopotamia	213/1	
Peacock B	1/7 W Yorks	Pte	25/05/18	Desertion	10yrs PS	F&F	213/22	914
Pearce G	RAMC	Pte	09/05/17	Cowardice x2	10yrs PS		213/15	
Pearse PH	Civilian	Sinn Fein	02/05/16	Rebellion	XXX 03/05/16	Dublin	213/8	223
Pearse William	Civilian	Sinn Fein	03/05/16	Rebellion	XXX 04/05/16	Dublin	213/8	235
Pearson A V	8 E Surrey	Pte	29/01/18	Desertion	10yrs PS	F&F	213/20	
Pearson AV	8 E Surrey	Pte	24/09/17	Desertion	10yrs PS	F&F	213/17	
Pearson JH	9 Yorks	Pte	19/02/17	Desertion	15yrs PS	F&F	213/14	
Pearson T	15 Highland LI	Pte	15/01/17	Desertion	10yrs PS	F&F	213/14	575
Peddar A	9 W Riding	Pte	25/01/18	Desertion	5yrs PS	F&F	213/23	
Peden William	ASC	Dvr	05/10/16	Mutiny	2yrs HL	F&F	90/6	470
Pedro Clyde	11 R Welsh Fus	Pte	06/01/16	Disobedience	5yrs PS	Salonika	213/7	
Pelly A	3 Royal Fus	Pte	12/06/15	Desertion	5yrs PS	F&F	213/4	
Peloquin C	22 Canadian EF	Pte	28/08/18	Desertion	7yrs PS	F&F	213/25	
Peloquin J	22 Canadian EF	Pte	28/03/17	Desertion	15yrs PS	F&F	213/14	
Pemberton J	1/7 W Yorks	Rfm	01/06/18	Desertion	10yrs PS	F&F	213/23	918
Pendlebury A	12 Manchester	Pte	14/05/18	Desertion	5yrs PS	F&F	213/22	
Penman J	6/7 R Scots Fus	Cpl	01/11/16	Desertion	5yrs PS	F&F	213/12	
Penn Major	1 R Welsh Fus	Pte	07/04/15	Desertion	XXX 22/04/15	F&F	213/3	59
Pennell A	3 Australian IF	Pte	15/03/17	Desertion	10yrs PS		213/14	
Penrose E	58 Canadian EF	Pte	19/09/17	Desertion	3yrs PS	F&F	213/17	
Peppard T	Civilian	Sinn Fein	04/05/16	Rebellion	3yrs PS	Dublin	213/8	270
Perkins W	78 Canadian EF	Pte	13/09/17	Desertion	10yrs PS	F&F	213/17	
Perks S	8 S Staffordshire	Pte	01/01/16	Desertion	10yrs PS	F&F	213/7	
Perrin T	1/8 Liverpool	Pte	01/07/16	Desertion	10yrs PS	F&F	213/9	391
Perris J	6 KOR Lancaster	Pte	25/09/16	Desertion	5yrs PS	Mesopotamia	90/7	459
Perry Eugene	22 Canadian EF	Pte	03/04/17	Desertion	XXX 11/04/17	F&F	213/14	618
Perry F	2 R Sussex	Pte	30/10/15	Losing Property	Quashed	F&F	213/6	
Perry J	4 Worcestershire	Pte	05/05/15	Cowardice	10yrs PS	Mesopotamia	213/4	
Pesochnikoff J	1 Slavo-British Legion	Sgt	13/07/19	Mutiny	XXX 00/07/19	N Russia	213/32	
Peters RA	RAMC	Pte	29/12/15	Desertion	10yrs PS		213/7	
Peterson VH	10 Australian IF	Pte	30/08/15	Sleeping	2yrs HL		213/5	
Petonhoff M	1 Slavo-British Legion	Pte	14/07/19	Mutiny	10yrs PS	N Russia	213/32	
Petro C	Civilian		23/05/16	Treason	XXX	Macedonia	213/12	317
Phelps E	1/22 London	Pte	02/08/17	Desertion	10yrs PS	F&F	213/16	
Phillips A	1 Canadian MGC	Pte	22/09/18	Desertion	5yrs PS	F&F	213/25	
Phillips E	7 Gloucestershire	Pte	09/01/17	Sleeping	5yrs PS	Mesopotamia	90/7	571
Phillips Lewis R	6 Somerset LI	Pte	08/08/15	Desertion	XXX 19/08/15	F&F	213/4	96
Phillips T	5 DAC	Dvr	12/09/16	Desertion	5yrs PS		213/11	
Phillips WTH	1 Coldstream Gds	Pte	24/05/16	Desertion	XXX 30/05/16	F&F	213/9	319
Philpott S	1 Hampshire	Pte	12/05/18	Desertion	5yrs PS	F&F	213/22	
Phipps GE	3 Worcestershire	Pte	01/04/17	Desertion	10yrs PS	F&F	213/14	
Phoraoh James T	2/5 York & Lancaster	Pte	06/10/18	Desertion	5yrs PS	F&F	213/25	
Picard H	2 Lincolnshire	Pte	31/10/17	Cowardice	10yrs PS	F&F	213/18	
Pickering G	9 Rifle Bde	Rfm	08/06/16	Quitting	5yrs PS	F&F	213/9	
Pingson W	2 R Welsh Fus	Pte	29/05/18	Desertion	5yrs PS	F&F	213/22	
Piper W	2 R Warwickshire	Pte	07/02/15	Desertion+	3mos FP1	F&F	213/3	35
Pitchford J	1 Northumb Fus	Pte	18/11/18	Desertion	5yrs PS	F&F	213/27	
Pither A	1 R Berkshire	Pte	15/08/16	Desertion	3yrs PS	F&F	213/10	
Pitts A	2 R Warwickshire	Pte	30/01/15	Desertion	XXX 08/02/15	F&F	213/3	28
Plant D	1 N Staffordshire	Pte	25/10/14	Cowardice	2yrs HL	F&F	213/2	
Plummer WR	4 Royal Fus	Pte	25/05/16	Desertion	10yrs PS	F&F	213/9	
Plummer WR	4 Royal Fus	Pte	12/10/16	Desertion	Not Conf	F&F	213/13	
Plunkett G	Civilian	Sinn Fein	04/05/16	Rebellion	10yrs PS	Dublin	213/8	271
Plunkett J	Civilian	Sinn Fein	04/05/16	Rebellion	10yrs PS	Dublin	213/8	272
Plunkett Joseph	Civilian	Sinn Fein	03/05/16	Rebellion	XXX 04/05/16	Dublin	213/8	236
Poirat A	14 Canadian EF	Pte	26/04/16	Desertion	Not Conf	F&F	213/9	
Pond A	7 Norfolk	Pte	15/06/17	Desertion	10yrs PS	F&F	213/15	
Poole Eric Skeffington	11 W Yorks	2 Lt	24/11/16	Desertion	XXX 10/12/16	F&F	90/6	519
Poole H	2 R Warwickshire	Pte	21/09/15	Desertion	2yrs HL	F&F	213/5	
Poole Harry	7 Yorks	Pte	11/10/16	Desertion+	XXX 09/12/16	F&F	213/12	478
Poole RS	1/4 KO Yorks LI	Pte	13/07/18	Desertion	10yrs PS	F&F	213/23	
Poole Vincent	Civilian	Sinn Fein	04/05/16	Rebellion	5yrs PS	Dublin	213/8	273
Porter WG	4 Canadian Mtd Rifles	Pte	15/09/17	Desertion	15yrs PS	F&F	213/17	
Porthouse J	22 Northumb Fus	Pte	02/01/18	Desertion	5yrs PS	F&F	213/20	852

Name	Unit	Rank	Date	Offence	Final sentence	Location	Ref	Note
Posdjeef N	1 Slavo-British Legion	Pte	14/07/19	Mutiny	XXX 00/07/19	N Russia	213/32	
Potter J L	11 A&S Hdrs	Pte	25/06/18	Desertion	10yrs PS	F&F	213/23	
Potts GC	50 Australian IF	Pte	26/04/17	Desertion+	10yrs PS		213/15	638
Potts T	5 Durham LI	Pte	09/07/18	Desertion	5yrs PS	F&F	213/24	
Potts W	19 Durham LI	Pte	30/12/16	Cowardice	10yrs PS	F&F	213/13	560
Potts William	2 Durham LI	Pte	19/07/16	Desertion	2yrs HL	F&F	213/10	
Poulter F	58 Canadian EF	Pte	30/12/17	Desertion	10yrs PS	F&F	213/19	
Pound F	2 R Berkshire	Pte	23/12/18	Desertion	2yrs HL	F&F	213/27	
Pounder J	RE	Spr	03/09/16	Desertion	15yrs PS		213/11	
Povey George H	1 Cheshire	Cpl	03/02/15	Quitting	XXX 11/02/15	F&F	213/3	30
Powell FB	18 Middlesex	Pte	24/11/16	Desertion	Quashed		213/13	520
Powell O	9 Rifle Bde	Rfm	08/06/16	Quitting	5yrs PS	F&F	213/9	
Powell W	Worcestershire	Pte	18/10/14	Sleeping	2yrs HL		213/1	
Power J	10 R Irish Rifles	Rfm	20/01/18	Desertion	Not Conf	F&F	213/20	865
Poynter EA	1 E Kent (Buffs)	Pte	05/02/16	Desertion	10yrs PS	F&F	213/7	
Prescott T	9 Rifle Bde	Rfm	08/06/16	Quitting	5yrs PS	F&F	213/9	
Presnell TW	11 Essex	Pte	27/12/16	Sleeping	10yrs PS	F&F	213/13	
Price E	2 Rifle Bde	Rfm	23/04/17	Sleeping	5yrs PS	F&F	213/14	
Price H	2 R Welsh Fus	Pte	01/02/15	Desertion	10yrs PS	F&F	213/3	
Price M	22 Northumb Fus	Pte	05/10/17	Desertion	5yrs PS	F&F	213/18	787
Priestley A	East Non Combat Corps	Pte	10/06/16	Disobedience	10yrs PS	F&F	213/9	345
Prince F	1 S Wales Bdrs	Pte	30/11/15	Desertion	10yrs PS	F&F	213/6	
Prince J	2 Welsh	Pte	21/10/15	Desertion	2yrs HL	F&F	213/6	
Prince LE	1 W Yorks	Pte	28/02/17	Desertion	5yrs PS	F&F	213/14	
Pringle J	10 Canadian EF	L/Cpl	26/02/16	Cowardice	5yrs PS	F&F	213/8	
Pringle JW	12 Northumb Fus	Pte	16/05/17	Desertion	10yrs PS	F&F	213/15	
Prinn J	12 Gloucestershire	Pte	10/02/17	Quitting	15yrs PS	F&F	213/13	592
Prior J	9 R Irish Rifles	Rfm	23/01/16	Desertion	2yrs HL	F&F	213/7	163
Prior V	1 R Berkshire	Cpl	24/09/14	Cowardice	2yrs HL/Red in rank	F&F	213/2	
Pritchard J	8 R Welsh Fus	Pte	09/11/17	Quitting	2yrs HL	Mesopotamia	90/7	826
Pritchard SP	6 Kings Shropshire LI	Pte	24/03/19	Mutiny	PS Life	F&F	213/29	
Pritchett WJ	8 E Yorks	Pte	20/01/17	Desertion	10yrs PS		213/14	
Proudfoot H	19 Durham LI	Pte	30/12/16	Cowardice	10yrs PS	F&F	213/13	561
Pugh C	52 Canadian EF	Pte	19/09/17	Desertion	2yrs HL	F&F	213/17	765
Pugh P	7 W Riding	Pte	29/07/16	Cowardice	Not Conf	F&F	213/10	
Pullen W	4 Royal Fus	Pte	25/03/15	Desertion	10yrs PS	F&F	213/3	
Purkin D	1 Gordon Hdrs	Pte	23/07/18	Desertion	10yrs PS	F&F	213/24	
Purnell G	3 Middlesex	Pte	26/08/15	Sleeping	10yrs PS	F&F	213/5	
Puttock A	1 Royal Fus	Pte	10/11/15	Disobedience	3yrs PS	F&F	213/6	
Putz PG	1/9 London	Rfm	09/12/16	Sleeping	5yrs PS	F&F	213/13	
Pyper D	1 Gordon Hdrs	Pte	12/12/16	Cowardice	10yrs PS	F&F	213/13	
Queen James	13 R Scots	Pte	23/03/16	Desertion	15yrs PS	F&F	213/8	
Quigley EJ	1 E Kent (Buffs)	Pte	09/05/16	Desertion	5yrs PS	F&F	213/9	
Quill	1 R Munster Fus	Pte	04/05/15	Cowardice	10yrs PS	Mesopotamia	213/4	
Quinn F	4 Rifle Bde	Rfm	29/06/15	Desertion	5yrs PS	F&F	213/4	
Rabjohn F	10 W Riding	Pte	17/01/18	Desertion	15yrs PS	Italy	213/19	
Radford J	1 Lincolnshire	Pte	31/12/14	Cowardice	10yrs PS	F&F	213/3	
Rae C	16 Trench Mtr Bty	Gnr	13/04/17	Desertion	10yrs PS		213/14	
Rafter James	Civilian	Sinn Fein	10/05/16	Rebellion	5yrs PS	Dublin	213/8	306
Raine H	2 Durham LI	Pte	14/12/17	Desertion	5yrs PS	F&F	213/19	
Raine Henry	2 Durham LI	Pte	29/06/17	Desertion	5yrs PS	F&F	213/16	
Ramage J	12 Highland LI	Pte	25/02/16	Desertion x3	10yrs PS	F&F	213/8	
Ramage J	12 Highland LI	Pte	20/03/17	Desertion	15yrs PS	F&F	213/14	
Ramazan Bairam O	Civilian		27/03/19	Aiding Enemy	PS Life	T'caucasia	213/34	1003
Ramscar W	18 Welsh	Pte	04/05/17	Desertion	5yrs PS	F&F	213/15	646
Randall C	9 Leicestershire	Pte	31/07/16	Desertion	10yrs PS	F&F	213/10	
Randall G	1 E Surrey	Pte	09/05/15	Sleeping	5yrs PS	F&F	213/4	
Randall ST	9 Northumb Fus	Pte	18/06/17	Desertion	5yrs PS	F&F	213/15	
Randle William H	10 Sherwood Fstrs	Pte	08/11/16	Desertion	XXX 25/11/16	F&F	213/12	502
Rascid S	Turkish Army	POW	10/07/18	Murder	XXX		213/24	
Ratcliffe F	4 Leicestershire	Pte	30/09/15	Sleeping	1yr HL	F&F	213/5	
Ratelle A	22 Canadian EF	Pte	03/04/17	Desertion	15yrs PS	F&F	213/15	
Ratican P	2 R Welsh Fus	Pte	02/11/17	Desertion	10yrs PS	F&F	213/18	
Ravenscroft A	1 KRRC	Rfm	24/04/16	Desertion	10yrs PS	F&F	213/9	
Rawlinson B	2 Worcestershire	Pte	20/05/16	Desertion	3yrs PS	F&F	213/9	
Raynor J	6 E Lancs	Pte	01/12/15	Quitting	5yrs PS	Gallipoli	213/7	
Raynor J	1/4 E Lancs	Pte	01/01/16	Cowardice	2yrs HL	Gallipoli	213/8	
Raynor J	2 New Zealand EF	Pte	03/08/17	Desertion	10yrs PS		213/16	718

Name	Unit	Rank	Date	Offence	Final sentence	Location	Ref	Note
Rayson A	7 S Wales Bdrs	Pte	13/11/17	Striking	10yrs PS	Salonika	213/18	
Rea TG	8 R Irish Rifles	Rfm	11/06/16	Sleeping	2yrs PS	F&F	213/10	348
Readhead H	1 Yorks	Pte	03/04/16	Desertion	5yrs PS	India	213/8	
Reavy F	1 R Irish Fus	Pte	21/12/14	Against Inhab	5yrs PS	F&F	213/3	
Redfern W	16 Northumb Fus	Pte	21/09/16	Desertion	15yrs PS	F&F	213/11	
Redmond D	1 R Irish Rifles	Rfm	28/07/15	Sleeping	56days FP1	F&F	213/4	
Reed F	2 Leicestershire	Pte	07/12/14	Sleeping	5yrs PS	Mesopotamia	213/1	
Reed G R	1 Canadian Mtd Rifles	Pte	13/02/18	Desertion	5yrs PS	F&F	213/20	
Reed WJ	38 Canadian EF	Pte	25/07/17	Desertion	10yrs PS	F&F	213/16	
Reen W	1 E Surrey	Pte	31/12/16	Cowardice	15yrs PS	F&F	213/13	
Rees DJ	13 Welsh	Pte	01/09/17	Desertion	2yrs HL	F&F	213/17	741
Reeson WH	1 E Surrey	Pte	28/10/16	Desertion	15yrs PS	F&F	213/12	
Reeves CE	11 KRRC	Rfm	12/10/15	Sleeping	3yrs PS	F&F	213/6	
Reeves Harry	1 S Staffordshire	Pte	18/12/15	Desertion	2yrs HL	F&F	213/6	
Reeves R	ASC	Dvr	13/04/17	Desertion	2yrs HL		213/14	
Reeves W	6 East Lancs	Pte	24/11/15	Sleeping	5yrs PS	Gallipoli	213/6	
Reid Alexander	16 Highland LI	Pte	18/01/17	Murder	XXX 31/01/17	F&F	213/13	576
Reid CF	46 Australian IF	Pte	04/09/17	Desertion	15yrs PS		213/17	
Reid Isaac	2 Scots Gds	Pte	26/03/15	Desertion	XXX 09/04/15	F&F	213/3	53
Reid James	6 Cameron Hdrs	L/Cpl	13/04/18	Desertion x2/Esc	XXX 11/05/18	F&F	213/22	888
Reid John J	Civilian	Sinn Fein	03/05/16	Rebellion	10yrs PS	Dublin	213/8	237
Reilly C	2 Highland LI	Pte	10/10/18	Desertion	5yrs PS	F&F	213/25	
Reilly T	1 Scottish Rifles	Pte	29/03/17	Desertion	1yr HL	F&F	213/15	
Reilly WP	Nelson Bn R Naval VR	A/B	17/05/17	Desertion	Not Conf		213/15	
Renton L	2 North Non Combat Corps	Pte	12/06/16	Disobedience	10yrs PS	F&F	213/9	357
Reynolds EJ	3 Canadian EF	Pte	08/08/16	Desertion	XXX 23/08/16	F&F	213/10	419
Rice A	1 Norfolk	Pte	12/08/15	Sleeping	10yrs PS	F&F	213/4	
Richard A	22 Canadian EF	Pte	25/06/18	Desertion	Not Conf	F&F	213/25	
Richards T	2 Welsh	Pte	05/05/18	Against Inhab	5yrs PS	F&F	213/22	
Richardson A	1 E Lancs	Pte	20/02/15	Desertion	10yrs PS	F&F	213/3	
Richardson A	1 York & Lancaster	Pte	20/05/15	Desertion	5yrs PS	F&F	213/4	
Richardson H	3 Canadian EF	Pte	27/04/16	Desertion	10yrs PS	F&F	213/9	
Richardson JW	19 Durham LI	Pte (L/C)	30/12/16	Cowardice	10yrs PS	F&F	213/13	562
Richardson T	1 D Cornwall LI	Pte	06/02/15	Desertion	10yrs PS	F&F	213/3	
Richardson TJ	2 KO Yorks LI	Pte	30/01/16	Sleeping	3yrs PS	F&F	213/7	
Richardson W	4/5 Black Watch	Pte	15/07/18	Desertion	10yrs PS	F&F	213/25	
Richman W	58 Australian IF	Pte	27/12/16	Striking	2yrs HL		213/13	
Richmond J	2/10 R Scots	Pte	23/11/18	Civil Offence	5yrs PS	N Russia	213/28	
Richmond Malcolm	1/6 Gordon	Pte	21/04/18	Desertion	XXX 26/05/18	F&F	213/22	891
Rickett E	10 W Riding	Pte	20/12/17	Desertion	10yrs PS	Italy	213/19	
Ricketts JC	Drake Bn RNVR	A/B	25/05/18	Desertion	5yrs PS		213/22	
Ricketts OG	East Non Combat Corps	Pte	10/06/16	Disobedience	10yrs PS	F&F	213/9	346
Rickman Albert	1 R Dublin Fus	Pte	07/09/16	Desertion	XXX 15/09/16	F&F	213/10	445
Riddell G	5 Highland LI	Pte	19/07/17	Sleeping	5yrs PS		213/17	
Ridding WH	2 Wiltshire	Pte	28/09/18	Desertion	1yr HL	F&F	213/26	
Riddle A	1 Welsh	Pte	13/07/15	Sleeping	3yrs PS	F&F	213/4	
Riddle J	11 Scottish Rifles	Pte (L/C)	24/02/19	Desertion	10yrs PS	Macedonia	213/28	
Ridgewell FH	24 Royal Fus	Pte	10/02/16	Sleeping	5yrs PS	F&F	213/7	173
Ridsdale W	6 Cheshire	Pte	22/07/18	Desertion	10yrs PS	F&F	213/24	
Rielly WG	18 Australian IF	Pte	07/09/16	Desertion	Not Conf	F&F	213/11	
Ries Irving Guy	Civilian	Alien	04/10/15	Espionage	XXX 27/10/15		92/3	120
Rigby H	2 Rifle Bde	Rfm	19/01/17	Desertion	5yrs PS	F&F	213/13	
Rigby Thomas Henry Basil	8 S Wales Bdrs	Pte	19/11/15	Desertion	3yrs PS	F&F	213/6	132
Rigby Thomas Henry Basil	10 S Wales Bdrs	Pte	22/10/17	Desertion	XXX 22/11/17	F&F	213/18	808
Riley J	1 Devon	Pte	25/04/17	Desertion	2yrs HL	F&F	213/14	
Ring J	East Non Combat Corps	Pte	02/06/16	Disobedience x2	Not Conf	F&F	213/10	326
Ring J	East Non Combat Corps	Pte	07/06/16	Disobedience	10yrs PS	F&F	213/9	334
Ritchie T	19 Durham LI	Pte	28/12/16	Quitting	15yrs PS	F&F	213/13	545
Rix JW	7 KOR Lancaster	Pte	04/10/16	Desertion	Not Conf	F&F	213/12	
Rix RH	10 Welsh (att 2 RW Fus)	Pte	21/09/16	Desertion	5yrs PS	F&F	213/11	
Riza Ali	Civilian	Alien	03/01/18	Espionage	5yrs PS		213/18	
Riza Mehmet N A [?]	Civilian		05/08/20	Poss firearms	PS Life		213/34	
Rizeli Elias	Civilian		22/09/20	Hostile Act+	XXX		213/34	1083
Roach T	11 W Yorks	Pte	16/10/15	Sleeping	2yrs HL	F&F	213/6	
Roach William	RFA	Dvr	04/09/14	Sleeping	2yrs HL		213/2	
Robe A	6 R Marines	Pte	04/10/19	Disobedience	5yrs PS	N Russia	213/30	
Roberts A	1 R Warwickshire	Sgt	23/08/16	Desertion	10yrs PS	F&F	213/11	
Roberts E	20 Liverpool	Pte	17/10/16	Cowardice	5yrs PS	F&F	213/12	

Name	Unit	Rank	Date	Offence	Final sentence	Location	Ref	Note
Roberts E	2/5 Gloucestershire	Pte	26/06/18	Desertion	2yrs HL	F&F	213/23	931
Roberts FJ	1/8 Worcestershire	Pte	25/09/17	Cowardice	15yrs PS	F&F	213/17	
Roberts J	1/8 Liverpool	Pte	29/06/16	Desertion	10yrs PS	F&F	213/9	387
Roberts John William	1 Canadian Mtd Rifles	Pte	15/07/16	Desertion	XXX 30/07/16	F&F	213/10	399
Roberts LL	8 Yorks	Pte	16/04/16	Cowardice	10yrs PS	F&F	213/8	
Roberts T	1 R Welsh Fus	Pte	06/11/16	Sleeping	2yrs HL	F&F	213/12	
Roberts T	96 MGC	Pte	04/01/17	Desertion	10yrs PS		213/13	
Roberts W	4 Royal Fus	Pte	25/05/15	Desertion	5yrs PS	F&F	213/4	
Roberts W	1/6 Welsh	Pte	25/04/16	Disobedience	3yrs PS	F&F	213/8	
Roberts William W	4 Royal Fus	Pte	20/05/16	Desertion/Esc	XXX 29/05/16	F&F	213/9	314
Robertson	Anglo-Indian	Pte	14/08/17	Sleeping	5yrs PS	Mesopotamia	90/7	729
Robertson H	47 Australian IF	Pte	26/04/17	Desertion	10yrs PS		213/15	
Robillard A	22 Canadian EF	Pte	07/07/17	Desertion	15yrs PS	F&F	213/16	
Robins John	5 Wiltshire	Sgt	08/12/15	Disobedience	XXX 02/01/16	Gallipoli	213/7	139
Robinson AH	9 Northumb Fus	Pte	24/01/16	Desertion	10yrs PS	F&F	213/7	
Robinson Arthur H	9 Northumb Fus	Pte	28/04/16	Desertion	XXX 10/05/16	F&F	213/9	215
Robinson H	2 E Surrey	Pte	24/03/15	Sleeping	3mos FP1	F&F	213/3	
Robinson H	9 W Yorks	Pte	14/12/15	Sleeping	2mos FP1	Gallipoli	213/7	
Robinson HJ	30 Australian IF	Pte	21/02/17	Desertion	Quashed		213/14	
Robinson John	3 Worcestershire	Pte	14/07/15	Desertion	XXX 26/07/15	F&F	213/4	90
Robinson R	17 Lancs Fus	Pte	15/12/16	Quitting	15yrs PS	F&F	213/13	532
Robinson R	Labour Corps	Pte	02/10/18	Desertion	5yrs PS	F&F	213/27	
Robinson RJ	12 Durham LI	Pte	24/07/16	Desertion	Quashed	F&F	213/11	
Robinson W	1 R Irish Rifles	Rfm	21/05/15	Striking	3mos FP1	F&F	213/4	
Robinson William	1 Sherwood Fstrs	Pte	24/03/17	Desertion	XXX 10/04/17	F&F	213/14	612
Robson D	1 Devon	Pte	21/08/15	Sleeping	10yrs PS	F&F	213/5	
Robson H	2 Lincolnshire	Pte	17/10/17	Desertion	10yrs PS	F&F	213/18	
Robson JR	16 Cheshire	Cpl	01/06/16	Quitting	5yrs PS	F&F	213/9	323
Robson L	148 RFA	Gnr	19/05/17	Cowardice	2yrs HL		213/15	
Robson R	7 Liverpool	Pte	04/04/17	Desertion	10yrs PS	Salonika	213/14	626
Rock JT	33 Bty RFA	Dvr	25/09/17	Desertion/Drunk	5yrs PS	Mesopotamia	90/7	
Rodgers C	Nelson Bn R Naval VR	A/B	09/06/17	Desertion	10yrs PS		213/15	
Rodgers S	1/8 W Yorks	Rfm	10/08/15	Sleeping	3yrs PS	F&F	213/4	98
Rodway W	9 KRRC	Rfm	16/03/18	Desertion	5yrs PS	F&F	213/21	
Rodwell E	2 Yorks	Pte	23/01/16	Desertion	5yrs PS	F&F	213/7	
Roe George	2 KO Yorks LI	Pte	26/05/15	Desertion	XXX 10/06/15	F&F	213/4	71
Roe W	1/11 London	Rfm	06/12/17	Desertion	5yrs PS	Egypt	213/20	840
Rogers D	1 Lancs Fus	Pte	09/10/15	Sleeping	10yrs PS	Gallipoli	213/6	
Rogers E	26 Ausralian IF	Pte	02/11/16	Desertion x2	10yrs PS	F&F	213/13	
Rogers John	2 S Lancs	Pte	01/03/17	Desertion	XXX 09/03/17	F&F	213/14	599
Rogers R	9 Northumb Fus	Pte	04/08/18	Desertion	5yrs PS	F&F	213/24	
Rogers SD	1 Liverpool	Pte	03/10/17	Desertion	10yrs PS	F&F	213/17	
Roggen Augusto Alfredo	Civilian	Alien	20/08/14	Espionage	XXX 17/9/15	UK	92/3	2
Rollin W	1 R Irish Rifles	Pte	06/10/17	Cowardice	15yrs PS	F&F	213/17	
Ronan J	9 Sherwood Fstrs	Pte	30/07/16	Against Inhab	3yrs PS	F&F	213/10	
Rookes TW	2 Yorks	Pte	01/11/16	Desertion	15yrs PS	F&F	213/12	
Roos Willem Johannes	Civilian	Alien	15/07/15	Espionage	XXX 29/07/15	UK	92/3	93
Rose A	Hawke Bn RNVR	A/B	04/06/18	Desertion	5yrs PS		213/22	
Rose Frederick	2 Yorks	Dmr	18/02/17	Desertion	XXX 04/03/17	F&F	213/13	594
Rose Thomas	2 Wiltshire	Pte	12/11/15	Desertion	3yrs PS	F&F	213/6	
Rosenthal Robert	Civilian		06/07/15	Espionage	XXX (Hanged)	UK	92/3	84
Rossington J	1 E Yorks	Pte	17/10/17	Desertion	10yrs PS		213/18	
Rossiter H	2 Durham LI	Pte	22/06/16	Desertion	10yrs PS	F&F	213/9	
Rothwell J	10 Lancs Fus	Pte	29/06/18	Desertion	5yrs PS	F&F	213/23	
Roundstein R	2 S Wales Bdrs	Pte	02/11/16	Desertion	5yrs PS	F&F	213/12	
Routledge JW	2 North Non Combat Corps	Pte	13/06/16	Disobedience	10yrs PS	F&F	213/9	368
Rowe J	22 Durham LI	Pte	17/10/17	Desertion	10yrs PS	F&F	213/18	802
Rowe L	6 D Cornwall LI	Pte	08/01/18	Cowardice +	Not Conf	F&F	213/20	857
Rowe T	2 Middlesex	Pte	19/11/14	Sleeping	1yr HL	F&F	213/2	
Royle J	1 Cheshire	Pte	10/11/14	Quitting	2yrs HL	F&F	213/1	
Rudge J	6 Dragoon Gds	Pte	15/10/15	Desertion	10yrs PS	F&F	213/6	123
Rue J	2 Essex	Pte	12/07/15	Quitting	3yrs PS	F&F	213/4	
Ruff N	DAC	Dvr	04/11/17	Desertion x2	5yrs PS		213/18	
Rumley R	19 Durham LI	Sgt	01/01/17	Cowardice	10yrs PS	F&F	213/13	567
Rummel C	2 New Zealand EF	Pte	16/06/17	Desertion	10yrs PS		213/15	679
Rushdi Ahmed	Civilian		31/08/22	Att Murder/Arms	XXX (Hanged)	Egypt	213/34	
Rushworth G	1 Sherwood Fstrs	Pte	29/04/17	Desertion	5yrs PS	F&F	213/15	
Rushworth J	1 Loyal N Lancs	Pte	12/01/18	Desertion	5yrs PS	F&F	213/19	

Name	Unit	Rank	Date	Offence	Final sentence	Location	Ref	Note
Russell C	1 Loyal N Lancs	Pte	15/01/15	Sleeping	2yrs HL	F&F	213/3	
Russell C	9 Black Watch	Pte	23/12/15	Desertion	5yrs PS	F&F	213/7	
Russell J	1/8 Liverpool	Pte	29/06/16	Desertion	10yrs PS	F&F	213/10	388
Russell J	RFA	Gnr	03/05/18	Desertion	10yrs PS		213/22	
Rutland E	RAMC	Pte	11/08/17	Desertion	5yrs PS		213/18	
Rutley L	7 Canadian EF	Pte	30/09/17	Desertion	5yrs PS	F&F	213/17	
Rutter N	38 Canadian EF	Pte	25/07/17	Desertion	10yrs PS	F&F	213/16	
Ryan EJ	51 Australian IF	Pte	12/09/17	Desertion	5yrs PS		213/17	
Ryan J	11 W Yorks	Cpl	28/10/16	Desertion	10yrs PS	F&F	213/12	
Ryan J	2 Leinster	Pte	03/02/17	Desertion	2yrs HL	F&F	213/13	
Ryan J	2 Leinster	Pte	20/08/17	Desertion	10yrs PS	F&F	213/16	
Ryan J	20 Lancs Fus	Pte	15/11/17	Quitting	2yrs HL	F&F	213/19	830
Ryan P	2 R Dublin Fus	Pte	01/09/15	Desertion	10yrs PS	F&F	213/5	
Ryan S	2 R Irish	Pte	02/03/16	Desertion	5yrs PS	F&F	213/8	
Ryder EE	9 Liverpool	Pte	13/03/16	Desertion	Not Conf		213/8	
Ryecroft W	1 Northumb Fus	Pte	09/09/16	Desertion	5yrs PS	F&F	213/11	
Sabongidda Samuel	3 Nigeria	Pte	03/07/17	Violence	XXX 27/07/17	East Africa	213/17	695
Saddington JW	5 Leicestershire	Pte	14/08/15	Sleeping	5yrs PS	F&F	213/4	
Sadik Arif O	Civilian		07/08/23	Pillage	XXX	Egypt	213/34	1105
Sadik Mashuk [?]	Civilian		28/08/20	Murder	XXX		213/34	
Saffer Samuel	1/18 London	Rfm	30/09/18	Desertion	5yrs PS	F&F	213/26	983
Sakharoff F	1 Slavo-British Legion	Pte	13/07/19	Mutiny	XXX 00/07/19	N Russia	213/32	
Salah AH [Gadalla Rageb]	Civilian		19/06/19	Murder + Riot	XXX (Hanged)	Egypt	213/32	1015
Salih Ali	Civilian		06/07/20	Hostile Act	10yrs HL	Turkey	213/34	1054
Salih Ibrahim O	Civilian		07/09/20	Murder	XXX	Egypt	213/34	1077
Salmon J	2 Essex	Pte	01/07/15	Desertion	Quashed	F&F	213/4	
Salter Harry	6 East Lancs	Pte	22/11/15	Desertion/Esc	XXX 11/12/15	Gallipoli	213/6	133
Sanches A	9 British West Indies	Pte	27/12/18	Mutiny	20yrs PS	Italy	213/27	
Sandelin HF	4 Canadian Mtd Rifles	Pte	24/09/18	Desertion	5yrs PS	F&F	213/27	
Sands Peter	1 R Irish Rifles	Rfm	30/08/15	Desertion	XXX 15/09/15	F&F	213/5	105
Sanford C	2 Lincolnshire	Pte	27/12/14	Sleeping/Quitting	2yrs HL	F&F	213/3	
Sanikidze Kerial	Civilian		09/03/20	Murder	XXX	S Russia	213/34	1042
Sarafede Demetre	Civilian		17/05/20	Murder	Not Conf	S Russia	213/34	1049
Sargeant Harry	9 Worcestershire	Pte	16/11/15	Sleeping	5yrs PS	Gallipoli	213/6	
Saunders GW	15 R Irish Rifles	Rfm	05/09/17	Quitting	5yrs PS	F&F	213/17	752
Saunders H	8 R Inniskilling Fus	Pte	06/05/16	Sleeping	2yrs HL	F&F	213/9	
Saunders W	14 DAC RFA	Gnr	26/08/16	Desertion	5yrs PS	F&F	213/11	
Sautier EG	35 Australian IF	Pte	30/07/17	Desertion	5yrs PS		213/16	
Savage EW	52 Canadian EF	Pte	03/12/17	Desertion	5yrs PS	F&F	213/19	837
Saville JW	1 Coldstream Gds	Pte	20/12/15	Desertion	3yrs PS	F&F	213/6	
Sawyer C	1 Leicestershire	Pte	26/10/16	Desertion	5yrs PS	F&F	213/12	
Saxby F	5 Dorset	Pte	13/09/17	Desertion	5yrs PS	F&F	213/17	
Scarffe A	9 R Inniskilling Fus	Pte	31/12/18	Desertion	5yrs PS	F&F	213/29	1001
Schofield E	2/8 Lancs Fus	Pte	08/09/17	Sleeping	5yrs PS	F&F	213/17	
Schofield S	1/5 E Lancs	Pte	24/10/17	Desertion	5yrs PS	F&F	213/19	
Schofield W	2 Lancs Fus	Pte	10/09/18	Desertion x2	10yrs PS	F&F	213/25	
Scholes R	11 E Lancs	Pte	24/08/16	Desertion	2yrs HL	F&F	213/11	436
Scholes William	2 S Wales Bdrs	Pte	14/11/17	Desertion	5yrs PS	F&F	213/18	828
Scholes William	2 S Wales Bdrs	Pte	06/07/18	Desertion	XXX 10/08/18	F&F	213/24	937
Schulman B	1/1 Oxon & Bucks LI	Pte	02/09/16	Cowardice	Not Conf	F&F	213/11	
Scott C	11 R W Kent	Pte	21/07/17	Desertion	10yrs PS	F&F	213/16	704
Scott D	10 Highland LI	Pte	25/08/15	Cowardice +	5yrs PS	F&F	213/5	103
Scott EH	19 Manchester	Pte	13/11/16	Cowardice	10yrs PS	F&F	213/12	508
Scott F	2 Lovat Scouts (TF)	Pte	11/10/15	Sleeping	5yrs PS	Gallipoli	213/6	
Scott H	1 Worcestershire	Pte	29/06/17	Desertion	5yrs PS	F&F	213/16	
Scott J	2 Durham LI	Pte	26/01/16	Desertion	10yrs PS	F&F	213/7	
Scott J	1/5 E Kent (Buffs)	Pte	21/07/16	Sleeping	5yrs PS	Mesopotamia	90/7	406
Scott J	2 Royal Fus	Pte	02/06/18	Desertion	15yrs PS	F&F	213/23	
Scotton William	4 Middlesex	Pte	28/01/15	Desertion	XXX 09/02/15	F&F	213/3	25
Scourfield D	6 R Munster Fus	Pte	18/12/15	Sleeping	Not Conf	Salonika	213/7	
Scrivener J	1/5 R Warwickshire	Pte	11/06/16	Quitting	2yrs HL	F&F	213/10	
Scrogge E	RFA	Dvr	12/11/17	Desertion	5yrs PS		213/18	
Scullard H	East Non Combat Corps	Pte	02/06/16	Disobedience x2	Not Conf	F&F	213/10	327
Scullard H	East Non Combat Corps	Pte	07/06/16	Disobedience	10yrs PS	F&F	213/9	335
Searle F	1 E Surrey	Pte	02/11/16	Desertion	5yrs PS	F&F	213/12	
Seed ER	14 Canadian EF	Pte	21/03/16	Desertion	5yrs PS	F&F	213/8	
Seed Robert	1/4 E Lancs	Pte	01/01/16	Cowardice	2yrs HL	Gallipoli	213/8	
Seed TG	1/4 Dragoon Gds	Pte	10/06/16	Disobedience	2yrs HL		213/9	

Name	Unit	Rank	Date	Offence	Final sentence	Location	Ref	Note
Sekum H	4 Canadian Mtd Rifles	Pte	23/01/17	Desertion	5yrs PS	F&F	213/13	
Selby J	1 KRRC	Pte	15/02/15	Sleeping	2yrs HL	F&F	213/3	
Selig M	13 Canadian EF	Pte	27/01/16	Desertion	Quashed	F&F	213/7	165
Semple G	1 Scottish Rifles	Pte	20/11/16	Cowardice	10yrs PS	F&F	213/12	
Senior CH	2 North Non Combat Corps	Pte	12/06/16	Disobedience	10yrs PS	F&F	213/9	358
Senior H	11 Hussars	Pte	28/01/15	Desertion	Quashed	F&F	213/3	
Sewell J	87 Canadian EF	Pte	13/09/17	Desertion	5yrs PS	F&F	213/17	
Seymour H	1 Grenadier Gds	Pte	05/02/15	Disobedience	3mos FP1	F&F	213/3	
Seymour John	2 R Inniskilling Fus	Pte	07/03/16	Desertion	10yrs PS	F&F	213/8	188
Seymour John	2 R Inniskilling Fus	Pte	12/01/18	Desertion	XXX 24/01/18	F&F	213/20	860
Shalders H	12 R Lancers	Pte	14/03/15	Desertion	Quashed	F&F	213/3	50
Shallcross G	1 KO Yorks LI	Pte	04/08/17	Sleeping	2yrs HL	Salonika	213/17	
Shamssedin	Egyptian Army	Colonel	19/08/20	Treason	5yrs PS	Egypt	213/34	1062
Shanahan A	1 R Munster Fus	Cpl	24/11/15	Sleeping	10yrs PS	Gallipoli	213/9	
Shannahan AJ	7 Australian IF	Pte	28/12/16	Desertion	5yrs PS		213/13	
Sharoff V	1 Slavo-British Legion	Pte	17/07/19	Mutiny	10yrs PS	N Russia	213/32	
Sharp G	12 R Sussex	Pte	02/06/16	Sleeping	3yrs PS	F&F	213/10	328
Sharp H	2 A&S Hdrs	Pte	24/02/15	Quitting	2yrs HL	F&F	213/3	
Sharpe GH	2 W Yorks	Pte	22/09/17	Desertion	10yrs PS	F&F	213/17	
Sharpe HL	50 Canadian EF	Pte	12/12/17	Desertion	7yrs PS	F&F	213/19	
Sharpe WL	14 York & Lancaster	Pte	05/08/16	Cowardice	10yrs PS	F&F	213/10	417
Shaw C	Royal Fus	L/Cpl	16/02/15	Desertion	10yrs PS		213/3	
Shaw C	37 Trench How Bty RFA	Gnr	08/08/15	Desertion	10yrs PS		213/4	
Shaw H	1 Lincolnshire	Pte	31/12/14	Cowardice	10yrs PS	F&F	213/3	
Shaw J	54 MGC	Pte	26/07/16	Desertion	Not Conf		213/10	
Shawcross A	1/7 Manchester	Pte	10/08/18	Desertion	5yrs pS	F&F	213/24	
Shea C	10 W Yorks	Pte	04/04/17	Desertion	10yrs PS	F&F	213/15	
Shebbeas W	2 Suffolk	Pte	11/12/15	Sleeping	5yrs PS	F&F	213/6	
Sheehan M	RFA	Bmdr	09/11/17	Desertion	10yrs PS		213/18	
Sheffield F	2 Middlesex	Pte	30/12/14	Desertion	XXX 12/01/15	F&F	213/3	17
Sheffield Sidney A	4 Australian IF	Pte	11/10/16	Mutiny	2yrs HL	F&F	90/6	479
Shefford E	5 R Berkshire	Pte	06/09/17	Desertion	5yrs PS	F&F	213/17	
Shepherd T	2 S Staffordshire	Pte	16/10/17	Desertion+	5yrs PS	F&F	213/18	799
Sheppard F	51 Australian IF	Pte	07/05/15	Desertion	10yrs PS		213/15	
Sheridan E	48 Australian IF	Pte	08/07/17	Desertion	10yrs PS		213/16	
Sherriff W	9 Sherwood Fstrs	Sgt	01/11/15	Cowardice	10yrs PS	Gallipoli	213/6	
Sherry D	36 Australian IF	Pte	13/08/17	Desertion	10yrs PS		213/17	
Shields EF	51 Australian IF	Pte (L/C)	19/01/17	Desertion/Esc	10yrs PS		213/13	
Shields J	2 R Munster Fus	Pte	02/04/17	Desertion	5yrs PS	F&F	213/14	
Shinton G	7 S Staffordshire	L/Cpl	31/07/15	Sleeping	2yrs HL	Gallipoli	213/5	
Ship CH	1/13 London	Pte	04/06/17	Desertion	5yrs PS	F&F	213/16	669
Shooter S	10 Sherwood Fstrs	Pte	27/02/16	Desertion	10yrs PS	F&F	213/9	
Short E	12 Highland LI	Pte	09/09/18	Desertion	10yrs PS	F&F	213/25	
Short Jesse R	24 Northumb Fus	Cpl	12/09/17	Mutiny	XXX 04/10/17	F&F	213/17	759
Shorthus William	2 Leicestershire	Pte	02/12/14	Sleeping	2yrs HL	Mesopotamia	213/2	
Shouldice John	Civilian	Sinn Fein	06/05/16	Rebellion	5yrs PS	Dublin	213/8	291
Shouliatieff T	1 Slavo-British Legion	Pte	13/07/19	Mutiny	10yrs PS	N Russia	213/32	
Sibun G	1/20 London	Pte	19/08/18	Desertion	5yrs PS	F&F	213/25	964
Siddall Clyde	2 S Lancs	Pte	24/11/17	Desertion	5yrs PS	F&F	213/18	
Silburn GH	36 Australian IF	Pte	20/09/17	Desertion	10yrs PS		213/17	
Sillitor LR	7 N Staffordshire	Pte	02/02/16	Cowardice	7yrs PS	Egypt	213/7	
Siman N	German Army	POW	29/10/17	Insubordinaion	168 days HL	Egypt	213/18	
Simeoni G	Macedonian Mule Coy	Muleteer	08/10/19	Murder x3	XXX 31/10/19	Turkey	213/31	1029
Simmonds W	8 Devon	Pte	19/02/16	Desertion	5yrs PS	F&F	213/7	
Simmonds William Henry	23 Middlesex	Pte	19/11/16	Desertion	XXX 01/12/16	F&F	213/12	513
Simons H	13 Canadian EF	Pte	10/08/16	Desertion	10yrs PS	F&F	213/10	
Simpson	R Scots Fus	Pte	18/12/14	Cowardice	2yrs HL		213/3	
Simpson J	ASC	Dvr	15/03/16	Desertion	10yrs PS		213/8	
Simpson J	8 Yorks	Pte	18/05/16	Desertion	2yrs HL	F&F	213/9	
Simpson R	1 Canadian DAC	Bmdr	27/05/16	Desertion	10yrs PS	F&F	213/9	
Simpson T	1/4 R Scots Fus	Pte	13/07/17	Disobedience	5yrs PS	Egypt	213/16	
Simpson W	9 Yorks	Pte	08/12/17	Desertion	10yrs PS	Italy	213/19	
Sims Robert W	2 R Scots	Pte	30/04/18	Desertion x2	XXX 19/05/18	F&F	213/22	900
Singh Mula	Hong Kong TMB RGA	A/Naik	24/04/16	Murder+	10yrs PS	Egypt	90/6	210
Sinicky Dimitro	52 Canadian EF	Pte	12/09/17	Cowardice	XXX 09/10/17	F&F	213/17	760
Sinna	W African	Pte	05/07/15	Cowardice	5yrs PS	Cameroon	213/4	
Sinsadze Elany	Civilian		21/09/19	Armed Robbery	XXX	S Russia	213/34	1023
Sizer B	1 E Yorks	Pte	19/10/17	Desertion	10yrs PS		213/18	

Name	Unit	Rank	Date	Offence	Final sentence	Location	Ref	Note
Skilton Charles WF	22 Royal Fus	Pte	09/12/16	Desertion	XXX 26/12/16	F&F	213/12	528
Skinner	2 Rifle Bde	Rfm	17/05/15	Desertion	2yrs HL	F&F	213/4	
Skinner P	2 E Surrey	Pte	20/03/15	Sleeping	5yrs PS	F&F	213/3	
Skone James	2 Welsh	Pte	28/04/18	Murder	XXX 10/05/18	F&F	213/22	899
Skuse SJ	19 Manchester	Pte	13/11/16	Cowardice	10yrs PS	F&F	213/12	509
Slade Frederick W	2/6 London	Rfm	14/11/17	Disobedience x2	XXX 24/11/17	F&F	213/18	829
Slattery Peter	Civilian	Sinn Fein	05/05/16	Rebellion	8yrs PS	Dublin	213/8	287
Sloan S	10 A&S Hdrs	Pte	20/09/16	Desertion	5yrs PS	F&F	213/11	
Sloane J	1/4 KOR Lancaster	Pte	29/06/16	Desertion	XXX 16/07/16	F&F	213/9	389
Smith A	4 Leicestershire	Pte	30/09/15	Sleeping	15yrs PS	F&F	213/5	
Smith A	2 Royal Fus	Pte	15/11/15	Sleeping	5yrs PS	Gallipoli	213/7	
Smith A	20 Liverpool	Pte	16/01/18	Desertion	10yrs PS	F&F	213/19	
Smith A	19 Durham LI	Pte	04/11/18	Desertion	10yrs PS	F&F	213/26	991
Smith B	42 Canadian EF	Pte	28/11/17	Desertion	15yrs PS	F&F	213/19	
Smith C	12 Liverpool	Pte	19/04/16	Desertion	10yrs PS	F&F	213/9	
Smith C	14 Trench Mortar Bty	Dvr	16/01/18	Desertion	5yrs PS		213/19	
Smith CE	RFA	Dvr	26/06/17	Desertion	PS Life		213/17	
Smith E	6 Northumb Fus	Pte	08/08/16	Desertion	5yrs PS	F&F	213/11	
Smith E	6 Northumb Fus	Pte	24/12/17	Desertion	5yrs PS	F&F	213/19	
Smith E	5 Scottish Rifles	Pte	09/09/18	Desertion	5yrs PS	F&F	213/25	
Smith F	2 Durham LI	Pte	29/04/16	Desertion	15yrs PS	F&F	213/9	
Smith F	58 Canadian EF	Cpl	06/11/17	Desertion	5yrs PS	F&F	213/18	
Smith G	2 E Surrey	Pte	19/03/15	Sleeping	3mos FP1	F&F	213/3	
Smith G	7 D Cornwall LI	Pte	16/10/16	Desertion	5yrs PS	F&F	213/12	
Smith GW	139 MGC	Pte	09/06/17	Sleeping	5yrs PS		213/15	
Smith GW	146 MGC	Pte	15/06/17	Murder	15yrs PS		213/16	
Smith H	4 Dragoon Gds	Pte	24/10/14	Sleeping	2yrs HL	F&F	213/2	9
Smith H	8 S Staffordshire	Pte	01/01/16	Desertion	10yrs PS	F&F	213/7	
Smith H	3 (att 11) Suffolk	Pte	18/09/16	Desertion	10yrs PS	UK	213/11	451
Smith H	2/7 W Yorks	Rfn	09/02/17	Desertion	Not Conf	F&F	213/14	590
Smith H	6 R Dublin Fus	Pte	02/04/17	Desertion	15yrs PS	Salonika	213/14	
Smith HE	20 Australian IF	Pte	18/06/17	Desertion	15yrs PS		213/15	
Smith HJ	2 R Irish Rifles	Rfm	13/03/16	Desertion	10yrs PS	F&F	213/8	
Smith J	10 Lancs Fus	Cpl	22/06/16	Cowardice	5yrs PS	F&F	213/10	
Smith J	10 Lincolnshire	Pte (L/C)	19/05/17	Desertion	10yrs PS	F&F	213/15	655
Smith J	Army Veterinary Corps	Pte	23/05/17	Desertion	10yrs PS		213/15	
Smith J	RE	Dvr	10/06/17	Disobedience +	10yrs PS		213/15	676
Smith J	2 R Scots	Pte	28/05/18	Desertion	10yrs PS	F&F	213/22	
Smith James	17 Liverpool	Pte	22/08/17	Desertion	XXX 05/09/17	F&F	213/17	732
Smith JL	45 Australian IF	Pte	13/05/17	Desertion	10yrs PS		213/15	
Smith John	1 Loyal N Lancs	Pte	17/06/16	Desertion	XXX 02/07/16	F&F	213/9	377
Smith L	4 Royal Fus	Pte	08/11/17	Desertion	5yrs PS	F&F	213/8	
Smith LP	1/24 London	Pte	12/10/18	Desertion	3yrs PS	F&F	213/26	
Smith R	2 Canadian EF	Pte	06/07/17	Desertion	5yrs PS	F&F	213/16	
Smith R	1 R W Surrey	Pte	19/11/18	Desertion	5yrs PS	F&F	213/26	
Smith S	2 Rifle Bde	Rfm	14/12/17	Desertion	2yrs HL	F&F	213/19	
Smith T	13 R Scots	Pte	29/09/16	Desertion	5yrs PS	F&F	213/11	
Smith T	1 R Irish	Pte	14/08/18	Murder	Not Conf	Egypt	213/29	
Smith W	2 Rifle Bde	Rfm	21/09/15	Desertion	XXX 03/10/15	F&F	213/5	116
Smith W	7 N Staffordshire	Pte	02/02/16	Cowardice	7yrs PS	Egypt	213/7	
Smith W	Div Am Sub Park	Pte	18/07/16	Indecency	Quashed		213/10	401
Smith W	7 KRRC	Rfm	10/10/16	Desertion	Not Conf	F&F	213/12	
Smith W	8 Devon	Pte	27/05/17	Desertion	10yrs PS	F&F	213/15	
Smith W	MGC	Pte	25/06/17	Disobedience	5yrs PS		213/16	
Smith W	3 Rifle Bde	Rfm	10/09/17	Desertion	10yrs PS	F&F	213/17	
Smith W	2 KO Yorks LI	Pte	03/06/18	Desertion	3yrs PS	F&F	213/22	
Smith W	4 Seaforth Hdrs	Pte	24/01/19	Desertion	5yrs PS	F&F	213/28	
Smith William	3/5 Lancs Fus	Pte	30/10/17	Desertion	XXX 14/11/17	F&F	213/18	816
Smoothy F	147 MGC	Pte	23/08/16	Sleeping	2yrs HL		213/10	
Smythe Alfred (Albert)	1 Irish Gds	Pte	19/01/15	Desertion	XXX 28/01/15	F&F	213/3	24
Sneddon HJ	20 Middlesex	Pte	30/06/17	Desertion	5yrs PS	F&F	213/16	688
Sneddon J	1 Black Watch	Pte	15/05/16	Desertion	2yrs HL	F&F	213/9	
Snell B	7 Norfolk	Pte	26/04/16	Insubordination +	2yrs HL	F&F	213/9	213
Sokol A	44 Canadian EF	Pte	29/11/17	Desertion	10yrs PS	F&F	213/19	
Southern A	1 Loyal N Lancs	Pte	24/03/16	Desertion	10yrs PS	F&F	213/8	
Southern W	20 Liverpool	Pte	26/02/16	Sleeping	3yrs PS	F&F	213/8	
Sparkes C	2 R Warwickshire	Pte	11/03/17	Desertion	15yrs PS	F&F	213/14	
Sparkes E	13 Hussars	Tpr	15/04/15	Desertion	Not Conf	F&F	213/3	

Name	Unit	Rank	Date	Offence	Final sentence	Location	Ref	Note
Sparkes JB	4 R Munster Fus	Pte	03/07/16	Desertion	3yrs PS		213/10	
Sparkisman A	7 E Yorks	Pte	09/08/15	Sleeping	5yrs PS		213/4	
Spear J	5 R Berkshire	Pte	12/06/18	Desertion	5yrs PS	F&F	213/22	
Speers D	9 R Inniskilling Fus	Pte	18/11/16	Sleeping	5yrs PS	F&F	213/12	512
Spencer ES	2 North Non Combat Corps	Pte	12/06/16	Disobedience	10yrs PS		213/9	359
Spencer J	9 Worcestershire	Pte	04/08/16	Sleeping	3yrs PS	Mesopotamia	90/7	416
Spencer James	RFA	Dvr	09/09/15	Desertion	XXX 29/09/15		213/5	108
Spencer T	2 E Surrey	Pte	20/03/15	Sleeping	5yrs PS	F&F	213/3	
Spencer Victor M	1 New Zealand EF	Pte	17/01/18	Desertion	XXX 24/02/18		213/20	864
Spicer T	1/1 Hertfordshire	Pte	23/05/18	Desertion	5yrs PS	F&F	213/22	
Spowart W	26 Ausralian IF	Pte	28/09/16	Desertion/Esc	Not Conf	F&F	213/11	
Spry W	2 Royal Fus	Pte	26/04/18	Des + Quitting	10yrs PS	F&F	213/21	895
Spry William	2 Royal Fus	Pte	02/06/18	Desertion	XXX 14/06/18	F&F	213/22	919
Squire J	5 KOR Lancaster	Pte	16/10/17	Desertion	15yrs PS	F&F	213/18	
Squires T	6 Leicestershire	Cpl	21/08/15	Sleeping	5yrs PS	F&F	213/4	
St Leger EF	RFA	Gnr	09/09/18	Desertion	10yrs PS		213/25	
Stafford W	10 Scottish Rifles	Pte	21/04/18	Desertion	5yrs PS	F&F	213/22	
Stainthorpe H	1 W Yorks	Pte	09/07/15	Desertion	10yrs PS	F&F	213/4	
Stainton T	11 W Yorks	Pte	26/06/17	Desertion	10yrs PS	F&F	213/15	
Stairs E	5 Canadian Mtd Rifles	Pte	24/09/17	Desertion	5yrs PS	F&F	213/17	
Stammers J	1 D Cornwall LI	Pte	16/05/16	Sleeping	2yrs HL	F&F	213/9	
Standed G	2 E Kent (Buffs)	Pte	19/07/15	Sleeping	3yrs PS	F&F	213/4	
Stannard O	1 Rifle Bde	Rfm	06/09/15	Desertion	15yrs PS	F&F	213/5	
Stanton HE	East Non Combat Corps	Pte	10/06/16	Disobedience	10yrs PS	F&F	213/9	347
Stanton P	RFA	Gnr	13/12/16	Desertion	2yrs HL		213/12	
Staunton M	24 Bty RFA	Pte	30/08/16	Sleeping	5yrs PS		213/11	
Stead F	2 W Riding	Pte	21/11/16	Desertion	5yrs PS	F&F	213/13	
Stead Frederick	2 W Riding	Pte	11/01/17	Desertion	XXX 12/02/17	F&F	213/13	574
Steadman WH	9 Worcestershire	Pte	04/09/17	Sleeping	3yrs PS	Mesopotamia	90/7	
Steben G	14 Canadian Bn	Pte	30/03/15	Desertion	Not Conf	F&F	213/3	
Stedman [Steadman] Joseph	117 MGC	Pte	26/08/17	Desertion	XXX 05/09/17	F&F	213/17	737
Steele E	1 Highland LI	Pte	01/09/15	Sleeping	2yrs HL	F&F	213/4	
Stepharnoff A	87 Canadian EF	Pte	13/09/17	Desertion	10yrs PS	F&F	213/17	
Stepharnoff A	87 Canadian EF	Pte	22/12/17	Desertion	15yrs PS	F&F	213/19	
Stephens A	8/10 Gordon Hdrs	Pte	26/11/17	Desertion x2	5yrs PS	F&F	213/18	
Stephenson JH	6 Durham LI	Pte	25/09/17	Desertion	5yrs PS		213/17	
Sterling P	2 R Irish Rifles	Pte	04/02/15	Cowardice	Not Conf	F&F	213/3	
Stevens A	DAC	Dvr	19/12/17	Desertion x2	5yrs PS		213/19	
Stevens J	16 DAC	Dvr	23/04/18	Desertion	5yrs PS		213/22	
Stevens JE	7 Gloucestershire	Pte	14/12/15	Quitting	2mos FP1	Gallipoli	213/7	
Stevens W	2 Gloucestershire	Pte	21/07/15	Sleeping	5yrs PS	F&F	213/4	
Stevenson A	1 R Scots Fus	Cpl	15/02/16	Desertion	10yrs PS	F&F	213/7	
Stevenson David	13 Middlesex	Pte	26/07/18	Desertion	XXX 18/07/18	F&F	213/23	951
Stevenson F	15 Lancs Fus	Pte	29/12/16	Desertion	10yrs PS	F&F	213/13	547
Stevenson J	2 Scottish Rifles	Pte	26/12/14	Drunk x2	2yrs HL	F&F	213/3	
Stevenson Richard	1/4 Loyal N Lancs	Pte	11/10/16	Desertion	XXX 25/10/16	F&F	213/12	480
Stewart A	6/7 R Scots Fus	Pte (L/C)	22/06/16	Desertion	15yrs PS	F&F	213/9	
Stewart F	58 Lab Coy	Pte	21/12/17	Desertion	10yrs PS		213/19	
Stewart J	2 Lovat Scouts (TF)	Pte	11/10/15	Sleeping	5yrs PS	Gallipoli	213/6	
Stewart Stanley	2 R Scots Fus	Pte	04/04/15	Desertion	Not Conf	F&F	213/3	55
Stewart Stanley	2 R Scots Fus	Pte	12/08/17	Desertion	XXX 29/08/17	F&F	213/16	725
Stewart W	3 Middlesex	Pte	01/11/18	Desertion	PS Life	Salonika	213/28	
Stokes RM	9 Durham LI	Pte	26/06/17	Desertion	5yrs PS		213/16	
Stokes T	2 KRRC	Pte	14/03/18	Quitting	2yrs HL	F&F	213/21	
Stokes W	RFA	Pte	15/10/17	Desertion	10yrs PS		213/18	
Stone AV	1/1 Cambridgeshire	Pte	09/10/17	Desertion	10yrs PS	F&F	213/18	
Stone C	7 R Sussex	Pte	27/02/17	Desertion	10yrs PS	F&F	213/15	
Stone EF	9 KRRC	Rfm	21/06/16	Desertion	10yrs Ps	F&F	213/9	
Stones Joseph W	19 Durham LI	L/Sgt	24/12/16	Casting Arms	XXX 18/01/17	F&F	213/13	537
Stovin E	14 E Yorks	Pte	24/11/16	Desertion	5yrs PS	F&F	213/12	521
Stovin E	10 E Yorks	Pte	12/08/18	Desertion	15yrs PS		213/25	959
Stow E	8 R W Kent	Pte	07/04/16	Sleeping	5yrs PS	F&F	213/8	
Stower E	2 S Staffordshire	Pte	22/10/18	Desertion x2	5yrs PS	F&F	213/25	
Stower EC	2/5 S Staffordshire	Pte	28/06/17	Desertion	5yrs PS	F&F	213/17	
Strachan A	6 Gordon Hdrs	Pte	15/02/15	Sleeping	84days FP1	F&F	213/3	43
Strathmere LG	1 Welsh Gds	Pte	28/04/17	Desertion	3yrs PS	F&F	213/15	
Strevens H	4 Bedfordshire	Pte	12/10/17	Desertion	15yrs PS	F&F	213/18	
Suddick Joseph	2 S Wales Bdrs	Pte	24/10/15	Sleeping	5yrs PS	Gallipoli	213/6	

Name	Unit	Rank	Date	Offence	Final sentence	Location	Ref	Note
Sukkar M (Dahan)	Civilian		01/06/19	Murder/Riot	XXX (Hanged)	Egypt	213/34	
Sulieman Khalil O	Civilian		23/08/20	Aiding Enemy	PS Life		213/34	1063
Sullivan	1 KOR Lancaster	Pte	21/04/15	Desertion	15yrs PS	F&F	213/4	
Sullivan RP	10 Royal Fus	Pte	31/01/17	Mutiny+	Not Conf	F&F	213/13	585
Summerfield J	1 Liverpool	Pte	28/04/16	Desertion	3yrs PS	F&F	213/9	
Sumner J	1 Middlesex	Pte	21/01/19	Desertion	2yrs HL	F&F	213/28	
Surtees T	19 Durham LI	Pte	30/12/16	Cowardice	10yrs PS	F&F	213/13	563
Sutton A	2 Wiltshire	Pte	02/02/15	Sleeping	Not Conf	F&F	213/3	
Sutton F	1 Liverpool	Pte	02/04/17	Sleeping	2yrs HL	F&F	213/14	
Swain John	5 R Berkshire	Pte	26/07/18	Desertion	XXX11/08/18	F&F	213/24	952
Swaine James W	RFA	Dvr	29/05/16	Desertion	XXX 09/06/16	F&F	213/9	322
Swann F	139 MGC	Pte	09/06/15	Sleeping	5yrs PS		213/15	
Swann T	3 Royal Fus	Pte	12/06/15	Desertion	10yrs PS	F&F	213/4	
Sweeney C	17 Highland LI	Pte	26/09/16	Cowardice	2yrs HL	F&F	213/11	460
Sweeney John J	1 New Zealand EF	Pte	13/09/16	Desertion	XXX 02/10/16		213/11	448
Sweeney P	2 R Munster Fus	Pte	10/10/16	Disobedience	10yrs PS	F&F	213/12	
Sweeney P	10 W Riding	Pte	17/10/17	Desertion	15yrs PS	F&F	213/18	
Sweeney PE	Civilian	Sinn Fein	03/05/16	Rebellion	10yrs PS	Dublin	213/8	238
Sweetapple W	1 Hampshire	Pte	26/02/15	Desertion	10yrs PS	F&F	213/3	
Swift J	115 MGC	Cpl	15/11/17	Sleeping	Not Conf		213/18	
Swift JC	2 KO Yorks LI	Pte	06/04/16	Desertion	5yrs PS	F&F	213/9	
Swinton GW	35 Australian IF	Pte	13/08/17	Desertion	10yrs PS		213/17	
Swords M	4 Australian Pnr Bn	Pte	05/07/17	Desertion	10yrs PS		213/16	
Sykes W	2 Essex	Pte	04/06/15	Cowardice	Quashed	F&F	213/4	
Syrett C	2 Manchester	Pte	29/07/17	Desertion	7 yrs PS	F&F	213/16	
Taffs J	ASC	Pte	13/11/16	Desertion	10yrs PS	F&F	213/12	
Tagg H	7 N Staffordshire	Sgt	01/12/15	Desertion	10yrs PS	Gallipoli	213/7	
Taggart J	1 N Staffordshire	Pte	26/02/15	Drunk	3yrs PS	F&F	213/3	
Tanner Edward	1 Wiltshire	Pte	13/10/14	Desertion	XXX 27/10/14	F&F	213/2	7
Taratin P	1 Slavo-British Legion	Pte	14/07/19	Mutiny	XXX 00/07/19	N Russia	213/32	
Tavarlkiladze Gerasin	Civilian		07/11/19	Murder	Not Conf	S Russia	213/34	1033
Taylor AW	3 East Non Combat Corps	Pte	13/06/16	Disobedience	10yrs PS	F&F	213/9	369
Taylor B	8 Cheshire	Pte	29/03/16	Disobedience	3yrs PS	Egypt	90/7	
Taylor C	8 E Kent (Buffs)	Pte	02/12/15	Sleeping	Quashed	F&F	213/6	
Taylor E	2/5 Lancs Fus	Pte	19/12/16	Sleeping	5yrs PS	F&F	213/13	
Taylor E	1/6 Welsh	Pte	26/11/17	Desertion	5yrs PS	F&F	213/19	833
Taylor ED	Lord Strathcona's Horse	Pte	06/06/15	Desertion	5yrs PS		213/4	
Taylor J	19 London	Pte	26/06/16	Desertion	10yrs PS	F&F	213/9	384
Taylor John	15 Lancs Fus	Pte	30/12/16	Desertion	XXX 27/01/17	F&F	213/13	564
Taylor John	2 S Staffordshire	Pte	17/10/17	Desertion x2	XXX 06/11/17	F&F	213/18	803
Taylor R	24 Bty RGA	Gnr	13/09/15	Desertion	18mos HL	F&F	213/4	
Taylor R	1 Liverpool	Pte	01/03/16	Desertion	5yrs PS	F&F	213/8	
Taylor R	2 Canadian EF	Pte	26/11/17	Desertion	5yrs PS	F&F	213/18	
Taylor T	1 Scottish Rifles	Pte	10/03/15	Desertion	10yrs PS	F&F	213/3	
Taylor T	2 Gloucestershire	Pte	21/07/15	Sleeping	5yrs PS	F&F	213/4	
Taylor W	6 R W Surrey	Pte	06/11/18	Desertion	10yrs PS	F&F	213/27	
Taysum Norman Henry	9 Black Watch	Pte	24/09/17	Desertion	XXX 16/10/17	F&F	213/17	771
Tchelidze Kondrat C	Civilian		07/11/19	Murder	Not Conf	S Russia	213/34	1034
Teague J	10 R Warwickshire	Pte	01/07/17	Desertion	10yrs PS	F&F	213/16	
Tempest J	RFA	Gnr	22/07/16	Desertion	5yrs PS		213/11	
Templeton J	15 R Irish Rifles	Rfm	27/02/16	Desertion	XXX 19/03/16	F&F	213/7	185
Templeton T	2 R Inniskilling Fus	Pte	10/04/16	Desertion	5yrs PS	F&F	213/9	
Tero Charles	1 Northants	Pte	06/02/15	Sleeping	2yrs HL	F&F	213/3	33
Terrington F	8 R W Surrey	Pte	11/12/16	Desertion	2yrs HL	F&F	213/13	
Terry CE	10 Royal Fus	Pte	22/04/18	Desertion	5yrs PS	F&F	213/22	
Thaourides Nicolas A	Muleteer	Foreman	12/06/17	Murder	XXX 06/07/17	Salonika	213/16	677
Thickett J	7 N Staffordshire	Pte	24/10/15	Sleeping	10yrs PS	Gallipoli	213/6	
Thickett W	8 S Staffordshire	Pte	19/02/18	Desertion	5yrs PS	F&F	213/20	
Thomas C	1 R Welsh Fus	Pte	25/01/15	Desertion	2yrs HL	F&F	213/3	
Thomas FC	15 R Irish Rifles	Rfm	05/09/17	Quitting	5yrs PS	F&F	213/17	753
Thomas H	2 Yorks	Pte	03/11/16	Desertion	Not Conf	F&F	213/12	
Thomas H	2 Hampshire	Pte	15/08/18	Desertion x2	10yrs PS	F&F	213/24	
Thomas J	2 Welsh	Pte	30/12/15	Desertion	5yrs PS	F&F	213/7	
Thomas J	2 Welsh	Pte	08/05/16	Desertion+	XXX 20/05/16	F&F	213/9	298
Thomas J	3 Liverpool (att 8 E Lancs)	Pte	27/09/16	Desertion	10yrs PS		213/11	
Thomas W	8 Welsh	Pte	09/09/15	Sleeping	1yr HL		213/5	109
Thomason TJ	2 E Lancs	Pte	12/06/18	Cowardice	5yrs PS	F&F	213/24	
Thompson A	2 Rifle Bde	Rfm	14/12/17	Desertion	5yrs PS	F&F	213/19	

Name	Unit	Rank	Date	Offence	Final sentence	Location	Ref	Note
Thompson Alfred	3 Worcestershire	Pte	14/07/15	Desertion	XXX 26/07/15	F&F	213/4	91
Thompson G	12 Northumb Fus	Pte	01/11/16	Desertion+	5yrs PS	F&F	213/12	
Thompson G	20 Durham LI	Pte	24/03/17	Desertion	15yrs PS	F&F	213/14	613
Thompson G	1/19 London	Pte	01/07/18	Desertion	5yrs PS	F&F	213/23	934
Thompson J	2 R Irish Rifles	Pte	29/03/15	Desertion x2	Quashed	F&F	213/3	
Thompson J	8 N Staffordshire	Pte	25/06/17	Desertion	10yrs PS	F&F	213/15	
Thompson JH	93 RFA	Dvr	04/06/17	Desertion	10yrs PS		213/15	
Thompson JH	RFA	Dvr	26/08/17	Desertion	Not Conf		213/17	
Thompson S	10 Royal Fus	Pte	22/04/18	Desertion	5yrs PS	F&F	213/21	
Thompson William Landreth	6 E Kent (Buffs)	Pte	04/04/16	Desertion	XXX 22/04/16	F&F	213/8	201
Thorne A	16 Canadian EF	Pte	08/01/18	Desertion	7yrs PS	F&F	213/19	
Thorne FR	2 Royal Fus	Cpl	23/11/16	Desertion	5yrs PS	F&F	213/13	
Thorne FR	2 Royal Fus	Pte	01/08/17	Desertion	5yrs PS	F&F	213/16	
Thornton G	1 R W Kent	Pte	04/01/17	Desertion+	15yrs PS	F&F	213/13	570
Thorpe W	17 Lancs Fus	Pte	07/11/16	Sleeping	10yrs PS	F&F	213/12	500
Tibble W	6 Northants	Cpl	11/01/16	Desertion	Quashed	F&F	213/7	
Tickle E	1/7 Manchester	Pte	10/08/18	Desertion	5yrs PS	F&F	213/24	
Tighe JJ	9 R Irish Rifles	Rfm	02/11/16	Sleeping	5yrs PS	F&F	213/12	495
Tilbrook W	2 Essex	Pte	04/06/15	Cowardice	Quashed	F&F	213/4	
Tilbury J	RFA	Gnr	16/08/17	Striking	5yrs PS		213/17	
Tilley S	1 Loyal N Lancs	Pte	10/08/16	Desertion	2yrs HL	F&F	213/11	
Timmins G	26 Australian IF	Pte	29/09/16	Desertion	Not Conf		213/11	
Timson GA	11 Northumb Fus	Pte	03/02/17	Desertion	10yrs PS	F&F	213/13	
Tite Reginald T	13 R Sussex	Pte	02/11/16	Desertion	XXX 25/11/16	F&F	213/12	496
Tobin A	52 Canadian EF	Pte	19/09/17	Desertion	3yrs PS	F&F	213/17	766
Tobin William	Civilian	Sinn Fein	03/05/16	Rebellion	10yrs PS	Dublin	213/8	239
Todd EH	1/20 London	Pte	19/08/18	Desertion	5yrs PS	F&F	213/25	965
Todd JW	6 R Marines	L/Cpl	04/10/19	Disobedience	5yrs PS	N Russia	213/30	
Todd T	7 Seaforth Hdrs	Pte	16/02/16	Disobedience	5yrs PS	F&F	213/7	
Tolley J	7 Liverpool	Pte	26/09/18	Desertion	Not Conf	F&F	213/26	982
Tolley T	112 Bty RFA	Gnr	08/03/16	Desertion	10yrs PS		213/8	
Tomalin GA	116 Canadian EF	Pte	26/01/18	Desertion	5yrs PS	F&F	213/19	
Tompkins CF	1 Canadian EF	Pte	09/01/17	Quitting	15yrs PS	F&F	213/13	
Tong F	15 Hampshire	Pte	19/04/18	Desertion	10yrs PS	F&F	213/21	890
Tongue James (Joseph)	1 Liverpool	Pte	22/01/17	Desertion	XXX 31/01/17	F&F	213/13	578
Tonkikh V	1 Slavo-British Legion	Pte	17/07/19	Mutiny	10yrs PS	N Russia	213/32	
Toomey N	1/4 London	Pte	14/06/17	Desertion	10yrs PS	F&F	213/15	678
Tootle TE	10 R Irish Rifles	Rfm	19/11/16	Sleeping	5yrs PS	F&F	213/12	514
Topps A	7 Kings Shropshire LI	Pte	25/04/18	Desertion	7yrs PS		213/22	
Torevell J	25 Northumb Fus	Pte	26/12/16	Desertion	Not Conf	F&F	213/13	539
Towey W	1 N Staffordshire	Sgt	18/03/15	Cowardice	10yrs PS	F&F	213/3	
Townsend HO	1 Canadian Mtd Rifles	Pte	11/11/16	Desertion	5yrs PS	F&F	213/12	
Townsend T	2 E Surrey	Pte	31/05/15	Desertion	5yrs PS	F&F	213/4	
Trainer H	1 R W Kent	Pte	19/04/16	Sleeping	5yrs PS	F&F	213/9	
Traynor J	1 Highland LI	Pte	10/04/15	Sleeping	2yrs HL	F&F	213/3	
Treveleyn V	38 Canadian EF	Pte	14/06/17	Desertion	15yrs PS	F&F	213/16	
Triptree HW	RFA	Dvr	27/04/17	Desertion	15yrs PS	F&F	213/15	
Trivett VJ	7 N Staffordshire	Pte	16/10/15	Sleeping	5yrs PS	Gallipoli	213/6	
Troughton Albert	1 R Welsh Fus	Pte	07/04/15	Desertion	XXX 22/04/15	F&F	213/3	60
Troughton W	2 R Warwickshire	Pte	23/01/15	Desertion	2yrs HL	F&F	213/3	
Tsangonria Philip	Civilian		09/03/20	Murder	XXX	S Russia	213/34	1043
Tseng Sung Kung	60 Chinese Lab Corps	Coolie	01/07/18	Murder	XXX 23/07/18	F&F	213/23	935
Tuke H	R Marines LI	Pte	13/09/18	Desertion	5yrs PS	F&F	213/25	
Tunnicliffe A	RAMC	Pte	15/09/17	Desertion	10yrs PS		213/17	
Turley G	94 MGC	Pte	20/09/16	Sleeping	2yrs HL		213/11	
Turnbull G	2 Rifle Bde	Rfm	21/08/16	Desertion	10yrs PS	F&F	213/10	
Turnbull W	2 KOR Lancaster	Pte	19/03/15	Sleeping	2yrs HL	F&F	213/3	
Turnbull W	85 Canadian EF	Pte	22/11/17	Desertion	10yrs PS	F&F	213/18	
Turner A	1 Bedfordshire	Pte	29/08/15	Sleeping x3	Commuted	F&F	213/5	
Turner C	RFA	Dvr	23/11/18	Desertion	5yrs PS		213/26	
Turner Frederick	6 Northumb Fus	Pte	11/10/17	Desertion x2	XXX 23/10/17		213/17	795
Turner G	1 E Yorks	Pte	15/01/15	Against Inhab	3mos FP1		213/3	
Turner G	2 Durham LI	Pte	14/05/15	Sleeping	5yrs PS	F&F	213/4	
Turner G	2 Royal Fus	Pte	13/10/15	Sleeping	5yrs PS	Gallipoli	213/6	
Turner G	2 Royal Fus	Pte	25/10/15	Sleeping	10yrs PS	Gallipoli	213/6	
Turner G	11 Sherwood Fstrs	Pte	16/06/17	Desertion	10yrs PS	F&F	213/15	
Turner H	1 Worcestershire	Pte	28/02/15	Desertion+	Not Conf	F&F	213/3	48
Turner H	9 Liverpool	Pte	27/04/16	Desertion	10yrs PS		213/8	

Name	Unit	Rank	Date	Offence	Final sentence	Location	Ref	Note
Turner H	9 Liverpool	Pte	14/10/17	Desertion	5yrs PS		213/17	
Turner HJ	28 Canadian EF	Pte	12/08/17	Desertion	Not Conf	F&F	213/17	
Turner J	1/8 Worcestershire	Pte	12/03/17	Desertion	5yrs PS	F&F	213/14	
Turner Percy	6 Dragoon Gds	Pte	04/11/14	Sleeping	2yrs HL	F&F	213/2	11
Turner R	1/8 Lancs Fus	Pte	15/09/15	Sleeping	Not Conf		213/5	
Turner R	1/8 Lancs Fus	Pte	20/09/15	Sleeping	Quashed	Gallipoli	213/5	
Turner R	6 S Lancs	Pte	10/10/15	Sleeping	5yrs PS	Gallipoli	213/6	
Turner SC	1 Gloucestershire	Pte	18/04/15	Cowardice	2yrs HL	F&F	213/3	
Turner W	8 Seaforth Hdrs	Pte	26/02/16	Desertion	10yrs PS	F&F	213/8	
Turner W	1 Northants	Pte	30/03/16	Sleeping	2yrs HL	F&F	213/8	
Turner W	8 Seaforth Hdrs	Pte	05/07/18	Desertion	10yrs PS	Egypt	213/31	
Turpie William	2 E Surrey	Pte	19/06/15	Desertion	XXX 01/07/15	F&F	213/4	78
Tye AE	10 Lincolnshire	Cpl	15/05/17	Desertion	10yrs PS	F&F	213/15	651
Tye FG	10 Lincolnshire	Cpl (L/S)	18/05/17	Desertion	10yrs PS	F&F	213/15	653
Ukovitch S	102 Canadian EF	Pte	16/02/18	Desertion	10yrs PS	F&F	213/20	
Underhill H	7 W Yorks	Pte	02/10/18	Desertion	5yrs PS	F&F	213/25	
Underhill RB	13 London	Pte	03/02/15	Disobedience+	3mos FP1	F&F	213/3	31
Underwood JT	1 Lincolnshire	Pte	31/12/14	Cowardice	5yrs PS	F&F	213/3	
Unwin J	8 N Staffordshire	Pte	22/01/19	Desertion	5yrs PS	F&F	213/27	
Urwin WA	14 Durham LI	Pte	26/10/16	Desertion	5yrs PS	F&F	213/12	
Vale Samuel	RFA	Gnr	20/11/14	Sleeping	2yrs HL		213/2	
Valler AJ	13 E Surrey	Pte	30/06/17	Desertion	5yrs PS	F&F	213/16	689
Vasadze Isak	Civilian		21/09/19	Armed Robbery	XXX	S Russia	213/34	1024
Vaughan T	1/7 W Yorks	Rfm	11/04/17	Desertion	5yrs PS	F&F	213/14	630
Vaughan W	8 N Staffordshire	Pte	28/06/18	Desertion	15yrs PS	F&F	213/24	
Vaughan W	8 N Staffordshire	Pte	17/11/18	Desertion	15yrs PS	F&F	213/27	
Veasey T	2 R Scots Fus	Pte	20/07/15	Desertion	2yrs HL	F&F	213/4	
Verpe Shakir [?] O	Civilian		17/08/20	Aiding Enemy	XXX		213/34	
Veryard Frederick G	13 Middlesex	Pte	25/09/18	Desertion	10yrs PS	F&F	213/25	
Vetters J	6/7 R Scottish Rifles	Pte	30/07/17	Desertion	2yrs HL	F&F	213/16	
Vickers G	10 R Warwickshire	Pte	15/10/17	Desertion	10yrs PS	F&F	213/18	
Viejra (Rikard) Leopold	Civilian	Alien	14/11/16	Espionage	PS Life	UK	92/3	510
Villiers V	2 Manchester	Pte	16/07/18	Desertion	10yrs PS	F&F	213/23	
Vogel E	1/19 London	Pte	12/03/18	Desertion	5yrs PS	F&F	213/21	882
Voice William	6 R W Surrey	Pte	26/06/16	Desertion	5yrs PS	F&F	213/10	
Volkoff P	1 Slavo-British Legion	Pte	14/07/19	Mutiny	XXX 00/07/19	N Russia	213/32	
Vose S	17 Lancs Fus	Pte	20/03/18	Desertion	10yrs PS	F&F	213/21	885
Wade W	1/4 York & Lancaster	Pte	28/01/18	Desertion	5yrs PS	F&F	213/21	867
Wadsworth A	64 MCG	Pte	24/08/16	Sleeping/Quitting	5yrs PS	F&F	213/11	
Wain H	10 Sherwood Fstrs	Pte	15/12/16	Desertion	2yrs HL	F&F	213/13	
Wain W	2 KO Yorks LI	Pte	30/01/16	Sleeping	3yrs PS	F&F	213/7	
Waite J	2 R Warwickshire	Pte	15/02/15	Desertion	2yrs HL	F&F	213/3	
Wakefield J	2 KO Yorks LI	Pte	14/05/15	Desertion	15yrs PS	F&F	213/4	
Wakefield W	8 S Lancs	Pte	31/05/16	Desertion	10yrs PS	F&F	213/9	
Wales EJ	8 KO Yorks LI	Pte	01/11/16	Cowardice	Not Conf	F&F	213/12	
Walker ABC	1 R W Surrey	Pte	17/10/15	Cowardice	Quashed	F&F	213/6	
Walker CE	19 Manchester	Pte	02/06/16	Sleeping	Not Conf	F&F	213/10	329
Walker E	10 R Welsh Fus	Pte	10/09/17	Desertion	5yrs PS	F&F	213/17	
Walker EH	3 East Non Combat Corps	Pte	13/06/16	Disobedience	10yrs PS	F&F	213/9	370
Walker F	7 R Sussex	Pte	28/09/18	Desertion	5yrs PS	F&F	213/25	
Walker GW	8 Sherwood Fstrs	Pte	27/06/18	Desertion	Not Conf	F&F	213/24	
Walker H	10 W Yorks	Pte	11/12/16	Desertion	2yrs HL	F&F	213/13	
Walker HH	1 New Zealand Rifle Bde	Pte	01/12/16	Desertion	10yrs PS		213/12	
Walker J	2 KO Scottish Bdrs	Pte	24/02/17	Desertion x2	15yrs PS	F&F	213/14	
Walker R	2 E Surrey	Pte	20/03/15	Sleeping	5yrs PS	F&F	213/3	
Walker T	1 Loyal N Lancs	Pte	16/01/15	Sleeping	2yrs HL	F&F	213/3	
Walker T	1 Border	Pte	01/05/17	Desertion	Not Conf	F&F	213/15	
Walker W	7 E Yorks	Pte	06/08/17	Desertion	15yrs PS		213/17	
Walker W	52 Australian IF	Pte	17/09/17	Desertion	10yrs PS		213/18	
Walker W	7 E Yorks	Pte	18/11/18	Desertion	15yrs PS		213/26	
Walklate GF	1 KOR Lancaster	L/Cpl	06/02/19	Desertion	5yrs PS	F&F	213/28	
Wall John Thomas	3 Worcestershire	Sgt	30/08/17	Desertion	XXX 06/09/17	F&F	213/17	739
Wallace J	24 Canadian EF	Pte	06/09/17	Desertion	5yrs PS	F&F	213/17	
Wallace J	6 Liverpool	Pte	26/09/18	Desertion	5yrs PS		213/26	
Wallace P	2 R Scots	Sgt	11/08/16	Desertion	5yrs PS	F&F	213/11	421
Wallace T	2 Lancs Fus	Pte	22/04/16	Cowardice	2yrs HL	F&F	213/8	
Wallen G	1 Sherwood Fstrs	Pte	11/11/16	Sleeping	2yrs HL	F&F	213/12	
Walley W	46 Canadian EF	Pte	30/05/17	Desertion	10yrs PS	F&F	213/15	

Name	Unit	Rank	Date	Offence	Final sentence	Location	Ref	Note
Walling AF	3 East Non Combat Corps	Pte	13/06/16	Disobedience	10yrs PS	F&F	213/9	371
Walls FR	21 Australian IF	Pte	01/09/16	Desertion	Not Conf		213/11	
Walls H	7 R W Surrey	Pte	29/01/18	Desertion	5yrs PS	F&F	213/20	
Walls L	2 KO Scottish Bdrs	Pte	12/02/15	Desertion	5yrs PS	F&F	213/3	
Walsh [?] J	1 R Inniskilling Fus	Pte	03/11/18	Against Inhab	15yrs PS		213/26	989
Walsh J	2 R Irish Fus	Pte	03/05/17	Plundering	1yr HL	Salonika	213/15	
Walsh J	22 Canadian EF	Pte	28/01/18	Desertion	5yrs PS	F&F	213/19	
Walsh JJ	Civilian	Sinn Fein	03/05/16	Rebellion	10yrs PS	Dublin	213/8	240
Walsh M	4 Royal Fus	Pte	25/05/16	Desertion	10yrs Ps	F&F	213/9	
Walsh M	4 Royal Fus	Pte	04/09/16	Desertion	10yrs PS	F&F	213/11	
Walsh WP	49 Australian IF	Pte	11/05/17	Desertion	10yrs PS		213/15	
Walshe D	39 Australian IF	Pte	01/09/17	Desertion	10yrs PS		213/18	
Walters G	1 Devon	Pte	07/04/15	Desertion	15yrs PS	F&F	213/4	
Walton H	8 S Staffordshire	Pte	27/09/16	Desertion	10yrs PS	F&F	213/11	
Walton T	1/7 Lancs Fus	Cpl	09/06/17	Quitting	7yrs PS	F&F	213/15	
Walton W	3 Rifle Bde	Pte	31/12/16	Sleeping	2yrs HL	F&F	213/13	
Walton William	2 KRRC	L/Sgt	12/03/15	Desertion	XXX 23/03/15	F&F	213/3	49
Wan Fa Yu	Chinese Lab Corps	Coolie	28/12/18	Against Inhab x2+	XXX 15/01/19	F&F	213/28	998
Wang Ch'un Ch'ih	Chinese Lab Corps	Coolie	14/04/19	Murder	XXX 08/05/19	F&F	213/29	1004
Wang En Yung	Chinese Lab Corps	Coolie	14/06/18	Against Inhab	XXX 26/06/18	F&F	213/24	926
Ward AP	4 Grenadier Gds	Sgt	21/11/15	Desertion	3yrs PS	F&F	213/6	
Ward E	2 York & Lancaster	Pte	05/07/16	Desertion	10yrs PS	F&F	213/10	
Ward G	1 R Berkshire	Pte	24/09/14	Cowardice	XXX 26/09/14	F&F	213/2	6
Ward H	11 Rifle Bde	Rfm	30/10/15	Sleeping	2yrs HL	F&F	213/6	
Ward H	13 KRRC	Rfm	13/09/17	Desertion	15yrs PS	F&F	213/17	
Ward J	2 KO Yorks LI	Pte	17/05/15	Desertion	15yrs PS	F&F	213/4	
Ward J	2 R Scots Fus	Pte	18/05/16	Desertion	2yrs HL	F&F	213/11	
Ward L	1 Loyal N Lancs	Pte	15/01/15	Sleeping	2yrs HL	F&F	213/3	
Ward T	1/4 Dragoon Gds	Pte	10/06/16	Disobedience	2yrs HL		213/9	
Ward T	10 Loyal N Lancs	Pte	13/07/17	Desertion	10yrs PS	F&F	213/16	
Ward Thomas	8/10 Gordon Hdrs	Pte	20/09/17	Desertion	XXX 16/10/17	F&F	213/17	767
Ward W	13 Canadian EF	Pte	25/05/17	Desertion	5yrs PS		213/15	
Wardlaw P	13 R Scots	Pte	25/09/16	Desertion	5yrs PS	F&F	213/11	
Wardlaw P	13 R Scots	Pte	21/10/16	Desertion	1yr HL	F&F	213/12	
Waring H	7 Leicestershire	Pte	08/08/17	Cowardice+	5yrs PS	F&F	213/16	721
Warren H	17 KRRC	Rfm	07/04/17	Sleeping	5yrs PS		213/14	629
Warren H	46 MGC	Cpl	17/05/18	Desertion	5yrs PS		213/22	
Warriner W	7 Lincolnshire	Pte	30/08/17	Desertion	5yrs PS	F&F	213/17	
Warrington E	2 Leicestershire	Pte	07/10/16	Sleeping	3mos FP1	Mesopotamia	90/7	471
Wassef Wissa	Civilian		09/08/22	Sedition	7yrs PS	Egypt	213/34	1101
Watchorn H	10 R Warwickshire	Pte	23/12/16	Desertion	10yrs PS	F&F	213/13	
Watchorn H	10 R Warwickshire	Pte	31/05/17	Desertion	15yrs PS	F&F	213/15	
Waterhouse A	2 Royal Fus	Pte	15/11/15	Sleeping	Remitted	Gallipoli	213/7	
Waters W	2 Durham LI	Pte	26/01/16	Desertion	10yrs PS	F&F	213/7	
Waterworth D	15 R Irish Rifles	Rfm	04/01/16	Desertion	5yrs PS	F&F	213/7	144
Watkins A	12 S Wales Bdrs	Pte	25/04/18	Desertion	5yrs PS	F&F	213/21	893
Watkins George	13 Welsh	Pte	29/04/17	Desertion	XXX 15/05/17	F&F	213/15	642
Watnough J	6 KOR Lancaster	Pte	25/09/17	Desertion/Drunk	5yrs PS	Mesopotamia	90/7	
Watson A	8 R W Kent	Pte	09/02/16	Desertion	10yrs PS	F&F	213/7	
Watson G	1 Highland LI	Pte	29/03/15	Desertion	5yrs PS	F&F	213/3	
Watson J	1 KRRC	Pte	13/01/16	Sleeping	3yrs PS	F&F	213/7	
Watson J	11 Suffolk	Pte	16/05/17	Cowardice	15yrs PS	F&F	213/15	652
Watson R	10 A&S Hdrs	Pte	12/11/17	Desertion	2yrs HL	F&F	213/20	
Watson T	9 Northumb Fus	Pte	25/11/15	Cowardice	10yrs PS	F&F	213/6	
Watson TE	2 KO Yorks LI	Pte	30/01/16	Sleeping	3yrs PS	F&F	213/7	
Watson W	1 Worcestershire	Pte	08/03/17	Desertion	Remitted	F&F	213/14	
Watts A	1 R Irish	Pte	28/08/16	Violence	10yrs PS	Salonika	213/11	
Watts Thomas W	7 E Yorks	Pte	10/08/17	Desertion	XXX 30/08/17	F&F	213/17	724
Watts William	1 Loyal N Lancs	Pte	18/04/16	Desertion	XXX 05/05/16	F&F	213/8	207
Wearne CA	1/5 E Lancs	Pte	20/07/17	Desertion	5yrs PS	F&F	213/16	
Weatherall W	2 R Irish Fus	Pte	03/05/17	Plundering	1yr HL	Salonika	213/15	
Weatherspoon P	20 Liverpool	Pte	29/10/16	Desertion	10yrs PS	F&F	213/12	490
Webb A	1 E Kent (Buffs)	Pte	20/01/16	Desertion	10yrs PS	F&F	213/7	
Webb E	1/5 Bedfordshire	Pte	06/04/18	Cowardice	Not Conf	Egypt	213/22	
Webb Henry J	2 KO Yorks LI	Pte	13/10/17	Desertion x2	XXX 31/10/17	F&F	213/18	798
Webb J	1 Loyal N Lancs	Pte	24/08/15	Sleeping	1yr HL	F&F	213/4	
Webber W	45 Australian IF	Pte	22/12/16	Desertion	10yrs PS		213/13	
Webber W	1 Border	Pte	28/05/17	Desertion	10yrs PS	F&F	213/15	

Name	Unit	Rank	Date	Offence	Final sentence	Location	Ref	Note
Webster J	2 KOR Lancaster	L/Cpl	20/09/16	Desertion	5yrs PS	Salonika	213/11	
Webster JA	32 Royal Fus	Pte	29/03/17	Desertion	10yrs PS	F&F	213/14	615
Weeks H	15 R Irish Rifles	Rfm	30/03/17	Desertion	15yrs PS	F&F	213/14	616
Weightman J	9 Black Watch	Pte	18/06/16	Desertion	5yrs PS	F&F	213/9	
Weightman J	9 Black Watch	Pte	18/09/16	Desertion	5yrs PS	F&F	213/11	
Wells A	3 Middlesex	Pte	10/07/15	Sleeping	3yrs PS	F&F	213/4	
Wells F	1/21 London	Rfm	01/08/17	Desertion	10yrs PS	F&F	213/16	713
Welsh C	8 Canadian EF	Pte	21/08/16	Desertion	5yrs PS	F&F	213/11	431
Welsh C	8 Canadian EF	Pte	12/02/18	Desertion	XXX 06/03/18	F&F	213/20	876
Welsh M	1 N Staffordshire	Pte	18/03/15	Cowardice	10yrs PS	F&F	213/3	
Welsh T	10 Royal Fus	Pte	13/08/18	Desertion	5yrs PS	F&F	213/25	
Welsh Thomas	Civilian	Sinn Fein	03/05/16	Rebellion	10yrs PS	Dublin	213/8	241
Wessell M	47 Australian IF	Pte	27/06/17	Cowardice	10yrs PS		213/16	
West J	8 R Berkshire	Pte	31/01/18	Desertion	5yrs PS	F&F	213/20	
Westaby A	1 Northumb Fus	Pte	27/02/18	Desertion	5yrs PS	F&F	213/20	
Weston G	12 Middlesex	Pte	11/07/16	Desertion	5yrs PS	F&F	213/11	
Westwood Arthur H	8 E Surrey	Pte	27/10/17	Desertion	XXX 23/11/17	F&F	213/18	811
Wheat H	1 Lincolnshire	Pte	31/12/14	Cowardice	5yrs PS	F&F	213/3	
Wheeldon JF	1 Lincolnshire	Pte	12/12/14	Quitting/Sleeping	5yrs PS	F&F	213/3	
Wheelton C	1 Middlesex	Pte	17/09/16	Desertion	5yrs PS	F&F	213/11	
Whicker WH	RE	Spr	07/07/17	Desertion	10yrs PS		213/16	
Whincup A	4 Dragoon Gds	Pte	04/09/14	Sleeping	2yrs HL	F&F	213/2	4
Whitbread W	1/5 Bedfordshire	Pte	06/04/18	Cowardice	Not Conf	Egypt	213/22	
Whitchard PG	2 Welsh	Pte	24/04/18	Desertion	5yrs PS	F&F	213/22	
White C J	RFA	Gnr	04/02/18	Desertion	5yrs PS		213/20	
White E	25 Australian IF	Pte	01/12/16	Desertion	10yrs PS		213/13	
White J	1 R Irish Fus	Pte	26/06/15	Desertion	2yrs HL	F&F	213/4	
White J	RFA	Dvr	28/09/15	Disobedience	Not Conf		213/5	
White J	1 R Irish Fus	Pte	03/04/16	Desertion	10yrs PS	F&F	213/8	
White J	9 Rifle Bde	Rfm	18/10/16	Desertion	10yrs PS	F&F	213/12	
White J	Leinster (att 1 R Dublin)	Pte	12/09/18	Desertion	10yrs PS	F&F	213/25	
White W	1 Hampshire	Pte	10/01/16	Desertion	10yrs PS	F&F	213/7	
Whitehead EG	13 R Welsh Fus	Pte	18/09/16	Quitting	10yrs PS	F&F	213/11	452
Whitehead H	1/10 Manchester	Pte	29/05/15	Cowardice	5yrs PS	Mesopotamia	213/4	
Whitehouse AE	1 Worcestershire	Pte	11/06/16	Desertion	15yrs PS	F&F	213/9	
Whitfield S	6 R W Kent	Pte	03/08/16	Cowardice +	10yrs PS	F&F	213/11	414
Whittaker J	1 Dorset	Pte	29/08/15	Sleeping	10yrs PS	F&F	213/5	
Whittaker R	1/4 E Lancs	Pte	03/01/16	Cowardice	2yrs HL	Gallipoli	213/8	
Whittle A	2 Dragoon Gds	Pte	23/08/14	Sleeping	2yrs HL	F&F	213/2	
Whittle T	7 N Staffordshire	Pte	18/01/16	Cowardice	7yrs PS	Gallipoli [?]	213/7	158
Whitworth W	RFA	Pte	21/08/17	Desertion	5yrs PS		213/16	
Whyte J	2 Yorks	Pte	27/10/18	Desertion	15yrs PS	F&F	213/26	
Wickens A	9 Rifle Bde	Cpl (L/S)	04/02/18	Murder	XXX 07/03/18	F&F	213/20	872
Widdows R	19 R Welsh Fus	Pte	17/07/17	Desertion	5yrs PS	F&F	213/16	700
Wiggham S	2 York & Lancaster	Pte	30/06/16	Desertion	10yrs PS	F&F	213/10	
Wigley J	2 S Staffordshire	Pte	07/10/15	Desertion	10yrs PS	F&F	213/6	
Wigmore A	7 Gloucestershire	Pte	12/01/16	Sleeping	5yrs PS	Gallipoli [?]	213/7	148
Wild Arthur	18 W Yorks	Pte	21/08/16	Desertion	XXX 05/09/16	F&F	213/10	432
Wilden H	1/5 Suffolk	Pte	06/09/18	Violence +	Not Conf	Egypt	213/27	973
Wiles W	2 Royal Fus	Pte	26/04/18	Desertion	10yrs PS	F&F	213/21	
Wilhams R	1 Somerset LI	Pte	18/05/17	Striking	2yrs HL	F&F	213/15	
Wilkes A	Kings Shropshire LI	Pte	09/12/17	Desertion	5yrs PS		213/19	
Wilkes H	8 N Staffordshire	Pte	07/12/16	Disobedience	15yrs PS	F&F	213/12	
Wilkinson E	4 KRRC	Rfm	14/10/15	Sleeping	1yr HL	F&F	213/6	
Wilkinson G	2 Essex	Pte	01/07/15	Desertion	3yrs PS	F&F	213/4	
Wilkinson W	RFA	Dvr	16/04/15	Desertion	5yrs PS	F&F	213/3	64
Wilks H	2 R Warwickshire	Pte	07/02/15	Desertion +	3mos FP1	F&F	213/3	36
Williams DG	14 Welsh	Pte	22/01/16	Sleeping	Quashed	F&F	213/7	162
Williams DH	9 R Welsh Fus	Pte	27/04/17	Desertion	10yrs PS	F&F	213/15	
Williams E	1 S Wales Bdrs	Pte	04/04/16	Desertion	5yrs PS	F&F	213/8	
Williams G	4 Royal Fus	Pte	26/10/18	Desertion	5yrs PS	F&F	213/25	
Williams Harry	1/9 London	Rfm	13/12/17	Desertion	XXX 28/12/17	F&F	213/19	843
Williams J	2/4 Oxon & Bucks LI	Pte	04/12/18	Desertion	5yrs PS	F&F	213/26	
Williams John	Civilian	Sinn Fein	03/05/16	Rebellion	10yrs PS	Dublin	213/8	242
Williams L	2 E Surrey	Pte	14/02/15	Desertion	1yr HL	F&F	213/3	
Williams T	13 Welsh	Pte	03/01/17	Desertion	10yrs PS	F&F	213/13	569
Williams T	RGA	Gnr	10/09/18	Desertion	10yrs PS		213/25	
Williams W	16 Lancers	Pte	01/10/14	Sleeping	2yrs HL	F&F	213/2	

Name	Unit	Rank	Date	Offence	Final sentence	Location	Ref	Note
Williams W	8 Somerset LI	Pte	10/09/16	Desertion	3yrs PS	F&F	213/11	
Williams WW	10 KO Yorks LI	Pte	24/06/17	Quitting	10yrs PS	F&F	213/15	
Willis Frank	RFA	Gnr	17/05/19	Murder	XXX 27/05/19	F&F	213/29	1011
Willis J	2 Wiltshire	Pte	13/06/18	Desertion x2	15 yrs PS	F&F	213/23	923
Willmot B	1 E Surrey	Pte	02/11/16	Desertion	3yrs PS	F&F	213/12	
Willoughby HO	5 Lincolnshire	Pte	15/05/15	Sleeping	3yrs PS	F&F	213/4	
Willoughby JW	2 R Berkshire	Pte	05/06/15	Sleeping	2yrs HL	F&F	213/4	
Wilson [?] CA	5 British West Indies	Pte	01/08/18	Striking x2	5yrs PS		213/26	956
Wilson A	1 R Irish Rifles	Pte	26/11/18	Desertion x2	10yrs PS	F&F	213/27	
Wilson EW	RGA	Gnr	04/09/17	Desertion	5yrs PS		213/17	
Wilson F	2 Bedfordshire	Pte	03/07/17	Desertion	10yrs PS	F&F	213/16	
Wilson H	4 A&S Hdrs	Pte	27/03/15	Desertion	15yrs PS	UK	213/3	54
Wilson H	4 A&S Hdrs	Pte	26/03/16	Desertion	PS Life	UK	213/8	198
Wilson H	7 R Irish Fus	Pte	02/08/16	Desertion	5yrs PS	F&F	213/10	
Wilson H	7/8 R Irish Fus	Pte	25/04/17	Desertion	Not Conf	F&F	213/15	
Wilson H	11 R Warwickshire	Pte	16/08/17	Desertion	10yrs PS	F&F	213/17	
Wilson H	1/20 London	Pte	08/10/17	Desertion	15yrs PS	F&F	213/19	793
Wilson H	100 MGC	Pte	22/11/17	Desertion x2	5yrs PS		213/19	
Wilson HF	16 Lancers	Pte	10/06/15	Sleeping	2yrs HL	F&F	213/4	73
Wilson J	5 Cameron Hdrs	Pte	07/01/16	Desertion	10yrs PS	F&F	213/7	
Wilson J	4 Canadian Mtd Rifles	Pte	13/02/18	Desertion	15yrs PS	F&F	213/20	
Wilson James H	4 Canadian EF	Pte	21/06/16	Desertion	XXX 09/07/16	F&F	213/9	380
Wilson JH	38 Canadian EF	Pte	25/07/17	Desertion	5yrs PS	F&F	213/16	
Wilson P	Civilian	Sinn Fein	04/05/16	Rebellion	3yrs PS	Dublin	213/8	274
Wilson PC	19 Durham LI	Pte	30/12/16	Cowardice	10yrs PS	F&F	213/13	565
Wilson T	1/5 W Riding	Pte	12/10/16	Desertion	5yrs PS	F&F	213/12	
Wilson W	Civilian	Sinn Fein	04/05/16	Rebellion	3yrs PS	Dublin	213/8	275
Wilson W	9 Liverpool	Pte	16/05/17	Desertion	10yrs PS		213/15	
Wilson W	2 Scottish Rifles	Pte	16/07/17	Desertion	10yrs PS	F&F	213/16	
Wilton Jesse	15 Sherwood Fstrs	Cpl	02/08/16	Quitting	XXX 17/08/16	F&F	213/10	413
Winter E	1 Essex	Pte	29/10/15	Disobedience	3mos FP1	Gallipoli	213/6	
Winter F	1 R Scots Fus	Pte	15/06/15	Desertion	10yrs PS	F&F	213/4	
Wishart J	7 R Inniskilling Fus	Pte	31/05/17	Desertion x2	XXX 15/06/17	F&F	213/15	665
Woitytzka W	German Army	POW	23/09/18	Striking +	1yr HL		213/26	981
Wolfe J	7 R Munster Fus	Pte	12/09/15	Desertion	Not Conf	Gallipoli	213/5	
Wood FW	1/6 Manchester (att RE)	Pte	28/09/17	Desertion	10yrs PS	Mesopotamia	90/7	779
Wood H	1 Lincolnshire	Pte	31/12/14	Cowardice	10yrs PS	F&F	213/3	
Wood H	12 KRRC	Rfm	29/03/17	Desertion	5yrs PS	F&F	213/15	
Wood J	2 R Scots	Pte	28/05/18	Desertion	10yrs PS	F&F	213/22	
Wood L	1/6 London	Rfm	19/02/18	Desertion	5yrs PS	F&F	213/20	
Wood T	2 Northumb Fus	Pte	01/04/18	Sleeping	2yrs HL	Salonika	213/21	
Wood T	12 E Surrey	Pte	16/07/18	Desertion	10yrs PS	F&F	213/24	944
Wood W	7 Highland LI	Pte	28/05/17	Desertion	5yrs PS	F&F	213/16	
Woodfield A	9 Rifle Bde	Rfm	10/10/16	Cowardice	10yrs PS	F&F	213/12	
Woodfield F	1/19 London	Pte	27/09/17	Desertion	5yrs PS	F&F	213/17	776
Woodhead J	18 Manchester	Pte	22/02/16	Sleeping	3yrs PS	F&F	213/8	180
Woodhouse G	7 Border	Pte	11/09/16	Desertion	5yrs PS	F&F	213/11	
Woodhouse G	7 Border	Pte	21/12/16	Desertion	5yrs PS	F&F	213/13	
Woodhouse G	7 Border	Pte	08/03/18	Desertion	5yrs PS	F&F	213/21	
Woodhouse J	12 KRRC	Rfm	26/06/16	Desertion	10yrs PS	F&F	213/9	
Woodhouse John	12 KRRC	Rfm	17/09/17	Desertion	XXX 04/10/17	F&F	213/17	763
Wooding E	2 R Warwickshire	Pte	18/10/17	Desertion	10yrs PS	F&F	213/18	
Woods CM	55 Canadian EF	Pte	03/08/16	Insubordination	5yrs PS	F&F	213/10	
Woods E	9 Rifle Bde	Rfm	04/04/16	Sleeping	5yrs PS	F&F	213/8	
Woods WJ	7 R Irish Fus	Pte	09/06/16	AWOL	5yrs PS	F&F	213/9	
Woolley F	10 R W Surrey	Pte	08/02/18	Desertion x2	15yrs PS	Italy	213/20	874
Wootton G	1 Devon	Pte	07/04/15	Desertion	10yrs PS	F&F	213/4	
Worgan F	5 Loyal N Lancs	Pte	23/10/16	Desertion	10yrs PS	F&F	213/12	
Worsley Ernest	2 Middlesex	Pte	08/10/17	Desertion	XXX 22/10/17	F&F	213/17	794
Worsley J	17 Lancs Fus	Pte	15/12/16	Quitting	15yrs PS	F&F	213/13	533
Wright	KOR Lancaster	Pte	04/06/15	Cowardice	Quashed		213/4	
Wright AE	RFA	Gnr	11/01/15	Sleeping	10yrs PS		213/3	
Wright FE	9 Gloucestershire	Pte	02/05/17	Violence	5 Yrs PS	Salonika	213/16	645
Wright Frederick	1 R W Surrey	Pte	10/01/17	Desertion	XXX 28/01/17	F&F	213/13	572
Wright H	6 R Marines	Pte	04/10/19	Disobedience	5yrs PS	N Russia	213/30	
Wright J	1 York & Lancaster	Pte	05/04/15	Sleeping	5yrs PS	F&F	213/4	
Wright J	2/2 London	Pte	07/11/17	Insub+	10yrs PS	F&F	213/18	824
Wright W	7 Lincolnshire	Pte	08/06/16	Striking	5yrs PS	F&F	213/9	

Name	Unit	Rank	Date	Offence	Final sentence	Location	Ref	Note
Wycherley William	2 Manchester	Pte	13/08/17	Desertion x2	XXX 12/09/17	F&F	213/17	727
Wyles C	2 Yorks	Pte	18/10/18	Desertion	10yrs PS	F&F	213/26	
Wyman A	60 Canadian EF	L/Cpl	05/09/16	Quitting	5yrs PS	F&F	213/11	
Wyniger G	3 Rifle Bde	Rfm	10/09/17	Desertion	10yrs PS	F&F	213/17	
Yang Ch'ing Shan	Chinese Lab Corps	Coolie	14/06/18	Against Inhab	XXX 26/06/18	F&F	213/24	927
Yarnold Anthony	3 Worcestershire	Pte	16/06/16	Desertion	2yrs HL	F&F	213/10	
Yates F	4 Grenadier Gds	Pte	10/09/17	Desertion	Not Conf	F&F	213/17	
Yazagi MH	Civilian		23/05/16	Treason	XXX	Macedonia	213/12	318
Yeoman W	1/12 London	Rfm	01/03/17	Desertion	15yrs PS	F&F	213/14	600
Yeoman Walter	1/12 London	Rfm	03/06/17	Desertion x2	XXX 03/07/17	F&F	213/15	668
Youll G	18 Northumb Fus	Pte	28/11/16	Desertion	10yrs PS	F&F	213/12	
Young Elsworth	25 Canadian EF	Pte	19/10/16	Desertion	XXX 29/10/16	F&F	213/12	486
Young G	2 R Irish Rifles	Rfm	27/03/15	Desertion	15yrs PS	F&F	213/3	
Young J	5 Yorks	Pte	02/03/18	Desertion	3yrs PS	F&F	213/21	
Young N	2 Canadian EF	Pte	15/07/16	Disobedience	2yrs HL	F&F	213/10	
Young P J	58 Canadian EF	Pte	07/04/17	Desertion	15yrs PS	F&F	213/14	
Young R	2 R Berkshire	Cpl	08/05/18	Desertion	10yrs PS	F&F	213/23	
Young Robert	11 Worcestershire	Pte	10/09/18	Desertion	XXX 18/09/18	Salonika	213/25	976
Zahab Salama MAE	Civilian		25/08/21	Murder	20yrs PS	Egypt	213/34	1092
Ziff S	38 Royal Fus	Pte	17/07/18	Sleeping	10yrs PS	Egypt	213/26	
Zorn F	78 Canadian EF	Pte	05/06/18	Desertion	10yrs PS	F&F	213/23	
Zuk G	38 Canadian EF	Pte	06/09/17	Desertion	5yrs PS	F&F	213/17	

Appendix: table of death sentences and executions

Regiment	Death sentences	Executions
Cavalry (all units)	26	0
Royal Artillery (all units)	104	13
Royal Engineers	13	4
Coldstream Guards	8	1
Grenadier Guards	12	0
Scots Guards	2	1
Irish Guards	7	3
Welsh Guards	4	0
Royal Scots	47	7
Royal West Surrey	29	3
East Kent	27	5
Royal Lancaster	41	5
Northumberland Fusiliers	66	8
Royal Warwickshire	51	5
Royal Fusiliers	64	8
Liverpool	62	6
Norfolk	22	1
Lincolnshire	32	3
Devonshire	14	1
Suffolk	16	1
Somerset Light Infantry	4	2
West Yorkshire	44	12
East Yorkshire	29	2
Bedfordshire	22	0
Leicestershire	34	2
Royal Irish	12	0
Yorkshire	30	2
Lancashire Fusiliers	52	8
Royal Scots Fusiliers	48	5
Cheshire	25	6
Royal Welsh Fusiliers	27	4
South Wales Borderers	23	3
King's Own Scottish Borderers	15	2
Scottish Rifles	34	5
Royal Inniskilling Fusiliers	29	5
Gloucestershire	26	0
Worcestershire	47	8
East Lancashire	31	1
East Surrey	53	5
Duke of Cornwall's Light Infantry	18	1
West Riding	22	1
Border	17	3
Royal Sussex	19	3
Hampshire	14	1
South Staffordshire	33	4
Dorsetshire	7	2
South Lancashire	25	6
Welsh	34	6
Royal Highlanders	28	5
Oxford & Bucks. Light Infantry	4	0
Essex	39	3
Nottinghamshire & Derbyshire	39	8
Loyal North Lancashire	31	5
Northamptonshire	14	2
Royal Berkshire	26	3
Royal West Kent	15	2
Yorkshire Light Infantry	49	3
Shropshire Light Infantry	9	0
Middlesex	49	8
King's Royal Rifle Corps	57	11
Wiltshire	15	3
Manchester	63	7
North Staffordshire	49	2
York & Lancaster	53	8
Durham Light Infantry	70	7
Highland Light Infantry	59	5
Seaforth Highlanders	16	1
Gordon Highlanders	17	3
Cameron Highlanders	10	3
Royal Irish Rifles	63	5
Royal Irish Fusiliers	29	2
Connaught Rangers	17	1
Argyll & Sutherland Highlanders	34	1
Leinster	23	3
Royal Munster Fusiliers	37	2
Royal Dublin Fusiliers	22	3
Rifle Brigade	50	3
Honourable Artillery Coy. T/F	0	0
Monmouthshire T/F	2	0
Cambridgeshire T/F	1	0
London T/F	63	5
Herefordshire T/F	0	0
Machine Gun Corps	55	3
Army Service Corps	14	1
Royal Army Medical Corps	12	0
D A C	14	0
Royal Naval Division	7	1
Total	2,699	293

Notes

1 Swedish citizen. GCM; DORA 1914, Reg. 48
2 Uraguayan citizen. GCM; DORA 1914, Reg. 48
3 GCM; DORA 1914, Reg. 48. Brazilian citizen. See also PRO WO71/1313
4 R Irish Dragoons
5 Aged 19. From Catford. Listed as 'died of wounds'. See also PRO WO71/387
6 Aged 20. See also PRO WO71/388
7 Aged 33. See also PRO WO71/389
8 Inniskilling Dragoons
9 R Irish Dragoons
10 aka Charles A Inglis. German citizen. GCM; Guildhall, Westminster; DORA 1914, Reg. 48. See also PRO WO71/1236
11 Inniskilling Dragoons
12 Inniskilling Dragoons
13 Inniskilling Dragoons
14 Prince of Wales' Dragoons
15 Aged 26. Mother: Mrs Elizabeth Browne, Greene St. Ingatestone, Essex. See also PRO WO71/390
16 Aged 20. Parents: Thomas & Emily Ball, 112 Lancefield St, Queens Park, London. See also PRO WO71/392
17 Aged 26. Brother: James Sheffield, 42 Franklin St, S Tottenham, London. See also PRO WO71/391
18 + Threatening
19 Aged 23. Parents: Mr & Mrs W. Latham, Islington, London. Husband of Elizabeth Latham, 5/69 Gt. Lister St, Nechells, Birmingham. See also PRO WO71/393
20 + Forgery
21 + Threatening + Insubordination
22 + Cowardice
23 Aged 27. Described as 'an excellent soldier' by unit commander. See also PRO WO71/395
24 Aged 22. See also PRO WO71/394
25 Aged 19. See also PRO WO71/396
26 Aged 17. See also PRO WO71/397
27 See also PRO WO71/397
28 See also PRO WO71/398
29 + Losing property
30 Aged 23. See also PRO WO71/400
31 Kensington Bn + Sec 40, behaviour prejudicial to discipline
32 Aged 20. See also PRO WO71/401
33 Discharged 22/04/16
34 Aged 20. See also PRO WO71/399
35 + Sec 20 ie Permitting prisoner to escape
36 + Sec 20 ie Permitting prisoner to escape
37 + Absence
38 + AWOL. Retried 10/02/15
39 + AWOL. Retrial: 10/02/15
40 + AWOL. Retrial from 08/02/15
41 + AWOL. Retrial from 08/02/15
42 Londonderry
43 Banff & Donside Bn
44 Possibly from Invergordon. See also PRO WO71/405
45 See also PRO WO71/404
46 Aged 24. See also PRO WO71/402
47 Aged 24. See also PRO WO71/403
48 + Cowardice
49 Aged 26. See also PRO WO71/406
50 Prince of Wales' R Lancers
51 Fired on British troops after surrendering. Rank of Gefreiter (L Cpl)
52 Not guilty of Desertion
53 Aged 20. See also PRO WO71/407
54 Extra Reserve Bn

55 Aged 19. Shot 29/08/17 for Desertion. Born: Liverpool. Son of Mrs Sarah Stewart, 12 Bentick St. Kilmarnock
56 Aged 19. See also PRO WO71/411
57 Aged 20. Son of Charles & Harriet Fox, 45 The Causeway, Chippenham, Wiltshire. See also PRO WO71/408
58 + Theft. See also PRO WO71/409
59 Aged 21. See also PRO WO71/414
60 Aged 22. Son of Nathaniel Troughton, 14 Ash Grove, Stoney Stanton Rd, Coventry. See also PRO WO71/413
61 + Escaping
62 Aged 20. See also PRO WO71/410
63 See also PRO WO71/412
64 See also PRO WO71/412
65 Shot at Sultan Hussein, British-backed Egyptian ruler
66 Aged 21. Shot 22/05/16 for Desertion. Born Pulborough. Son of Charles Alfred & Fanny Burrell, Mill House, Fishbourne, Chichester
67 Aged 19. Listed as 'Killed in Action'. Previous offence commuted (first such case). See also PRO WO71/427
68 Aged 31. Armentieres. MID (posthumous). Parents:James & Hanna Taylor Chisholm, Heaton. Wife: (Janet) emigrated to Manitoba, Canada. See also PRO WO71/415
69 + Escaping
70 See also PRO WO71/416
71 Aged 19. See also PRO WO71/417
72 Aged 21. See also PRO WO71/420
73 The Queen's Bn
74 Aged 27. Parents: James William & Ann Beaumont, 35 Russell St, Cambridge. See also PRO WO71/418
75 Aged 21. Listed as 'died'. Born Greenwich S.E. London. Domicile: Gravesend, Kent. See also PRO WO71/419
76 + Striking
77 Reserve Bn
78 Aged 24. Arrested in Dover. See also PRO WO71/421
79 Aged 21. See also PRO WO71/431
80 Aged 34. See also PRO WO71/422
81 Aged 17. See also PRO WO71/424
82 Aged 20. See also PRO WO71/433
83 See also PRO WO71/429
84 GCM. Guildhall, Westminster
85 Aged 30. See also PRO WO71/428
86 Isle of Man Bn + Quitting
87 Isle of Man Bn + Quitting
88 Aged 29. Parents: James & Emma Fellows, 65 Moseley Rd, B'ham. Wife: Mary Annie Crosby, 5 Court, 5 House, Dymoke St, Birmingham. See also PRO WO71/426
89 Aged 32. See also PRO WO71/426
90 Aged 31. Parents: Mr & Mrs Edward Robin, 1 Back, 120 Long Acre, Nechells, Birmingham. See also PRO WO71/425
91 Aged 25. See also PRO WO71/425
92 Dutch citizen. GCM. Guildhall, Westminster; DORA 1914 Reg. 48. See also PRO WO71/1312
93 Dutch citizen. GCM; Guildhall, Westminster; DORA 1914. Reg. 48. See also PRO WO71/1312
94 Wellington Bn Journalist. KIA 08/08/15
95 Leeds Rifles Bn
96 Aged 23. See also PRO WO71/430
97 The King's Bn
98 Leeds Rifles

99 Pioneer Bn
100 Ardwick Bn
101 Renfrewshire Bn
102 Retrial
103 + Quitting
104 Ardwick Bn
105 Aged 27. See also PRO WO71/432
106 Hackney Bn
107 Pioneer Bn
108 See also PRO WO71/433
109 Pioneer Bn
110 Aged 21. + Theft x4, Civil x2. Born: E London. Mother: Mrs Pilling, 142 Mortlake Rd. Prince Regents Lane, London. See also PRO WO71/436
111 Offence unspecified
112 Conviction quashed following act of gallantry
113 Conviction quashed following act of gallantry
114 See also PRO WO71/435
115 Aged 30. False surname. Parents: Henry William (decd) & Margaret Ann Irish, 4 Salt Lane, Salisbury, Wilts. Listed as'KIA'. See also PRO WO71/434
116 Aged 37. See also PRO WO71/434
117 Fife Bn
118 + Threatening + Insubordination
119 Offence unspecified
120 Pseudonym; real identity unknown. GCM; DORA 1914, Reg. 48. US citizen. See also PRO WO71/1238
121 Renfrewshire Bn
122 Aged 25. Shot 01/10/17 for Desertion. Parents: Arthur & Louisa Mackness, 3 Dundonald Rd. Leicester
123 Att to Life Gds
124 + Drunk
125 Killindoni, East Africa
126 Argyleshire Bn
127 Danish citizen. GCM; DORA 1914, Reg. 48
128 Aged 28. See also PRO WO71/437
129 Fife Bn
130 Mafia Island, East Africa. Poisoned garrison water supply
131 Mafia Island, East Africa. Failed to inform British of enemy positions
132 Aged 21. Shot 22/10/17 for Desertion. Known as 'Harry'. Wife: Gladys May Lloyd Jones Rigby
133 Aged 24. Son of Daniel & Charlotte Salter, Bridgewater, Somerset. See also PRO WO71/439
134 Dundee Bn
135 Aged 20. Pleaded Guilty. Son of Michael & Mary Downey, 1 Kellys Range, Wiyes Fields, Limerick. Ireland. Attached to ANZAC. See also WO71/441
136 Aged 19. Parents:(late) Samuel James & Anne Dennis, Cheetham Hill, Manchester. First XXX confirmed by Haig as C in C. See also PRO WO71/430
137 + Insubordination
138 East Belfast Bn
139 See also PRO WO71/442
140 Aged 21. See also PRO WO71/438
141 Attached to ANZAC. + Escaping
142 Aged 20. XXX 15/02/16 for further offence. + Disobedience
143 Indian Army
144 North Belfast Bn
145 Aged 27. XXX 24/02/16 for further offence
146 + Striking
147 Princess Charlotte of Wales Bn
148 Peninsula evacuated 8/1/16. Egypt?

149 Peninsula evacuated 8/1/16. Egypt?
150 Peninsula evacuated 8/1/16. Egypt?
151 Peninsula evacuated 8/1/16. Egypt?
152 Peninsula evacuated 8/1/16. Egypt?
153 Peninsula evacuated 8/1/16. Egypt?
154 Peninsula evacuated 8/1/16. Egypt?
155 Peninsula evacuated 8/1/16. Egypt?
156 Peninsula evacuated 8/1/16. Egypt?
157 Peninsula evacuated 8/1/16. Egypt?
158 Peninsula evacuated 8/1/16. Egypt?
159 West Belfast Bn
160 Aged 21. See also PRO WO71/433
161 + Disobedience
162 Swansea (football & cricket clubs) Bn
163 West Belfast Bn
164 2nd North Wales (Llandudno) Bn
165 Guilty of AWOL
166 Aged 20. Previous XXX sentence 30/12/15 suspended. See also PRO WO71/444
167 Extra Reserve Bn Ireland
168 Aged 20. Parents: James & Margaret Hunter, 55 Coronation St. North Shields, Northumberland. See also PRO WO71/445
169 Sheikh Saad. Indian Army
170 2nd Rhondda Bn
171 Aged 20. Born nr Canterbury. Parents' address: 10 Staplegate Place, Canterbury, Kent. See also PRO WO71/448
172 Aged 21. See also PRO WO71/447
173 Sportsman's Bn
174 Aged 27. Previous XXX sentence 05/01/16 suspende. Born: Kingston upon Thames. Se also PRO WO71/449
175 Aged 18. West Belfast Bn See also PRO WO71/450
176 Pioneer Bn
177 + Escaping
178 Aged 23. Born Stockton on Tees. Domicile:Darlington. See also PRO WO71/446
179 While drunk, killed friend. See also PRO WO71/451
180 3rd City Bn
181 See also PRO WO71/452
182 North Belfast Bn
183 Aged 19. Father: John McCracken. North Belfast Bn. See also PRO WO71/453
184 West Belfast Bn
185 Son of Mr Templeton, 12 Enfield St. Belfast. North Belfast Bn. See also PRO WO71/454
186 Aged 21. False surname. Son of Rebecca & Joseph Beverstein, 48 Anthony St., London E1. See also PRO WO71/456
187 See also PRO WO71/455
188 Shot 24/01/18 for Desertion
189 Aged 26. Arrested, Hornsey, London. See also PRO WO71/458
190 GCM. Hanged. See also PRO WO71/457
191 First Canadian shot. From Montreal
192 + Quitting
193 Peruvian citizen. GCM; DORA 1914, Reg. 48
194 Arrested at Ince, Lancs. See also PRO WO71/459
195 2nd City Bn
196 Extra Reserve Bn
197 Extra Reserve Bn
198 Extra Reserve Bn
199 + Quitting
200 See also PRO WO71/462
201 Aged 27. Parents: Mary & Moses Thompson. Wife:Florence Rossetta Hedley, 180 Canning St. Benwell Grove, Newcastle upon Tyne. See also PRO WO71/460
202 + Disobedience
203 + Threatening + Disobedience.
204 Aged 18. See also PRO WO71/461
205 See also PRO WO71/466
206 Indian Army
207 Aged 29. Listed as 'Killed in Action'. Arrested on Xmas Eve whilst with wife, Mary Ann Watts at home,144 Upper Frederick St, Liverpool. See also PRO WO71/463
208 Indian Army
209 Aged 20. See also PRO WO71/464
210 GCM; Assuit. + Desertion
211 Indian Army

212 Fife Bn
213 + Disobedience
214 West Ham Bn
215 See also PRO WO71/475
216 Aged 23. aka Hasemore.See also PRO WO71/465
217 Easter Rising, Dublin. PRO WO71/347 (currently closed) also refers
218 Easter Rising, Dublin
219 Easter Rising, Dublin
220 aka Ceannt Eamonn. Easter Rising, Dublin. PRO WO71/348 (currently closed) also refers
221 Easter Rising, Dublin. PRO WO71/346 (currently closed) also refers
222 aka McBride Sean. Easter Rising, Dublin. PRO WO71/350 (currently closed) also refers
223 Easter Rising, Dublin. PRO WO71/345 (currently closed) also refers
224 Easter Rising, Dublin
225 Easter Rising, Dublin
226 aka Daly. Easter Rising, Dublin. PRO WO71/344 (currently closed) also refers
227 aka Doherty. Easter Rising, Dublin. PRO WO71/358 (currently closed) also refers
228 Easter Rising, Dublin
229 Easter Rising, Dublin
230 Easter Rising, Dublin
231 Easter Rising, Dublin
232 Easter Rising, Dublin
233 Easter Rising, Dublin
234 Easter Rising, Dublin. PRO WO71/357 (currently closed) also refers
235 Easter Rising, Dublin. PRO WO71/358 (currently closed) also refers
236 Easter Rising, Dublin. PRO WO71/349 (currently closed) also refers
237 Easter Rising, Dublin
238 Easter Rising, Dublin
239 Easter Rising, Dublin
240 Easter Rising, Dublin
241 Easter Rising, Dublin
242 Easter Rising, Dublin
243 Easter Rising, Dublin
244 Easter Rising, Dublin
245 Easter Rising, Dublin
246 Easter Rising, Dublin
247 Easter Rising, Dublin
248 Easter Rising, Dublin
249 Easter Rising, Dublin
250 Easter Rising, Dublin
251 Indian Army
252 Easter Rising, Dublin
253 aka Dorrington. Easter Rising, Dublin
254 aka Heuston Sean. Easter Rising, Dublin. PRO WO71/351 (currently closed) also refers
255 Easter Rising, Dublin
256 Easter Rising, Dublin
257 Easter Rising, Dublin
258 Easter Rising, Dublin. PRO WO71/356 (currently closed) also refers
259 Easter Rising, Dublin. First woman elected as MP (1918)
261 Easter Rising, Dublin
262 Easter Rising, Dublin
263 Easter Rising, Dublin
264 Easter Rising, Dublin
265 aka Cornelius Colbert. Easter Rising, Dublin. PRO WO71/352 (currently closed) also refers
266 Easter Rising, Dublin
267 Easter Rising, Dublin
268 Easter Rising, Dublin
269 Aged 35. Address: 13 Sussex Rd, Watford, Herts. Parents: John & Ellen Parker. See also PRO WO71/367
270 Easter Rising, Dublin
271 Easter Rising, Dublin
272 Easter Rising, Dublin
273 Easter Rising, Dublin
274 Easter Rising, Dublin
275 Easter Rising, Dublin
276 Easter Rising, Dublin
277 Easter Rising, Dublin
278 Aged 21. Previous XXX suspended 30/04/15. See also PRO WO71/469

279 Easter Rising, Dublin
280 Easter Rising, Dublin
281 Easter Rising, Dublin
282 Easter Rising, Dublin
283 Easter Rising, Dublin. PRO WO71/353 (currently closed) also refers
284 Dundee Bn
285 Easter Rising, Dublin
286 Easter Rising, Dublin
287 Easter Rising, Dublin
288 Easter Rising, Dublin
289 Easter Rising, Dublin
290 Easter Rising, Dublin
291 Easter Rising, Dublin
292 Easter Rising, Dublin
293 Easter Rising, Dublin
294 aka Eamonn. Easter Rising, Dublin
295 Easter Rising, Dublin
296 Easter Rising, Dublin
297 Easter Rising, Dublin
298 Aged 44. + Escaping. Had 5 children. Son of Mrs M Davies, Lampha, Pembroke. See also PRO WO71/468
299 Easter Rising, Dublin. PRO WO71/354 (currently closed) also refers
300 aka MacDermott Sean. Easter Rising, Dublin. PRO WO71/355 (currently closed) also refers
301 From Enniscorthy. Easter Rising, Dublin
302 From Enniscorthy. Easter Rising, Dublin
303 From Enniscorthy. Easter Rising, Dublin
304 From Enniscorthy. Easter Rising, Dublin
305 aka de Lacy. From Enniscorthy. Easter Rising, Dublin
306 From Enniscorthy. Easter Rising, Dublin
307 + Insubordination
308 4th Salford Bn Bantam
309 From Galway. Easter Rising, Dublin
310 Easter Rising, Dublin
311 Easter Rising, Dublin
312 Aged 31. + Quitting. Parents: Samuel & Mary Holland, Northwich, Cheshire. See also PRO WO71/470
313 Karaissi, Macedonia
314 Aged 34. Londoner. See also PRO WO71/472
315 Aged 20. Stated to be of 'Poor intellect'. Bantam Bn. Sister: Mrs E Gray, 9 Rosevale Place, Leith, Edinburgh. See also PRO WO71/473
316 Karaissi, Macedonia
317 Karaissi, Macedonia
318 Karaissi, Macedonia
319 Aged 24. See also PRO WO71/471
320 Karaissi, Macedonia
321 Karaissi, Macedonia
322 Wife: R Swaine, 82 Herga Rd, Wealdstone, Middlesex. See also PRO WO71/474
323 2nd Birkenhead (Bantam) Bn
324 From Cambridge
325 From Pinner, Middlesex
326 From Barnet, Hertfordshire
327 From Sutton
328 2nd South Down Bn
329 4th City Bn
330 + Disobedience
331 See also PRO WO71/476
332 From Cambridge
333 From Pinner, Middlesex
334 From Barnet, Hertfordshire
335 From Sutton
336 + Quitting
337 5yrs remitted. GCM; Dublin; DORA 1914, Reg. 50
338 GCM; Dublin; DORA 1914, Reg. 50
339 GCM; Dublin; DORA 1914, Reg. 50
340 GCM; Dublin; DORA 1914, Reg. 50
341 From Pinner, Middlesex
342 From Luton
343 From Merton
344 From Burgess Hill, Sussex
345 From Stafford
346 From Petworth, Sussex
347 From Luton
348 East Belfast Bn
349 From Leeds
350 From Cleveland
351 From Leeds

352　From Darlington
353　From Darlington
354　From Stansford, near Ely
355　From York
356　From Cleveland
357　From Leeds
358　From Leeds
359　From Leeds
360　From Edmonton, Middlesex
361　From Conisborough
362　From Edmonton, Middlesex
363　From East Bolton, Sunderland
364　From Leeds
365　From Leeds
366　From Little Milton, Berkshire
367　From Tottenham
368　From Leeds
369　From Edmonton, Middlesex
370　From Edmonton, Middlesex
371　From Edmonton, Midlesex
372　GCM; Dublin; DORA 1914, Reg. 50
373　Pioneer Bn
374　Aged 21. See also PRO WO71/479
375　Indian Army
376　5th City Bn
377　See also PRO WO71/481
378　See also PRO WO71/477
379　See also PRO WO71/478
380　Born: Ireland. Ex-Connaught Rangers
381　See also PRO WO71/480
382　R Fus Bn
383　GCM; Londoner. Head injury affected behaviour
384　St Pancras Bn
385　+ Quitting
386　3rd Gwent (Bantam) Bn
387　Liverpool Irish Bn
388　Liverpool Irish Bn
389　See also PRO WO71/482
390　From Merseyside. Liverpool Irish Bn. See also PRO WO71/483
391　Liverpool Irish Bn
392　+ Escaping + damaging property
393　Aged 26. American, ex-US Army
394　Surrendered then killed British soldier with bomb
395　Aged 25. From Birmingham. Brother: G Grove, Providence Terrace, Friston St. Ladywood, Birmingham. See also PRO WO71/485
396　Indian Army
397　2nd Barnsley Bn
398　See also PRO WO71/484
399　Aged 20. Central Ontario Bn
400　Isle of Man Bn
401　Quashed by Sec of State on 23/08/16
402　Aged 36. Welbeck Rangers Bn. Had 5 children. aka Lawton. See also PRO WO71/486
403　Aged 22. Welbeck Rangers Bn See also PRO WO71/487
404　2nd Glamorgan (Bantam) Bn
405　Ross Highland Bn
406　Indian Army
407　Aged 25. Parents: Luger & Eugenie LaLiberte, 170 Ferdinand St., Montreal
408　Aged 27
409　Aged 27. See also PRO WO71/491
410　Aged 22. See also PRO WO71/490
411　Aged 24. Parents: Henry & Alice Nelson, 10 Back Adelaide Rd, Seaham Harbour. See also PRO WO71/488
412　Nottingham (Bantam) Bn
413　Aged 40. Nottingham (Bantam) Bn. See also PRO WO71/489
414　+ Disobedience
415　Canterbury Bn + Sleeping. Labourer. KIA 24/08/18
416　Indian Army
417　2nd Barnsley Bn
418　Shoreditch Bn
419　Central Ontario Bn
420　British Empire League (Pioneers) Bn
421　Sentence later reduced
422　Auckland Bn
423　Aged 28. Canterbury Bn. Labourer. Mother: M Hughes, Peter St, Wellington, NZ
424　Pioneer Bn

425　Pioneer Bn. See also PRO WO71/494
426　Aged 19. Son of John Bennett, 37 Vernon Rd, Bow, London. See also PRO WO71/492
427　Indian Army
428　See also PRO WO71/493
429　Aged 32. From Bradford. 2nd Bradford Pals Bn See also PRO WO71/495
430　Bantam Bn
431　Manitoba Bn. Shot 06/03/18 for Desertion
432　Aged 24. Policeman. Parents: Thomas Wild, Bradford, Yorks. 2nd Bradford Pals Bn. See also PRO WO71/496
433　See also PRO WO71/500
434　+ Sleeping
435　Aged 32. Father: Edwin Haddock, 21 Ranskill Rd, Tinsley Park, Sheffield, Yorks. Sheffield. See also PRO WO71/499
436　Accrington Pals
437　+ Quitting
438　Otago Bn. UK-born chemist
439　Indian Army
440　Aged 30. Father: Charles Depper, Rock Hill, Bromsgrove, Worcs. See also PRO WO71/501
441　Aged 30. Born Manchester. See also PRO WO71/497
442　Dundee Bn. See also PRO WO71/502
443　Indian Army
444　Manitoba Bn
445　Aged 27. Parents: Charles & Ann Rickman, 4 Carrington Terr. Milford on Sea, Hants. See also PRO WO71/498
446　Aged 23. From Bow. British Empire League (Pioneer) Bn. See also PRO WO71/503
447　St. Helens (Pioneer) Bn
448　Aged 37. Born Tasmania. Labourer. Otago Bn
449　Dundee Bn
450　Sheikh Saad. Indian Army
451　Reserve Bn. Remained in UK
452　1st North Wales Bn
453　+ AWOL. See also PRO WO71/538
454　Indian Army
455　Aged 22. Son of Archibald & Elizabeth Hamilton, 28 Stewartfield, Broxburn, West Lothian. See also PRO WO71/505
456　See also PRO WO71/506
457　4th City Bn
458　Pioneer Bn. See also PRO WO71/504
459　Basrah. Indian Army
460　3rd Glasgow Bn
461　Aged 21. From Stepney. See also PRO WO71/507
462　Aged 28. + Desertion. See also PRO WO71/508
463　Aged 23. See also PRO WO71/509
464　GCM; Blargies Prison riot
465　GCM; Blargies Prison riot
466　Aged 30. GCM; Blargies Prison riot. See also PRO WO71/510
467　GCM; Blargies Prison riot
468　GCM; Blargies Prison riot
469　GCM; Blargies Prison riot
470　GCM; Blargies Prison riot
471　Indian Army. Filahinyah (Fallahiyeh),
472　Born: St Phillips, Bristol. WIA June 1915. Nervous breakdown, Nov. 1915. Brother (same Bn) killed in action, 10/09/16
473　4th Glasgow (Bantam) Bn. See also PRO WO71/518
474　Aged 35. GCM. Blargies Prison riot. Australian, enlisted Dunedin. Mother: Mrs M Braithwaite, Auckland, NZ
475　GCM; Blargies Prison riot
476　GCM; Blargies Prison riot
477　FGCM recommended mercy. Said to be of 'low intellect'. See also PRO WO71/512
478　+ Quitting. Father: Mr A. Poole, 9 Bernard St Park, Sheffield. See also PRO WO71/530
479　GCM; Blargies Prison riot
480　Aged 23. See also PRO WO71/511
481　Kensington Bn
482　Kensington Bn
483　Glasgow Bn
484　2nd Rhondda Bn
485　Liverpool Irish Bn
486　Aged 19. Nova Scotia Bn Son of Mrs Emma Young, King Edward St, Glace Bay, Cape Breton,

Nova Scotia
487　Liverpool Irish Bn. See also PRO WO71/513
488　Aged 34. Wife & 3 children domiciled Keighley. Son of the late Robert & Margaret MacDonald of Cumberland. See also PRO WO71/514
489　4th Glasgow (Bantam) Bn. See also PRO WO71/519
490　4th City Bn
491　West Ham Bn
492　Wearside Bn
493　Wearside Bn
494　Aged 20. Orphan from Manchester. 3rd City Bn. See also PRO WO71/516
495　West Belfast Bn
496　Aged 27. Londoner. Domicile: East Grinstead. 3rd South Down Bn. See also PRO WO71/527
497　Aged 29. Parents: Ann & Henry John Ansted (decd), 9 Wood End Cottages, Northolt, Middlesex. See also PRO WO71/517
498　Bantam Bn
499　From Montreal. British Columbia Bn
500　South East Lancs (Bantam) Bn
501　Aged 22. Shot 09/02/18 for Desertion. Son of William Henry & Elizabeth Louisa Clarke, 20 Garrick St. Stanhope Rd. South Shields
502　See also PRO WO71/523
503　See also PRO WO71/521
504　St. Pancras Bn
505　Aged 20. Mother: Mrs M Moon, 5 Blue Coat School, Chester. See also PRO WO71/520
506　4th City Bn
507　4th City Bn
508　4th City Bn
509　4th City Bn
510　Dutch citizen. GCM; Guildhall, Westminster; DORA 1914, Regs. 48 & 18A
511　See also PRO WO71/528
512　Tyrone Volunteers Bn
513　Aged 23. 2nd Football Bn. Parents: William & Emily Simmonds, 18 Sidney Terrace, Bedfont Lane, Feltham, Middlesex. See also PRO WO71/522
514　South Belfast Bn
515　Public Schools Bn
516　Aged 24. Listed as 'Died of Wounds'. Clerk from Salford. Son of George Edward & Elizabeth Ann Ingham, Atherton Cottage, Lower Kersal, Manchester. 3rd City Bn. See also PRO WO71/526
517　Aged 21. Clerk from Salford. Wife:Mary Francis Longshaw, 21 Milnthorpe St, Pendleton. 3rd City Bn. See also PRO WO71/525
518　See also PRO WO71/524
519　Aged 31. Listed as 'died of wounds'. GCM; Poperinghe. History of shell-shock. Parents: Henry Skeffington & Florence Hope Gibson Poole, 2 Rectory Place, Guildford, Surrey. Born Nova Scotia. See also PRO WO71/1027
520　1st Public Works (Pioneers) Bn
521　Further conviction 12/08/18
522　West Belfast Bn
523　See also PRO WO71/529
524　Aged 24. Western Ontario Bn. Son of David & Emma Higgins, 24 Gwynne Ave. Toronto. Born Charlottetown, Prince Edward Island. 'Died of Wounds'
525　Extra Reserve Bn
526　GCM; Officer
527　Aged 21. GCM. History of shell-shock. Parents: May Constance Dyett, Rock Ferry, Cheshire & (late) Comdr WHR Dyett, RN
528　Aged 20. Kensington Bn. See also PRO WO71/531
529　Bn from Ayr/Kilmarnock. See also PRO WO71/532
530　Aged 25. Shot 06/11/17 for Desertion. Son of Henry & Elizabeth Hanna
531　South East Lancs (Bantam) Bn
532　South East Lancs (Bantam) Bn
533　South East Lancs (Bantam) Bn
534　Indian Army
535　Reserve Bn UK
536　2nd County (Bantam) Bn
537　Aged 25. 2nd County (Bantam) Bn. Coalminer. Wife & children. From Crook, Co. Durham. See

also PRO WO71/535

538 Aged 28. Born Ireland. Coachpainter. Auckland Bn
539 Tyneside Irish Bn
540 2nd County (Bantam) Bn
541 Bantam Bn
542 2nd County (Bantam) Bn
543 Aged 21. 2nd County (Bantam) Bn. Coalminer. Wife: M Goggins, 58 South St. Southmoor, Stanley, Co. Durham. See also PRO WO71/534
544 Aged 28. 2nd County (Bantam) Bn. Labourer with young daughter. Son of Malcolm & Johnina McDonald, 29 Hartleys Buildings, Millfield, Sunderland. See also PRO WO71/534
545 2nd County (Bantam) Bn
546 Aged 22. Shot 12/08/18 for Desertion: 21/06/17. Eastern Ontario Bn. Son of Albert & Fanny Ling, 1125 Dovercourt Rd. Toronto, Canada
547 1st Salford Pals Bn
548 2nd County (Bantam) Bn
549 2nd County (Bantam) Bn
550 2nd County (Bantam) Bn
551 2nd County (Bantam) Bn
552 2nd County (Bantam) Bn
553 2nd County (Bantam) Bn
554 2nd County (Bantam) Bn
555 2nd County (Bantam) Bn
556 2nd County (Bantam) Bn
557 2nd County (Bantam) Bn
558 2nd County (Bantam) Bn
559 2nd County (Bantam) Bn
560 2nd County (Bantam) Bn
561 2nd County (Bantam) Bn
562 2nd County (Bantam) Bn
563 2nd County (Bantam) Bn
564 1st Salford Pals Bn. See also PRO WO71/533
565 2nd County (Bantam) Bn
566 1st Birkenhead (Bantam) Bn
567 2nd County (Bantam) Bn
568 Shot 22/11/17 for Desertion
569 2nd Rhondda Bn
570 + Escaping
571 Indian Army
572 See also PRO WO71/544
573 Indian Army
574 Aged 20. Previous XXX sentence 11/16, suspended. See also PRO WO71/546
575 1st Glasgow (Tramways) Bn
576 Aged 30. 2nd Glasgow (Boys Bde) Bn. See also PRO WO71/540
577 See also PRO WO71/545
578 From Liverpool. See also PRO WO71/536
579 Pioneers Bn
580 Aged 42. See also PRO WO71/543
581 Aged 20. Parents: Edward & Lavinia Harris, 90 Nether Edge Rd, Sheffield. See also PRO WO71/542
582 Perthshire Bn
583 Aged 22. Brother (11 Suffolk) killed at Passchendaele. Son of Charles & Emma Hart, 101 Fore St, Ipswich, Suffolk. See also PRO WO71/537
584 Mother: Mrs Jane Murphy, Blackridge, West Lothian. See also PRO WO71/541
585 + Sleeping
586 Aged 22. 4th City Bn. See also PRO WO71/548
587 Aged 24. Indian Army. See also PRO WO71/631
588 Aged 22. Indian Army. See also PRO WO71/632
589 Aged 40. See also PRO WO71/630
590 Leeds Rifles
591 Tyneside Irish Bn
592 Bristol Bn
593 Aged 31. See also PRO WO71/550
594 Aged 23. Mother: Mrs E Rose. See also PRO WO71/547
595 Quebec Bn
596 US citizen. GCM; Guildhall, Westminster; DORA 1914, Regs. 48 & 18 (x2) & 18 A (x3)
597 See also PRO WO71/553
598 Aged 25. Kensington Bn
599 See also PRO WO71/549
600 Rangers Bn
601 Aged 38. Father of Mrs BM Major, 56 Blakes Road, Peckham, London. See also PRO

WO71/556

602 + Cowardice
603 Aged 21. See also PRO WO71/554
604 Retried 06/04/17
605 Labour Bn
606 South Belfast Bn
607 Aged 21. Shot on 15/06/17 for similar offence. Son of John & Eliza Allsop, 5 Club Row, Bagthorpe, Nottingham
608 Tyneside Irish Bn
609 7th City Bn
610 Son of Mr W Malyon, 1 Myrtle Villas, Miltoson St. Swanscombe, Kent. See also PRO WO71/551
611 Aged 21. See also PRO WO71/555
612 See also PRO WO71/552
613 Wearside Bn
614 + Disobedience. Rhondda Bn
615 East Ham Bn
616 North Belfast Bn
617 Shot 25/10/17 for Desertion
618 Aged 21
619 1st Barnsley Bn
620 + Quitting
621 + Quitting
622 + Quitting
623 1st Barnsley Bn
624 + Sec 40, ie Behaviour prejudicial to military discipline
625 + Quitting
626 Isle of Man Bn
627 Aged 21. Son of George H & Milly Carter, 143 Cumberland St. Toronto, Ontario. Canada
628 Aged 21. Retrial from 09/03/17. Son of Albert & Mary Lewis, 1 Factory Rd, Barking, Essex. See also PRO WO71/539
629 British Empire League. Pioneers
630 Leeds Rifles
631 Aged 33. Labourer. Otago Bn
632 6th City Bn
633 Bermondsey Bn
634 Bermondsey Bn
635 Tyneside Irish Bn
636 + Quitting. See also PRO WO71/575
637 + Disobedience
638 + Disobedience
639 + Escaping
640 Lonsdale Bn
641 Aged 20. See also PRO WO71/558
642 Aged 31. WIA x2 in 1915. 2nd Rhondda Bn. See also PRO WO71/559
643 Aged 31. Real name: Hogan. Co. Tyrone Volunteers. See also PRO WO71/557
644 Finsbury Bn
645 Bristol Bn
646 2nd Glamorgan (Bantam) Bn
647 Tyneside Irish Bn
648 Aged 20. Born Blackfriars, Glasgow. See also PRO WO71/560
649 Shot 30/08/17 for further offence
650 Finsbury Rifles
651 Grimsby Bn
652 Cambridge & Isle of Ely T/F
653 Grimsby Bn
654 Grimsby Bn
655 Grimsby Bn
656 See also PRO WO71/565
657 Aged 20. Retried 30/06/17 then shot
658 Shot 10/09/17 for further offence. Son of Mr C Bateman, 3 Kilton St. Sheffield. Yorks. Hallamshire Bn
659 Indian Army
660 Liverpool Irish Bn
661 R Fus
662 Liverpool Irish Bn
663 Aged 25. Previous XXX suspended 01/03/17. + Esc. Son of Mrs M E Mayers, 193 Morning Lane, London E9. See also PRO WO71/564
664 Aged 21. XXX 13/03/17 suspended. Brother recently KIA. Son of John & Eliza Allsop, 5 Club Row, Bagthorpe, Nottingham. See also PRO WO71/561
665 Aged 24. See also PRO WO71/563
666 Born: Barony, Glasgow. See also PRO WO71/577
667 + Escaping
668 Aged 22. Rangers Bn. See also PRO WO71/566

669 Kensington Bn
670 Aged 22
671 Aged 24. From Littlehampton. Possibly suffering from shell shock. See also PRO WO71/567
672 Aged 21
673 Aged 23. See also PRO WO71/571
674 Aged 24. See also PRO WO71/568
675 Aged 23. Londoner. Bermondsey Bn. See also PRO WO71/562
676 + Quitting
677 aka Thaudis. See also PRO WO71/574
678 R Fus
679 Aged 20. Labourer. Wellington Bn
680 Tyneside Scottish Bn
681 Aged 23. Previously wounded. Son of Rosena Elizabeth Hull, Fulham, London. See also PRO WO71/572
682 St Helens (Pioneer) Bn
683 1st Barnsley Bn
684 Sheffield Bn
685 Aged 28. Born: Bicton, Shropshire. Parents: George C & Sophia Blakemore, 3 St Georges St, Mountfields, Shrewsbury. See also PRO WO71/569
686 R Fus. See also PRO WO71/570
687 Aged 20. Retrial from 21/05/17. Mancunian. Son of William & Alice Ashton, Blackburn, Lancs. See also PRO WO71/573
688 Shoreditch Bn
689 Wandsworth Bn
690 Indian Army. Samarra(h). See also PRO WO71/633
691 Tyneside Scottish Bn
692 Aged 29. Born Australia. Labourer. Tunnelling Coy
693 St. Pancras Bn
694 Shot 19/08/17 for Desertion
695 East Africa. See also PRO WO71/576
696 Aged 26. Carter. Auckland Bn. WIA 17/08/17. Jailed 17/11/17
697 Reserve Bn, UK
698 Shot 15/11/17 for Desertion
699 Shot 19/09/17 for Desertion
700 Bantam Bn
701 Liverpool Irish Bn
702 See also PRO WO71/576
703 Indian Army
704 Lewisham Bn
705 1st Glasgow (Tramways) Bn
706 Tyneside Scottish Bn
707 Banff & Donside Bn
708 Sportsman's Bn
709 + Desertion x2
710 + Desertion
711 Ardwick Bn
712 Post Office Rifles
713 1st Surrey Rifles
714 City of Glasgow Bn
715 Previous XXX suspended 03/07/17. See also PRO WO71/578
716 See also PRO WO71/580
717 Tyneside Scottish Bn
718 Aged 33. Born Australia. Bridgebuilder. Auckland Bn. WIA 23/11/17. WIA 01/09/18. DOW 7/11/18
719 Aged 32 (?). Born Australia. Miner. Canterbury Bn
720 + Violence. See also PRO WO71/595
721 + Desertion
722 Hallamshire Bn
723 See also PRO WO71/585
724 Aged 21. From Houghton le Spring. Son of Robert Watts, 135 Lewis St., Middle Rainton, Co. Durham. See also PRO WO71/581
725 Aged 21. History of shell-shock. Previous XXX sentence suspended 04/04/15. See also PRO WO71/579
726 + Cowardice
727 Aged 24. Wife: May Wycherley, 18 Queen St. Cheetham Hill, Manchester. See also PRO WO71/591
728 Guilty of Absence only
729 Indian Army. Baghdad,
730 KIA 16/06/18
731 Renfrewshire Bn
732 Aged 26. Parents: James William & Elizabeth

Smith, 52 Noble St. Bolton, Lancs. See also PRO WO71/588

733 Aged 20. Parents: John James & Susanah Maria Abigail, 17 Distillery Yard, Oak St. Norwich. See also PRO WO71/592

734 Aged 19. See also PRO WO71/583

735 Father: Mr W Hyde, 35 Ridgedale St, Bow, London. See also PRO WO71/587

736 Previous XXX suspended 09/05/17. See also PRO WO71/584

737 Aged 25. aka Steadman. Parents: Henry Patrick & Sarah Stedman, Liverpool. See also PRO WO71/589

738 Norwegian citizen. GCM; Guildhall, Westminster

739 Aged 22. Parents: William & Harriet Wall, Hill Cottages, Brockleton, Tenbury, Worcs. See also PRO WO71/582

740 See also PRO WO71/586

741 2nd Rhondda Bn

742 Aged 40. Compositor, born Scotland. Otago Bn

743 + Disobedience + Escaping

744 Bristol Bn

745 Aged 30. Listed as 'killed in action'.Son of Mrs E Everill, 40 Mount Pleasant, Shelton, Staffs. Wife: Mrs L Everill, 7 Southampton St. Hanley, Stoke on Trent, Staffs. See also PRO WO71/593

746 Liverpool Irish Bn

747 Aged 38. Labourer. Auckland Bn

748 North Belfast Bn

749 North Belfast Bn

750 Previous XXX suspended 16/07/17. See also PRO WO71/590

751 + Desertion

752 North Belfast Bn

753 North Belfast Bn

754 Aged 32. Wife: D.C. Kirman, 10 Radnor St, Southsea, Portsmouth, Hants. See also PRO WO71/604

755 Aged 17. Parents: William & Ophelia Morris, Riversdale PO, St. Catherine, Jamaica. See also PRO WO71/594

756 Aged 19. Pre-war soldier from Kent. See also PRO WO71/609

757 Civil Service Rifles

758 R Fus

759 Aged 31. Etaples mutiny. Welsh coalminer. Wife: Dinah & children domiciled: Felling, Co. Durham.Tyneside Irish Bn. See also PRO WO71/599

760 Aged 22. Labourer. Born: Kiev, Russia. Enlisted Winnipeg. Manitoba Bn

761 Aged 25. Previous XXX suspended 09/10/15. See also PRO WO71/598

762 Blythswood Bn

763 See also PRO WO71/597

764 Ross Bn

765 Manitoba Bn

766 Manitoba Bn

767 Aged 23. Mother: Mrs Ward, 31 Society St, Glasgow. Wife: Fanny Watt. See also PRO WO71/601

768 West Ham Bn

769 Aged 33. Gentleman's servant. Wounded in both legs in July 1916. See also PRO WO71/616

770 Belgian citizen. GCM; Guildhall, Westminster

771 Aged 25. Parents: Henry Alfred & Mary Ann Taysum. See also PRO WO71/602

772 + Violence/Drunk

773 Indian Army. Amara

774 Indian Army. Amara

775 Sutherland & Caithness Bn

776 St. Pancras Bn

777 Rioter at Marseilles, 16/09/17. See also PRO WO71/600

778 Considered a 'good soldier' by own commanding officer. Stretcher bearer. Previous XXX suspended 02/04/17. See also PRO WO71/608

779 Indian Army. Amara

780 Aged 37. Londoner. Boer War veteran, emigrated to Canada. x2 Good Conduct Medals

781 + Insubordination

782 Aged 29. Born: Redhill, Surrey. Wife: Rebecca, 84 Dale Rd, Canning Town, London. See also PRO WO71/607

783 Divisional Ammunition Column

784 Tyneside Scottish Bn

785 Aged 28. Born: Brompton Ralph, Somerset. Previous service with SLI. Mother: Louisa Mudford, West Chinnock, Crewkerne, Somerset

786 Tyneside Scottish Bn

787 Tyneside Scottish Bn

788 Arts and Crafts Bn

789 Tyneside Irish Bn. See also PRO WO71/612

790 Blackheath & Woolwich Bn

791 Aged 19. Born Middlesborough. Twin brother killed, Ypres 10/10/17. Parents: Alexander & Catherine Nicholson, 11 Levin St., Middlesborough. See also PRO WO71/619

792 Aged 31. Born: Devonport. Parents: Richard (Customs official) & Julia Isabel Oyns. See also PRO WO71/613

793 Blackheath & Woolwich Bn

794 See also PRO WO71/605

795 Aged 31. Wounded:11/09/17 & allegedly 'acutely depressed'. Parents: William & Mary Turner, 62 First St, Bensham, Gateshead. Listed as 'died'. See also PRO WO71/606

796 Poplar & Stepney Rifles

797 Aged 30. Served as 'M Monaghan'. Real name Byrne, Stephen. Brother: Thomas Byrne, 32 Ushers Quay, Dublin. See also PRO WO71/613

798 See also PRO WO71/615

799 + Disobedience

800 Grimsby Bn

801 Aged 20. Londoner. Brother (Patrick) KIA 05/11/16. Church Lads Bde. See also PRO WO71/614

802 3rd County (Pioneer) Bn

803 Aged 24. See also PRO WO71/610

804 Aged 26. Previous XXX suspended 15/12/16. Parents: Henry & Elizabeth Hanna. See also PRO WO71/611

805 Manitoba Bn

806 Aged 22

807 6th City Bn

808 Aged 21. Known as 'Harry'. Previous XXX suspended (19/11/15). Wife: Gladys May Lloyd Jones Rigby. See also PRO WO71/618

809 Previous XXX suspended (13/07/17). See also PRO WO71/617

810 Civil Service Rifles

811 Aged 20. Parents: William & Ellen Westwood, 27A Leagrave Rd., Fulham, London. See also PRO WO71/625

812 + Disobedience

813 Leeds Rifles

814 Not recorded by WO71; no ref. in *Shot at Dawn*

815 Hackney Bn

816 Aged 20. Parents: Robert & Ada Smith, 16 Lord St., Pendleton, Manchester. See also PRO WO71/624

817 Aged 30. See also PRO WO71/620

818 Aged 21. Parents: Thomas (decd) & Ellen Foulkes. See also PRO WO71/623

819 See also PRO WO71/621

820 Tyneside Scottish Bn

821 Probably F&F (Nov. 1917 Bn moved to Italy)

822 Previous XXX suspended (03/01/17). See also PRO WO71/622

823 Aged 21. Father: John Lawrence, 101 Clifton Rd, South Norwood, London. See also PRO WO71/634

824 + Disibedience. R Fus (disbanded June 1916)

825 Shot 04/06/18 for Desertion

826 Indian Army. Tijdari,

827 Hackney Bn

828 Aged 25. Shot 10/08/18 for Desertion. Parents: Mary Ann & (late) Job Scholes

829 Aged 24. See also PRO WO71/626

830 4th Salford (Bantam) Bn

831 Hallamshire Bn

832 Tyneside Scottish Bn

833 Glamorgan Pioneer Bn

834 Aged 26. WIA at Neuve Chapelle. Invalided home 1916 (heart failure/nerves). See also PRO WO71/628

835 Manitoba Bn

836 Manitoba Bn

837 Manitoba Bn

838 Bantam Bn

839 Said to be 'a petty criminal & mental defective'. Medically examined. Wife: M A Hopkins, 6 Vine St., Birkenhead, Lancs. See also PRO WO71/635

840 Finsbury Rifles

841 Banff & Donside Bn

842 XXX for desertion 19/06/18

843 See also PRO WO71/637

844 Argyllshire Bn

845 Aged 18. Att rape, murdered victim's husband. See also PRO WO71/629

846 Liverpool Irish Bn

847 1st Barnsley Bn

848 Swansea (football & cricket clubs) Bn

849 1st Barnsley Bn

850 4th Salford (Bantam) Bn

851 Alexandria

852 Tyneside Scottish Bn

853 Aged 22. Carpenter

854 Merged Bn

855 Alexandria

856 Name not recorded

857 + Disobedience

858 Shoreditch Bn

859 2nd Glasgow (Boys Bde) Bn

860 Previous XXX suspended (07/03/17). See also PRO WO71/679

861 1st Glasgow (Tramways) Bn

862 6th City Bn

863 Aged 23. Previous XXX suspended (08/11/16). Parents: William Henry & Elizabeth Louisa Clarke, 20 Garrick St., South Shields. See also PRO WO71/678

864 Aged 20. Maori engineer in non-Maori Bn. Shell-shocked, July 1915

865 South Belfast Bn

866 Aged 32. Retried: 26/02/18. XXX on 15/03/18. Often sick or AWOL. From Montreal. Wife: Hettie Dagesse, Thorold, Ontario

867 Hallamshire Bn

868 Aged 22. Shot 22/04/18 for Desertion. From Lancs

869 Aged 26. Said to be 'mentally weak'. Parents: Edmond & Sarah Horler, 3 Harfield Terr., South St., Yeovil. See also PRO WO71/617

870 French-Canadian. August 1918 shell-shocked. Wife: Jessie Henry, 66 Big Vennel, Cromarty, Rosshire. See also PRO WO71/637

871 3rd Glasgow Bn

872 Aged 28. Killed prostitute. See also PRO WO71/636

873 Aged 23. Parents: Mr & Mrs Franklin Fairburn, 11 Maple St., St. Catherine, Ontario. Canada

874 The Queen's Bn

875 Victoria Rifles

876 Manitoba Bn. Previous XXX suspended (21/08/16)

877 Kensington Bn

878 3rd South Down Bn

879 Aged 32. Retrial from 28/01/18. From Montreal. Wife: Hettie Dagesse, Thorold, Ontario

880 Public Schools Bn

881 Aged 22. Previous XXX suspended (30/01/18). Married, from Lancs. See also PRO WO71/646

882 St. Pancras Bn

883 Aged 27. Parents: John Charles & Ellen Hughes, 5/3 Gilpin St. Sheffield. See also PRO WO71/638

884 GCM; Durban

885 1st South East Lancs (Bantam) Bn

886 City of Glasgow Bn

887 Aged 24. Ironmonger. Auckland Bn

888 Aged 26. See also PRO WO71/642

889 2nd Portsmouth Bn

890 2nd Portsmouth Bn

891 Aged 22. + Escaping x3. Banff & Donside Bn. Possibly mentally ill. See also PRO WO71/643

892 3rd Gwent Bn

893 3rd Gwent Bn

894 Aged 24. See also PRO WO71/639

895 Shot 14/06/18 for Desertion

896 + Disobedience

897 Aged 27. Listed as 'died of wounds'. Parents: William & Margaret McFarlane, 14 Gerard St. Byrom St. Liverpool. Enlisted Bootle. See also PRO WO71/644

898 Shot 22/05/18 for Desertion

899 Aged 39. Shot Sgt whilst drunk. Son of Mrs Mary Skone, 13 Thomas St. Orange Gdns, Pembroke. See also PRO WO71/641

900 Aged 25. + Escaping + Striking. See also PRO WO71/645

901 Aged 25. Labourer. Parents: Phillipe & Hectorine Larose Delisle, 1553 Jeanne Mance St., Montreal

902 Holder of Military Medal

903 During rifle inspection, shot 2nd Lt Wynell Lloyd. See also PRO WO71/640

904 1st Glasgow (Tramways) Bn

905 Aged 25. Labourer. Canterbury Bn

906 Aged 22. Parents: George & Lilian Earl, 14 Earl St. Lower Broughton, Manchester. See also PRO WO71/647

907 Further conviction 29/12/18

908 Aged 21. Previous XXX suspended (08/11/17). See also PRO WO71/649

909 Considered not responsible for his actions

910 Aged 21. Previous XXX suspended (12/12/17)

911 Renfrewshire Bn

912 Previous XXX suspended (28/04/18)

913 2nd Football Bn

914 Leeds Rifles

915 + Quitting. Blackheath & Woolwich Bn

916 + Striking

917 Kensington Bn

918 Leeds Rifles

919 Aged 29. Londoner, Married, x2 children. Previous XXX suspended (26/04/18). See also PRO WO71/648

920 4th Glasgow (previously Bantam) Bn

921 Aged 26. Shot 27/08/18 for Desertion. Son of Mrs E Butcher, 24A Park St. Folkestone

922 Aged 22. Parents: William & Lily Dossett, Sheffield. Hallamshire Bn. See also PRO WO71/650

923 Guilty (x1) of AWOL

924 Blythswood Bn

925 Blythswood Bn

926 Murdered French woman during robbery. Coolie No.10299. See also PRO WO71/654

927 Murdered French woman during robbery. Coolie No. 10272. See also PRO WO71/654

928 2nd Salford Bn

929 + Violence

930 Gloucester Bn

931 Gloucester Bn

932 East Africa. After re-trial (23/10/18) XXX on 10/11/18

933 St Pancras Bn

934 St Pancras Bn

935 WO213 cites Coolie No. 53497. See also PRO WO71/651

936 Aged 27. Mother: Harriet Briggs, 7 R'way View, Locksford Lane, Brimington, Chesterfield. Newly-wed + baby. Father and brother 'KIA'. See also PRO WO71/653

937 Aged 25. Previous XXX suspended (14/11/17). Parents: Mary Ann & late Job Scholes. See also PRO WO71/656

938 Sec 4·5, ie Aiding enemy whilst POW. GCM; Guildhall, Westminster

939 Real name James Charlton, a middle-aged Scotsman. See also PRO WO71/657

940 Aged 22. Deserted 21/06/17. Previous XXX suspended (29/12/16). Eastern Ontario. Parents: Albert & Fanny Ling, 1125 Dovercourt Rd. Toronto

941 Middle-aged Scotsman. See also PRO WO71/657

942 Aged 20. From Sheffield. See also PRO WO71/658

943 + Violence

944 Bermondsey Bn

945 + Escaping

946 Aged 26. Previous XXX suspended (07/06/18). Son of Mrs E Butcher, 24A Park St. Folkestone, Kent. See also PRO WO71/664

947 + Insubordination

948 Killed fellow Chinese Labourer. Identified in WO213 & WO71/655 as Coolie No. 46090. See also PRO WO71/655

949 Aged 23. Parents: James & Mary O'Connell,

950 Bankers' Bn. See also PRO WO71/650

951 Aged 23. See also PRO WO71/652

952 See also PRO WO71/662

953 Indian Army. Aden

954 Finsbury Rifles. + Violence

955 Aged 46. US citizen. Oldest man to be XXX. See also PRO WO71/661

956 Entry (name) unclear

957 Aged 26. See also PRO WO71/663

958 Hallamshire Bn

959 Prior conviction 24/11/16

960 1st South East Lancs (ex-Bantam) Bn

961 Leeds Rifles

962 Aged 20. London Territorial Bn. See also PRO WO71/667

963 1st County Bn

964 Blackheath & Woolwich Bn

965 Blackheath & Woolwich Bn

966 + Desertion + Esc x2. Pioneer Bn

967 1st Barnsley Bn

968 1st County Bn

969 WO213/25 cites Coolie no.42476. See also PRO WO71/665

970 Aged 28. Father: Mr C Bateman, 3 Kilton St. Sheffield. Yorks. Previous XXX suspended (21/05/17). Hallamshire Bn. See also PRO WO71/666

971 Tyneside Scottish Bn

972 + Quitting

973 Alexandria. + Escaping

974 Enlisted 1914. Previously wounded. See also PRO WO71/670

975 Aged 25. Arrested: Glasgow. Parents: John & Jane Gibson, Bridgeton, Glasgow. Wife: Agnes Gibson, 338 1/2 Gallowgate, Glasgow. See also PRO WO71/668

976 Aged 21. Claimed shell-shock in defence. See also PRO WO71/669

977 Aged 28. GCM; Boulogne. + Desertion

978 Ross Bn

979 Aged 28. See also PRO WO71/671

980 Nottingham Bn. Bantam

981 + Insubordination

982 Isle of Man Bn

983 London Irish Bn

984 1st Barnsley Bn

985 Aged 32. Londoner. Sportsmen's Bn. See also PRO WO71/673

986 Aged 23. + Desertion. Born London, domiciled Leeds. Parents: Abraham & Harriet Harris, 41 Cooper St. Meanwood Rd. Leeds. See also PRO WO71/672

987 Previous trial sentence not confirmed (01/07/18). See also pRO WO71/674

988 Tyneside Scottish Bn

989 Entry (name) unclear

990 Bantam Bn

991 2nd County Bn. Bantam

992 Shoreditch Bn

993 Carmarthenshire Bn

994 GCM; Taranto. See also PRO WO71/675

995 + Murder

996 + Murder

997 + Murder. Commited suicide before XXX. See also WO71/676. No name cited

998 + Murder. See also WO71/676 which cites name as FY Wan

999 Previous conviction 16/05/18

1000 Arts and Crafts Bn

1001 Co. Tyrone Volunteers Bn

1002 London Rifle Bde

1003 Fired at British troops

1004 Coolie No. 44735. See also PRO WO71/680

1005 Pera, Constantinople. Russian national. Released 28/11/22!

1006 Coolie No. 16174.See also PRO WO71/681

1007 Rank of Sgt

1008 Rank of Sgt

1009 Rank of Sgt

1010 Batoum

1011 Aged 20. Shot NCO while being arrested. See also PRO WO71/682

1012 Killed fellow burglar. See also PRO WO71/683

1013 15/05/19 + Suspension of Sentences Act not applicable to Chinese Labourers

1014 Kebir

1015 Mehalla Kebir

1016 Aged 24. Killed Belgian woman. Parents: Mrs A Davids, 8 Vrede St., Cape Town, SA. See also PRO WO71/685

1017 Aged 23. Killed Belgian woman. See also PRO WO71/684

1018 Batoum

1019 Constantinople

1020 Baghdad. Rank of Pte

1021 Abbassia. Rank of Pte

1022 Batoum

1023 Batoum

1024 Batoum

1025 Aged 19. Parents: A & J Boos, Cape Town, SA. See also PRO WO71/686

1026 Constantinople. See also PRO WO71/687

1027 Constantinople. See also PRO WO71/687

1028 Constantinople. See also PRO WO71/687

1029 Constantinople. See also PRO WO71/687

1030 Batoum

1031 Batoum

1032 Batoum

1033 Batoum

1034 Batoum

1035 Abbassia. Rank of Sgt

1036 Constantinople

1037 Coolie No. 97170. See also PRO WO71/688

1038 Coolie No. 44340. See also PRO WO71/688

1039 Batoum

1040 Batoum

1041 Batoum

1042 Batoum

1043 Batoum

1044 Batoum

1045 Batoum

1046 Batoum

1047 See also PRO WO71/689

1048 Batoum

1049 Batoum

1050 Constantinople. Fired at British troops

1051 Constantinople. Fired at British troops

1052 Constantinople. Fired at British troops

1053 Constantinople. Fired at British troops

1054 Constantinople. Fired at British troops

1055 Constantinople. Trafficking explosives

1056 Constantinople. Trafficking explosives

1057 Moda

1058 Mevda

1059 Mevda

1060 Mevda

1061 Mevda

1062 Mevda. Released 25/10/20

1063 Released 19/08/21

1064 Mutiny at Jullunder. India Office Library & Records Ref: L/Mil/7/13314

1065 Mutiny at Jullunder. India Office Library & Records Ref: L/Mil/7/13314

1066 Mutiny at Jullunder. India Office Library & Records Ref: L/Mil/7/13314

1067 Mutiny at Jullunder. India Office Library & Records Ref: L/Mil/7/13314

1068 Mutiny at Jullunder. India Office Library & Records Ref: L/Mil/7/13314

1069 Aged 21. Mutiny at Solon. India Office Library & Records Ref: L/Mil/7/13314

1070 Mutiny at Solon. India Office Library & Records Ref: L/Mil/7/13314

1071 Mutiny at Solon. India Office Library & Records Ref: L/Mil/7/13314

1072 Mutiny at Solon. India Office Library & Records Ref: L/Mil/7/13314

1073 Mutiny at Solon. India Office Library & Records Ref: L/Mil/7/13314

1074 Mutiny at Solon. India Office Library & Records Ref: L/Mil/7/13314

1075 Mutiny at Solon. India Office Library & Records Ref: L/Mil/7/13314

1076 Mutiny at Solon. India Office Library & Records Ref: L/Mil/7/13314

1077 Ismid

1078 Ismid

1079 Moda

Tinnarath, Foulkesmills, Wexford, Ireland. See also PRO WO71/659

1080	Moda
1081	Moda
1082	Ismid
1083	Bacos. + Murder
1084	Shileh. + Rape. Released 28/11/22
1085	Moda. Released 16/07/21 (insane)
1086	Constantinople
1087	GCM
1088	See also pRO WO71/690
1089	Ireland
1090	Possession of explosives etc
1091	Kantara
1092	Alexandria
1093	Alexandria
1094	Alexandria
1095	Cairo
1096	Cairo
1097	Cairo
1098	Cairo
1099	Cairo
1100	Cairo
1101	Cairo
1102	Cairo. + Possession firearms
1103	Cairo. Details of offence unspecified
1104	Cairo. Details of offence unspecified
1105	Ismid
1106	Ismid
1107	Details of offence unspecified. Moda

Bibliography

Primary sources – unpublished

Public Record Office:

WO71/387 – WO71/1238 inclusive: Judge Advocate
General's Records of Courts Martial.

WO86/62-90 inclusive: Register of Charges at home and
abroad 1914-1920.

WO90/6 – WO90/8 inclusive: Register of General Courts
Martial (abroad).

WO92/3 & WO92/4: Register of General Courts Martial
(home).

WO93/42-45 inclusive: Nominal Role of Courts Martial of
Australian and Canadian Forces (all ranks) 1915–1919.

WO93/49 – WO93/51 inclusive: Judge Advocate General's
statistics.

WO213/1 – WO213/34 inclusive: Register of Field General
Courts Martial.

Primary sources – published

Blake, R. (ed.), *The Private Papers of Douglas Haig* (London, 1952).

Catholic Bulletin, August 1917 (Dublin, 1917).

Crozier, F. P., *A Brass Hat in No Man's Land* (Bath, 1968).

Crozier, F. P., *The Men I Killed* (London, 1937).

Dunn, J. C., *The War the Infantry Knew* (London, 1987).

Imperial War Graves Commission, *Registers of War Cemeteries
and Memorials*.

Manual of Military Law (London, 1914).

Mitchell, T. J. and Smith, G. M., *Official History of the War,
Medical Services* (London, 1931).

*Report of the Committee Constituted by the Army Council to
Inquire into the Law and Rules of Procedure Regulating Military
Courts Martial* – Darling Committee (HMSO, 1919).

*Report of the War Office Committee of Enquiry into 'Shell-
Shock'* – Southborough Committee (HMSO, 1922).

Sinn Fein Handbook (Dublin, 1917).

Thurtle, E., *Shootings at Dawn* (London, 1924).

War Office, *Statistics of the Military Effort of the British Empire
in the Great War 1914–1920* (London, 1920).

War Office, *Soldiers Died in the Great War*, Volumes 1–80
inclusive (London, 1920).

Secondary sources – published

Babington, A., *For the Sake of Example* (Barnsley, 1993).

Babington, A., *Shell-Shock: a History of the Changing Attitudes
to War Neurosis* (Barnsley, 1997).

Beckett, I. F. W. and Simpson, K. (eds.), *A Nation in Arms. A
Social Study of The British Army in the First World War*
(Manchester, 1985).

Bourne, J. M., *Britain and the Great War 1914–1918* (London,
1991).

Brown, M., *The Imperial War Museum Book of the Western
Front* (London, 1993).

Clark, A., *The Donkeys* (London, 1991).

Freedman, L., (ed.) *War* (Oxford, 1994).

Fussell, P., *The Great War and Modern Memory* (Oxford, 1977).

Gammage, D., *The Broken Years: Australian Soldiers in the
Great War* (Canberra,1974).

Gilbert, M., *First World War* (London, 1994).

Hichberger, J.W.M., *Images of the Army; The Military in British
Art 1815–1914* (Manchester, 1988).

Hynes, S., *A War Imagined* (London, 1992).

James, E. A., *British Regiments 1914–1918* (London, 1993).

James, L., *Mutiny* (London, 1987).

Joll, J., *The Origins of the First World War* (Harlow, 1984).

Joll, J., *Europe Since 1870* (Harmondsworth, 1990).

Keegan, J., *The Face of Battle* (Harmondsworth, 1976).

Keegan, J., *A History of Warfare* (London, 1993).

MacDonald, L., 1915: *The Death of Innocence* (London, 1993).

Marwick, A., *The Deluge*, Second Edition (Basingstoke, 1991).

Middlebrook, M., and M., *The Somme Battlefields*
(Harmondsworth, 1994).

Moore W., *See How They Ran* (London, 1970).

Moore, W., *The Thin Yellow Line* (London, 1974).

Morton, D., *When Your Number's Up: The Canadian Soldier in
the First World War* (Toronto, 1993).

Pugsley, C., *On the Fringe of Hell* (Auckland, 1991).

Putkowski, J. and Sykes, J., *Shot at Dawn* (Barnsley, 1989).

Stevenson, J., *British Society 1914–45* (Harmondsworth,
1990).

Taylor, A.J.P., *The First World War* (Harmondsworth, 1963).

Terraine, J., *Douglas Haig: The Educated Soldier* (London,
1963).

Travers, T., The Killing Ground: *The British Army and the
Emergence of Modern Warfare on the Western Front
1900–1918* (London, 1990).

Westlake, R., *British Battalions on the Somme* (London, 1994).

Wilson, T., *The Myriad Faces of War: Britain and the Great War
1914–1918* (Cambridge, 1986).

Winter, D., *Haig's Command* (Harmondsworth, 1991).

Winter, J. M., *The Great War and the British People* (London,
1986).

Woodward, D., *Armies of the World 1854–1914* (London,
1978).